FREEDOM AND THE HUMAN PERSON

STUDIES IN PHILOSOPHY
AND THE HISTORY OF PHILOSOPHY

General Editor: Jude P. Dougherty

Studies in Philosophy
and the History of Philosophy   Volume 48

Freedom and the Human Person

edited by Richard Velkley

THE CATHOLIC UNIVERSITY OF AMERICA PRESS
Washington, D.C.

The paper used in this publication meets the minimum requirements of American
National Standards for Information Science—Permanence of Paper for
Printed Library Materials, ANSI z39.48-1984.
∞

LIBRARY OF CONGRESS CATALOGING-IN-PUBLICATION DATA
Freedom and the human person / edited by Richard Velkley.
     p. cm. — (Studies in philosophy and the history of philosophy ; v. 48)
    Includes bibliographical references and index.
    ISBN 978-0-8132-3208-9 (pbk : alk. paper)   1. Liberty.   I. Velkley, Richard.
    II. Title.   III. Series.
  B824.4.F735 2007
  123´.5—dc22

                      2007015318

Contents

INTRODUCTION

RICHARD VELKLEY

The essays collected here were with two exceptions delivered in the Fall 2001 lecture series of the School of Philosophy, the Catholic University of America. As the lectures were being planned in the academic year 2000–2001 it could not be foreseen how events political and personal would place their grim stamp on the series. The attacks of September 11 transpired just days before the first of the lectures, delivered by Robert Sokolowski. Seth Benardete, who was scheduled to lecture on September 28, was struck by a fatal illness shortly before that date and died on November 14. This pairing of events—the beginning of a new era with the 9/11 calamity and the passing of one of the major interpreters of classical thought—seemed strangely fitting, like an augury for the series' speakers and listeners concerning the somber urgency of the themes of their discussion, freedom and the human person. Fortunately Benardete completed his paper for the series and it is included here as he sent it. One of the virtues of this volume is its making us more mindful of his extraordinary legacy. The passing of outstanding persons dear to us can lead us to be yet more grateful for the enduring, brilliant achievements they leave behind.

The very notions of "freedom" and "person" could have no meaning for human beings if they did not have historical experience. The human good has permanent and universal features and human freedom is intelligible only in relation to them. But the conditions under which the good is pursued are indeterminately various and unforeseeable, and wholly definable limits on the choice of means to ends are accordingly not available. Morality and politics cannot be precise sciences, and consequently a permanent, satisfactory attainment of the good in the practical realm is simply beyond conceiving. The human goods are not only diverse but diverging. The requirements of intellect and body, of freedom and order, of individuality and community, are always in some tension and never to be reconciled by formulae or even by some arduously attained habit of the soul. The human capacity to address this inescapable indeterminacy is constitutive of what we call "freedom" and "personhood."[1] It belongs to the nature of freedom and personhood that they reveal what they are in concrete historical efforts to realize the good, and thus investigations of the history of thinking about these concerns are not just exercises in documenting the application of universal principles but disclosures of possibilities that enlarge our theoretical understanding.

All but two of the essays in this collection approach these themes through historical inquiries having this theoretically illuminating character. It is a distinguishing feature of this volume that it gives strong emphasis to the relations between theological and philosophical treatments of these often-examined topics, while frequently underlining their political dimension, as well. A thread running through most of the essays is the world-historical transformation of notions of freedom, will, and person which occurred when the infinite divine being of biblical faith, as object of desire and intelligence, was introduced into European life. This transformation came after the discovery by Greek philosophy of the philosophical life as the dedication to free inquiry, that based life in reason rather than mere convention. How the European soul was deepened by the encounter of philosophy with biblical faith is an ever-renewable theme of inexhaustible reflection to which, it is hoped, this volume contributes. Another great revolution was the modern era's turn to freedom as grounded in natural rights rather than natural ends, and therewith the various ideals of self-sovereignty that shape modern moral and political life. These three pivotal moments bring forth questions which are central to the essays here: Is freedom grounded in knowledge

---

1. This line of thought may sound modern but has solid support in Thomas Aquinas, who follows Aristotle in his account of the contingency and variability of human affairs and of the imprecision of practical reason as concerned with them. "Although there is necessity in the general principles, the more we descend to matters of detail, the more frequently we encounter deviations" (ST I-II, q. 94, a. 4). In deriving human law from natural law it is sometimes possible as in the sciences to proceed by drawing conclusions from premises. Thus "one must not kill" can be derived from "one should do harm to no man." But in attending to the details of practical life the procedure is more like that of a craftsman who particularizes or determines general forms to a particular shape, clearly a nondeductive procedure. The law of nature states that the evildoer should be punished, but "that he be punished in this or that way" does not follow directly from natural law and requires a judgement of the particular case. "The general principles of the natural law cannot be applied to all men in the same way on account of the great variety of human affairs." Accordingly Thomas endorses what "the Philosopher says in such matters" (cf. Nicomachean Ethics VI, 1143b11), that "we ought to pay as much attention to the undemonstrated sayings and opinions of persons who surpass us in experience, age, and prudence as to their demonstrations" (ST I-II, q. 95, a. 2). Finally, it could be said that the inevitability of moving beyond natural law toward prudential judgment belongs to the freedom of persons, and makes evident that personhood cannot be defined solely in terms of natural ends, even the highest.

of the natural order or in apprehension of the supernatural? Is freedom the compliance with a transcendent order, natural or divine, or is it the capacity for self-determination apart from such order? How does freedom relate to teleology? How does the self-determination so prized in modern life relate to community, tradition, nature, and the sacred? Ultimately such questions lead one back to the examination of human powers and human nature: Are speech, thought, and judgment bound up in some way with the capacity for freedom? Does a human life as rational necessarily involve some exercise of freedom? And since "living rationally" might, it seems, mean many things, is not freedom as intrinsic to rational life also multifarious in meaning?

Each author in the volume is a prominent authority in a particular historical period or figure in Western thought, and thus the series of essays provides an invaluable source for considering crucial moments in the effort of this tradition to achieve satisfactory accounts of freedom and the human person. A tendency of all thinking is to lapse into uncritical contentment with contemporary terms of discourse and to be unreceptive to other possible terms. Historical inquiries can always be useful in acting against this tendency, but for the reasons given above, the provocation of historical reflection may be exceptionally needful in the present subjects. To those considerations one can add that the very words "freedom" and "person" have an overwhelming power in the modern world, so that their thunderous clamor in the rhetoric of public life tends to drive into oblivion the quieter voices of the true thinkers. The present collection seeks to bring more audience and authority to the latter.

The essays can be broadly classified into four groups: treatments of classical and biblical sources of thinking about freedom and the human person (Benardete, Kass, Sokolowski); Christian and medieval treatments (Rist, Shanley, Stump); early modern accounts (Gillespie, Tarcov, and Zuckert et alia) and accounts that can be called late modern (Shell, Pippin, Rethy) on the premise that Kant marks a turning-point in modern thought. Sokolowski's approach is the least historical of all the contributors insofar as he develops systematic concerns without extensive comment on earlier thinkers. But since his essay draws deeply from Aristotelian-Thomist sources as well as from Husserl, I believe it is rightly placed in the first group. Robert Pippin is also less concerned with the exegesis of a primary thinker, but his argument as engaging contemporary Kantian thought is everywhere under the shadow of Kant and his greatest critic, Hegel. A general difficulty in thinking about the relations among the essays arises from the fact that they do not employ fundamental terms (freedom and person) with univocal senses. The Western tradition of thought on these subjects is so manifold and complex that a well-defined linguistic field of primary terms, transmitted through texts and translations that would secure an enduring base of unambiguous concepts, is hardly to be hoped for. What the study of this tradition does grant us is a remarkable wealth of insight and debate about problems that all humans face in an "existential" way. And it should be evident that we cannot think of advancing toward solutions before we have an adequate account of problems.

Seth Benardete's essay introduces several related approaches to the meaning of freedom in classical authors, thus pointing to some broadly unifying themes. He shows that classical accounts of freedom are inseparable from accounts of necessity, and that both freedom and necessity are bound up with the political context of human thought and action. Indeed classical thought calls into question the assumption or hope that there can be human activity entirely free of compulsion or necessitation, or any pure grace either inside or outside the city. Furthermore there is a profound tension between two senses of freedom: freedom of the spirit, culminating in philosophy, and freedom from rule by others, the freedom of self-defense, grounded in the needs of the body. Philosophic freedom promotes the appearance of human beings with weaker ties to the city (e.g. Alcibiades' betrayal of Athens), and the political form of freedom, the freedom of self-rule, is based on habit and easily corruptible. In sum the eros for knowledge behind philosophic freedom is rarely combinable with the unswerving attachment to "one's own" required for political freedom. What is more, the desire dominant in political life is "freedom for oneself and rule over others," which naturally leads to injustice—and thus the ordinary citizen is akin to the tyrant, whom he both envies and decries. This is the truth about the city which the city hides from itself: there is no political greatness (nor any high attainment in the arts and sciences) without the subjugation of others. The high depends on, and yet is contradicted by, the low, and so the natural order seems paradoxical. Reflection on freedom occasions doubt that the cosmos is teleological. In any case, the coincidence of political greatness and justice is a matter of unmasterable chance, and all human affairs are infected with this contingency.

Modern ideas of freedom that offer the promise of human mastery of chance surely have a different cast: they postulate an ultimate coincidence of the low and the high as something attainable by properly regulated ("methodical") efforts, if not by a logic internal to history itself.

Leon Kass gives an account of a biblical view of freedom, in which freedom is not solely a power of choosing but relates essentially to reason and speech as distinguishing marks of the human. It belongs to the human as a dual being bound to the body yet capable of transcending it; and although such transcending in thought and speech reveals human dignity it is also the source of misery. Kass claims that the Bible exposes more strikingly the darker side of human freedom and reason than Aristotle and the Greek classics. Genesis as read by Kass is not the story of a unique historical event, the "fall," but a moral lesson about the permanent condition of the human and a warning about the pitfalls of that condition. The original disobedience and punishment of Adam and Eve are revelatory of human nature as created rather than the result of particular acts of will. As created, human reason and speech have the potential for the imagining of what is absent, the merely possible, which humans desire and pursue at their peril. The comprehending of the divine prohibition ("Eat not . . .") as grasping the difference between good and evil, and as making the absent (the prohibited) present, already contains the power of questioning the prohibition and the seed of defiance. The fact that humans understand the prohibition is the proof of their need for it. Human speech is a "world-ordering" power that discloses what is the case, but the truth it makes manifest is inevitably distorted by self-interest and pride, as Kass illustrates with his brilliant exegesis of Adam's naming of the creatures and Eve. Adam becomes self-aware (of his humanity and masculinity) through Eve, but the name he gives her is derived from himself, reflecting the possessive desire which compels him to see her similarity to himself as sameness. Speech reveals otherness, sameness, and sameness within otherness; yet possessiveness and pride powerfully are at work in the usual misjudging of sameness and otherness, so that human thought and desire require correction by the law. In Kass's reading of the Bible, the existence of law points to a deep flaw in human reason and speech, a flaw that the life of autonomous inquiry is unable to overcome. The Bible does not present the life of reason as the fulfillment of the natural order or of natural law.

In another discussion linking freedom to human speech and reason, although with a more positive accent, Robert Sokolowski argues that the syntactic order of speech, as enabling us to make the absent present and conversely to put the present at a distance, grounds the possibility of responsible acting and thinking. Syntax establishes rationality. To support this position Sokolowski appeals to Aristotle's account of apprehension as inherently judgmental and Husserl's analysis of the categorical structuring of experience by wholes and parts. Sokolowski advances beyond the description of mere judging to characterize, as a fundamental form of human freedom, the responsible appropriation of judgment wherein we declare ourselves as affirming a judgment. As responsible for what we affirm we are "agents of truth" directed toward the telos of achieving the truth. Such freedom is not an a priori faculty, but a predicative capacity generated out of prepredicative experiences that include a crucial intersubjective dimension: we develop the capacity to assume a position on a state of affairs in our relations to others. Therewith we acquire the ability for attention to a common point of reference and the willingness to accept truth pertaining to it. In stressing the social aspect of rationality in the "agency for truth," Sokolowski goes beyond Husserl and provides the basis for an account of personhood in something deeper than just the power of choosing: he discloses the freedom that is inherent in human thought as such. As inhabitants of a "space of reasons" we are beings called on to account for what we say, think, and do. Thus Sokolowski seeks to reveal a positive ontological sense to the human self-distancing that Benardete and Kass, in commenting on their respective traditions, presented as a more problematic self-transcending.

A critical approach toward both classical and modern accounts of freedom and the person, argued from a theological perspective, is found in John Rist's essay. In classical accounts, freedom is the capacity to remove obstacles to attaining the good, our ultimate end. These accounts have the strength of relating freedom to an objective goal, unlike modern accounts, which start from the self's capacity for choice. Classical accounts are "agent-centered" in that self-improvement of the soul, or approximation to the divine, is essential to the objective good. In the Platonic version the objective good, the soul as unified whole, is erotic and not only cognitive. But nowhere in classical thought does the individual have worth as a unique being, since classical metaphysics provides no ground for regarding the individual human soul as irreplaceable. Even when Boethius defines the person as "individual substance of a rational nature," his sense of "rational" derives from the highest teleological object in the whole. Although certain thinkers of late antiquity (the Stoics, Cicero, Plotinus) begin to ascribe importance to the individual's history as constitutive of personhood, they lack the theistic framework required for establishing the absolute value of the individual. When modern (most notably Kantian) accounts of the absolute worth of the individual turn to autonomy, the power of choosing rationally, as the ground of value, they forfeit the objective telos of both classical and Christian thought. The true but forgotten ground of the modern accounts is the doctrine of the divine persons, which has been replaced by a formalistic and legislative view of freedom: humans qua rational are bearers of rights.[2] Supposing that "person" could be thus defined, what would make it wrong to act

2. Rist's thought on the person is a form of twentieth-century Christian personalism seeking to advance beyond modern subjectivism and individualism through accounts of personhood grounded in the Trinitarian doctrine of the divine persons. Twentieth-

against persons? Rist denies that the possession of reason and speech, seen apart from their divine creative ground, is sufficient to secure human dignity. The natural teleology of truth fails to define personhood. But Rist also observes that the desire to establish the reality of personhood cannot serve as a proof of theism.

The Thomist account of freedom and the human person is the theme of the essays by Brian Shanley and Eleonore Stump. Thomas offers both an objective, rational account of the good and a view of the human person as a free being responsible (to some extent) for the virtues that bring him closer to the good. The highest good is the completion of the love of God in the vision of the all-powerful and all-knowing God. Every human soul has infinite worth as created by the infinite ground of all being. Yet early in the Christian era thinkers saw the possibility of a contradiction between the infinite causal power of the divine and human freedom. In some cases they were not content to resolve the problem by appeal to the unfathomability of the divine will. Shanley elaborates the Thomist metaphysics of creation, which offers an account of the divine will as intelligibly good and compatible with human freedom. God, the efficient and final cause of all being, is that to which the human will is ordered (in the *visio dei*) by necessity and not by choice. But this ordering is a moving of the human will by interior means, i.e., by its own nature, and not by external means, i.e., temporally antecedent, predetermining events. This non-coercive ordering by God is neither a "libertarian" account of freedom in which all movement originates in human choosing as the first cause, nor a "compatibilist" view that seeks to reconcile causal determinism with human freedom. What ultimately moves the human will is not choice but something prior to choice, the intellectual apprehension of the good (or God as ultimate intelligible object), which belongs to the nature of the will as rational appetite. While the human will

century personalism has also found inspiration in vitalist, existentialist and phenomenological (often non-Christian) thinkers such as Bergson, Blondel, Berdyaev, Scheler, Jaspers, and Buber, who critique classical realism (or "objectivism") as well as modern thought for their inability to account for the reality of the person. This has led to attempts to combine Thomist philosophy with "relational" and action-centered personalism, efforts that in several cases have entailed criticism of Thomas. See Gabriel Marcel, *The Mystery of Being* (Lanham: University Press of America, 1950), Emmanuel Mounier, *Personalism* (New York: Grove Press, 1952), Jacques Maritain, *The Person and the Common Good* (Notre Dame: University of Notre Dame Press, 1966; original 1947), Karol Wojtyla, *The Acting Person* (Boston and Dordrecht: Reidel, 1979). For some recent work see W. Norris Clarke, *Person and Being* (Milwaukee: Marquette University Press, 1993), Robert Spaemann, *Personen* (Stuttgart: Klett-Cotta, 1996), John F. Crosby, *The Selfhood of the Human Person* (Washington, D.C.: The Catholic University of America Press, 1996), and by the same, *Personalist Papers* (Washington, D.C.: The Catholic University Press of America, 2004). For a penetrating assessment of the entire movement of Christian personalism see Kenneth Schmitz, "Personalism and the Existential Act," *Fides Quaerens Intellectum* 1, no. 1 (Summer 2001): 184–99.

is necessarily inclined toward that ultimate good which perfects its own nature, it is not necessitated in its choice of every object. In a seeming paradox the human will is most free when it recognizes that to which it is necessarily ordered, or when it acknowledges its dependence on God. Clearly this account of freedom is not the Ockhamist one in which the will is free to act independently of reason. Thomas's account of freedom is neither "voluntarist" nor "intellectualist." The true subject of freedom is the human person in which reason and will form a whole. Since human freedom becomes more perfect as it approaches the perfect unity of will and intellect in God, the capacity to choose evil forms no part of freedom rightly defined. Indeed freedom of choice is a mere contingency with respect to the concept of will; God has no need of choice. Divine action with respect to human beings cannot be construed according to the model of finite choosing and acting but involves a special sort of causality between persons.

Eleonore Stump brings forward another aspect of Thomas' thought on freedom—a problem that demands a purely theological solution. In the Christian interpretation of Genesis the primal progenitors of the human species experience a fall with the consequence that a sinful condition of will is borne by all their descendants. How can the human will be converted to a condition of righteous willing? To suppose this could occur through the will's own efforts is to commit a heresy (Pelagian) which denies that God is the source of all good. But to assume that the conversion to a righteous will seeking God is simply the result of divine infusion is apparently to leave no room for human freedom. Thomas does indeed claim that there is divine infusion of the "grace of justifying faith"—the turning of the will to assent to God's justice—which Stump describes as a "second-order willing": a will to will righteously, which must be followed by progress in the "first-order willing" of righteous acts. But again, such grace would seem to remove responsibility from the human for the primary turn to the good. (Note that Shanley's account of the will as non-coercively ordered by its nature toward the intelligible good does not address this problem, since sin impairs the natural inclination and fallen nature by itself cannot overcome this impairment.) Stump proposes a solution she says is "available to Aquinas" although "whether Aquinas held the position I suggest will always be controversial." The divine will does not act upon the human will as an external efficient cause producing "violent" change contrary to the latter's nature; thus, infusion of grace cannot be an instance of giving the human will a configuration or form contrary to its existing configuration or form. Rather it is the replacing of a simple privation of form in a "quiescent" will that neither refuses nor accepts grace, with the form of the faith that justifies. The quiescent will does not yet actually will the good but no longer rejects it. Rather it judges that it would be good to conquer its sinful nature. The intellect is divided against itself, as it no longer wants to be sinful but has not converted to righteousness. But this quiescence, which is a state of readiness for grace, is within human power. Thus ceasing to refuse grace is an act of the will as free: although a meritorious act of free will cannot produce grace, the will can impede itself from receiving grace. It should be noted that this subtle solution arises out of the need to reconcile contradictory theological claims (of grace and freedom) and not through a phenomenological analysis of natural moral experience.

With Michael Gillespie's essay on the notions of individual and state sovereignty we enter the modern era of thinking on freedom. He notes that crucial in the background to this change is the breakdown of the reconciliation of reason and revelation achieved by Thomas and other Aristotelians of the thirteenth century. The nominalism of William of Ockham rejects the notion that the free will is fulfilled within a given, unchosen order of ends known by reason. Universals, which are only fictions invented by reason, cannot be binding on any will, divine or human. The divine will, free to act independently of reason, reveals itself in acts of radical individual creation. Such doctrine would favor the submission of the human will to an utterly inscrutable divine will, but would also encourage the stress on human individuality that appears in the humanism of the late Middle Ages (Petrarch, etc.). But the distinctively modern move occurs in Descartes' ascribing to the human will the infinite will of the nominalist God, and to human reason a new sort of sovereignty in revealing a limitation in the divine will: no higher creative power can deceive human thinking about its own existence. Human intellection, no longer principally contemplative, undertakes the mastery of nature. The political counterpart of the Cartesian doctrine is the new approach to state sovereignty that postulates purely humanly instituted, contractual grounds for legitimating the powers of the state in order to overcome the devastation of theological and philosophical controversies. From this arises the problematic tendency in all modern thought to assert imaginary, absolute, godlike forms of independence for individuals and states. And a new kind of conflict appears: if both individuals and states claim absolute self-sovereignty, without a higher cosmic-divine order to limit and sanction human conduct, how can they peacefully coexist? Hence the manifold disputes between "libertarian" or individualist programs and "communitarian" or collectivist programs which characterize the modern era. Gillespie argues that the limited liberal state offers the best solution available within the terms of modernity: a moderate version of both state sovereignty and individual autonomy, eschewing grandiose versions of creative self-origination. Its spirit is in accord with the insight that there can be no theoretically rigorous solution to the problem of the dual nature of the human. Yet both forms of sovereignty—and therewith modern ideas of freedom and personhood—now need rethinking, since globalization forces on us the recognition that individual and political identities are more interrelated and less self-sovereign than had been thought.

Nathan Tarcov offers further insight into the ambiguity of the modern approach to freedom in his essay on one of the founding works of modern political philosophy, Machiavelli's *The Prince*. This work, most frequently read as a daringly innovative essay in "realistic" thinking about the state, power, and the art of princely rule, is shown by Tarcov to contain a subtext of careful reasoning on behalf of republics and political freedom. Partially vindicating the claims of Spinoza and Rousseau that *The Prince* is a republican book addressed to free peoples, Tarcov argues it is a book addressing princes while subtly encouraging republican policies. Thereby he closes the gap between *The Prince* and *The Discourses on Livy*, the second of which is clearly concerned with teaching how republics can best preserve their freedom. Machiavelli makes a promise in *The Prince* to limit his discussion to princes and principalities and to be silent on peoples and republics, but he does not keep it. He appeals to practices of the Roman republic, such as its holding of provinces by sending colonies, for models of "what all wise princes should do," whereas the prime instance of failure in the acquiring and holding of additions to the state is a prince. One of *The Prince*'s examples of a great princely founder of "new modes and orders" is Romulus, praised in the *Discourses* for founding laws that favor "a free and civil life." But if *The Prince* indeed encourages princes to imitate the founders of republics, the question arises: What is in it for the prince? The answer is that republics secure "the greatest advantages of preserving the state and glory" for the prince, but this answer occasions doubt that princes are motivated by love of virtue and freedom even as they take actions that promote virtue and freedom. In the cases of both princes and peoples, Machiavelli exposes their self-misunderstanding and implicitly asserts his superiority to both. He is a new princely founder of republics who looks to the Roman republic as a model and yet points to its defects: Rome eventually destroyed itself through destroying other republics. Tarcov concludes that Machiavelli's new republicanism is based on a new account of political freedom allied to a larger concept of human freedom as the ability of humans to become free of *their own natures*, in particular, the natural tendency to be the slave of habit. This proves, however, to be a limited freedom: not freedom in the choice of ultimate goods (such as riches and glory) but freedom in how the given ends are pursued. In this area Machiavelli surely emerges as a radical critic of traditional moral teachings.

Michael Zuckert, Jesse Covington, and James Thompson were invited to contribute to this volume their essay on the philosopher usually regarded as the father of modern liberalism. They examine closely John Locke's complex engagement with Christian political theology, weighing in particular the strategy of his critique of Robert Filmer in the *First Treatise of Government* and thereby shedding light on the relation between modern notions of freedom and Christian thought. The *First Treatise* supplies the elements of Locke's doctrine that the end of politics is "the preservation of every man's right and property, by preserving him from the violence and injury of others," which is fully expounded in the *Second Treatise*. Already in the first work "Locke attempts to reorient the human attitude toward the world from one of gratitude toward the provident God to one of rational industry in response to the scarcity and near valuelessness of the given that is man's birthright." This fundamental change also entails reducing the sense of dependence on God and therewith guilt over original disobedience. Locke attacks Filmer's claim of having biblical authority for grounding political rule in divine creation of the world and the donation to Adam, and his consequent denial that humans are naturally free. By separating Filmer from the Bible, Locke seems to argue that the Bible is more in accord with reason, which is Locke's "star and compass." Yet Locke makes clear his departures from the Bible, as well, thus denying biblically sanctioned parental power of life and death over children and according the power of life and death only to the humanly constituted state. Through subtle manipulations and distortions of Filmer, Locke gives the impression that the Bible is closer to his own views than to Filmer's. In the process Locke puts forth a purely rational theology according to which man in the original natural state has rational grasp of the law of nature teaching one's primary rights and the obligation to respect the rights of others. The use of all creatures for the end of self-preservation, contradicting the Bible's more restricted donation of creatures, is the rational response to natural scarcity, which replaces human error or sin as the ground of the human need to labor. Human freedom or "self-ownership" is the root of labor and of labor's fruit, property, and the human transformation of given nature is affirmed as progress—an advance upon original creation. And simply human prudence and consent settle the question "Who possesses the legitimate title to rule?" which Locke argues cannot be resolved by attempts to derive political power from divine creation.

Perhaps the most radical version of human autonomy in the modern era is Kant's account of personality, or practical reason in the human as having absolute responsibility for determining the will. One could say that Kant modifies Locke's idea of human self-ownership (and the modern concern with self-sovereignty in general) so that it becomes an "ideal" task of radical self-overcoming. Susan Shell's essay on Kant's late treatise *Religion within the Boundaries of Bare Reason* treats Kant's grappling with difficulties within the execution of this task. Without regard for any external end, practical reason must be able to determine itself so that obeying the moral law is its only incentive. Yet it is a natural limitation of our finite reason that it must think of ends in order to determine itself toward any action. Indeed the moral law gives rise to the idea of the "highest good," the goal of moral perfection accompanied by an appropriate happiness, to whose realization all humans must apply their efforts. Since this is an infinite project, its actualization requires the assistance of a divine author of the world, and hence pure morality leads to religion. The danger of lack of religion is misanthropy: hatred of the species in light of its inability to attain moral perfection wholly unaided. But the danger of religion is moral laxity: the introduction of the divine will into human moral self-improvement weakens the purity of the moral incentive. (Here one sees a kind of reversal of the Thomist problem regarding freedom and grace.) In clarifying this problem Kant notes a tendency toward evil in the human makeup, a tendency to make obedience to the moral law conditional on happiness. This is not simply to reject the moral law, but it is to regard external freedom (which is indeed a moral good) as the highest end in place of the moral law itself. It involves this self-deception: supposing ourselves morally justified solely through external compliance with duty. The great difficulty is that, given the wholly non-sensible character of the moral motive, human beings can never make present to themselves whether their motivations are pure. The various historical religions respond to this sublime failure of reason to know itself with discursive-sensible means to absolve the will of its arduous self-responsibility: acts of penitence, confessions of faith, and reliance on the letter, rather than the spirit, of the law. The heart of Kant's effort to uncover a "pure rational religion" in the Bible is to show that reason's "sublime failure" is ground for wonder and admiration, and thereby moral inspiration. The moral agent assumes responsibility for the natural flaw of reason, reason's need to represent an end. But Shell raises the question whether this doctrine of radical autonomy does not promote intolerance of all those forms of religion that the pure moralist regards as hindering human progress.

Starting with another problem in Kant's account of autonomy, Robert Pippin moves to recent reconstructions of Kant's thought, which he criticizes from a Hegelian perspective. If the problem Shell addresses is "How can one be certain that one is making progress in realizing the pure moral good?" the question Pippin raises with Kant is "How is being autonomous compatible with the emphasis on unconditional obedience to the moral law?" Kant demands a reflective "a priori endorsement" of any determinations to action, whereby all norms are imposed from a "first-person standpoint" without regard for existing institutions, traditions, and social attachments. But, Pippin asks, why should self-imposed norms be absolutely binding on the agent? How can "pure reason" be absolutely authoritative? (Shell asked, "How can we know that we are fulfilling the moral demands that are binding?" Pippin now asks "How can we know that the moral demands are binding in the first place?") Kant's moral principle, the categorical imperative, requires that the moral agent, in subjecting himself to the law, be at the same time a universal legislator. But what is the moral agent before this self-subjection, if not a lawless being of some sort? Noting that the language of self-subjection suggests a temporal sequence that can only be metaphorical, Pippin observes (with approval) that Kant is developing an understanding (taken further by Fichte and Hegel) of rationality as active achievement rather than as metaphysical substance. But the difficulty of first-person self-subjection to the pure noumenal law leads recent Kantians (thus Christine Korsgaard) to think of moral bindingness or "normativity" as a universal or transcendental condition for rational agency in general, so that even instrumental or hypothetical reasoning ("I must do X because I desire Y") presumes a form of self-obligation: If I rationally commit myself to end Y then I rationally commit myself also to means X. To acknowledge this rational implication is what it means to exist as a rational agent. In valuing this capacity for rational agency, I value "humanity in my own person" and recognize it as something valuable in all other rational beings. Thus in failing to follow the norms of practical reasoning I fail to exist as a rational agent. Pippin asks various pointed questions about this conception—above all, what it could mean to be responsible for a failure of reasoning if I cease to exist as rational agent. How can the failure be *mine?* Pippin argues that Korsgaard should follow through with her admission that "human identity has been constituted differently in different social worlds," which would lead her to Hegel's account of socially constituted identity and the abandonment of Kant's account of rational agency as a self-imposed identity. A priori–deductive methods in ethics give way to ethics as collective legislation over time. Still, a version of John Rist's question might be posed here: Are we now truly out of the woods with respect to the grounds of moral authority? Why should collectively legislated duties be more binding than self-legislated ones?

Robert Rethy concludes the volume with an essay on Nietzsche's intricate, indeed labyrinthian, reflection on freedom. Before presenting Nietzsche's ultimate positions, he summarizes the phases of this reflection: a juvenile conception of an antinomy of freedom and necessity; a Schopenhauerian period of regarding freedom as recognition of the will's unchanging intelligible character behind the phenomenal flux; an Enlightenment-skeptical phase in which freedom (with all of metaphysics) is an illusion underlying the illusion of moral responsibility. From the start the status of human freedom within the whole was a vital center of Nietzsche's thought. In his final phase he still regarded freedom of the will as an error—the greatest of "the four great errors" expounded in *Twilight of the Idols*—to be overcome by affirming the redemptive vision of the "fatality of all that is" in a renewal of Greek tragic (Dionysian-Heraclitean) wisdom. Rethy shows that this final fatalism is entwined with a radical version of modern self-sovereignty, such that Nietzsche can still speak of "my concept of freedom" in a positive sense, and that this concept can be grasped only through an "agonal dialectic," a movement of thought transforming the will. The dialectic begins with the "free spirit" rejecting all goals and all responsibility, wandering homelessly, reflecting on infinite possibility, denying God and all metaphysical support. This stance proves to be only a preparation for recognizing that life is impossible without limited perspectives, commitment, and hierarchy, and so the thinker takes on a new responsibility, a "will to free will," a willing of a new "thou shalt." This is "the great health," the morality of life itself as will to power—will to exploitation, violence, appropriation—for which the term "tyranny" is "too weak a metaphor." It is the morality of the higher human beings who live "beyond good and evil" but not beyond the noble, who practice the virtues of reverence and gift-giving. The higher men seek not freedom from responsibility (the slave's account of freedom) but danger and resistance, which make the will stronger through making self-mastery necessary. They attain the freedom of the warrior, wherein the manly instincts dominate over the other instincts and a ruling passion creates a hierarchy without settled law among passions. This freedom, hovering between mastery and servitude, which "one has and does not have," can arise only in the act of conquering, and so it calls for endless warfare. It also involves a hovering between solitude and social engagement, a hovering reflected in Nietzsche's elusive way of writing, which denies the luxury of fixed principles and proceeds through "thought-skirmishes" which emphasize the unsaid, the spaces between aphorisms of the "hermit's philosophy."

As with Kant's autonomous agent, the will of Nietzsche's higher man is not directed toward natural ends, and the "fall" into natural or dogmatic teleology is a constant temptation. And although here the imperative is of life rather than of reason, and drastically anti-egalitarian (freedom conceived as rights being the great enemy), the problem of whether one ever truly possesses this higher freedom recalls a similar problem in Kant with respect to the self-certification of moral progress. At the same time, Nietzsche goes well beyond Hegel in calling into question the unity and integrity of the self, and in viewing all thought as historically constituted.

All contributions to this volume make evident that, for every major thinker engaged with freedom, the nature of freedom is problematic and approachable only through oppositions and limitations. In other terms, the reality of freedom seems bound up with the peculiarly human task of determining and delimiting what it is to be human, for in seeking answers to that question, thought exercises the highest freedom. Thus one can recognize the centrality of the problem of freedom in the two roots of the Western tradition, Greek philosophy and the Bible, where the diverse estimates of the nature and goodness of human freedom may obscure but cannot conceal a common insight: the human is the one being that transcends itself in thinking toward a higher fulfillment, and therefore is led toward the question of its own nature and end.

1   FREEDOM
Grace and Necessity

SETH BENARDETE

Before the start of the Isthmian games at Corinth in 196 B.C., a Roman herald proclaimed that with the conquest of Philip of Macedon all the cities of Greece and Asia Minor were to be free, exempt from tribute, and under their own laws. The crowd was so astonished that they demanded that the herald repeat his message. "Not only was there happiness at the moment," Livy goes on to say, "but for many days it was freely renewed in thoughts and speeches: 'There was a people on earth that at their own expense and by their own effort waged war for the freedom of others, and they bestowed this not on a neighboring people or one on adjoining lands, but they crossed the sea so that there not be anywhere on earth an unjust empire, but instead law and right, both sacred and profane, be most powerful everywhere. The single voice of a herald had liberated all the cities of Greece and Asia: It was characteristic of a bold spirit to conceive of such a hope, it was the work of immense virtue and mighty fortune to carry it into effect.'"[1] Fifty years later a Roman general sacked Corinth, and Greece became a province of the Roman empire.

Thucydides would have held the imperial expansion of Rome to be due to necessity; and he would have doubted that her motives were ever as generous as those which the people at the Isthmian games ascribed to the Romans. He would have indicated that Rome would prefer to have to her East a collection of independent and quarrelsome cities than a single rival empire. It was enough for the moment that Macedonia was out of the way; she did not have to take over its territory in order to be safe. In discussing the Trojan War he says that Agamemnon gathered the expedition because he had the greatest power and not because the suitors of Helen were bound by an oath. It was fear rather than *charis*—an uncompelled graciousness—that made for that still un-Greek expe-

---

1. Livy, *History of Rome*, 33.32–33.

ditionary force.[2] Thucydides certainly doubts whether anything like *charis* operates either within or outside the city. If it shows up anywhere it is among uncivilized people—those who have not yet united knowledge with freedom. Such a unity is as rare as it is unstable, for it involves simultaneously, to use a Platonic pair of contraries,[3] a restriction on Scythian freedom—a people with ancestral graves but no settlements—and a liberation from Phoenician servility—a people equipped with all the latest in the arts but addicted to the love of gain. (This contrariety may remind you of the contemporary debate whether democratic institutions or economic development are to have priority; and the fruitlessness of the debate may be taken as a sign that if it is considered by itself it admits of no rational solution.) Herodotus speaks of the Scythians as the wise discoverers of the greatest human things—to be without cities and walls—but he does not admire the rest of their ways, for they have no depth and lack the wisdom Pythagoras represents.[4] If Greekness in a nontribal sense stands in for the proper mix of Scythian freedom and Pythagorean wisdom, then it is always threatened by a rebarbarization in which either a refined cruelty or an unexpected graciousness can reemerge. Themistocles, Thucydides tells us, saved his life in his flight from his pursuers by holding the son of the Molossian king Admetus at his hearth and not merely by giving a plausible argument why his prior thwarting of the king's wishes before the Athenians should not now be reckoned just grounds for retaliation. As soon as Themistocles, however, eluded his pursuers with the help of the king and returned to civilization he saved his life once more by the use of money and fear.[5]

The necessity that rules political life consists of two kinds. The first is chance, everything that is outside human providence and control. The Athenian Stranger of Plato's *Laws*, when he is about to propose legislation for a new city in Crete, stops himself short and says, "I was about to say that no human being ever legislates anything, but chance and circumstances of every kind in falling out in every sort of way legislate all things for us. Either some war overturns regimes violently and alters laws, or the bafflement of a harsh poverty affects them; and diseases too often compel revolution, when plagues swoop down, and often over a long time there is the untimeliness of a drought for many years. So if one looked ahead to these things one would give a start as I just did and say, 'No mortal legislates anything, but pretty nearly all of human affairs are chance.'"[6] Insofar as modern science offers a way to overpower or

---

2. Thucydides, *Historiae,* 1.9.1; 9.3.   3. Plato, *Republic,* 435e3–436a3.
4. Herodotus, *Historiae,* 4.46.2; cf. 4.95.2.   5. Thucydides, *Historiae,* 1.136–137.2.
6. Plato, *Laws,* 709a1–b2.

outwit chance, it seems to have built into it an incapacity to anticipate the innovations of chance and nature: it is doomed to catch up and never be ahead of the curve. Science stands in need of a history of its own future or a predictive science of science—a universal Hilbert-program as it were—for only then would it know whether there is no problem it cannot solve. Without such a map science too, in its conquest of chance, is subject to chance.

The second kind of necessity that is at the heart of political life itself involves an inner tension within two political principles that are never found consistently together except by chance. The city wants to be both free and great, but it can never become great unless it deprives others of their freedom. For ourselves, the vanishing of the American Indians represents at once the pride in absolute freedom for which we stand but they embodied and the condition for our establishing what seems to be a free people on free soil. Herodotus lays out these two principles at the beginning of his *Histories,* and they run their course throughout his story until the end, where the last word about an imperial people is "to be a slave." Herodotus begins his *Histories* with the Persian understanding of justice. Their understanding is designed to become the reader's. Paradoxically, Herodotus's typical audience is Persian, for the Persian view is prevalent almost everywhere and always: Herodotus never uses *Dike*, right and just punishment, of Athens and Athenians.[7] The *Persians* of Aeschylus strikingly confirms Herodotus' silence on this point, for though the play is in some sense a celebration of Athens' victory over Persia and of freedom over tyranny, the word *dike* never occurs. The Persians, on the other hand, believe that justice consists in the effective realization of the pattern of right: every violation of right leads and should lead to an equal and opposite vindication of right. Almost one-third of the expression *dikas didonai* in Herodotus—to pay the penalty of right—occurs in the first three chapters of the first book. The ordinary view of justice, Herodotus implies, is poetic justice. It is justice on paper and drained of the experience of right. When the Phoenicians seized Io, some Greeks—the Persians, in not knowing who they were, betray the nonexperiential and storybook character of their understanding—took Europa in exchange—*isa pros isa* (tit for tat), as the Persians say. The Greeks then began the second round of injustice by seizing Medea, and when Paris in retaliation raped Helen, the Greeks proved to be unjust because they sacked a city for the sake of a woman and thus did not

---

7. The remark at 7.133.2, in contrast with the Spartan story (7.134–37), can be said to represent Herodotus' view in general about Athens. It is particularly telling because the Spartan story links their piety with human freedom, which consists in the refusal to bow down before any man.

keep to the due measure of right.[8] Herodotus does not say whether he agrees with the Persians or not; instead, he says he will start his own account from him who he knew first acted unjustly against the Greeks, for up to Croesus' time all Greeks were free.[9] Injustice, then, for Herodotus consists in the permanent subjugation of a foreign people; it is not to be found in a raid no matter how destructive: "The expedition of the Cimmerians that came into Ionia, though it was older than Croesus', was not," he says, "a conquest of its cities but a raid of plunder."[10] In implicitly defining injustice as the characteristic of empire, Herodotus justifies his procedure to go through small and large cities alike, "for of those that were once great many have become small, and those in my own time that were great were formerly small. So knowing that human happiness never remains in the same place I shall make mention of both alike."[11] Herodotus' indifference is ultimately an indifference to the issue of right in itself, for human happiness depends unqualifiedly on empire, and empire is unjust. The city or the center of civilization cannot exist without the injustice that alone makes it possible. The city therefore can justify itself if and only if it can appeal to something higher than justice. Herodotus calls it happiness. Following Plato we can say that the good and the beautiful must ultimately rank higher than the just. One finds Plato's radicalization of Herodotus' thought in the *Republic*. There Socrates sets out to prove that the good coincides with the just. Such a coincidence founders on the need for the true city to encroach on its neighbors in order to support the unproductive but indispensable guardians who are meant to be merely defensive once they have satisfied their own needs. That the good of the city, however, is at the expense of the just does not entail that the city itself accept this truth. The good city lives in the element of justice while it violates justice from the start. This veil of false opinion is on the whole good too.

If one faces squarely the inner tension between a city's freedom and a city's injustice, one is forced to ask whether there is a way to minimize the effects of necessity, so that unlimited imperial expansion will not ultimately wipe out the very freedom for which empire may have been undertaken initially. In Herodotean terms, one wants to know how the necessity that makes greatness possible leaves room for freedom, and the Roman peace does not prove to be a specious name for the Roman desert.[12] Whatever the ratio turns out to be when a proper balance has been struck, it seems to be incalculable in advance: Aristotle's beautiful ex-

---

8. Herodotus, *Historiae*, 1.1–4.   9. Ibid., 1.5–6.
10. Ibid., 1.6.3.   11. Ibid., 1.5.4.
12. Cf. Tacitus, *Agricola*, 30.5; Pliny, *Natural History*, 14.1.

pression for this is *kat' euchen*, "in accordance with prayer." Material and final causes do not fit together before the fact, and after the fact they are indistinguishable. Socrates remarks that illness turned his companion Theages to philosophy, and in his own case the *daimonion*—whatever made Socrates unlike anyone else—had the same effect, but he did not know of another who experienced the same consequences as he did. This human and political problem seems to cancel the very possibility of any plausible teleological cosmology.

In order for us to observe a situation where necessity is perfectly adjusted for the production of the best possible fruit, we have to turn to the Platonic dialogue. There a certain question gets approached through conditions that seemingly are not most favorable for the discovery of the truth. Glaucon wants to know what justice and injustice are, and he wants justice to be praised in the most fitting way and injustice condemned. He wants the unvarnished truth and its veneer. Cebes and Simmias want Socrates to prove the immortality of the soul, and they want him to console their childish fear within. Socrates criticizes the previous speakers in the *Symposium* for not telling the truth about Eros, but he proposes to tell the truth while selecting only those elements of Eros that are most beautiful. Plato, however, was able, not to get around the conditions he seems to have arbitrarily imposed on himself, but to make those very conditions the indispensable way to the truth. It is not the arguments in Plato that convey the truth but the conditions for the arguments that carry the *logos*. In the Platonic universe necessity is the teleology. The Platonic dialogue, in accomplishing in the element of logographic necessity what cannot be accomplished otherwise, lays bare the limits that necessity puts on us in deed and dispels any illusion we might have had that it could be overcome. Through the transparency that necessity there has for *logos*, it teaches us about the opacity that haunts our freedom.

The city, as the ancients never tire of repeating, consists of men. It is therefore inevitable that the freedom and greatness of the city insinuate themselves into the makeup of citizens. They first imitate and then emulate the city on their own. Just as freedom reaches its politically established peak, insofar as it shows up individually, in the refusal to bow down before any other human being,[13] but then individually adopts the banner "the freedom to do whatever one likes," so the city's greatness inspires the tyrant. The tyrant is the ultimate patriot. Democracy and tyranny thus belong together. Plato has devoted an entire dialogue to the working out of the experiential equivalents to the structure of the city. It

13. Herodotus, *Historiae,* 7.136.1; cf. Plutarch, *Artaxerxes,* 21.8 (1022D).

is there where we can see what consequences the necessarily incoherent structure of the city has for individuals: the *Republic* can handle classes of men, it cannot bring to light the tumbling effect that mixes experientially the apparently separate parts of the soul. In the *Gorgias*, whose setting *per impossibile* is almost the entire length of the Peloponnesian War, Socrates finally gets Gorgias, after some stubborn misunderstanding on his part, to declare that rhetoric is equally responsible for the freedom of human beings themselves and the rule over everyone else, each in his own city.[14] Gorgias assigns to rhetoric what is in truth the nature of the city itself. Rhetoric is the self-deceived and self-deceiving reapplication to an individual of the city's own twin drives; it thus adopts, according to Socrates, the disguise of the art of justice, for it expresses the greatest public indignation at tyrannical ambitions while it privately fosters envy of the tyrant's success as the peak of true happiness.[15] Rhetoric in short exposes tragedy as an essentially popular form of literature: there are equal portions in it of satisfaction and distress, for we take open delight in the fated fall of him whom we secretly desire to be.[16] The published scandals of Hollywood are the contemporary version of this element in Greek tragedy. Of the three interlocutors in the *Gorgias*, Callicles expresses perfectly the doubleness of this experience while appearing to be the embodiment of what occasions this experience in everyone else. He contemplates with equanimity his subjugation to his natural ruler who does whatever he likes. Callicles is the tyrant's satellite; he is the essence of the vicarious life. "How would a human being be happy," he asks Socrates, "should he be a slave to anyone or anything whatsoever? This is what is noble and just according to nature—I'm now speaking to you frankly: he who is to live rightly must let his desires be the greatest possible, and he must not curtail them, but be capable of serving them while they are the greatest possible, and fulfill whatever his desire is at any time."[17] One notices at once that the condition for not being a slave *(douleuon)* to anything is to serve *(uphretein)* one's own desires. Callicles conceals this paradox from himself through a shift in vocabulary, but he had already confirmed it when he cited, as his only examples, Darius' expedition against the Scythians and Xerxes' against the Greeks. They both failed. Their *impotentia*, or reckless immoderation, is the same as their impotence. To fulfill one's desire is to act on it, it is not to achieve its goal. Callicles means without knowing it that only if one's desires exceed one's capacity to satisfy them, can one be certain that one has not unconsciously limited one's

14. Plato, *Gorgias*, 452d5–8.
15. Plato, *Gorgias*, 471a4–d2; *Laws*, 661b1–4.
16. Plato, *Minos*, 321a4–5; cf. *Laws*, 658d2–3; Homer, *Iliad*, 2.270.
17. Plato, *Gorgias*, 491e5–492a3.

desires to one's capacity and thus failed to be without restraints. This is an essentially tragic view of life, for the moral of Greek tragedy is that the happy life is the criminal life, and hence one cannot choose what one most desires: Oedipus must accept as fate what he wants but cannot will. Socrates puts this to Callicles with a quotation from Euripides: "Who knows whether to live is to die, and to die to live?" Callicles prompted the question by asserting that those who are not in need of anything are not the happy but rather stones and corpses; he implies that to be filled with desires is to be fully alive. Socrates therefore tells the story of the Danaids who are eternally compelled to carry water in a sieve to a leaky jar. Socrates informs Callicles that only in the unconditionality of Hades, where the soul is by itself and apart from the body with its built-in limitations, would Callicles find the life he is looking for. Only if he were dead would he be fully alive. Only if he were the shadow of a dream would he truly be. Only then would he avoid what he most dreads—the contempt that a slap in the face inscribes on the soul.

To slough off necessity is to jump out of one's own skin. It is to make oneself into an exhibition of oneself, for the dream of individual freedom leads inevitably to the dissolution of the boundary between self and other, of inside and outside. It involves the same necessity as that which the city undergoes in losing its freedom in pursuing greatness. This necessity is the burden of most ancient poetry, for, for the poet, character is destiny. Achilles believes he has a choice; he can go home and live a long life or die young and achieve glory at Troy. His future, however, is closed. He can no more be Odysseus and go home than he can become a god and give up his version of immortality, just as Odysseus' own choice, to be a god or to go home, seems likewise not to be a genuine offer. The emergence of fate behind apparent choice determines the plot of both the *Iliad* and the *Odyssey*. Fate is the name we give to the rightness of the fit between inside and outside, when what is in a name—the most arbitrary of signs—turns into the inner truth of a man. Aeneas, who seems to walk through Vergil's poem without taking any part in it, comes into his own when at the end he kills Turnus in a rage. We would have seen it coming had we kept in mind that the city Aeneas founded after the fall of Troy was named after himself and meant Terror *(Ainos-ainos)*. Usually, however, the hero, in defying his fate, defies himself. Ajax, whose name is a cry of woe *(aiai)*, believes he is Achilles' superior, for Achilles' virtue was not entirely his own but relied on divine support: at the beginning of the *Iliad* Achilles shies away from a criminal act only because Athena appears to him alone and yanks his hair.[18] Ajax, on the other hand, is

18. Sophocles, *Ajax,* 764–65; Homer, *Iliad,* 1.197–98.

entirely his own man. On his failure to demonstrate this by slaughtering the Greek army he resolves to kill himself. He reasons as follows. To kill everyone is to punish on the greatest possible scale all who denied the reality of his supremacy; they were dazzled by Achilles' beauty and Odysseus' cunning. When, however, Athena thwarts his plans and makes him believe that a flock of sheep is the Greek army, and thus reveals to him that what he took for the real is at the whim of the gods, Ajax turns to himself: Athena cannot get at that and transform who he is into an illusion. Suicide is for him the proof that there is something of his own that is immune from the gods. The gods cannot get inside him. He is mistaken: Hades is the ingression of the gods into the supposedly integral self. Although Ajax's original plan was to kill himself inside the tent where, in the midst of other dead cattle, he had been torturing whom he believed to be Odysseus, he changes the scene of his death at the last minute and withdraws to a place uncontaminated by carnage. At the last minute Ajax refuses to understand himself as carrion, as more deserving, as Heraclitus put it, to be cast out than dung. He finds he needs the consolation of the sacred, or the claim that even in death he is still human. He needs, he believes, Hades if he is not to be a prey to birds and dogs. He needs Hades in order to tell his story to those below.[19] When Odysseus descends there and addresses him, Ajax remains silent, for he has nothing to say.[20]

Greek tragedy presents man as ordained as much to become what he is as the city embodies in principle the inevitability of a conflict between its freedom and its greatness. The sign of their coincidence is in the history of Rome. Once Rome had defeated all of its external neighbors it began to devour itself, until with freedom wiped out with the death of Brutus and Cassius at Pharsalus, Augustus established on its exhausted body a tyranny that could never legitimize itself over time, for it could never acknowledge that it had not restored the republic but buried it. On account of the limbo in which the Julio-Claudian dynasty lived, it had to assume the guise of Greek tragedy. What had been up to then stories about the remote past, with an internal *logos* that did not either seek or need any confirmation in political events, now became the truth of the present. Vergil, in grounding the reality of Rome in the fiction of Homer, pointed the way. The word one finds throughout the Greek histories of the first century A.D. is tragic: there is even a play, *Octavia Praetexta*, falsely ascribed to Seneca, that puts Nero on the same stage as where he often acted tragic roles. Nero is merely the culmina-

---

19. Sophocles, *Ajax*, 826–30, 865.
20. *Odyssey*, 11.563.

tion of the sudden recrudescence of myth that haunts the early principate. His murder of his brother Britannicus brings back the truth that the fraternity for the city is against the grain of the fratricidal principle of rule. His murder of his mother is the ultimate playing out of incestuous *erôs* in the realm of the political. We read of the first inkling of this descent into the roots of political crime in Tacitus. He reports that Tiberius, when he had had killed indiscriminately everyone with whom Sejanus was connected, stationed spies along the way when their corpses were being dragged to the Tiber, in order for them to note down those who displayed any sorrow. We are forcibly reminded of Creon's decree that forbade female lamentations at the death of Polynices, though he could not bring himself to convict Ismene for her tears.[21] The tearlessness of Antigone baffled him.

This perfect match up between tragedy and politics makes one suspicious precisely because it is perfect. People, after all, often surprise and say and do things that are seemingly above or below them. When Prometheus defies Zeus and refuses to reveal to him the secret of his future he does so in full knowledge that Zeus will punish him for his obstinacy. He believes that his foreknowledge makes the threats of Zeus' henchmen harmless; but what he does not understand is that there can be no foreknowledge of experience. He cannot know whether Zeus will break him. The facts of the future are not the facts then and there. Event is not affect. The tragic formula for this is *pathei mathos*, "by experience understanding." It announces that the relation of action to reaction is in principle unpredictable. Tragedy seemingly shows the impossibility of prudence. To be fearless is not yet to have been confronted with the terror that overwhelms you. To be moderate is not yet to have been seduced by the temptation that ensnares you.[22] After Odysseus, just before his departure from her island, rejects Calypso's offer of immortality, she warns him that he will soon regret his decision. He assures her that he will not: "And if one of the gods once more on the wine-dark sea shipwrecks me, I shall patiently endure it, for I have already suffered much and toiled much on waves and in war."[23] No sooner does Odysseus leave Calypso than he regrets it and, though he does not take back his refusal to be immortal, he expresses the wish to have died at Troy and received a proper burial. Odysseus gives up at that moment all the experiences he had had after the Trojan War that allowed him to reject Calypso's offer and made him interesting to us. Through those experiences he had

---

21. Tacitus, *Annals*, 6.19; Sophocles, *Antigone*, 28–29, 204, 527.
22. Cf. Seneca, *De beneficiis*, 7.11.
23. Homer, *Odyssey*, 5.221–24.

come to choose to remain a human being, but he did not know that he thereby had chosen self-opacity. Despite his knowledge of what it meant to be a human being, with this body and this mind, he did not know that it entailed a permanent ignorance.[24]

If, then, there is this curious room for freedom on the part of man, we can well ask whether the conditions for either foreclosing or expanding such freedom can be worked out. The risk in the realization of those conditions is clear: one opens up the possibility of the better and the worse almost equally. The Sparta of Thucydides would seem to represent the kind of regime in which any departure from its norms would prove disastrous for an individual. Thucydides holds up Pausanias as the model of the corrupt deviation that must follow any relaxation from Spartan rigidity. No sooner did Pausanias lead the victory over the Persians at Plataea, and in its aftermath display several signs of what we call Greek sobriety and humanness, than he conceived the desire to be the tyrant of Greece and entered into treasonous correspondence with the Persian king. He betrayed his plans by his arrogant behavior and luxurious garb and table, and did not hesitate to hand over his trusted boyfriend to execution in order to further his designs. Spartan virtue, it seems, is cloistered virtue; it cannot go outside without turning inside out. Indeed, Socrates asserts in the *Republic* that even in his own best city every citizen who is virtuous by habit but without philosophy would necessarily choose, if given the chance, to be a tyrant and only express a vain remorse if he knew beforehand that he was condemned to eat his own children.[25]

A Spartan in Plato's *Laws* makes the case for Athens. It is a common saying, he reports, that Athenians who are good are exceptionally so, for they alone without compulsion but by nature are truly and not feignedly good.[26] Thucydides' Pericles makes a somewhat similar claim. "To sum up," he says, "I say the city as a whole is the education of Greece and individually the same man in my opinion would show himself to be self-sufficient over the largest number of kinds of affairs and dexterously display the most grace or charm *(meta chariton)*."[27] The two men who come closest to this ideal Athenian and are in Thucydides his end-pieces are Themistocles and Alcibiades: Pericles did not have either of them in

---

24. Aeneas says: *omnia praecepi atque animo mecum ante peregi* (Vergil, *Aeneid*, 6.105). It is a question whether he is shown to be right or not.

25. Plato, *Republic*, 619b7–d1.

26. Plato, *Laws*, 642c6–d1; cf. 951b4–7; cf. Plutarch, *Dion*, 58.1: "It seems to be truly said that that city [Athens] bears men who when good are the best in virtue and when knaves the most wicked in vice, just as its land produces the finest honey and the fastest-acting hemlock."

27. Thucydides, *Historiae*, 2.41.1.

mind. Both saved Athens when it most needed saving, and the Athenians condemned them both for treachery. The city most shows its greatness if it can produce citizens who can be accepted anywhere, not as experts in some craft but as their true rulers. The city breeds its best at its own expense. They are the political equivalent of the philosopher who dwells in his own city and not in his fatherland.[28] The harm they do, however, is greater and their benefit more short-lived.

We began with Rome and now end with Rome. In the *Annals,* Tacitus implicitly connects the freedom L. Brutus established along with the consulship when he expelled the last of the Roman kings with the freedom Republican writers had to write up the deeds of the Roman people, and which they lost once Augustus had firmly rooted the principate; but in the *Agricola* he comments that Nerva inaugurated a blending of things that had long been incompatible, the principate and freedom, and in the *Histories,* in praising the rare felicity of his own time, in which it was allowed to think whatever you wanted and say whatever you thought, he lets us infer that the two kinds of freedom, political and intellectual, do not necessarily go together, and the universal domination of a one who is not freely chosen can let freedom flourish that does not have to have its roots in the free soil of a free people. This inference is a pale reflection of Plato's *Republic.* Socrates there argues at length that the city cannot put together except in an illusory way the needs of the body and the needs of the soul, and the fulfillment of the needs of the body is to be found in the defense of the city, which, inasmuch as it is mounted no less against internal than external enemies, cannot afford the luxury of the mind's freedom: the city envelops its citizens from their earliest youth in the shadows of fictions.

Longinus, or whoever wrote *On the Sublime,* lived under the Roman empire, probably in the middle of the first century, when Rome had lost any reason for existing unless it was for the maintenance of its own existence.[29] At the end of his treatise, he appends the following:

A philosopher recently put this question before me in saying: "I am as surprised as of course many others are, how in the world there are in our time highly persuasive and political natures, keen, skilled, and particularly inclined to the pleasures of words, but as for very lofty and magnificent natures they no longer, except rarely, come to be. Or must one trust," he went on to say, "the common talk, 'Democracy is the good nurse of the greatest, in which it was pretty nearly the case that those skilled in speeches flourished and died along with it?' Freedom, one says, is capable of fostering and giving hope to the proud thoughts of

---

28. Plato, *Republic,* 592a7–8.
29. Cf. Lucan, *The Civil War,* 1.21–23.

those who think great things, and in doing so awakens rivalrous zeal and ambition for the first prizes. Furthermore, on account of the rewards proposed in such a regime the orator's soul is given a sharp edge by practice and once rubbed smooth, as it were, is likely to flash out in freedom in the course of actions. But we nowadays," he said, "seem to be the childish pupils of a just slavery, just about wrapped up as we are in the swaddling clothes of the same habits and practices from the time when our minds are still malleable and without a taste of the most beautiful and fertile stream of speeches: I mean," he said, "freedom. It is for this reason we come out as nothing but naturally gifted flatterers." Accordingly he said that all other conditions square with household servants but no slave becomes an orator. To be caught in the impossibility of speaking freely is to live in a prison and endure constant beatings by way of habit. For as Homer says, "The day of slavery takes away half of virtue." Just as the flute cases in which the so-called dwarf Pygmies are raised—so I hear by report and am convinced—check the growth of those locked within and on account of the bonds that circumscribe the body damage them, so one would declare that total slavery, even if it is most just, is the gag of the soul and a universal prison.[30]

30. Longinus, *On the Sublime*, 44.1–5.

2

THE FOLLIES OF FREEDOM AND REASON
An Old Story

LEON R. KASS

The story of Adam and Eve in the Garden of Eden is perhaps the most famous story in Genesis, indeed, in the whole Hebrew Bible. Read simply and superficially, it tells the tale of man's disobedience and its doleful consequences: the loss of ease, innocence, and psychic wholeness, the gain of a burdened and painful mortal existence. But read carefully and searchingly, with attention to all its details, it offers profound insights into our permanent human nature and the human condition. First among these are insights into the follies of human freedom and reason.

A careful reading of the Garden of Eden story begins by noticing that it presents a view of our humanity vastly different from the one offered in Genesis 1, the so-called "first creation story," in which man is said to be made in the God's image and given dominion over the earth. If read "historically," the Garden of Eden story shows *how* and *when* human life got to be so difficult. If read "philosophically" and "anthropologically," it makes clear *why* human life is *always* so difficult. And if read "morally," it enhances our moral education by enabling us to see clearly and to experience powerfully the primary sources of many of our enduring moral dilemmas and much of our unhappiness. Like every truly great story, it seeks to show us not what happened (once) but what *always* happens, what is always the case. Like every truly great story, its truth may lie not so much in its historical or even philosophical veracity as in its effects on the soul of the reader.

If they are read as "historical" accounts, the two creation stories contradict each other, but read philosophically they in fact complement one another and form part of a coherent whole. As the first story shows, there is an eternal, intelligible, and hierarchic order of the world, in which we human beings stand at the top of the visible beings; the cosmos itself is not divine, for it has a higher, invisible, and (partly) mysterious source.

Man, not the sun, is godlike. But, as the second story shows, human life, considered here on earth and in its own terms, is, for the most part, hardly godlike: it has a sorrowful content for which we sense that we are somehow responsible. A life of sinless innocence and wholeheartedness is virtually impossible for a human being, thanks to freedom, reason-and-speech, and human pride linked to freedom, reason, and speech.

Taken together, these two separate stories combine to teach the reader that neither cosmic nature nor human reason will suffice to help us live well. Knowledge of nature cannot heal our self-division or teach us righteousness, not least because—as we learn from the first story—the cosmos is neither divine nor a source of such moral-political teaching. And—as we learn from the second story—our own native powers of mind and awareness, freely exercised on the world around us, are inadequate for discerning how to live happily or justly.

In short, Genesis 1 challenges the dignity of the natural objects of thought and the ground of natural reverence; Genesis 2–3 challenges the human inclination to try to guide human life (solely) by our own free will and our own human reason, exercised on the natural objects of thought. Ordinary human intelligence, eventually culminating in philosophy, seeks wisdom regarding how to live—that is, knowledge of good and bad—through contemplation of the nature of things. The Bible opposes, from its beginning, this intention and this possibility, first, in chapter one, by denying the dignity of the primary object of philosophy, the natural things, and second, in chapter two, by rebutting the primary intention of philosophy, guidance for life found by reason and rooted in nature. God, not nature, is divine; obedience to God, not the independent and rational pursuit of wisdom, is the true and righteous human way. Having stated the conclusion at the beginning, we turn now to the text and to this story's account of the primordial human being.

I. SPEECHLESS INNOCENCE:
THE BASIC STRATUM OF HUMAN LIFE

The text's picture of man—his powers, his activities—comes to us sequentially in layers, built up in order from the inside out; for this reason, we must not ascribe human capacities to "our hero" before they are explicitly presented in the text. I repeat: we can learn most from the story by regarding it as a mythical yet realistic portrait of permanent truths about our humanity, rather than as a historical yet idealized portrait of a blissful existence we once enjoyed but lost.

Every shrub of the field was not yet in the earth, and every herb of the field had not yet sprung up; for the Lord God had not yet caused it to rain upon the earth, and there was not a man (*ʾadam*) to till [or 'serve'; *laʿavod*] the ground (*ʾadamah*). (2:5)

As our story opens, the earth is hard, dry, and lacking in vegetation. The earth's fruitfulness needs both the rain of heaven and the workings of man. Even before we meet him, man is defined by his work, man has his work cut out for him: less the ruler over life, more the servant of the earth, man will till and toil, needily waiting for rain, anxious about the future. The story begins convincingly, conveying a nearly universal truth about human life.

But *why* is this our life? What is responsible for its being so difficult? The sequel intends an answer.

> Then the Lord God formed the human being (*ʾadam*)
> of the dust of the ground (*ʾadamah*),
> and breathed into his nostrils the breath of life;
> and man became a living creature.
>
> (2:7)

A beginning clue regarding human troubles may be contained in man's dual origins: he is constituted by two principles, the first one low ("dust of the earth"), the second one high ("breath of life"). The human being here first comes to sight not as "image of God" but as formed and animated dust of the ground. Higher than the earth, yet still bound to it, the human being has a name, *ʾadam* (from *ʾadamah*, meaning "ground" or "earth," from *ʾadam*, meaning "ruddy" or "tawny"), which reminds us of his lowly terrestrial origins. A groundling or earthling, man is, from the start, up from below.

Although formed from the ground, man is not alienated from it. On the contrary, simply as a living creature, he appears at first to be right at home, in a world that seems absolutely "made for him."

> And the Lord God planted a garden eastward, in Eden;
> and there he put the man whom He had formed.
> And out of the ground made the Lord God to grow every tree that is pleasant
> to the sight and good for food;
> the tree of life also in the midst of the garden,
> and the tree of the knowledge of good and bad. . . .
> And the Lord God took the man and put him into the garden of Eden
> to work it [or "to serve it"; *leʿavdah*] and to keep it [or "to guard it" or "to
> watch it"; *leshamrah*].
> And the Lord God commanded the man, saying,
> "From every tree of the garden thou mayest surely eat; . . ."
>
> (2:8–16)

This prototypical human being, what is he like? The text does not explicitly tell us. Yet this very silence suggests that he is a simple being, with a simple soul, living a simple life. In body he looks like one of us: upright, naked, and hairless. But in mind and heart he seems proto-human, more childlike than godlike. He is ignorant, speechless, and (above all) innocent; as yet, he knows no complex or specifically human passions or desires: neither shame nor pride, anger nor guilt, malice nor vanity, wonder nor awe visit his soul. Very likely, he also lacks both fear of death and erotic desire. With his simple needs—for food, for drink, for repose—simply met, he is content. Experiencing little gap between desire and its fulfillment, and feeling no opposition either from without or from within, he knows neither self-division nor self-consciousness. Solitary and independent, he lives for himself, immediately and here-and-now, in a world that provides him peace, ease, and the satisfaction of his basic needs.

Read as history, the text fails to persuade the skeptical reader. Man probably never lived as a solitary or in an edenic garden. But read anthropologically and morally, the story is both revealing and moving. Whatever else human beings are or become, they are, always and at bottom, *also* beings with an uncomplicated, innocent attachment to their own survival and ease, beings who experience and feel, immediately and without reflection, the goodness of their own aliveness. This stratum of all *animal* being—private bodily need, privately satisfied and enjoyed—is an ineradicable part of *human* being. All human beings know hunger, thirst, and fatigue. No man, no matter how altruistic or saintly, meets his own hunger by putting food into someone else's mouth. Moreover, from the point of view of simple necessity—for food and drink—the world is a rather generous place; were it not for the depredations of civilized man, it would be so still.

Most readers, no matter how sophisticated and civilized we have become, respond to this portrait of our mythical remotest "past" with something that feels, in fact, like nostalgia. With at least part of our souls, we long for a condition like this. We envy "original man" not only his contentment with life but also his simple innocence and goodness, his psychic wholeness and spontaneity, and his lack of troublesome self-division and corrosive self-consciousness. We envy his apparent being at home in the world, at one with and in command of his surroundings. Even though we probably would not, on balance, exchange our life for his, we are made poignantly to experience "what we have lost" and to wonder why. The text's answer is right before us.

II. DISTURBING KNOWLEDGE, DANGEROUS FREEDOM

The simple, primordial human being, because he is primordially *human*—or perhaps, instead, *potentially* human—is not quite simple. As the story already hints, there is something disquieting in his original nature. Some innate capacities or potentialities in the human soul dangerously threaten to upset the tranquility of man's simple and innocent life. Two possible sources of disturbance are subtly identified, metaphorically, in the form of the two special trees, trees which are distinguished from those "pleasant to the sight and good for food" (2:9), each an object of potential desire: the tree of life (in the midst of the garden) and the tree of knowledge of good and bad.

The tree of life, offering deathlessness, stands in the center of man's garden. As is true of other living animals, man's immediate attachment to his own life implies an instinctive fear of death, which, should it become active by becoming conscious as an *actual* fear, could—and does—greatly disturb man's tranquillity. But unless the fear of death is accompanied by something like self-conscious knowledge of death as a badness, the creature will have no interest in trying to overcome death by seeking immortality from the tree of life. The original human being shows no interest in the tree of life; indeed, he never eats of it prior to his expulsion from Eden, presumably because concern with death does not penetrate the consciousness of his simple soul.

The more important threat to the contentment of elementary human life is represented by the tree of knowledge of good and bad. That tree stands as the object or goal of an (at least) latent human tendency to seek a certain kind of knowledge or a certain kind of awareness. Once attained, this knowledge will necessarily disturb the psychic peace and harmony of the living creature. In its presence the human being cannot without trouble enjoy his own existence. In its presence he cannot remain undivided within himself. To reinforce the threat that such knowledge poses to his own health and happiness, the danger is here revealed to human beings—both the one in the story and the ones reading it—by the highest authority. Not mere local custom, but the highest principle of Being attests to the trouble that comes with and from a certain kind of dangerous knowledge. The warning the story puts in the form of a divine command.

And the Lord God commanded the man, saying,
"From every tree of the garden thou mayest surely eat;
but of the tree of the knowledge of good and bad, thou shalt not eat of it;
for in the day that thou eatest thereof thou shalt surely die."
(2:16–17)

We take it as an axiom that God is unlikely to waste His commandments and prohibitions, issuing them where there is no need. Thus, from the fact that it is here prohibited, we infer the existence of a human propensity that leads toward the tree. Man must be the kind of being that has at least a potential to seek the kind of knowledge represented by the tree. Man must be the kind of being for whom such knowledge is always in his vicinity, so to speak but an arm's reach away. To see why a benevolent God might try to keep His creature from it, we need first to try to say what this prohibited tree *is* and why knowledge of good and bad might be deadly.

We note first that one should regard the knowledge it represents as knowledge of "good and *bad*" rather than "good and evil." The Hebrew word translated "bad" has a much broader meaning than "moral evil." Pain is bad and so are sickness, ugliness, and disorder. It is therefore better to begin with this very broad, and not exclusively moral, understanding of "bad." Second, the tree of knowledge is obviously a metaphor; knowledge does not grow on trees. Nevertheless, the metaphor is powerful. Why does the Bible present knowledge as if it were embodied *in a tree*, obtainable by eating? What, for openers, is a tree?

A tree is a seemingly independent being, self-developing, self-sustaining, and apparently self-caused. But seeming is not being. God caused this tree to come out of the ground—like all trees. The tree's appearance of independence—its "on-its-ownness"—is deceptive. Though separate and distinct, the tree in fact belongs to the earth. Though it appears lofty to the human eye, it is in fact of lowly origins and contains no breath of life. A tree may be attractive to sight and tempting for food, but it is silent; it has nothing useful to teach about life. In short, a tree is a natural, terrestrial, low but seemingly lofty, attractive but amoral being, seemingly—but only seemingly—autonomous and self-sufficing.

Consider next the name of our special tree. The name "knowledge of good and bad" is ambiguous. Some have held that it is an idiom meaning knowledge of all things, others that it means political knowledge, especially knowledge of how to rule. But on its face, the name suggests rather knowledge of how to live, of what we would call practical knowledge, including but not limited to moral knowledge. Yet, it is unclear whether it signifies knowledge only *that there are* good and bad, or, in addition, also a *concern* with good and bad, or, further, *true* knowledge of what good and bad *really are*. In the light of the sequel, I am inclined to think that the tree offers the human being not *true* knowledge of good and bad, but merely a concerned awareness of their presence and difference, coupled with (not necessarily reliable) opinions about which is which.

Putting together our discussion of "tree" with the discussion of this tree's name, we get the following suggestion: the tree of knowledge of good and bad stands for some autonomous "knowledge" of how to live, derived by human beings from their own experience of the visible world and rooted in their own surroundings (nature; trees in the garden). Once the potential for human freedom and choice emerges, human beings live by their own lights, learning solely from their own experience. It is precisely this natural and uninstructed human way that the Bible warns us against by having God attempt to prevent man from attaining (or even pursuing) that freedom and its correlative, autonomous knowledge. By means of the image of a divinely prohibited tree, the story means to make clear to the reader that human freedom—or, what is the same thing, human reason—is itself deeply questionable, and the likely source of all our unhappiness.

The point is even better made if we pursue a purely formal analysis, dealing not with the substance of the tree but only with the fact that it was prohibited. Man in this story is defined as being in need of a prohibition, that is, as a free being, or as a "too-free" being. Accordingly, the crux of the story is prohibition and interdiction, which is to say—by negation—freedom and autonomy. The Bible knows that the only way to show human freedom as a problem is to come at it from its opposite: constraint. Here is how the story's logic works.[1]

The man is told to obey a command. Obedience is therefore called for, its opposite is proscribed. The opposite of obedience is nonobedience or disobedience, or, in other words, choosing-for-yourself. *Any* free choice is, by definition, an act of non-obedience. To make this truth absolutely clear, the story makes free choice appear as disobedience to command.

Free choice is tied to knowledge; free choice implicates reason. Whereas obedience means necessarily "no *independent* knowledge of good and bad," disobedience necessarily means, at least implicitly, independent or autonomous knowledge of good and bad. *Any* free choice implies reaching for and acting on our own "knowledge" (or opinion) of good and bad, better and worse. *Every* free choice implies some (at least) tacit judgment that the thing being chosen is, in some sense, good.

The meaning of the tree of knowledge of good and bad should now be clear: the knowledge prohibited is in fact the knowledge implied in violating *all* prohibitions, or, in other words, the knowledge implied

---

1. I am indebted for the analysis that follows (in the next three paragraphs) to a marvelous essay by Leo Strauss, "On the Interpretation of Genesis," *L'Homme* 21, no. 1 (January–March 1981): 5–20.

in *any* act of *free* choice. As everybody knows, the human being indeed chose to disobey, never mind why. He (they) chose therewith the principle of disobedience, which is to say, the principle of freedom and independence. The name that Genesis gives to the principle of freedom or disobedience is "knowledge of good and bad," knowledge freestanding and autonomous (that is, just like a tree).

In the story, the human being, in the act of disobedience, appropriates to himself knowledge of good and bad. But please note: *to reach for the forbidden fruit is already to have tasted it.* The woman, *before* she eats of it, has already made a judgment that the tree is "*good* for food and a delight to the eyes and to be desired to make one wise." The woman judges for herself, on the basis of her own autonomous "knowing" of good and bad, that "to eat is good." Formally speaking, the eating merely ratifies, after the fact, the human way of freedom and autonomy.

Some will argue that the problem that God sought to address (or, to speak strictly anthropologically, the problem at the heart of our troubles) is not freedom itself but rather only its abuse. On this account, freedom is itself a good, even a blessing, but a blessing which can be used for both good and bad. When it is badly used, the fault lies not with freedom or reason itself but with human appetite: desire (concupiscence) frequently leads human freedom astray. Or, alternatively, human pride distorts free will.

Supporters of this interpretation emphasize that the prohibition seeks to limit human eating, an activity born of desire. But the context shows that eating, by itself, is not the problem: God generously provides a whole garden full of trees "good for food," and the tree of knowledge is clearly distinguished from the trees of nourishing. The text seems to imply not that freedom is corrupted by desire, but rather the reverse: natural desire and its satisfaction are threatened as a result of human freedom and reason and a certain kind of knowledge. Because we have free choice—that is, because our desires are not simply given by "instinct"—and because our reason, through its working on our imagination, influences and alters natural appetites, human appetite increases beyond what is necessary and good for us. Precisely because we are rational and, hence, free, we can freely desire vastly more things than we should, things that are harmful to life, health, and well-being. The proscriptive limitation on human omnivorousness metaphorically (and perfectly) highlights the dangers freedom poses to healthy natural desire.

As an empirical matter, it is no doubt true that desire and pride can and do warp human choice. But our biblical text has a much more radical teaching about the problem of freedom. Every act of uninstructed free choice, the text seems to intimate, is an implicitly prideful act, presupposing as it does the possession of knowledge of what is good for a human being. Every act of choice implicitly expresses a judgment of good and bad, better and worse. Every act of choice presupposes that the human agent knows—or thinks he knows—what is good for him (or someone else), on which basis he chooses accordingly. On this interpretation of the text, the fact that God wants to keep man from the tree of knowledge of good and bad suggests that He wants man to remain an innocent, contented, and un-self-divided being who follows "instinctively" the path to his natural good. Or, better, reading morally rather than historically, through God's command about the tree the text teaches us readers that it is our own freedom—and its implicitly yet necessarily disobedient character—that is the cause of all human troubles. Freedom—independence, choice, will—is the problem, and not only once upon a time, but always.

To sum up: for a human being, as for any human child, the possibility of choosing for oneself lies always within reach. To be a human being *means* that judgments of good and bad are always in one's mental garden, no more than a thought away. And, as every parent teaches, and as we children learn painfully by ourselves much later, a free choice is not necessarily a good choice, not even for oneself. In the story, the generous God paternalistically seeks to keep man from sacrificing his simple and innocent happiness; yet the need for such a restraint shows that the autonomous source of trouble lies already deep within, at least potentially. Moreover, man's ability presumably to understand the prohibition, however partially, proves that he needs it: because he already has mind enough to distinguish the trees by name, he will soon enough have a mind of his own—just like the reader—and, with it, the ability to make himself miserable. Self-chosen knowledge of good and bad is not *true* knowledge of good and bad; human beings on their own will not find true knowledge of how to live. This must be supplied by (what is later called) "revelation."

III. SPEECHLESS ALONENESS:
WEAKNESS OR STRENGTH?

So much for the picture of "original" solitary man, the poetic incarnation of the first and deepest stratum of human nature. The story that follows concentrates on the transgression and its sequellae, which it narrates dramatically, in stages, through the following episodes: God's attempt to remedy man's aloneness, through the creation, first, of the animals, second and successfully, of woman; man's first reaction to the woman; the woman's conversation with the serpent; the act of disobedience; the discovery, interrogation, and "punishment"; and the expulsion from the garden. Embedded in the narrative are deep and subtle clues to the next layers or levels of human nature. We shall follow the tracks of human speech, reason, and freedom.

The human being as we have met him so far in the Eden story has been silent. He offered no comment of any kind regarding the garden, his appointed task, or even the prohibition. Speech is no part of the fundamental human beginning, of the basic or lowest stratum of human life. Or, to put it another way, our basic engagement with life is speechless and sub-rational. In addition, the primordial human being is alone: what need is there to speak, and with whom? We will hear him speak only after the creation of woman; his speech on that occasion will reveal deep truths about the character of human speaking altogether.

The original human being is not only silent. He evinces no other clear evidence of the possession or exercise of reason. True, God appears to be addressing the man's understanding when He informs him of the plenitude of food and when He pronounces the prohibition. By implication, one could argue, the primordial man must have sufficient reason to understand the prohibition. Fair enough. However, it is possible also to think that man in the original condition, being not yet fully free or fully human, lacks any active inclination toward the forbidden knowledge, which is to say his reason is still merely potential and dormant. Only when dormant reason begins to stir (as it has, of course, for every reader of the text) will the *enunciation* of the prohibition *as a prohibition* become important: only then will the prohibition be understood for what it is; paradoxically, only then will it become necessary. On the basis of this analysis, one can argue that human reason is, to begin with, merely potential. Or, to say the same thing in non-temporal ways, the basic stratum of human life—represented in the story by the tableau of a solitary human being, before the coming of the animals and before woman—is non-rational and "suspicious" of or deaf to reason, even as reason sleeps alongside, waiting to be awakened.

We readers, unlike original ʾ*adam*, have enough reason to understand all this. Thanks to our reason and its ability to understand the speech of the text, the story can teach us about the trouble with reason and speech, and hence, with human freedom. We are now alerted to watch closely what happens when reason and speech finally appear.

The itch in his soul that could destroy his contentment is, as we have argued, not manifest to the simple human being. Neither is a second difficulty: his aloneness. It is not man (who, as yet, knows not good and bad), but the Lord God who notices: "It is not good that man should be alone; I will make him a help opposite him *(ʿezer kᵉnegdo)*" (2:18). This observation sets in motion the rest of the story: it leads to and explains the creation of woman, which in turn leads to both sexuality/sociality and speech/reason, which in turn issue in the transgression, which in turn leads to and explains human life as we know it. We need carefully to consider its meaning.

Why and for whom is man's aloneness not good? Is it not good for the man or not good for the world around him or not good for God? Is it not good because of present circumstances or because of likely future possibilities? That is, might God be anticipating human death—which He had just mentioned as the inevitable consequence of gaining knowledge of good and bad—in response to which He will now provide the means of perpetuation? Or is it not good for the same reason that gaining knowledge of good and bad is not good: it invites the illusion of self-sufficiency? Much depends on how we understand the meaning of man's solitariness.

It is common and appropriate to think that "alone" means "lonely" or "in need of assistance," that is, that "aloneness" is a badge of weakness. Weakness cries out for help, whether as companion, partner, or co-worker; and God in fact offers to make a "help" for the human being. But "alone" could also mean "self-sufficient" or "independent"; it could be a mark of strength—real or imagined. Aloneness as strength and apparent self-sufficiency might be bad or dangerous in a variety of ways. For example, a solitary being, lacking a suitable mirror, might be incapable of self-knowledge. Or, lacking self-knowledge and, hence, believing himself independent, the solitary man, though he dwelt in the Lord's garden, might have no real awareness of the presence of God. Or, seemingly self-sufficient, he might be inclined to test the limits—like the hero Achilles or like the original circle-men in Aristophanes' tale (in Plato's *Symposium*) of the birth of *eros*—seeking evidence for or against his own divinity. For "aloneness" as strength, the proper remedy is weakening, caused by division, opposition, conflict.

Fittingly, God proposes an ambiguous helper. Man's helper is to be (in Hebrew) *neged*, that is, *opposite* to him, *over against* him, *boldly in front* of him, *in his face:* the helper is to be (also? instead?) a *contra*, an opponent. Putting together "partner" and "opposition," God proposes to make man a *counterpart.* What is called for, whatever the reason, is not just another, but an *other* other—fitting and suitable ("meet"), to be sure, but also opposed. Company here comes with difference; and *la différence* will turn out to make a very big difference, both for good and ill.

IV. NAMING: THE ELEMENTARY USE OF REASON

Though He promises to make man a counterpart, God does not do so straightaway. Instead, He makes the animals. Encountering the animals activates the mental and emotional powers that permit man to recognize and receive his fitting counterpart. The result of man's first encounter with the animal "others" is remarkable.

> And the Lord God formed from out of the ground (*'adamah*) all the beasts of the field and all the fowl of the air, and He brought them to the man *to see what he would call them;* and whatsoever the man called every living creature, *that would be its name.* And the man gave names to all cattle and to the fowl of the air, and to all the beasts of the field; but for the man there was not found a help-opposite-him [a "counterpart"]. (2:19–20; emphasis added)

When God brings the animals to the man to see what he will call them, human reason is summoned to activity, to its primordial activity, naming. Indeed, here the man acts for the first time: the prototypical or defining human act is an act of speech, naming. Encountering the non-human animals actualizes the potential of human speech, thereby revealing the human difference. For the ability to name rests on the rational capacity for recognizing otherness and sameness, for separating and combining. It requires reason's separating power that sees each animal as a distinct unit, separate from all others; it requires reason's combining power that sees also the samenesses that run through individual animals. Reason collects the same animals under their own singular idea, each idea corresponding to a singular species, each deserving and receiving its own general name, one common noun for each kind. Human speech does not create the creatures of the world. As the text indicates, the creatures themselves (the animals) are given; man "creates" only their names. The names he gives them—say, "camel" rather than "porcupine"—may be arbitrary, but the distinctions among the creatures that the names recognize and celebrate are not: the camel and the porcupine, by their clearly different natures, clearly deserve and invite different names. Human naming is (in part) reason's fitting acknowledgment and appreciation of the ordered variety of an articulated world.

Yet human speech, even at its most disinterested, is not a purely responsive act of mirroring the given world. For one thing, naming is selective and therefore partial. Names bear the same relation to things as map does to territory. A map, necessarily selective, is not a mirror image of the land; the only truly complete map would *be* the territory. Like mapping, naming is always partial and incomplete. Less a passive mirroring, more an active choosing, even simple naming is a form of acting on the world. Even when it is born of appreciative wonder, it therefore represents the germ of appropriation and mastery.

Human acts of selection are shaped by interests. And interests spring from desire. The same is true of human speech, even of simple naming. Although the ability to name rests on the powers of reason, the *impulse* to name is rooted in desire or emotion. Like every act of speech and thought, an act of naming is not only a cognitive response to the articulated character of the world. It is also an expression of some inner urge, need, or passion, such as fear or wonder, anxiety or appreciation, interest or just plain curiosity. Even the most disinterested act of speech, such as naming the animals, is not an act of unmotivated reason; it is humanly important to know one animal from the other, since some may be dangerous, others may be tasty, while still others may strike the human perceiver as amusing or awe-inspiring or potentially useful. To generalize: what A says about B *always* tells you something also about A. This does not mean that speech is necessarily arbitrary and distorted by passion. But it does mean that, as we listen to the content of speech, we should be attending also to the soul of the speaker.

The text tells us that the man gave names to all cattle, to the fowl of the air, and to every beast of the field, but, unfortunately, we are not told what those names are; we do not even hear him speak. Yet this unfortunate "silence" invites us to wonder what motivates the allegedly simple human acts of naming. For we do not know whether the name-giving was (primarily) disinterested, reflecting, say, the look or activity of the animal, or (primarily) interested, reflecting human hopes and fears. We do not know, that is, whether the man called the horse "swifty" or "strong-backed," the elephant "thick skin" (pachyderm) or "ivory" (*elephas*, in Greek), the tiger "stripes" or "fang," the porcupine "thorny pig" or "don't touch," the camel "humpy" or "burden-bearing" (*gamal* is from a Hebrew root meaning "to benefit or requite"). But as we shall soon see in the naming of the woman, human naming is hardly unmotivated.

Knowledge of the animals is, of course, not part of forbidden knowledge. Yet, human reason thus aroused will not stay innocently confined to the activity of naming. Indeed, there are potential difficulties in the activity of naming itself. Even naming is not altogether "innocent."

Human naming, while it does not create the world, creates a linguistic world, a second world of names that shadows the first world of creatures. As the text indicates, human beings not only practice speech, they create it. Names are the first human inventions: although they point to the things named, they have a certain independence from them. Names (and other words) and the ideas they represent constitute a mental human world that is necessarily separated from the world it means to describe. The gap between the "two worlds"—the world of words and the world of things—raises the question of how well human speech can capture and reveal the truth about the world it attempts to bespeak: are our words adequate to the things? to what extent is speech revelatory, to what extent obfuscating? As we will see shortly, these difficulties, which adhere even to the relatively disinterested uses of speech, become magnified when reason's view of the world is colored by the presence of desires and passions. Under these circumstances, speech becomes a vehicle for projecting human wish and desire. Down the road, the somewhat independent, somewhat interested realm of language can become the medium for human independence altogether. For human beings can productively imagine, with the help of the creative possibilities open in speech, a world different from the one they now inhabit. All that is required is the growth of the requisite self-consciousness.

The encounter with the animals, in fact, stirs the germ of human self-awareness, and, with it, the germ of a "new"—that is, previously invisible—human desire. Man's naming of the animals reveals to him his human difference: he names the animals but they cannot name him. Man alone among the animals can name. Accordingly, man's powers of discernment turn back upon himself, and with feeling. He inwardly discovers: "I am not alone, but I am different from them. They are different from me, indeed, too different to satisfy my newly awakened desire for a mate. Now that I am not alone, I am beginning to feel 'lonely.'" To be accurate, this "discovery" is still latent in the man; it is only the text that notes, "but for the human being there was not found a help-opposite-him" (2:20). Why not? What was lacking among the animals? Was it speech and the possibility of conversation? Or was something else required in a counterpart that could properly remedy the problem of man's aloneness?

V. PREDICATING AND SELF-NAMING: AWARENESS OF SELF AND OTHER

The suitable counterpart arrives in the immediate sequel:

And the Lord God caused a deep sleep to fall upon the man [or 'human being'; ʾadam], and he slept; and He took one of his ribs (tselaʿ) and closed up the place instead with flesh. And the Lord God built the rib which He had taken from the man (ʾadam) into a woman (ʾishah), and He brought her to the man. And the man said:

> "This one at last [literally, 'the time,' hapaʿam] is bone of my bones
>   and flesh of my flesh;
> This one shall be called Woman (ʾishah),
>   because from Man (ʾish) this one was taken."

(2:21–23)

The counterpart is created out of man himself; God builds a woman (*'ishah*) out of the man's (*'adam*'s) rib, and brings her to the man. We concentrate here only on the unfolding account of speech, reason, and self-consciousness.

The appearance of the woman prompts the first full human sentence, indeed, the first speech of any human being directly quoted in the text. In his paradigmatic speech, the human being is not only a namer, he is also a predicator, displaying an advanced capacity to see sameness within otherness. Most significantly, he not only names the woman, he states a *reason* for the name he chooses: "This one shall be called Woman (*'ishah*) *because* from Man (*'ish*) this was taken." The offering of articulated explanations, as well as the linguistic structure displayed in the naming, reveal the creative, world-ordering power of human speech.

But there is more to human speech than creative dexterity. Man's counterpart stirs his soul to a new level of self-awareness. As she stands before and against him, he also sees *himself* for the first time. As a result, he now names himself: no longer (as God named him) *'adam*, earthling, generic human-being-from-the-earth, but *'ish*, individual male human being, man as *male* in relation to female woman. The woman, *'ishah*, gets from the man the lexically derivative name; her name, like her origin, is derivative. Yet her place in this speech of self-discovery and self-naming is, in fact, first: only because the woman stands first before him and comes first to mind is he able to know and name himself and to recognize his "maleness" as a decisive aspect of his own humanity. This deep and far-reaching insight about complementarity and selfhood is beautifully conveyed by the text: in the man's speech, *'ishah*, although lexically derivative, is spoken first.

Whereas the appearance of the animals elicited names, the appearance of the woman elicits poetry. Human speech is not just neutral description; it also expresses human desire, a desire that had been stimulated by the encounter with the animals ("*This* one *at last* . . ."). In fact, the man's entire speech seems to have been incited by desire, almost certainly by sexual desire: as the names indicate—"she Woman, me Man"—the appearance of woman makes man feel his masculinity, which is to say, his desire for her. Regarded as an expression of sexual desire, the speech may accurately reveal the state of the man's soul; but, at the same time, the presence of powerful desire may distort his view of woman. Though he acknowledges the woman's otherness (she gets her own name, different from his), the man is much more impressed by her similarity; indeed, because of his desire, he exaggerates and treats similarity as sameness: "This is my flesh and bone; this is mine; this is me." In naming the woman with reference to her derivation from himself, the man is not just neutrally playing with his words; he is *defining* the woman in the light of his possessive desire for her. The name, like the desire it expresses, is a form of capture, a "taking-hold" of her, a verbal act of (anticipatory) appropriation. As if to underscore his self-centered outlook, the text makes clear that he is speaking not to her but only about her. Human speech, we are shown, is dangerous not only because it can reconstruct the world through language, but because any such reconstruction will likely carry the distortions born of human passion and human pride. Even before we get to the transgression, the careful reader who attends to the nuances of the text will not simply be celebrating man's powers of speech and reason.

VI. QUESTIONING AND ANSWERING, FALSE AND TRUE: THE ROAD TO INDEPENDENCE

After the private acts of naming, expostulation, and predication, human speech and reason rise to the level of dialogue, propelled by acts of asking and answering. These are displayed in the discourse between the woman and the serpent, presented as the Bible's first quoted conversation and begun by the Bible's first question. The voice of developed reason, sibilant and seductive, comes from the mouth of a snake.

Now the serpent *(nahash)* was more cunning [or 'subtle' or 'shrewd' or 'crafty'; `*arum*] than any beast of the field which the Lord God *(YHWH ʾelohim)* had made. And the serpent said unto the woman, "Indeed, [or, 'Could it be'] that God *(ʾelohim)* hath said 'Ye shall not eat of any tree of the garden'?"

And the woman said unto the serpent: "Of the fruit of the trees of the garden we may eat; but of the fruit of the tree which is in the midst of the garden, God hath said: 'Ye shall not eat of it, neither shall ye touch it, lest ye die.'"

And the serpent said unto the woman: "Ye shall not surely die; for God doth know that in the day ye eat thereof, then your eyes shall be opened, and ye shall be as gods *(ʾelohim)*, knowing [*yodʿey;* plural participle] good and bad." (3:1–5)

We have here a paradigm of conversable speech, interrogative speech, and responsive speech. On display is the human willingness and ability to answer—that is, to look within oneself for a response to—a question. Also evident is reason's capacity to negate and contradict, to consider opposed alternatives, and to think that things need not be as they seem or as they are.

Needless to say, the presence of a talking serpent is something of a mystery. Nevertheless, here he is, seemingly out of nowhere, and we must not try to get much beyond this surface fact. Two other facts about the serpent may be inferred. First, the serpent in this tale shares with human beings not only speech but perhaps also upright posture (only later is he cursed to crawl on his belly), long associated with the theoretical attitude and the possibility of disinterested viewing of the natural whole. This makes it all the more plausible to regard the serpent as an external-ized embodiment of certain essentially human (rational) capacities. Sec-ond, the serpent was presumably among the animals that were rejected as a suitable counterpart for the human being. If this is correct, three further inferences follow. First, the rejection of the serpent despite his ability to speak and think implies that suitability, for the human coun-terpart, means something other than rationality: a sexual counterpart, not a fellow dialectician, is what is required. Second, though he is one of God's creatures, the serpent, because he is rational, acts entirely on his own, displaying that dangerous independence to which he will lead the human being. Third, the serpent's rejection (by God and man) as an appropriate partner could motivate his desire to punish the man for choosing woman instead of himself (for preferring sex to philosophy?). It would explain also his clever decision to do so by corrupting the wom-an, and precisely through the use of subtle speech.

The text says the serpent "was *more cunning* [or *'subtle,'* etc.] than any beast of the field which the Lord God had made" (3:1). The word "cun-ning," in Hebrew *ʿarum*, echoes and puns on *ʿarumim*, "naked," that ap-pears in the preceding sentence: "and they were both naked (*ʿarumim*)"; 2:25). The root sense of *ʿerum*, "naked," is *smooth:* someone who is naked is hairless, clothesless, smooth of skin. But, as the pun suggests, someone who is clever is also smooth, a facile thinker and talker whose surface speech is beguiling and flawless, hiding well his rough ulterior purposes. The serpent is indeed a smooth speaker, his true intention craftily hid-den beneath his silky speech. He asks the first question, initiates the first conversation, and challenges God's benevolence and truthfulness. He implies that knowledge of good and bad will provide immunity against death; he challenges hearsay, the oral tradition, and law, implicitly coun-seling that one should see and experience for oneself; and he beckons the woman to unite with natural knowledge. All these are further rea-sons for an allegorical reading of the serpent: an embodiment of the separated and beguiling voice of autonomous human reason speaking up against innocence and obedience, coming to us as if from some at-tractive source "outside" us that whispers doubt into our ear. In making his rationalist mischief, speech is the serpent's only weapon.

And the serpent said unto the woman, "Indeed, [or, 'Could it be'] that God hath said, 'Ye shall not eat *(loʾ toʾchlu)* of *any* tree of the garden?'" (3:1; empha-sis added)

What kind of question is this? Surely not a question seeking the truth. Rather it intends to *call into question*—authority, opinion, law. It seeks to make simple obedience impossible, in this case, by challenging the goodness of the commander. The serpent's question implies that God is a being who is, or might be, not only arbitrary but also hostile to human beings: God is the sort of being who could have put human beings into a fruitful garden but denied them access to *all* the trees. Says the serpent, "Is it really true that God has denied you all sustenance?" The serpent's question is a perfect example of mischievous speech.

The radical effect of the serpent's question does not, however, depend on his subversive intent. The question itself is deeply disquieting. Like any question, it intrudes upon silent and unselfconscious activity, disturbing immediate participation in life and forcing introspection and reflection. Like any question, it puts thoughts before the mind, thoughts that collect and stimulate feelings: just as the question as asked had meaning for the questioner apart from its logical content, so the question as received gains meaning from interacting with the addressee's desires and concern. Questions are more than verbal interrogatives: questions stir the soul.

The particular question put by the serpent is perfect for provoking self-reflection. In order to answer it, the woman must rise to self-consciousness about food and eating, about God's commands and the world's hospitality to her needs, and about herself in relation to her needs, to God, and to her world. As long as any need is easily and simply satisfied, it goes virtually unrecognized; in the absence of obstacles, food is taken for granted and eating proceeds mindlessly. By raising the prospect of opposition to human eating, the serpent's question brings need into consciousness, against the imagined possibility of its denial. And by blaming (albeit falsely) this denial on a nay-saying God, it stirs a sense of precarious selfhood pitted against an inhospitable world and threatened by outside imperatives. The woman is forced to discover that she has needs independent both of God's power to command them and the world's ability to satisfy them: pondering the question, she begins to feel both her vulnerability and her independence.

Self-awareness grows largely through the encounter with error and opposition. As long as experience seems reliable and appearances go unchallenged, human life proceeds with a childlike trust in the truthfulness of things. By asking the woman about the veracity of God's (alleged) speech, but imputing to Him words God did not say, the serpent's question introduces the issue of truth and falsehood and, what's more, provokes the desire to correct error. The mind opens up by discovering—and caring about—the gap between the false and the true, between what merely appears to be so and what truly is. Appearances (and utterances) are scrutinized, judged, and corrected. In the space between the apparent and the real, the human imagination takes wing. As a result, the mind will soon be able to project a gap between what is and what might be; affirmation and denial will give rise to deliberate pursuit and avoidance. The free play of imagination and thought will soon direct the free exercise of choice. All that is required is a more developed sense of self, one that recognizes itself as thoughtful and free. This, too, the serpent's question generates.

Questions about oneself necessarily summon one to reflect—to look back—upon oneself and to discover oneself as a being that thinks. By forcing thoughts about her food and eating, the serpent's question creates a "doubleness" in the woman's soul: her awareness of her belly is separate from her belly, her thoughts about hunger are not rumblings in her stomach. By focusing on her body's need for food, the woman awakens to herself *as mind*. She discovers that "she herself" is not simply identical to her needy body. She experiences herself not only as a being with desires, but also as a being with thoughts, a being that can inquire into the truth about her desires (and about much else).

This momentous act of self-discovery is liberating not only for thought but also for action. For to think about appetite is to cease to be its slave. It becomes possible freely to decide whether to eat or not to eat, whether to obey the imperatives of necessity (or 'nature' or 'Being' or God). In time, imagination and reason can even create new objects for human desires. In short: merely facing the serpent's *question* means discovering and exercising one's autonomy.

The woman's answer clearly reveals her emerging and risk-filled freedom of mind:

And the woman said unto the serpent: "Of the fruit of the trees of the garden we may eat; but of the fruit of the tree which is in the midst of the garden, God hath said: 'Ye shall not eat *(loᵓ toᵓchlu)* of it, neither shall ye touch *(loᵓ tigᶜu)* it, lest ye die.'" (3:2–3)

The woman's response implicitly denies the serpent's tacit accusation against God, but she does not in fact explicitly reaffirm God's generosity. In answering, "Of the fruit of the trees of the garden *we may eat*," she forgets to remember that this is part of God's bounty; she treats it instead as a matter merely of human freedom and choice. Now aware that the imperative behind her eating resides within her belly rather than with any outside authority, she does not say, "*God said* that we may eat." Following the lead of the serpent, she too has God speak only as a naysayer.

The woman's answer demonstrates another danger of speech: the problem of mistake and misunderstanding. The woman says the thing which is not, albeit in innocence. Eager to correct the serpent's error, she herself commits multiple errors of speech. She answers not the question that the serpent asked (to which the right answer was simply "No"). She says more than was called for. She *mis*identifies the forbidden tree as the one "in the midst of the garden" (that one was the tree of life [2:9]), she adds "neither shall ye touch it" to the prohibition, and, most importantly, she converts the predicted dire consequences of disobedience ("for in the day thou eatest thereof, dying you will die" [2:17]) into the reason for obedience ("ye shall not eat of it . . . *lest* you die" [3:3]). She "does not remember" that it was to be avoided *because* it was forbidden and commanded, not in order to avoid the deadly consequence. To put the matter universally: Exactly because she is expanding her newly emerging freedom of thought, she (predictably) has no use for obedience.

The addition "neither shall ye touch it" exemplifies one or another of some common yet misleading uses of speech. It might represent a protective addition, born of solicitude, provided by the man, in communicating the prohibition to the woman (who had not heard it in the first place); or it could be an addition, born of fear, advanced by the woman herself. Or it could be a simple misunderstanding that arose in the transmission, as happens so often in the children's game of telephone. But whatever the explanation, sloppy speech is itself a corruption of law, and it opens the door to corruption in deed.

In the serpent's rejoinder, he exploits the fact that the woman respects the prohibition solely to avoid the bad consequence of death. He appeals to her awakened pride in her own powers of understanding.

And the serpent said unto the woman: "Ye shall not surely die; for God doth know that in the day ye eat thereof, then your eyes shall be opened, and ye shall be as gods (*'elohim*), knowing [plural participle] good and bad." (3:4–5)

In one short speech, the serpent manages both to impugn God's veracity and His motives and to provide the inducement for disobeying Him. By insisting "you won't die," the serpent implies that God is a liar. By offering reasons for what God said—implicitly claiming, as reason frequently does, to know more than what is at the surface of things—he goes behind God's explicit words to expose (so he thinks) their hidden meaning and motive. By asserting that God knows that the forbidden knowledge will make you godlike, the serpent implies that the prohibition stems from God's jealous and self-protecting wish to avoid sharing His special privileges with human beings. By suggesting the existence of many gods (through the use of the plural participle, *yod'ey*), the serpent encourages a belief in the possibility of apotheosis. Most remarkable, by his implicit chain of reasoning, the serpent clearly suggests that knowledge makes one not only godlike but perhaps, therefore, also immune to death. In this sense especially, the serpent is like a proto-philosopher, one who respects no authority but the truth and who promises that knowledge gives one a share in immortality. We see here, perhaps, the reason why the serpent was passed over as a possible counterpart for the human being.

Crucial to the serpent's successful seduction of the woman is the rational power of doubt, opposition, negation, and contradiction: in the Hebrew text, the first word of the serpent's final response ("Ye shall not surely die") is "Not." The idea of "Not" is essential to human speech and reason. It also anchors the human imagination in its abilities to go beyond appearances, both its creative ability to conjure images and its ability to recognize an image as merely an image, not the true thing. These powers the serpent in fact displays in this final speech. For he shows his cunning not only as a proto-philosopher but also as a poet, creating the Bible's first metaphor: "your eyes shall be opened," meaning, "you will have insight." Finally, in combination with this power of non-literal speech, reason's assertion of the possibility of "Not so" liberates the imagination to picture new alternatives for what is or could be "So": not only may things not be what they seem—even better, things need not remain as they are. Thus, speech and reason contribute to disobedience not only, negatively, by undermining authority, but also, positively, by conjuring new possibilities for choice.

VII. FREEDOM AND ENLIGHTENMENT: THE MELANCHOLY RISE OF MAN

The force of this first conversation, begun by the Bible's first question, is to call into question both authority and obedience. By challenging the goodness and the truthfulness of the author, by denying the announced consequences of disobedience, and by suggesting attractive alternative benefits of transgression, speech and reason completely erode the force of the prohibition. Once the prohibition is undermined, once reason awakens, *simple* obedience—whether to God or to fixed instinct—becomes impossible. With alternatives now freely before her, the woman's desire grows on its own, partially enticed by the serpent's promise of wisdom, mostly fueled by her own newly empowered imagination. Having heard the voice of serpentine reason, the woman now sees the world through eyes imaginatively transformed by what was said:

And the woman *saw* that the tree *was good for food,* and that it *was a delight to the eyes,* and a tree *to be desired to make one wise,* and she took of the fruit thereof, and did eat and gave also to her husband with her, and he did eat. (3:6; emphasis added)

Independent reason, having mentally eroded the force of the prohibition and suggested new possibilities, now takes control also of action. Speech issues in the momentous and transforming act of free choice. Thanks to the growth of human mental powers, the woman "sees" in a new light; mind and desire both color and reflect the new powers of a liberated imagination. In ascending order, she looks to the tree for meeting animal necessity ("good for food"), for aesthetic pleasure ("delight to the eyes"), and for enlightenment, insight, or judgment (desire for wisdom). True, as the text tells us in the immediate sequel, her imagination did not get it right: when their eyes are opened, the human beings discover not (the good news) that they are godlike (as the serpent had promised) but (the bad news) that they are naked. Nevertheless, the human beings in transgressing display the (albeit problematic) powers of rational choice, distinctive of our humanity, based upon a conscious and autonomous (even if mistaken) judgment of what is good (and bad). Their eating merely ratifies (or symbolizes) the autonomous act of *choosing* to eat, a free act of choice that was based on the self-generated belief that eating would be *good.* Only a being who already distinguishes good and bad, and who has opinions about which is which, can make such a choice.

Traditional interpretation (especially Christian) refers to this act of transgression as signaling the "fall of man"—though the expression nowhere occurs in the text. But if we read anthropologically, and in a wisdom-seeking spirit, what we have here instead is in fact the *rise* of man to his mature humanity as a free and rational being—to be sure, in all its pathos and ambiguity. Such a reading, by the way, was offered already by Kant, commenting precisely on our passage, in his "Conjectural Beginnings of Human History" to which I refer you.

The first discovery of our humanity, or, better, the discovery that *constitutes* our humanity, is a discovery about our sexual being (not, as others would say, about our mortality):

And the eyes of them both were opened, and they knew that they were naked; and they sewed fig-leaves together and made themselves girdles. (3:7)

Human self-consciousness is radically sexual self-consciousness. Moreover, the discovery of nakedness is made not indifferently but with passing judgment: nakedness is viewed as shameful (that is, bad, rather than good or neutral), and action is taken to cover it up and to keep it from being seen. Here we note only the new, judgmental dimension of human self-consciousness. Shame, a peculiarly human passion, expresses pain over the gap between our wished-for estimable or idealized self-image and the now discovered fact of our lowliness or baseness. Shame presupposes a concern for self-esteem and the presence of pride: only a being concerned with self-esteem could have his pride wounded and experience shame.

The response to the discovery of shameful nakedness represents yet another important aspect of human reason: the disposition to art. The fig leaf, or rather the needle, is the first human invention. Like all human craft and technology, it manifests both enterprise and cleverness. More important, like any invention, it tacitly asserts the insufficiency of the world and expresses the human urge to do something about it—what Rousseau would call "perfectibility." Moreover, it symbolizes man's path of violent opposition to nature. Unlike weaving, which gently and harmoniously binds threads together without destroying anything, sewing invades and does violence to the elements it unites. The technological mentality and disposition emerge out of this very modest beginning.

Thanks to the needle, the girdle is produced. It may be flimsy, but its meaning is profound. Like all more sophisticated clothing, it provides protection, but more importantly, dissimulation, beautification, and adornment. Standing as an obstacle to the immediate gratification of sexual desire, it represents the beginning of the rule of reason over desire. As an instance of enhancing self-esteem, it gives rise also to a concern with the beautiful; and it also represents and at the same time augments human *amour propre*. And, as the first human transformation of the naturally given, the fig leaf girdle stands as the first mark of society and civilization; at one stroke, it manifests human reason's propensity to *techne*, custom, and law.

VIII. LEARNING THE LIMITS OF REASON: CIVILIZATION AND ITS DISCONTENTS

Human art does not sufficiently provide for human needs, not even for the needs of the body: fig-leaf girdles are hardly adequate for protection or concealment. But human art is especially weak in addressing the needs of the soul once it knows about good and bad and assesses itself under these judgments. A being that experiences shame needs to know more than his own cleverness—and he knows it. Right after they make themselves girdles, the human beings show their first real openness to or awareness of the divine:

And they heard the voice of the Lord God walking in the garden in the evening breeze; and the man and his woman hid from the presence of the Lord God in the midst of the trees of the garden. (3:8)

This is the first explicit mention that any human being *really* attended to or even noticed the divine presence. Only in recognizing our lowliness can we also discover what is truly high. The turn toward the divine is founded on our discovery of our own lack of divinity, indeed, of our ugliness.

It is a delicate moment: having followed eyes to alluring temptations that promised wisdom, human beings came to see instead their own insufficiency. Still trusting appearances but seeking next to beautify them, they set about adorning themselves, in order to find favor in the sight of the beloved. Lustful eyes gave way, speechlessly, to admiring ones, by means of intervening modesty and art. Yet sight and love do not alone fully disclose the truth of our human situation. Human beings must open their ears as well as their eyes, they must hearken to a calling, for which sight and the beautiful beloved do not sufficiently prepare them. The prototypical human pair, opened by shamefaced love, was in fact able to hear the transcendent voice.

The ensuing conversation with this transcendent voice is, on its face, hardly encouraging; God conducts an inquest, extracts a confession, pronounces sentence. In the course of the examination, new uses of human speech emerge: rationalization, evasion of responsibility, and shifting of blame. The inquest concluded, God pronounces sentence on the serpent, the woman, and the man, in three short speeches that we shall not analyze here. But we observe, in passing, the major features of the new human condition, announced and foretold in these divine remarks to the newly awakened pair, the condition within which the story of human life will hereafter—and irreversibly—unfold. (1) There is the (partial) estrangement of humankind from the world (or nature), evidenced by (a) enmity between serpent and woman (3:15); (b) partial alienation of man from the earth, upon which he must now toil for his food (3:17–19); and (c) pain of childbirth, implying conflict even within the (female) human body (3:16). (2) There is division of labor, defined relative to work: the one gives birth, the other tills. (3) There is the coming of the arts and crafts: no more just picking fruit and gathering nuts, but agriculture—the artful cultivation of the soil, the harvesting of grain, its transformation into flour, the making of bread, and, eventually, also astronomy (to know the seasons and to plan for sowing), metallurgy (to make the tools), the institution of property (to secure the fruits of one's labor), and religious sacrifices (to placate the powers above and to encourage rain). (4) And there is rule and authority (3:16). To sum it up in one word: civilization. The "punishment" for trying to rise above childishness and animality is to be forced to live like a human being.

The so-called "punishment" seems to fit the so-called "crime," in at least two ways. If the crime of transgression represents the human aspiration to self-sufficiency and godliness (free choice necessarily implying humanly grounded knowledge of good and bad), the so-called punishment thwarts that aspiration by opposition: human beings instead of self-sufficiency receive estrangement, dependence, division, and rule. Second, and more profound, the so-called punishment fits the crime simply by making clear the unanticipated meaning of the choice and desire implicit in the transgression itself. Like Midas with his wish for the golden touch, like Achilles with his desire for glory, the prototypical human being gets precisely what he reached for only to discover that it is not exactly what he wanted. He learns, through the revealing conversation with God, that his choice for humanization, wisdom, knowledge of good and bad, or autonomy really means at the same time also estrangement from the world, self-division, division of labor, toil, fearful knowledge of death, and the institution of inequality, rule, and subservience. The highest principle of Being insists that, given who and what we humans are, we cannot have the former without the latter.

This analysis leads me to believe that the so-called punishment is not really a newly instituted condition introduced by a willful God against the human grain. It is rather a making clear of just what it means to have chosen enlightenment and freedom, just what it means to be a rational being. The punishment, if punishment it is, consists mainly in the acute foreknowledge of our natural destiny to live out our humanity under the human condition.

For Adam and Eve, the end of the story is grim. But for the *readers* of the story it is edifying, for the story of man in the Garden of Eden helps us on our way to finding the path to a life well lived. It enables us to reflect on our basic nature and to discover the perils inherent in our special gifts of speech, reason, self-consciousness, and freedom. In following the emergence of human reason and human speech, we have pondered their morally ambiguous activity in naming, predicating, celebrating, self-naming, explaining names, asking, answering, conversing, questioning, calling into question, denying, mistaking, challenging, and shifting blame. We have considered the multiple manifestations of self-awareness and the emergence of passions to which self-awareness gives rise. We have examined the meaning of free choice and recognized its inherently disobedient character. We have seen the birth of craft, reason's prodigal son, as well as conscience, reason's judge, and awe, the seed of piety, reason's recognition of its own limits. And we have thought about all these matters not with neutral detachment but with judgmental engagement.

The early verdict on human reason and human freedom is, to say the least, mixed. The Bible agrees with Aristotle in holding that man alone among the animals has *logos*, thoughtful speech, but it takes a much less celebratory view of our distinctiveness. Speech can be an instrument of mischief and error, deception and falsehood, pride and domination. Reason creates a divided consciousness and overstimulates the imagination. Free choice is not necessarily wise choice. Judgmental self-consciousness yields vanity, shame, and guilt. Artfulness separates man from nature and creates new needs and desires, without bringing contentment.

But human speech and reason, in the form of this remarkable story and our ability to ponder its meaning, hold out a redemptive possibility. The remedy begins with our being willing to recognize and acknowledge the follies of which we human beings are capable, indeed, precisely because of our special intellectual capacities and the freedom they make possible. The ill-clad human protagonists in our story become aware of their own inadequacies from hearing and experiencing the voice of the Lord God walking in the garden. Similarly, thanks to the special kind of speech that we are reading, we psychically ill-clad human readers become aware of our own inadequacies from hearing and experiencing the voice of the text. The source of our troubles, dear reader, is not in our stars but in ourselves, not in our weakness but in our peculiarly human strength. Suitably humbled, we are prepared to be educated by the rest of the text.

3   FREEDOM, RESPONSIBILITY, AND TRUTH

ROBERT SOKOLOWSKI

There are three nouns in the title of my essay. If we stay with only two of them, *truth* and *freedom,* and if we try to think these two things together as a coherent whole, we might seem to run into a paradox or an aporia. Truth seems to necessitate us, and therefore it seems to exclude freedom. If something shows up as true, we seem to have no further choice about the matter. Truth seems to bring along with it a kind of intellectual determinism. Freedom, on the other hand, seems to undermine truth. If we are to be truly free, it might appear, we should be free even to accept or not accept what seems to us to be true. If we do not have freedom in this respect, are we not being "forced" by the truth? Are we not being determined and hence not free? Thus, at first glance, truth and freedom might seem to be incompatible. The relativism we so often encounter in our society is a symptom that people think that we must choose between truth and freedom; we can't have them both.

The third word in my title, however, *responsibility,* seems to straddle the other two and it may help us find a way out of paradox, aporia, and incoherence. Responsibility is obviously associated with freedom, but etymologically it is also related to truth, because it carries the overtone of answering to something. To be responsible is to respond in an appropriate way to something that shows up, and it also implies that we take the trouble to find out what the truth is, to find out what we must answer to. Truth seems to imply and demand responsibility and responsibility seems to demand truth. The resolution of our apparent aporia, therefore, is to think more carefully about truth and freedom, and to relate both of them to responsibility. We can understand them in such a way that we shall not only avoid paradox when we bring them together; we shall also see that each demands the other.

Before we carry out this task, however, I would like to exclude one sense of truth from our immediate discussion. We can be said to be truthful when we tell the truth, when we avoid lies and falsehoods. Obviously, our freedom comes into play in such truthfulness; we can decide to tell a lie or we can choose to tell the truth. This relationship between truth and freedom is relatively noncontroversial. I wish to explore a more elementary question, the kind of freedom that comes into play when we discover the truth or when we face the truth. This sort of truthfulness, the ability to manifest or disclose the truth of things, is more basic than the ability to tell the truth, because we can choose to tell the truth or to tell a lie only after we have acquired the truth in some manner.

I

The first point I wish to develop is drawn from the work of an American linguist, Derek Bickerton.[1] He claims that human language and human rationality are established by the power to use syntax in speech. It is syntax that makes human discourse different from animal sounds and cries. Grammar is the linguistic emblem of rationality. What syntax makes possible is a hierarchic embedding, a Chinese-box or Russian-doll structure, in which phrases are embedded within other phrases. In order to bring this structure out more clearly, Bickerton makes an important distinction between language and protolanguage.[2] Protolanguage is like baby talk. It uses signs, but they are merely concatenated, strung out one after the other. Protolanguage involves a sequential continuum, but does not achieve discrete, hierarchic enclosures and hence it does not reach the grammar that marks true speech. It has semantics but not syntax.

Protolanguage can be illustrated by five different kinds of expression. First, it is found in real baby talk, in the "speech" of children before the age of about two years. Second, it is found in people who have not developed properly; they may be autistic, or they may have been abused or deprived of linguistic training and hence missed the window of opportunity during which linguistic learning is still possible. Like the speech of small children, theirs also lacks the full use of syntax. Third, protolanguage is found, according to Bickerton, in animals, such as apes or

1. See Derek Bickerton, "Pidgin and Creole Languages," *Scientific American* 249 (1983): 116–22; *Language and Species* (Chicago: University of Chicago Press, 1990); *Language and Human Behavior* (Seattle: University of Washington Press, 1995); Derek Bickerton and William H. Calvin, *Lingua ex Machina: Reconciling Darwin and Chomsky with the Human Brain* (Cambridge: The MIT Press, 2000).

2. For the following material, see Bickerton, *Language and Species*, 106–29; also chapter 6: "The World of Protolanguage," and chapter 7, "From Protolanguage to Language." In an appendix to *Language and Human Behavior*, Bickerton provides samples of protolanguage from pidgins, child language, and ape "language"; see 162–66.

chimpanzees, who have been trained to enter into something approximating human speech. Fourth, it can be found in normal human speakers who lose their grip on their language and their rationality, when they fall into emotional distress, confusion, or intoxication.

The fifth instance of protolanguage that Bickerton offers is extremely interesting. He claims that protolanguage comes into play in pidgin languages. Pidgins occur when adult speakers from two unrelated language groups are put into contact with one another. Both groups begin uttering what seems very much like baby talk, sequential sounds that lack the hierarchic embedding of true language. What is especially fascinating is the fact that in such a situation the very next generation of speakers go beyond pidgin into a creole language; they insert syntax into the "names" that the pidgin offered them, and the resulting grammatical structures can be as complex as those of other developed languages.[3]

An important difference between protolanguage and language is the fact that protolanguage is a reaction to the immediate surroundings of the speaker and listener. It needs the direct presence of what it talks about in order to disambiguate a statement, to show what the speaker means. True language, on the other hand, can be spoken and clearly understood even in the absence of the things to which it refers. Syntactic speech works "off-line," so speak, in the absence of its target. True speech allows human beings to master absence.[4]

As a marginal comment, may I add that human depiction, in painting, for example, also involves a kind of syntax, a composition of elements analogous to phrases. A painter who paints a canvas is something like a speaker who formulates a complex sentence; both articulate wholes into parts, and the viewer of a painting has to "read" the painting properly, to see how the parts fit into the whole, if he is to understand it. Just as speech has phrases within phrases, so a picture has images within images. The syntax that structures full human speech finds a parallel in the syntax that structures human imaging.

I find Bickerton's description of language so appealing because it can easily and fruitfully be blended with Husserl's doctrine of categoriality. One of the great contributions of Husserl's philosophy has been his doctrine of categorial intending and categorial intuition, in which we intend or register not simple objects but syntactically articulated ones, objects in which parts and wholes have been explicitly differentiated and recognized as parts and as wholes. We do not just see a tree, we see that

---

3. Bickerton, *Language and Species*, 169: "pidgin . . . is structureless, whereas a creole exhibits the same type of structure as any other natural human language."

4. Bickerton, *Language and Species*, 107–8; *Language and Human Behavior*, 59–61, 90–92.

the tree is blossoming; we do not just think about Janice, we think that Janice is industrious.[5] Husserl claims that human rationality is constituted precisely by categoriality, and Bickerton's studies in linguistics can be used both to confirm and to amplify what Husserl offers.

I would also claim that syntax and categoriality find an interesting parallel in Thomas Aquinas's theory of knowledge. We recall Thomas's analysis of knowing: the exterior senses react to their formal objects; the external perceptions are coordinated and amplified by the internal senses (the common sense, imagination, sensory memory, the cogitative sense); the phantasm in the imagination is illuminated by the agent intellect, which establishes an intelligible species in the passive intellect. At this point the knower has grasped and is able to express what Thomas, following Aristotle, calls an "indivisible," the quiddity of the thing in question. This abstractive and expressive achievement of the intellect is then followed by the activities of composition and division or judgment, in which the mind returns to the existence of the things that it knows. In this process, we should not suppose that for Thomas the grasp of indivisibles is temporally prior to the activity of judgment. We should not think that the mind collects a lot of ideas and then only later, only subsequently, starts to compose and divide them. Rather, the apprehension of indivisibles and the judgment come together; they are simultaneous. This interpretation of Thomas is expressed by John Wippel when he says he is inclined to endorse the following statement: "These two intellectual operations [simple apprehension and judgment] are simultaneous, with the understanding of indivisibles depending on judgment in the order of formal causality, while judgment would depend on the understanding of indivisibles in the order of material causality."[6] In other words, we cannot discuss the activity of knowing without relating it to judgment and hence to articulation as its *telos*, as that in view of which it must be understood. I would say that what Thomas describes as composition and division is what Bickerton refers to as syntactic thinking and what Husserl describes as categorial intentionality. There is, I think, an interesting convergence in all these approaches.

This, then, is my first point: the importance of syntax in the establishment of human speech and human thinking.

5. The theme of categoriality is introduced in its full form in Husserl's *Logical Investigations*, trans. John N. Findlay (New York: Humanities Press, 1970 [1900–1901]), Sixth Investigation, 773–802.

6. John F. Wippel, *The Metaphysical Thought of Thomas Aquinas* (Washington, D.C.: The Catholic University of America Press, 2000), 40.

II

My second point is to introduce a distinction between two uses of the term *I*. I wish to distinguish between what I shall call the *informational* and the *declarative* uses of the first-person pronoun.

The informational use of the pronoun can be illustrated by statements such as "I weigh 150 pounds" and "I am standing in front of the door." The declarative use of the pronoun can be illustrated by statements such as "I believe that it will rain" and "I know that Helen is coming."

The first-person pronoun is used informationally by a speaker to refer to himself as an entity in the world and to say something about himself as an ordinary subject of predication. The informational use of the word could just as well be replaced by a third-person description: "John weighs 150 pounds" and "Henry is standing in front of the door."

The declarative use of the pronoun, in contrast, endorses or appropriates or confirms the speaker as an agent of truth, as someone who has engaged his power to reveal and express the way things are. The pronoun is used to "declare" the speaker as exercising his truthfulness here and now. It refers to the speaker not as a mere entity in the world but as one who has a world and is responsible for manifesting and expressing things. In Husserlian terms, the declarative use expresses the transcendental ego in one of his activities. It expresses the agent of truth at work in a particular instance. This usage is self-ascripting in a way that the informational usage is not. It expresses a user of language precisely as using the language in a speech act at that very moment. It expresses the judger precisely as judging. In Thomistic terms, it expresses the composer and divider as composing and dividing.

There are different kinds of declaratives and I wish to distinguish four. First, the most obvious is the kind we have been describing, the *cognitive* use of first-person pronouns: "I know," "I suggest," "I suspect," "I think," "I remember." A second kind comprises *emotive* declaratives, such as "I hate," "I love," "I fear," "I enjoy." Such emotive uses have a dimension of truthfulness and judgment in them, because they implicitly are saying that we judge the target of our emotion as deserving of such an emotion. If I say "I hate you," I imply that in my judgment you are hateful. Emotive declarations do not merely say what sort of feeling I happen to have at the moment. If that were all that they did, they would be informational and not declarative. A third kind of declaratives is used in acts of commitment or choice, such as "I promise," "I refuse," or "I christen this ship the USS *Nimitz*." These involve what could be called a *performative* use of declaratives. Here again, there is an articulated or propositional core to what we are doing or committing ourselves to. Fourth, I think we could also distinguish something we might call *existential* declaratives, such as "I am still here." In all four kinds of declaratives we mention ourselves as acting as agents of truth, as exercising our rationality here and now as we use the term. We have something analogous to declaratives in the artist's signature on a painting. Another analogue might be the imprint of a hand in a prehistoric cave painting, if in fact that imprint was made to record someone's involvement in creating the images.

The declarative usage of the first-person singular depends, of course, on the possibility of syntax. It can come into play only after the syntactic articulation of experience has occurred. It is one form, but a special form, of the hierarchic embedding that syntax makes possible. It is a special form, because declaratives do not simply add one more clause within a complex sentence; rather, they take responsibility, they appropriate, they endorse, they self-ascribe the exercise of reason and syntax to which they are added. They mention the agent of truth precisely as being responsible in the articulation that he is carrying out. In this way, they bring to a higher completion an instance of composing and dividing, of judging, that is being carried out by the speaker.

If declaratives have such a perfective role in speech, then we would be deficient if we stopped with judgment, with composition and division, in our philosophical study of human cognition. We have to go beyond judgment to the appropriation of judgment that is always potentially there whenever we exercise syntax, whenever we act as an agent of truth. Declaratives provide the more complete whole, the more ultimate *telos*, that we have to keep in mind if we are to recognize the full nature of cognition and rational activity.

If we recognize the role of declaratives, we will be less likely to take human cognition as merely a natural process, as something almost naturalistic. Sometimes the impression is given that even the scholastic theory of knowledge belongs in the philosophy of nature, that it describes a kind of inevitable and impersonal process—from external senses to internal, from phantasm to intelligible species—that takes place without any involvement of the human person as such.[7] Once we introduce judgment as the telos of cognition, and once we introduce declaratives

---

7. Some medieval critics of the doctrine of intelligible species rejected the theory of knowledge associated with it because it seemed to them to have presented knowing as a purely natural process. See Leen Spruit, *Species Intelligibilis: From Perception to Knowledge*, vol. 1, *Classical Roots and Medieval Discussions* (Leiden: E. J. Brill, 1994), 177: "In general, critics of intelligible species do not focus on a specific author or position; their target is an eclectic, widespread 'communis opinio,' embodying—in particular after Thomas's death—quite evident naturalistic assumptions."

as a completion of judgment, we make it clear that cognition is not a process but a human achievement, one that involves responsibility and freedom.

This, then, is the second part of my paper: the role of declaratives in knowledge. Please notice, incidentally, that my own paper is an exercise in syntactic embedding on a large scale, and that from time to time I declare my own involvement in bringing it about, as I have just done.

III

The third part of my paper takes another look at judgment, the activity of saying something of something, the activity of predicating a feature of a subject. I think we can take it for granted that judging is the core syntactical activity. We might have a sentence that is very complex grammatically, but the heart of the sentence, and the core of each of the subordinate clauses, is judgment. Aristotle, Aquinas, Kant, Frege, and Husserl would all agree on this, and Bickerton says, "If nouns and verbs are the most basic elements of syntax, then predication is its most basic act."[8] He also says that predication is "the very core of universal syntax."[9]

But where does predication come from? How does judgment arise from prejudgmental experience? I would like to develop this point by bringing out some contrasts with some other thinkers. First of all, let us examine two approaches that can be called "nativist" or "innatist." In the work of Chomsky and some of his followers, we find what we could call a biological nativism.[10] Syntactic structures in general, and predication in particular, come about because of certain developments in the evolution of the brain. At a certain point in evolution, something called a "language acquisition device" is formed.[11] Bickerton speaks of the development of a "syntactic engine."[12] Human beings use syntax because their brains developed in a certain way. In contrast with this biological

8. Bickerton, *Language and Species*, 59.

9. Ibid., 61.

10. See Fiona Cowie, *What's Within? Nativism Reconsidered* (New York: Oxford University Press, 1999).

11. Ibid., 170: "[Chomsky] holds not just that the learner possesses whatever conceptual resources are necessary to her theorizing about language, but also that she possesses them innately, as a consequence of her biology." See Noam Chomsky, *Language and Thought* (Wakefield, R.I.: Moyer Bell, 1993), 29: "The child's language 'grows in the mind' as the visual system develops the capacity for binocular vision, or as the child undergoes puberty at a certain stage of maturation. Language acquisition is something that happens to a child placed in a certain environment, not something that the child does." In contrast with Chomsky, I would claim that an element of responsiveness and responsibility is engaged when a child learns to speak. Something is being done and not just undergone.

12. Bickerton and Calvin, *Lingua ex Machina*, 150.

nativism, Kant would offer us a kind of intellectual nativism: human understanding comes equipped with certain categories, certain pure concepts that are blended into our experience and enable us to think objects.[13] These categories enter into our judgments and yield the various forms of judgments that Kant catalogues for us.

Over against these two forms of nativism as the explanation of where our judgments come from, Husserl offers us a description of the stages by which judgments arise from prejudgmental or prepredicative experience.[14] In Husserl, judgment and its formal categories are not simply the a priori contribution of our brains or our minds. Rather, there is something like a genealogy of the judgment. One can describe, philosophically, how judgment arises from perception. Perception itself involves a certain grasp of an identity persisting throughout a continuum or multiplicity of aspects and profiles. Such prepredicative experience does have some stability and it achieves some identification, but it does not rise to the level of judgment. Perceptual identities could be the things that are expressed in protolanguage. However, at a certain point human experience enters into categorial registration: the identity that is grasped in perception can become an explicit theme, and we can begin to distinguish, explicitly, between the thing and its features, between the whole and its parts, between the object and its predicates. Judgment arises out of perception as a new cognitive level. I find that Husserl's analysis of judgment is more satisfactory than those provided by structural linguists and by Kant. It is less a priori.

However, I would like to propose an improvement on Husserl's approach. I want to claim that the achievement of a judgment or of a predication is a more intersubjective activity than it is taken to be either by Husserl or by the nativist approaches we have mentioned. I would claim that predication occurs primarily not in the solitude of a single mind but between a speaker and a listener. It is true that judgments are sometimes made in solitude or privacy, in a single mind, but in that form they are derivative on a public structure. A judgment made in privacy is like a promise made to oneself. The original and standard way of predicating is public, and it takes place among speakers and listeners.

What happens in predication is that a speaker identifies a topic for a listener and then says something about it. The speaker establishes a referent for someone else and then declares something about it. No matter

---

13. Immanuel Kant, *Critique of Pure Reason*, A66–83.

14. Husserl's most complete description of the genesis of judgment from experience can be found in *Experience and Judgment: Investigations in a Genealogy of Logic*, ed. Ludwig Landgrebe, trans. James S. Churchill and Karl Ameriks (Evanston, Ill.: Northwestern University Press, 1973 [1948]).

how complex a conversation may become, no matter how many qualifications, subordinations, contrasts, emphases, and modifications may occur, the inevitable center of what is said remains a referent and a predicate. The speaker establishes the reference in a manner suitable for the particular listener or audience; he may use a name, or point at something, or give a description, or speak around the topic, but whatever he does he manages to hold the topic up to the listener in such a way that the listener waits for what is going to be said about it. This intersubjective situation, this elementary context for speech, is where the formal predicative structure, "S is p," comes about. This subject and predicate structure is not a structure of the mind, nor does it arise from private experience through categorial constitution alone. It arises because one speaker identifies a subject for a listener and declares something about it. Logical form arises from the interplay of minds; it does not arise within a mind. We compose and divide primarily *for* someone.

Of course, the two or more speakers enter reciprocally into the conversation. They respond to one another. When they do so, they may have to take a more explicit possession of what they have said, and they do so by mentioning themselves and reappropriating their statements. Instead of just saying, "The tree is swaying in the wind," they will say, for example, "I know the tree is swaying," or "I doubt that it is," or "I see that it is." In other words, they use the declarative form of the first-person pronoun. Once we see that predication and judgment belong primarily in the public domain, it becomes obvious that such declarative usage is inevitable. It is part of the logic of judging that sooner or later we will highlight ourselves as the ones who take this or that position in the company of the persons among whom we speak.

In this third section we have discussed how syntax, declaratives, and intersubjective predication work together.

IV

In the fourth part of my essay, I wish to return to the role of freedom and responsibility in the achievement of truth. I hope that the role of syntax, declaratives, and intersubjectivity will give us more room in which to speak of the way in which truth depends on human freedom. It should be obvious that when we make use of declaratives, when we say "I know . . ." or "I suspect . . ." we express a certain kind of responsibility that we must have had in bringing about and stating our claims to various forms of truth. When we use declaratives, we do not only *say* something; we also express that it is *we* who have said it and that the saying is *ours;* we make this declaration before other people, and we take responsibility for what we have said. If I were to say "I suspect that he is coming," I show that I am warranting something as being suspect, as perhaps being the case, as deserving of this or that modality. I am indicating that you and the others can count on me as having acted as an agent of truth in this case, and hence as having exercised a certain kind of freedom.[15]

Can we explore what kind of freedom this is? Let us move into it by listing four ways in which freedom is associated with truth.

First of all, the action of telling the truth, or the action of telling a lie, which I mentioned at the beginning of my paper, obviously fits into the interaction between speakers and listeners, and it obviously engages the freedom of the speaker. However, the ability to tell either the truth or a lie depends on our prior ability to obtain the truth. An important moral virtue that is involved in obtaining the truth is what we could call teachability or docility, the willingness to accept the truth from others. This is a second kind of freedom associated with truth; it is the freedom from an excessive love of our own opinions, the freedom to learn from others. Yves Simon has written eloquently about this topic.[16] Still deeper than such docility is a third kind of freedom, the ability and the willingness to pay attention to things. This exercise of freedom deals not with our relations with other people who are trying to help us attain the truth, but with our own willingness to bring our cognitive powers to bear on what needs to be focused on, to take the steps that are appropriate in discovering the truth. We can turn our minds toward the issue at hand, or we can turn them away; we can do our best not to think about the issue, or we may not think about it with the care that the issue demands.

We might think that these three kinds of responsibility in regard to truth—telling the truth, learning from others, paying attention—are all

15. The role of declaratives comes especially to the fore when people deliberate about a project they are undertaking. A statement beginning with the phrase, "What *I* think should be done is this . . . ," underscores dramatically the practical opinions of the speaker in question, and calls up the character of the speaker as well: Is he reliable? Prudent? Honest? Does he know what he is talking about? Bernard Williams, in *Truth and Truthfulness: An Essay in Genealogy* (Princeton: Princeton University Press, 2002), distinguishes between Sincerity (not misrepresenting my beliefs) and Accuracy (taking the appropriate steps to discover the truth): "If others are to rely on what you tell them, you need, as well as not misleading them about what you believe, to take the trouble to make sure that your belief is true" (149). These two dimensions of truthfulness are implicated in the use of declaratives.

16. See Yves R. Simon, *A General Theory of Authority* (Notre Dame: University of Notre Dame Press, 1962), 148–56. Simon says that true honesty requires that a scholar be willing "to make himself independent of himself and to side with truth" (151). The fact that human beings can fail to seek the truth, "that human freedom should be restricted in this high order of the mind's relation to truth is a moral and metaphysical disaster of the first magnitude" (151–52). What happens then is that an idea of my own "instead of leading my mind to truth acts as a screen between truth and the mind" (152).

that there are. I think, however, that there is a fourth kind, one that underlies these three. Just to give it a name, let us call it *veracity*. Another term for it might be *responsiveness*. Suppose we have gotten to the point where we do take in what others say and where we pay attention to the things that are appearing. Even listening and paying attention are not enough; even then, the truth does not come to light automatically. We still need one more form of responsibility: we have to be willing to *accept* the things to which we are paying attention. We have to be willing to face facts; we must *want* the truth, for ourselves as well as for others. It is possible for us to be focused on something, to avoid distraction, and still to avoid seeing what is there before us, and we can fail willingly. We *want* not to see, and hence we *don't* see. We can hide things not just from others but also from ourselves. We fail to be responsive. Our relation to the truth cannot be automatic and impersonal; it must be free, responsible, and most essentially our own doing. This deep responsibility is intimately related with human cognition, and it is the most elementary kind of freedom, more basic than a choice that we might make within a range of options. It is associated with our being as persons, as agents of truth. It is the essential honesty, the rudimentary love of truth. It unfolds ultimately into the theoretical life and even into the moral life, since moral action itself is a form of responding to the way things are. This veracity is at the heart of the scientific enterprise, but it is not guaranteed by academic certification or training in a methodology; the willingness to face facts can be found in the illiterate as well as the learned and clever.

Veracity can be an issue for people who cannot read, but not for those who cannot speak, those who are incapable, in David Braine's phrase, of "thinking in the medium of words."[17] If a human being cannot speak, if he cannot exercise his rationality, he cannot truly act as a person (even though he still *is* a person). As we have seen, speech, the use of language, is dependent on the ability to exercise syntax. Veracity is associated with syntax.

V

The fifth and final section of my paper is even more speculative than the earlier parts. I wish to present as a hypothesis the claim that syntax is involved with what the ancient and medieval philosophers call the agent intellect. In the classical theory of knowledge, the agent intellect illuminates the phantasms we have in our imagination. It thereby causes the

---

17. See David Braine, *The Human Person: Animal and Spirit* (Notre Dame: University of Notre Dame Press, 1992), 5, 439, 448.

intelligible species to be abstracted and possessed by the passive intellect. It brings to light the indivisibles that are received into the passive intellect. Syntax comes into play in this process. I would suggest that syntax is like a stick that the agent intellect uses to poke into the phantasms of things in order to make their intelligibility show up.[18] I would suggest that it is the combination of syntactic speech and imaginative presentation that dislodges the intelligibility of things.

In other words, we do not just have a phantasm confronted by a simple, glowing, undifferentiated agent intellect hovering above it like the sun over a landscape. What we have, more tangibly, is a phantasm along with speech. We imagine the thing or the situation we are trying to think about, and we use words to try to understand it. Normally, we use "inner" or silent speech as we try to get the point of what we are imagining. We imagine the thing or the situation that we are trying to think about, and words are spoken as we do so. It is, however, not the case that we are only imagining that we are speaking; our internal speech is real speech, not an imagined conversation with ourselves. This internal or solitary speaking, as ragged and fragmentary as it may be, does engage syntax. If we take syntax as involved with the activity of the agent intellect, we may be able to see that freedom and responsibility have a place in the abstraction of indivisibles, in the abstraction of an intelligible species and its articulation in a judgment or definition, because the syntactic wholes we utter do involve some verbal choices on our part. The active and receptive intellect are not automatic or necessitating powers, but part of the rationality of a human person. We have to be willing to let the intellect do its work. It will not do so if we do not let it.

Thomas Aquinas, drawing on Aristotle's *De Anima*, says that the intellect does not come with any innate ideas or structures. It is empty and purely formal. It has to be, if it is to be open to all of being. If the intellect had any structures or contents of its own, these structures or contents would serve to block out certain things and hence limit what the intellect could know, just as the organic structure of a particular external sense limits that sense's exposure to its specific formal objects (we can see colors, but we do not see sounds; we can hear sounds, but we do not hear colors). Aquinas does claim, however, that the intellect is not entirely simple, but differentiated into two powers. It is one intellect but it has two dimensions. It has an active power and a passive or receptive one; it is an agent and a passive intellect. These are the only two parts or powers in it, and each of them is without content. The intellect

---

18. I note that my use of this simile, of syntax's being like a stick used to poke something, is an attempt to offer you a phantasm from which you might abstract an intelligibility.

needs these two powers, and it specifically requires the active intellect, because the senses by themselves, even the internal senses, could not rise to the level of intellectual cognition; there must be an intellectual causality that brings about rational cognition. We must, therefore, posit the active intellect.[19]

I would suggest that the power that provokes rational cognition is connected with syntax. It is what we could call grammaticality, the power to articulate the intellectual target, to structure it in such a way that its intelligibility can be manifested. I do not wish to say that the agent intellect *is* any syntactic structure. It is not even the basic structure of predication. The agent intellect is the more fundamental power to structure, the ability to distinguish formal parts and wholes that then become more fully articulated in appropriate judgments and definitions. To bring this out, we must make some distinctions concerning the way words are used.

Words are sometimes used in a rather passive, associative way. They are tied to the things we are experiencing, but our experience remains on the level of perception and imagination. We remain with phantasms. We do not rise to the level of logic. We might employ linguistic syntax, but it is more a habitual, associative use of grammatical terms than a true and thoughtful usage. We indulge in what Husserl calls vague or confused thinking.[20] As we continue to talk in this manner, we often wind up contradicting ourselves and falling into incoherences. On this level, obviously, the agent intellect has not yet kicked in, at least not in full force.

At other times, we may engage in clear, distinct thinking, we may use syntax thoughtfully, but we are engaged in what Husserl calls the truth of correctness.[21] We make judgments, and we try to confirm whether they are true or not by matching them to the things that we experience. We try to verify the judgments we make. The categories we use, the predicates we assign to subjects, are all taken from our standard stock of concepts, and we try to see whether the thing or situation in front of us does indeed fall under the concept we are using. Such cognition is thoughtful and legitimate, but it is somewhat derivative. I want to get to still another kind of thinking.

I wish to get to what we could call the truth of disclosure or manifes-

---

19. In *Summa theologiae* I q. 79 a. 7, Aquinas shows that the intellect needs these two powers and none other. The senses are incapable of generating an understanding: ibid., I q. 84 a. 6.

20. On the extremely important phenomenon of vagueness in speech, see Edmund Husserl, *Formal and Transcendental Logic*, trans. Dorion Cairns (The Hague: Nijhoff, 1969 [1929]), §§16, 88, 89. See also Robert Sokolowski, *Introduction to Phenomenology* (New York: Cambridge University Press, 2000), 105–8, 171–72.

21. Husserl, *Formal and Transcendental Logic*, §46.

tation.[22] In this case, we do not have a ready-made concept waiting to be applied, or a judgment waiting to be verified. In this case, we start with a perception and tease out the predicate. We originally distinguish the predicate from the subject, the feature from the object. We establish a certain concept for the first time. We may have to use metaphors to bring out what we are trying to say. Suppose, for example, that we were dealing with a very difficult human situation and didn't have a term to describe it exactly. We try to identify *what* is going on, and if we succeed we abstract an indivisible, we dislodge a predicate, we have an insight into something we did not know before. We also realize that if we have truly captured an intelligibility, it must transcend this learning situation, that is, we realize that it is a universal.[23] This activity of disclosure is what Husserl describes in his analysis of the origins of predication in *Experience and Judgment*.

I would say that it is in such an achievement of truth that the agent intellect and the syntactic possibilities of the human mind most vividly come into play. Such thinking is very concrete, and hence it is very Aristotelian. We do not intuit predicates by themselves; we intuit the predicate in the concrete object that we experience and imagine. We dislodge the predicate and hence the category and the universal, we do not just apply it. Such thinking has to be differentiated especially from the kind of associative, vague, imaginational thinking that does not rise to the level of logic. In the present case, we *think*, we do not just feel, and we try to think about something we have not thought about before. To pull this off, we have to bring our syntactic concerns to the thing, and we also have to bring the intelligibilities that we already have. We have to elevate what we are experiencing into the space of reasons, as John McDowell, following Wilfrid Sellars, has called it.[24] We use the syntax and predicates we already have, but we do not impose them on what we are experiencing. Our agent intellect may profit from these acquired syntactic and conceptual structures, but it is not caged by them. Our agent intellect is, in principle, not confined to any structure, and so it can be flexible in the face of something new, and it can distill the intelligibility of something we had not experienced before. When we do grasp this intelligibility, it has to blend in with what we already know, and it has to become involved with all the syntactic possibilities available in our lan-

22. Ibid. Husserl calls this the truth as *Wirklichkeit*, but this term does not translate well into English.

23. On transcending the learning situation and universality, see Braine, *The Human Person*, "We are not tied in our use of words to the learning situation" (359).

24. John McDowell, *Mind and World* (Cambridge: Harvard University Press, 1994), 5. McDowell goes on to say, "In a slogan, the space of reasons is the realm of freedom."

guage. If we have truly elevated the thing we experience beyond phantasms and into logic, the principle of noncontradiction will come into play, and we go on from here toward further definitions, compositions, and divisions that can spring from the thing in question.

Much more needs to be said about the relation between syntax and thinking. I think an especially promising line of argument would be to show that grammatical elements in speech serve as signals of the acts of thinking that lie behind them, and thus reveal the speaker as a speaker, as someone taking responsibility for his speech.[25] They signal the activity that the speaker ascribes to himself when he uses the first-person declarative. When we speak in this way, when we say *I* in a declarative manner—"I know this is so," "I suspect that this will happen"—we *authorize* what we declare, and we thus implicitly show that we were responsible for the truth that we disclosed. It is that kind of responsibility or veracity, this responsiveness, that underlies all our exercises in truth. We cannot be truthful if we are not willing to be so; truth and freedom go hand in hand.

25. On grammar as signaling the speech acts of the speaker, see Robert Sokolowski, *Presence and Absence: An Investigation of Language and Being* (Bloomington: Indiana University Press, 1978), 122.

4   FREEDOMS AND WOULD-BE PERSONS

JOHN M. RIST

The apparently simple title of this lecture series as a whole is "Freedom and the Human Person," but those five words conceal problems: What is freedom? And how do we identify a person? Starting with freedom, we can recognize at least two different accounts in circulation, so that saying that we all agree that freedom is very important in human life is often confusing rather than helpful. The first view, which dominates antiquity and the Middle Ages, is that freedom is secured by the removal of encumbrances in the way of our choosing the good. There have been varying ways of formulating and developing this idea. Some people (such as Pythagoreans) said that a man is free if he follows God; others, like Augustine, said that since we live in a fallen world we cannot choose the good without divine assistance, so that to be genuinely free entails that we must be freed: *liber* entails *liberatus*.

In contrast to all such ideas, though not entirely without predecessors, grew up a post-Cartesian view—which we would normally associate especially with modern orthodoxies deriving from or influenced by Hume and Mill—that to be free means enjoying the right to choose in the broadest sense, that is, having the right to use and abuse what is one's own or in one's power. In other words, whereas the older view indicates that to be free is to be able to choose the good, the Humean version is that to be free is to be able to choose whatever one likes if one can or if one has the right. One of the obvious difficulties is that if everyone were able to choose in this way without limitation, the rights of one of us would be the disadvantages of many others, or even of everyone else. Hence non-nihilist accounts usually introduce some sort of Lockean caveat: one is free to choose so long as one's choices do not impede the equal right of everyone else to do the same.

But that suggestion is itself not without difficulties: what sort of caveat have we introduced? Is it a moral caveat or a caveat of expediency or convenience, or are the two identical? A problem about supposing that to be moral is simply to be expedient is revealed by the following example. When Hitler ordered the Holocaust of the Jews, was that simply inexpedient or inconvenient, or is the problem much more serious? There are various ways in which people try to defuse this sort of difficulty. It may be said that the inexpedient is converted into the moral insofar as it is unfair—though that is to introduce a whole series of new problems, such as what is always so bad about being unfair. Perhaps it is bad because it is irrational.

That too looks rather counter-intuitive, or at least incomplete, though Kantians seem to adopt it *faute de mieux*. Is *all* that is wrong with the Holocaust that it was irrational? Indeed the very claim that it *was* irrational needs justification, since it depends *inter alia* on the premise that everyone has as much value as everyone else. But what kind of value: intrinsic or extrinsic? Are people really valuable intrinsically—and, if so, how is that to be understood, and what does it imply? Or are they valuable simply because they claim to be valuable, or because we claim value on their behalf? It is worth noticing that to say that all men are equal is often also merely to *assert* that they are all valuable; but they may all be equally devoid of any value whatever. The origin of value is really quite a difficult matter. As L. W. Sumner observed, it was easy for Locke;[1] he could assume that men are valuable because they are somehow created such by God, but without God there seem to be problems. In brief, there are all sorts of difficulties down the road if we scrutinize the implications of the "Humean" concept of freedom instead of unthinkingly assuming it to be the lightship to guide us on our moral journey.

Which is not to say that what I dub the post-Humean position does not highlight significant facts as well as possible weaknesses in its rival as traditionally proposed. To understand these facts we should turn back to the roots of the alternative account of freedom, that of Plato and Aristotle, of Plotinus and Augustine, etc, whereby freedom is the deliverance from impediments preventing one from leading the good (including the moral) life. For in this earlier landscape we can readily identify problems about the nature of the individual human being: not, that is, about the nature of humanity as such, but about the significance of the individual human being as such. A basic difficulty is whether he is or should be, or is not and should not be, a substitutable unit, and if not, why not. For there is reason to think that much of the pre-modern philosophical tradition was inclined to imply either that the metaphysical individual is not particularly important as such or, alternatively, that philosophy (or at least metaphysics) has nothing to say about him.

Of course, as with most Greek and medieval philosophy, the picture

1. L. W. Sumner, *The Moral Foundation of Rights* (Oxford 1987).

looks much more complex and confusing once we start to go beyond generalities, whether about the tradition as a whole or even about individual philosophers and their internally differing views. But we can perhaps see our present problem at its clearest if we look first at a modern thinker, and the thinker I have in mind is a recent Pope. As Karol Wojtyła, John Paul II had quite a lot to say in philosophy, and he continued to speak regularly enough about philosophy, as in the encyclical *Fides et Ratio*. When I was trying to review a book by Rocco Buttiglione about Wojtyła's philosophical stance, I was constantly brought back to the well-publicized fact that he wants to combine much of the so-called perennial philosophy, in some sort of Thomist guise at least as regards the theory of substance, with claims derived from his own philosophical background in Scheler and other phenomenologists who take their starting point from something like the so-called "acting person"—now we come to the second problem word in the name of this lecture series—viewed as the center of something like a Cartesian consciousness and as a modern center of freedom to act. And that no doubt led Wojtyła and others, in Vatican II and elsewhere, to emphasize at times something more like the post-Humean right to use and abuse, namely the right to pursue an erroneous course in good faith, especially in matters of religion. Here the primacy of the individual's freedom to choose is proposed as paramount (lest human dignity be infringed)—though we should remember that the Pope was far from playing such Humean notes in other areas: he did not advocate the freedom to choose to abort, let alone to kill one's children if they are not up to standard. He was thus committed to say that in some cases, such as that of freedom of religion, the right to choose is a fundamental condition of human dignity, but in others it is to be overruled.

In the case of religious freedom (though perhaps even here there are limits) the right to choose "freely" (in some sense) is to be promoted absolutely along with a similar freedom for others *even though* it may have harmful social consequences—something like a Lockean caveat again—but elsewhere such freedom is to be denied precisely or not least because it does have damaging social consequences. Or is that the only reason? We shall shortly consider an alternative and platonizing possibility. But at least many of the objections to more contemporary versions of the Lockean caveat do not apply: clearly the Pope did think that all men are equal precisely because they are so created as uniquely and incommensurably valuable individuals by God.

So what has happened to the difficulty which I identified in many pre-modern accounts of the individual? Is the modern "personalism" a complete break with the pre-modern past? Some years ago George Grube claimed that according to Plato individuality is something to outgrow. This is far from a mindless comment, but in several respects it is misleading, not least in that it was always the aim of the Platonic Socrates—protagonist *par excellence* of an agent-relative morality—to proclaim that the aim of the good man is to make his soul better. Socrates is continually presented as arguing that the end-state, the material result achieved, is not the key to morality. Thus when he refused to take part in the illegal arrest of a certain Leon of Salamis, he knew that his refusal would do nothing for Leon; there were plenty of others ready and willing (or fearful enough) to commit the crime; his point was that *he* would not commit the crime, thereby, *inter alia*, making his soul worse. And Socrates certainly seems to have thought that it is a function of a good and hopefully binding law to promote the well-being of the citizens who are compelled to obey it.

So unless individuality is wholly unrelated to individual responsibility, Grube's comment about the unimportance of individuality is somehow misleading—yet not entirely so. Plato's aim seems to be that each individual become a good enough member of a perfect group: in the *Republic*, for example, he pays little attention to possible differences within the Guardian class. Some Guardians, of course, are male and some are female, others are weaker or stronger, or more or less intelligent. But little attention is paid to what might be crudely called the sum of all such possible differences. And yet it needs to be. Consider the following example. I say that I know Dean Pritzl. Someone asks me what that amounts to. In answer I come up with an ever-expanding set of propositions about Dean Pritzl, but when I reach the end of my list (or say, "and so on"), if I am asked, "Is that all there is to him?" I will say "No." There is an important sense in which I cannot "capture" the nature of an individual human being within a set of propositions.

That is not to say that some propositions about any individual are not much more informative and truthful than others. I would not want to make the mistake commonly made even by philosophers of supposing or implying that because I cannot "capture" an individual (or an event, or even a stone) in a propositional framework, I do not know anything, or anything worth knowing, about that individual (or event or stone). So it seems that, as the Stoics already argued against what they took to be the views of Plato and Aristotle, there is something philosophically interestingly about *any* individual in his uniqueness—as Plotinus also seems to have concluded with his anti-Platonic theory set in a Platonic frame about forms of individuals, at least of individual humans. Perhaps indeed this individual uniqueness has something to do with the notion of a person—though adding that idea by itself would still not induce me to accept (at least without a great deal of further glossing for a contemporary audience) the classic Boethian definition that a person is an individual substance of a *rational* nature. For the usefulness of that definition would also depend on what is entailed by the notion of a rational nature, and here again the ancients and the mainstream moderns after Descartes would differ radically. For the Platonic tradition in particular, reason (and therefore the rational nature) is quite inseparable from its own highest form of erotic desire for the best possible sort of teleological object.

Perhaps I have neglected a fundamental point in my rather cavalier remarks about individuals, a point which my own argument about the behavior of Socrates in the case of Leon should have made obvious. To see the objection I have in mind, consider the remark of Aristotle in *Metaphysics Zeta* (similar things can be found elsewhere) that of the individual there is no definition, but that individuals are recognized by the mind or the senses. This, one might suppose, need not be read as proposing that *philosophy* has nothing to say about individuals except insofar as they can be considered as members of classes, only that *metaphysics* as defined by Aristotle has nothing to say about individuals. After all, Aristotle has plenty to say about the way in which individuals should behave, both in his various ethical writings and in his *Politics*. Clearly his whole discussion of virtues and vices is in the best Platonic tradition of how each of us should best lead his life. But my concern is not so much about the general point that Aristotle (or Plato) has little to say metaphysically about the nature of individuals or even about individual persons, but more specifically that the effect of this silence is that it is difficult to see how he would explain how and why individual *persons* should be so important. Clearly they are or seem to be important in a way that individual pigs are not, but is that a matter of what would now be called speciesism, or is there available a better explanation of their importance?

Perhaps Plato and Aristotle did not discuss such a basic point because it seems obvious that human beings are important. But the answer that they are important because they are important does not take us very far. In fact both Plato and Aristotle suppose that our importance, our being more "valuable"—*timiōteroi* as Aristotle might put it, along the lines by which he says that the unmoved mover thinks of himself rather than of less important subjects—has something to do with some sort of capacity for divinity we seem to possess. Four times Plato refers to the search for likeness to God as being the goal for man, and famously in the tenth book of the *Nicomachean Ethics* Aristotle urges us to immortalize ourselves as far as possible. But making oneself divine, what does that mean? Something like developing the finest part of the human being, identified as his capacity to think about what is eternal and unchanging.

So are the Kantians substantially right after all? Certainly Aristotle says in the ninth book of the *Nicomachean Ethics* that *nous* is "us" or mostly us. That looks like an assertion that some sort of cognitive power is what makes a man, and Aristotle also suggests on a number of occasions—openly or by implication—that those in some way incapable of deliberative activity, that is, of running their own lives, are natural slaves, or "manimals" as I once called them.[2] So are we somehow back not only to Kant but to the "individual substance of a rational nature"? I do not want to discuss Aristotle in this context, because I am not sure what his view is, and I do not want to talk about the Stoics because their view is too rationalist, too much like a foreshadowing of Kant, to fulfil the apparent requirements for "personhood"—that elusive word slips back in again—for my present purposes. Rather I want to talk about Plato and the Platonic tradition on the subject of the mind, because it was the gradual weakening of this Platonic concept of mind—a concept which via Augustine and others largely persisted until late Scholastic times—which precipitated so many difficulties in contemporary moral philosophy and philosophical psychology: about freedom, the person, choice, and all the rest.

I have already observed that the Platonic mind is not a merely cognitive phenomenon; hence, *inter alia*, it *cannot* be merely instrumental in the Humean manner. Rather it is properly an erotic and teleologically driven phenomenon: a power rationally desirous of the Good; when freed from distraction—I now rather anachronistically use Scholastic terminology—ordered towards the good. That is also one reason why it is so misleading to talk in the same breath of Cartesian and of Platonic dualism.

In the Platonic tradition an erotic, good-seeking intelligence is the mark *par excellence* of a human being. I have already commented that such a phenemonon was more easily recognized in *moral* philosophy. Our present problem arises when it is not allowed for explicitly in metaphysics, and here again I must indulge in some broad-brush work. Generally speaking there have been two ways of approaching the question, What is man? The first is metaphysical, and then we normally find some kind of ontological account of the relationship or otherwise between form and matter, between soul and body. Such accounts are in the broadest sense scientific in that they can be—though they need not be—expounded in value-free language. But in the Platonic tradition the most

2. Cf. J. M. Rist, *The Mind of Aristotle* (Toronto 1989), 153–57, 249–52.

basic answer to the question, What is man? is that he is a subject capable of choosing, identifying, and loving the good. The earliest and in some ways the most interesting text on this matter in the Platonic dialogues themselves is to be found in the *Phaedo*. Socrates speaks of his staying in prison: he knows he could escape; if it were up to his body, he suggests, he would now be in Thebes, but he has *decided* to remain where he is. That decision indicates that he is a real philosopher, and Plato's point is not to be neglected, because in the *Phaedo* he still argues that a basic clash between the goods of the soul and those of the body provides the explanation of virtue and vice. In any case, by the time he comes to write the *Republic* Plato has realized that if the soul is so easily tempted by the body there must be something problematic about the soul itself—hence the so-called tripartite soul, but that is another story.

Or is it? The tripartite soul—though Plato never uses the word "tripartite" and even prefers "kinds of soul" to "parts of soul"—plays many roles, but one of them is to draw attention to the fact that we are many potential people: we might be philosopher kings if all our "souls" are in the proper relationship to each other, or we might be Humeans—our minds being no more than slaves of our passions—if the so-called desiring element, that which commercializes and materializes everything, including sexual relations, is able to treat the erotic and good-desiring "self" as a mere instrument. But now I have introduced a new term, "self," a term which is not in Plato's text, though something like it occurs in the pseudo-Platonic, crudely Platonic and therefore very influential dialogue entitled the *Lesser Alcibiades*. In that dialogue it is said that we are our souls, something which the authentic Plato never quite says. Thus a question arises about all the different concepts Plato (and other Greeks) are trying to get at when they use the word "soul" *(psyche)*. In some sense we are our souls, perhaps, but the Platonic soul is divided. or, as I would prefer to put it, we are compartmentalized: in modern jargon we are a narrative, and all of us have in varying degrees lost the plot.

So in a sense we are not one soul, or in the more modern jargon one self, but several, or at least three. We are all familiar with the myth (or is it a myth?) of the Mafia hit man who comes home to play with his children or to pat the dog. And we are familiar with ourselves, who dress differently in all the different lives we engage in, and behave differently too—to the point of living in contradiction to ourselves—from one "life" to the next; in our home-life, love-life, work-life; are we still the same person or self in all these "lives"? It really is puzzling that Plato could see that Dr. Jekyll and Mr. Hyde are the same person. But certainly Dr. Jekyll is not like Socrates, who seems to have regarded it as the part of a good man to be all of a piece—not merely, like the apocryphal Wittgenstein, not to care what he eats so long as it is always the same—but in the sense that a good man should be a harmonious, or at least a compatible, whole. And that compatibility should extend not merely synchronically over the different roles we are forced to engage in, but in the attitude we adopt to our remembered past. The good man, in the Socratic tradition, cannot rationalize his past actions; he is responsible for appropriating them as they are, and contradictory as they are, on pain of becoming further divided.

I have said enough for the moment about all these ramifications of the problems of freedom, and I have at least insinuated others about which self is free to do what and whether we have any overall freedom over and above the freedom we exercise within the different selves of our lives. It is now time to turn to our other problem-word, namely "person," though in speaking of freedom and in introducing the term "self" I have already come close, if obliquely so, to certain possible features of the person: if, that is, a person is an individual with *(inter alia)* some sort of facility to be free, or at least to be freed.

"Person" itself is an odd term, deriving from the Latin *persona* which means a mask, thus perhaps invoking something of the role-playing and compartmentalization to which I have already alluded. But first a bit more history, and the more history we learn the more surprised we shall be about the roots of some of the ideas lying behind the modern notion of "person." For it may seem that we somehow "know" (or think we know) what a person is without being able to say what it is, "person" being some sort of rigid designator in Kripke's sense. Perhaps a little more historical reflection will help us to see why the contemporary term "person" seems not only slippery but often indeed little more than a source of muzzy thinking when bandied about in a secularized, deplatonized, and post-Christian philosophical culture.

Any starting point is more or less at random, but a convenient one is a passage of Cicero's *De Officiis* (1.107–15), probably dependent on the Stoic philosopher Panaetius and a possible source for a notorious and hardly understood distinction of Augustine's between our "common life" and our "individual life" which—since as human beings we are one in Adam—plays such an important part in his theories about original sin. Be that as it may, Panaetius (and Cicero) identify four *personae*. The first, the *communis persona*, seems to be that set of characteristics by virtue of which we can identify ourselves as men; the second, the *propria natura*, those by which, as individuals, we are marked off from other men, but in what seems to be something of a hypothetical sense: that is, before we have experienced the actual events of our ongoing daily lives and acted in accordance with our individual decisions—something like our own unique genetic make-up which exists within what is a possible genetic make-up for any human being whatsoever. The third *persona* indicates the effects on our character of external (especially social) circumstances and expectations and of the passage of time, while the fourth reveals the effects of our own decisions in relation to those external circumstances: our actions, that is, as distinct from the events which befall us.

This passage, striking though it is, may seem far from much modern talk about persons, which (as typically in Dennett) is largely stipulative, but there is one significant common feature: Panaetius was apparently concerned to point out—doubtless in line with the standard Stoic attack on Plato and Aristotle to which I alluded before—that within humanity as a whole, and within the "genetic" structures of each particular individual, we must also consider the way in which individual and historically rooted nature works itself out in light of our individual experiences and our resultant decisions. Thus "personhood" will be recognizable in a set of human possibilities for each individual personality, while the *persona* we finally exhibit will be the combined presentation of the other *personae* which it seems to enclose.

This "historical" thesis about "persons," however Panaetius himself might have chosen to develop it, seems to have entered the Western tradition in a rather strange fashion; hence it was to receive little immediate attention, though now perhaps something like it may be—somewhat oddly—of more interest. It apparently entered the tradition through a Stoicizing theologian—a development Panaetius himself could hardly have looked for. For it is a curious fact that in antiquity the most interesting and influential talk of "persons" occurs not in the context of disagreement about developing human souls or selves or (as in Epictetus) about role-playing, but in heated debate about the fixed and unchanging nature of the Christian God. So from Panaetius we would need to move first to Tertullian, who comes to think of a divine Person as a distinct individual existence with particular reference to that Person's perfect inner life, and then to the classical Christian thinkers of the Latin fourth century and beyond to the Council of Chalcedon. Persons—who in the Stoic tradition presupposed a perfect standard—in the strictest sense are the distinct persons of the Christian Trinity, and hence human persons (necessarily) are an incomplete though developing image of that divine personhood.

Why have I introduced this apparently strange material? I suppose because I am asking myself whether the contemporary difficulties about identifying the nature of the person—the word, as we have seen, seems to be some kind of semi-rigid designator—may be another instance of the phenomenon much discussed by Elizabeth Anscombe and others in her wake, that much modern talk in ethics and in philosophical psychology derives from a coherent but theistic world-view from which, however, God has later been removed as inconvenient or indefensible. I am suggesting, that is, that the reason why we think we *know* what persons are, but cannot *explain* what they are, is because any good explanation can be and must be (and originally was) theological—though I do not like the modern distinction of philosophy and theology which has always tended, apart from mere biblical fundamentalism, to leave theology without a properly intellectual subject-matter.

But am I jumping ahead, giving too much respectability to the modern concept of a person? For it seems to be the case that we do *not* know, but, as I said, merely stipulate—"we," meaning our society, certainly do not agree—what a person is and who are persons. Must they be able to experience pain? That eliminates the newly conceived. Are they those who can deliberate or choose or claim? That eliminates the newborns and many of the handicapped. Do they include those senile or in a coma? If I leave the University and am knocked down by a bus, remaining alive in a vegetative state, am I still a person? Or should it then be said of me that I *was* a person. All these difficulties arise because persons are being defined somehow as individual members of the human race (that is, with human parents) capable of some sort of action or ability to experience. But all such accounts would seem to introduce various forms of the Sorites paradox (or the slippery slope). How much damage does the bus have to do to cause me to change my status, short of being dead, to that of an ex-person? No compelling answers to such questions are forthcoming—a fact which helps to generate many of the puzzles and paradoxes to which philosophers like Derek Parfit have drawn our attention.[3]

For it seems that although the word "person" may function up to a point as a rigid designator—though the rigidity becomes rather more flexible when it is pressed by ideological concerns—the interpretation of the word remains in a haze. Indeed it may be the case, as we have suggested, that apart from some rather limited and legalistic purposes, the word "person" is merely a further source of muddled thinking. By "legalistic purposes" I mean that it may be decreed or determined by some law-making body that blacks or whites are to be treated as persons. But if such determinations are scrutinized historically, we recognize that many

3. See *Reasons and Persons* (Oxford 1986).

to whom particular societies wished to deny the status of persons (as blacks at the time of the American Declaration of Independence) would (in theory) have been able to advance logically persuasive but socially—and therefore legally—unacceptable claims to some revision of their status. Or in more Aristotelian fashion we might decree that a person is someone whose IQ is at least X + 1.

As an alternative to positive law, philosophers are sometimes inclined to resort to dictionary definitions when trying to identify at least the core usage of a word, and indeed a glance at the OED is informative in the case of "person," if not in ways we might expect. The predominant sense proposed is "an individual human being." (This is emphasized in those cases where "person" seems to indicate either the individual body or "the actual self.") But the impreciseness of all this historically based suggestion is ironically confirmed by the theological entry for person: here we read what is traditionally a heretical description of the Divine Persons as "The three modes of the divine being in the Godhead"—a definition of which old Sabellius (and of course his modern imitators) would have been proud. And the OED curiously omits an older usage, apparently first recorded in a juridical context in the Straits Times of Singapore of 1821, where a young lady complained of someone who had interfered with her person. Apparently the only conclusion to be drawn from the dictionary is that "person" seems to be used to indicate something about human animals which is very important, uniquely individual (though the sense of an actor's mask still lurks in the background), and perhaps somehow intimate, but that no one is sure how to proceed further.

If my instinct is correct, we have to consider the possibility, as I indicated earlier, that when we discuss persons, a chasm will open up between secular and non-secular ways of thinking. Before looking at how the Christian might be able to put some less confused interpretation on the word "person," I should like to prospect this chasm in a little more detail: that is, before urging that we are confronted with another instance of a fairly common difficulty in contemporary debate. On grounds of brevity, however, I offer only one example—indeed, an example to which I have already alluded, but one which introduces a theme where much more realistic thinking is required. I refer to the question of rights, a topic on which, I would argue, the secularist has the right to pronounce only if—brazenly or covertly—he filches religious premises and assumptions. Rights, you remember, were described by Jeremy Bentham—from his point of view not unrealistically—as "nonsense on stilts," and the contemporary philosopher Alasdair MacIntyre has argued forcefully that, at least from most secular perspectives, natural rights are fantasies. But rights-theory is illuminating not least because it overlaps with theories about persons: as when it is claimed, opaquely, that persons qua persons have rights.

Take a disturbing example. Every moment of each twenty-four-hour period somewhere in the world someone is being tortured. Most of us would say that these victims have the right not to be so mistreated, that persons should not be treated in that way. Leave aside for the moment the rights, if any, of those apparent humans, say in a coma, who may be legally denied the title of persons, and ask what kind of a right these present torture-victims could lay claim to. Their claim must be that *persons* just should not be treated in this way in any place and for any reason, that such treatment is "just wrong." But what does that mean? We have already considered the apparent illogicality—and consequent impotence against moral nihilism—of the modern version of the Lockean caveat in accounts of freedom.

Our first problem is that of self-serving and selective relativity. Many people, confronted, say, with an accusation of fornication, would say that their sexual behavior, so long as they do no "harm" to anyone else— I leave aside the obvious problems of that—is a matter of free choice: roughly that what is wrong is what I or we agree to be wrong. But many of the same people, confronted with the activities of some notorious and sadistic torturer, would say that his behavior is *just wrong.* So, a principle has been established; there are intrinsically evil acts, and anyone who might wish to say, for example, that certain sexual activities are by stipulation of a wholly different moral sort, must recognize that he bears the burden of proof to establish his case. And of course, as we saw earlier, when we say of the torturer that his acts are just wrong, we do not mean that they do not contribute to the greatest good of the greatest number—I suppose that on some calculations they might even do that at times—nor do we mean that they are inconvenient, antisocial, etc. We mean, rightly or wrongly, that they are much more gravely wrong than any such description would allow.

Let us assume for the sake of argument that offenses against the person are more serious than those against property: in most jurisdictions murder is regarded as among the most serious crimes. So let us consider the sadistic and cold-blooded murder of an innocent person. But now that word "person" has come up again, and this time we cannot evade it. Clearly here to use the term "person" is merely a way of referring to a human being, and the principle to which we refer is that it is just wrong to torture to death an innocent human being. But why? Perhaps because it is the unnecessary infliction of pain, but that would include animals, and I am still working on the common assumption that though it would be just wrong to do an animal to death in an unnecessary and sadistic fashion, it is worse to do so in the case of a human being, of a person. At this point, therefore, I would move—as I intimated might be necessary—to an explicitly theistic position. In a theistic universe we can do justice to the dreadfulness of sadistic killings, while in a non-theistic universe we cannot. In the latter universe we cannot identify adequate guidelines for thinking of acts being simply wrong at all: Nietzsche, wise in his own way, as so often, got that one right.

But be careful not to attribute to me a view I am not proposing, namely that one must be a theist to appeal to, and to feel the force of, the notion of something's being simply wrong. What I am proposing is that just as it very hard for the non-theist to *justify* any appeal to natural rights, so more generally it is difficult for him to *justify* any significant notion of the person as a specially privileged human subject: in other words, that the behavior of many non-theists, insofar as they fall back on an appeal to notions of the inviolable person and of natural rights to which they are not entitled, is better than the theories they can propose to account for their actions.

So I am arguing that within a theistic context, and specifically within a Christian context—I shall return to that in a moment—we can make sense of notions like "person" (as used in modern ethical discussion), "rights" (other than merely legal rights) and ultimately also of "freedom," for in such a world, as we saw at the start, freedom must have to do with following the teleologically set path toward the good and the ability to remove the encumbrances on that path. In the end, therefore, the free person, accepting and defending his rights, will be, as Augustine especially wanted to point out, the human being all of whose moral acts will *seem* to be predetermined (when viewed from a non-theistic prospective). If that seems bizarre, consider your position when you enter a bank with a gun, properly licensed, in your pocket. You are also in possession of Gyges' famous ring, which, as Plato tells it, grants its bearer the gift of invisibility. Why then, your more unscrupulous friend later asks you, did you not rob the bank, starting by threatening death to various of its employees? At first, in response to such a suggestion, you laugh, but if your interlocutor persists, you probably give him the right answer. Which is, "What sort of a man do you think I am?" or "I just wouldn't do that," or "I could not bring myself to do it: in that sense I had no option."

For the theist this kind of non-option is desirable; it is even godlike. For clearly there is a sense in which one could say that God *could* decide directly to cause a major atomic explosion in an American city. But any intelligible account of God would also say that he is not the kind of Per-

son (capital P) to do that sort of thing. It is not that he couldn't physical-
ly do it—in that sense he is free to do it—but it is the case that he could
not morally (though the word here is obviously inadequate) do it. Hence
when I am sufficiently determined by goodness and my love of it not to
hold up the teller, I am enjoying the highest freedom, in the pre-modern
sense of the word with which we started, and I would say also that, in behaving in a manner which in a sense approximates to that of God, I am
behaving as a person in the image and likeness of a divine Person.

One of the major difficulties we noted in the way of determining
whether an individual is a person or not is resolved in such a theistic
context, and perhaps in no other. I have argued elsewhere—I alluded to
this above—that Plato is right in speaking of our divided selves, of the
possible selves we could become.[4] Where he is wrong is in thinking that
we are, somehow underneath, *already* that undivided self or soul—but
that is another story. What I would propose is that if we recognize that
we are all persons only in the image of a divine Person, other more obviously defective persons are less liable to be written out of the class of
persons altogether. The Sorites problem to which I alluded before then
begins to seem illusory. For if, as seems to have been largely the case in
late-Christian antiquity, the term "person" is used to refer in the first instance not to human beings at all but to divine being, then human beings, that is those produced from human beings, are all approximations
to that divine Person.

Perhaps to give some sort of more obviously philosophical explanation of my proposal, I can turn to a famous thesis of Aristotle's. The thesis is that the perfect instance of a thing can explain the nature of imperfect specimens, but that the converse is not true. If I know what a
good watch is, and what it is for, I can identify a bad watch as a watch; if I
have seen a bad watch, I cannot so easily identify a good one. So, in one
of Aristotle's own examples from the *Nicomachean Ethics*, if I know what
true courage is, I can understand various deficient kinds of behaviors
of which we might say, "Oh yes, that is courageous in a way." Courage,
that is, gives both sense and an object of reference to what we may label
"courage"; or in more current linguistic parlance—though the matter is
ontological and not solely a question of language—we may say that the
perfect example of courage provides some sort of "focal meaning" to
various approximate ways in which we speak of "courage."

In the course of this discussion I have implied, if not formally stated, two general principles of philosophical enquiry, with particular ref-

---

4. Cf. J. M. Rist, *Real Ethics* (Cambridge 2001), 61–118.

erence to ethics and philosophical psychology, though I am convinced that the same approach would be helpful in other areas of philosophy as well. These principles are, first, that in philosophy we have often forgotten or been induced to forget what we once knew: in our particular case we have forgotten that there was once a very prominent notion of freedom to be found among philosophers who in many other respects were radically diverse, a notion very different from the choice theories which dominate the contemporary scene.

The second principle is the Anscombian dogma, which historical research constantly confirms, that much modern ethical debate is conducted on the basis of assumptions, as about rights, which essentially depend on metaphysical claims to which their modern proponents no longer wish to subscribe. And I have suggested that not only is rights-talk infected in this way but that many contemporary notions of the person make no real sense when divorced from a set of theological claims developed much earlier, whereby personhood is primarily to be expounded with reference to God. Then, by the use of some sort of focal account, personhood is extended to man—provided, that is, we can introduce the specifically Christian side constraints that man is constructed in God's image and that he is a "person" as yet incomplete. (Indeed, in his ongoing condition he is a possible set of persons, each of which is still "striving" to dominate—in fact, to become—the complete human individual.)

But my assessment of what Anscombe called "modern moral philosophy" and its psychological accompaniments is not perhaps as negative as hers. I have accepted, that is, that the personalist turn is important in that it highlights what we can call the necessary conditions of that agent-relative morality the origins of which go back to Socrates and Plato. The emphasis on starting with the human subject, which goes back to Descartes and is refined by criticism emanating from the Humean tradition, can help illuminate and develop many of the underlying themes of traditional (i.e. pre-modern) ethical theory. Yet, like all positives, the emphasis on the self has its dangers and its price. If ethics remains at the level of the subject and what he can construct, it can never provide a moral, but only a conventional response to nihilism, as of course it does in Hume himself. It needs, in fact, the old objective world, that world first proposed by Plato, if it is going to function as one would hope, that is, as a defense for natural rights and natural obligations.

That is where the theistic option, in particular its Christian form, can come in. The challenge the theist can make is to propose a hypothesis which will do the ethical work required. That of course does not make it true, but it is certainly an argument for the likelihood of its truth. This has always been a method of Christian philosophy, though it was much more strongly emphasized in patristic than in later times. Take for example Augustine's use of the Pauline concept of original sin. The theistic thesis is offered to explain, better than any other, certain apparently observable features of human life. Clearly Augustine would be refuted if his observations of human life are erroneous, but he can make a good defense of many of them. And in this regard Augustine is in a certain sense, though perhaps unwittingly, following the example of the great agent-relativist Plato himself. In the *Republic* no knock-down syllogisms are offered in favor of the view that the life of the tyrannical man is worse than the life of the philosopher-king. But there is a powerful argument all the same. It is as though Plato had said: here is the character of the vicious man, as I can best describe him (let us say in modern times he might paint a portrait of Hitler); here is a portrait of some widely recognized saint or moral paragon. Plato then asks which life we would prefer. If we say we would rather be like Hitler, he can do no more than paint a picture of Hitler's soul over again, and if we still would prefer to be like that—if, that is, we agree that the portrait is accurate—he has no more to say, except perhaps that hell is possible.

In ancient times Parmenides of Elea offered a very strange account of the universe: motion, he claimed, did not exist. When others argued that if Parmenides is right the world seems totally bizarre, his disciple Zeno retorted that if Parmenides is wrong the world is even more peculiar. In a sense contemporary ethics is in a similar condition, and it is no solution to revert to what has been unkindly called the all-American solution of such as John Rawls in his *Political Liberalism*—namely, that no agreement about first principles is needed, because we can hammer out a solution around the table in a democratic manner. Certainly a solution of some sort can be found in this way to practical problems, but it is the solution of a wheeler and dealer, not of a moral philosopher. And so long as theistic models are on offer which provide some sort of intelligible story about such notions as freedom and persons, we do not yet need to despair about the possibilities and the future of moral philosophy. Or have I proposed to explain the obscure by the more obscure? I think not.

5   BEYOND LIBERTARIANISM AND COMPATIBILISM
Thomas Aquinas on Created Freedom

BRIAN J. SHANLEY, O.P.

Contemporary philosophers approaching the writings of Thomas Aquinas on human freedom naturally look to him for answers to the kinds of questions that vex us. For several centuries now, philosophical discussions of freedom have focused on the problem of the relationship between human choice and causal determination. Are human choices the end-products of causal chains originating outside of and antecedent to the agent in such a way as to determine the agent to one and only one outcome? If the answer is yes, then one is either a determinist or a compatibilist. A determinist is someone who argues that causal determination makes freedom an illusion, while a compatibilist is one who argues that significant human freedom is consonant with causal determination. If the answer to the original question is no—that human actions are not determined to one outcome by antecedent causal conditions—then human beings are free in the sense that they exercise a peculiar kind of indeterministic agency, generally thought to be rooted in something called the will and somehow connected to acting for a reason or intelligently. To defend freedom in this more robust sense is to be an incompatibilist, a locution that stresses the negative claim regarding the connection between causal determinism and freedom, or a libertarian, a locution stressing the positive side of the claim. Presuming these divisions to be exhaustive, contemporary philosophers want to know how to classify Aquinas—is he animal, vegetable, or mineral?

I know of no one who claims that Aquinas is a straightforward determinist. There are just too many texts where he argues explicitly for significant human freedom and moral responsibility against what we may retrospectively identify as antecedent versions of determinism. So that leaves either libertarianism or compatibilism. The most eloquent and interesting interpreter of Aquinas as a kind of proto-libertarian is Eleonore Stump.[1] In a series of intriguing papers, Professor Stump has offered an interpretation of Aquinas as belonging to the species of libertarians who deny that the Principle of Alternative Possibilities (PAP) is central to human freedom. According to her definition of the PAP:

A person has free will with regard to (or is morally responsible for) doing an action A only if he could have done otherwise than A.[2]

Stump's argument builds upon the so-called Frankfurt-style counterexamples to the PAP, where some agent is represented as choosing *A* in a self-determining manner without any external coercion but without any real option to do otherwise because of the presence of a coercive mechanism that would have forced the choice of *A* in any event; because the choice was not made under the influence of the mechanism, however, the action is genuinely free and so it would seem that freedom does not require the PAP. Once we eliminate the PAP as a necessary condition for freedom, and so allow Aquinas to count as free a number of highly significant cases of willed action without the PAP—God, angels, and the blessed in heaven—Aquinas can be claimed for the libertarian camp. In the libertarian interpretation of Aquinas, the analytical focus is placed primarily on the act of choice as the locus of human freedom.

While I have learned much from Professor Stump's analysis, nonetheless I do not find her interpretation of Aquinas as a proto-libertarian to be persuasive. In much of what follows, the first two sections of the paper, I want to explore the multiple ways in which Aquinas's account of freedom strains against broadly libertarian presuppositions until it finally contradicts a central libertarian tenent in such a way as to appear to make Aquinas into a proto-compatibilist instead. The breaking point is that, according to Stump, it is a necessary condition for libertarian freedom that "the causal chain resulting in any voluntary act on an agent's part has to originate in the system of the agent's own intellect and will [because] if it originates in some cause external to the agent which acts with efficient causation on the agent's will, what results will not be an act of will at all."[3] If this is so, then Aquinas cannot be a libertarian, for it is

---

1. "Aquinas's Account of Freedom: Intellect and Will," *The Monist* 80 (1997): 576–97. See also her earlier "Intellect, Will, and the Principle of Alternative Possibilities," in *Perspectives on Moral Responsibility*, ed. John Martin Fischer and Mark Ravizza (Ithaca: Cornell University Press, 1993), 237–62, and "Libertarian Freedom and the Principle of Alternative Possibilities," in *Faith, Freedom, and Rationality*, ed. Jeff Jordan and Daniel Howard Snyder (Savage, Md.: Rowman & Littlefield Publishers, Inc., 1996), 73–88. Scott MacDonald also interprets Aquinas as a libertarian in "Aquinas's Libertarian Account of Free Choice," *Revue internationale de philosophie* 21 (1998): 309–28.
2. "Aquinas's Account of Freedom," 591.
3. Ibid., 586.

a central feature of Aquinas's account of *all* human action[4] that the will is moved by God as first efficient cause. Libertarian readings of Aquinas tend to dismiss such claims as "theological" and therefore outside the scope of philosophical concern. Yet Aquinas's argument for a divine motion with respect to the will is based on metaphysical claims rather than theological ones. Indeed, on the basis of such claims for divine causality it seems obvious to philosophers such as Anthony Flew[5] and Thomas Loughran[6] that Aquinas must be classified as a compatibilist; Anthony Kenny even labels Aquinas's position as "soft determinism."[7] While I think the libertarian interpretation is untenable in the face of Aquinas's account of the relationship between divine causation and human freedom, I do not think this makes him a compatibilist in the contemporary sense by default. I will spell out my reasons for this in the third part of this paper. Having rejected the applicability of either libertarian or compatibilism as inappropriate and anachronistic conceptual categories for interpreting Aquinas, I shall argue that the ultimate reason for this rejection is Aquinas's doctrine of creation. Human freedom coming from God as its exemplar causal source and ordered to God as its final end demands a model beyond libertarianism and compatibilism.

I. THE NATURAL NECESSITY OF THE WILL AS THE ORIGIN OF FREEDOM

Libertarian accounts of freedom in Aquinas typically begin with a brief account of Aquinas's doctrine on the will in general and then move to a focus on *liberum arbitrium* or *electio* as the locus of freedom. In this section I want to argue that a focus on the nature of the will as rational appetite is the real ground of human freedom. Paradoxically, the will is free to choose because of what belongs to it necessarily by virtue of its nature.

Aquinas uses the term "appetite" to describe the relationship of every being to its appropriate good.[8] Since in every being except God perfection or fulfillment as an instance of its kind is not given by its natural constitution but must rather be achieved through action, the good is

---

4. Evil is a separate and complicated problem.
5. "Compatibilism, Free Will, and God," *Philosophy* 48 (1973): 231–44.
6. "Aquinas, Compatibilist," in *Human and Divine Agency*, ed. F. Michael McLain and W. Mark Richardson (New York: University Press of America, 1999), 1–39.
7. *Aquinas on Mind* (New York: Routledge, 1993), 73–78.
8. "Cum omnia procedant procedant ex voluntate divina, omnia suo modo per appetitum inclinatur ad bonum sed diversimodo." *Summa theologiae* I, 59, 1. All citations of this text (henceforth abbreviated as ST, followed by the part, question, and article) will be from the 1941 Ottawa edition. All translations are my own.

conceived as the object of striving and all things are said to have a natural appetite, or an inclination, or a desire for their appropriate good. The substantial form of a thing, called its nature when considered as the principle of action, causes the thing to act in a way commensurate with its substantial form to achieve a perfected state appropriate to its kind. Aquinas typically distinguishes three different kinds of appetites.[9] The first characterizes material beings lacking the capacities for sensation or intellection: their self-perfective activities are determined by their natures to a specified kind of activity; it is of the nature of fire to heat, of a stone to fall, of a plant to grow according to a determinate pattern. A second kind of appetite characterizes animals with sensation but no intellection. Such beings have a more complex interaction with their environment in their self-perfective activities. Their striving is characterized by a kind of indeterminacy regarding particular objects on the basis of how they are sensed on particular occasions; a lion may pursue prey on one occasion because hungry and ignore it on another occasion because tired, wounded, or full. A third kind of appetite is characteristic of intellectual beings. Because their substantial form is characterized by an immaterial intellect capable of grasping the entire range of being, their striving for self-perfection is not restricted in its range to only certain kinds of actions regarding certain kinds of objects. Rather, they are able to engage through knowing any object that is possibly perfective or good and so desire it in a conscious way. Intellectual beings therefore have an unrestricted appetite for their own good *as known*. That appetite is called will.[10] As rational creatures, it belongs to the nature of human beings to desire through will the human good as known. This inclination to the good belongs necessarily to human beings as rational natures prior to any choice.

Thomas describes the will, the appetite for the human good as known, as a power or capacity for activity. Like any power, the will has its own proper object which motivates and specifies its activities. The will's proper object is what makes all things good *(bonum in commune)* understood precisely as such *(sub ratio boni)*.[11] Wherever goodness is perceived, the

9. For a detailed discussion of the different ways in which Aquinas distinguishes the kinds of appetites, see David Gallagher, "Thomas Aquinas on the Will as Rational Appetite," *Journal of the History of Philosophy* 29 (1991): 559–84.

10. "Quaedam vero inclinatur ad bonum cum cognitione qua cognoscunt ipsam boni rationem, quod est proprium intellectus. Et haec perfectissime inclinatur in bonum, non quidem quasi ab alio solummodo directa in bonum, sicut ea quae cognitionem carent; neque in bonum particulare tantum, sicut ea in quibus est sola sensitiva cognitio; sed tantum inclinata in ipsum universale bonum. Et haec inclinatio dicitur voluntas." ST I, 59, 1.

11. "Similiter etiam principium motivum voluntariorum oportet esse aliquid naturaliter volitum. Hoc autem est bonum in communi, in quod voluntas naturaliter tendit, sicut etiam quaelibet potentia in suum objectum." ST I-II, 10, 1.

will can become engaged with it as an object of desire precisely as known to be good (even if mistakenly so). It is important to note the ordination of the will to the *bonum in commune* is not a claim that the will is attracted to some univocal universal property in general or a particular abstract object, but rather a description about the formality under which the will engages its objects. It is the same as saying that the formal object of sight is color or that the intellect's object is truth. Because something is the kind of power that it is, it engages its objects under a certain description. This natural ordination or inclination of the will to objects as good is prior to and explanatory of all the will's explicit acts; we do not have any choice about our ordination to the good—it belongs to the will by natural necessity. But precisely because it is an ordination to goodness wherever it is found *(bonum universale vel absolute)*,[12] it is not an ordination to any particular good and hence not a determination to pursue only one kind of good.[13] The will's orientation to the universal good is the reason why no particular good attracts it necessarily.

In addition to this natural ordination to the good, Aquinas argues that the will is naturally inclined to happiness as the perfect fulfillment of its capacities or its ultimate end *(beatitudo* as *bonum perfectum* or *ultimus finis)*.[14] It is of the very nature of the good to be an object of desire, and the desire is for perfection in actuality or existence commensurate with the nature. Every being has a desire for its own proper perfection. The term we use to designate human fulfillment as the conscious object of desire is happiness. Every human being desires what it understands to be perfective for itself as a human being and so wills happiness. Obviously this is not to say that all human beings will the same thing under the rubric of happiness, but rather that what formally and fundamentally motivates all human willing is the good-as-perfective, beatifying, completing of human beings taken as a whole and in the context of a lifetime. This kind of willing characterizes all human striving once one is able to reflect upon the good. It too is not a matter of choice but nature: human beings naturally will what they do for the sake of happiness. But

12. "Objectum autem voluntatis, quae est appetitus humanus, est universale bonum; sicut autem objectum intellectus est universale verum." ST I-II, 2, 7.

13. "Vnde cum actus sint in singularibus, in quibus nullum est quod adequet potentiam uniuersalis, remanet inclinatio uoluntatis indeterminate se habens ad multa." *De malo* 6, 1. All citations of this text will be from the Leonine edition of the *Opera omnia*, V. 23 (Rome, 1982).

14. ". . . cum unumquodque appetat suam perfectionem, illud appetit aliquis ut ultimum finem, quod appetit ut bonum perfectum et completivum sui ipsius." ST I-II, 1, 5. "Ratio autem beatitudinis communis est ut sit bonum perfectum, sicut dictum est. Cum autem bonum sit obiectum voluntatis, perfectam bonum est alicuis quod totaliter eius voluntati satisfacit. Unde appetere beatitudinem nihil aliud est quam appetere ut voluntas satietur." ST I-II, 5, 8.

precisely because there is no one object or activity available in natural human experience that perfectly and definitively completes the human person, the natural desire for happiness is the ground of human freedom. We are free to choose any particular good at any time precisely because none of them can completely satisfy our natural desire for happiness.[15] It should also be noted that our natural desire for happiness can also be described as a natural love of happiness, since love is the principle of all motion tending toward the end.[16] And since love is always a two place relation in Aquinas—*amare est velle alicui bonum*—our natural love of happiness involves a natural friendship love of self as the one to whom the good of happiness is willed.[17]

Finally, and most importantly, Aquinas argues that there is an existing good that perfectly finalizes and completes human nature and its rational appetite: God. The natural desire for the beatifying good is de facto an ordering to God, even though most people do not recognize this. Thomas argues that the only intelligible object that could satisfy the intellect's natural desire for knowledge would be a vision of the essence of the first cause of things.[18] Likewise, the only object that could satisfy the will's desire for the absolutely perfect good is God.[19] By nature then we desire God, even if at the level of conscious choice we deny his existence. All human striving for the perfective good is an implicit yearning for God. If we were actually to see God in all his perfect goodness, we would will him necessarily and naturally and not as an object of free choice.[20] Once a person enters into the beatific vision, the will's na-

15. It should be noted that there are some goods that we naturally recognize as constituent means to human happiness and so will naturally and necessarily. We cannot not will to know the truth, to be, or to live; all of these are recognized as necessarily connected with human flourishing: "Si igitur dispositio per quam alicui uidetur aliquid bonum et conueniens fuerit naturalis non subiacens uoluntati, ex necessitate naturali uoluntas preeliget illud, sicut omnes homines naturaliter desiderant esse, uiuere et intelligere." *De malo*, 6.

16. "Amor autem respicit bonum in communi, sive sit habitum, sive non habitum. Unde amor naturaliter est primus actus voluntatis et appetitus. Et propter hoc omnes alii motus appetitivi praesupponunt amorem quasi primam radicem." ST I, 20, 1.

17. "Manifestum est autem quod in rebus cognitione carentibus, unumquodque naturaliter appetit consequi id quod est sibi bonum; sicut ignis locum sursum. Unde et angelus et homo naturaliter apetunt suum bonum et suam perfectionem. Et hoc est amare seipsum. Unde naturaliter tam angelus quam homo diligit seipsum, inquantum aliquod bonum naturali appetitu sibi desiderat." ST I, 60, 3. For more on this see David M. Gallagher, "Desire for Beatitude and Love of Friendship," *Mediaeval Studies* 58 (1996): 1–47.

18. ST I-II, 3, 8.

19. "Beatitudo enim est bonum perfectum, quod totaliter quietat appetitum; alioquin non esset ultimus finis, si adhuc restaret aliquid appetendum. Obiectum autem voluntatis, quae est appetitus humanus, est universale bonum; sicut obiectum intellectus est universale verum. Ex quo patet quod nihil potest quietare voluntatem hominis, nisi bonum universale. Quod non invenitur in aliquo creato, sed solum in Deo, quia omnis creatura habet bonitatem participatam." ST I-II, 2, 8.

20. "Est autem impossibile quod aliquis videns divinam essentiam velit eam non videre.

ture has come to rest in its proper object. Precisely because its nature is made to find completion in the infinite good that is God, the will is not necessitated with respect to any other object. This side of the beatific vision, no object can compel and quiet the will's orientation to the good.

What emerges from the rather cursory account of what belongs to the very nature of the will antecedent to choice is a paradoxical conclusion: we are free precisely because we are naturally and so necessarily ordered to the perfect good who is God.[21] What we call freedom of choice presupposes as its condition what is not a matter of choice but given in human nature: the orientation to the infinite good as known and loved. While it is customary to couple nature with necessitation and determination and so oppose it to the free—and there is a sense in which Aquinas endorses this opposition when he distinguishes natural appetite from voluntary appetite—nonetheless there is a sense in which the internal necessity rooted in the nature as ordered to its end is not inimical to freedom but rather its ground.

The libertarian focus on choice as the locus of freedom thus obscures the truth that choice is neither the origin of freedom nor the end of the will. Choice must be understood as grounded in the nature of the will as ordered to rest in the perfect good. Also, it is important to note that Aquinas's account of the will as ordered to the good means that freedom cannot be understood to be rooted in indifference to the good or independence from natural desire. It is a feature of extreme voluntaristic libertarianism to want to ground freedom in the will's indifference to the good, even understood as happiness or God, and in its freedom from natural inclination. In such a view, the will must also be free even to act independently of reason.[22] As we have seen thus far, Aquinas understands freedom of the will to entail an essential orientation to the good, happiness, and God that is rooted in nature. Now we shall discuss how it is essentially connected to reason in the act of choice.

Quia omne bonum habitum quo aliquis carere vult, aut est insufficiens, et quaeritur aliquid sufficientis loco eius; aut habet aliquod incommodum annexum propter quod in fastidium venit. Visio autem divinae essentiae replet animam omnibus bonis, cum coniungat fonti totius bonitatis." ST I-II, 5, 4.

21. Jacques Maritain notes this pardox by saying: "Voilà une surprenante conséquence! Saint Thomas déduit la liberté (ici) de la necessitaté (là); c'est parce que la volunté est intérieurement et naturellement nécessitée au bonheur, au bonheur absolument saturant, qu'elle est libre à l'égard de tout le reste; a l'égard de tout le reste, c'est-à-dire à l'égard de tout ce qu'elle peut vouloir ici bas,—car où est le bonheur absolument saturant?" "L'Idée thomiste de la liberté," *Revue Thomiste* 45 (1939): 443.

22. On the contrast between Aquinas's notion of freedom and that originating in the voluntarism of William of Ockham, see Servais Pinckaers, O.P., *Les sources de la morale chrétienne*, 3e édition (Fribourg, Switzerland: Editions Universitaires, 1993), 250–63, 335–405.

II. FREE CHOICE AS AN ACT OF INTELLECT AND WILL

It is central to Aquinas's account of free choice that it comprises *both* intellect *and* will acting together in consort. In contrast to contemporaries who postulated a separate faculty of *liberum arbitrium* and to subsequent libertarian voluntarists who located free choice solely in the will, Aquinas offers an analysis of choice as involving an essential unity in mutual interpenetration of the practical judgment of reason and the election of the will. Like Aristotle before him, Aquinas thinks reason and will are so closely intertwined in the act of choice that it is hard to decide whether it is better described as desiderative thinking or intellectual desiring.[23] While Aquinas adopts the latter position as properly Aristotelian, he takes great pains to stress that both intellect and will are active in choice. As we shall see, the analysis of just how that works is complex, but before we enter into that story it is important to understand that it is precisely because Aquinas wants to give both powers their proper due that the complexity arises.[24] Too many expositors of Aquinas assume that either intellect or will must have the final say in freedom and seek to assign primacy to one faculty so as to make Aquinas into either an intellectualist or a voluntarist.[25] Such an approach misses the whole point of Aquinas's analysis.[26] Ultimately, if one single ultimate subject of freedom must be identified, it is the person as a whole rather than one of its powers.

As we have already seen, the human will is naturally orientated toward perfect happiness as its end. Strictly speaking, the domain of choice is *ea quae sunt ad finem:* the goods to be pursued for the sake of the end. In Aquinas's analysis of human action, the will's abiding inten-

---

23. "Et ideo Aristoteles in VI Eth. sub dubio derelinquit utrum principalius pertineat electio ad vim appetitivam, vel ad vim cognitivam; dicit enim quod electio *vel est intellectus appetitivus, vel appetitus intellectivus.* Sed in III Eth. in hoc magis declinat quod sit appetitus intellectivus, nominans *electionem desiderium consiliabile.*" ST I, 83, 3.

24. The best analysis of Aquinas's complex account of human action is found in the notes and appendices by Servais Pinckaers, O.P., in *Somme théologique. Les actes humains, Tome Premier, 1a-2ae, Questions 6–17,* trans. H.-D. Gardeil, O.P., Nouvelle Édition (Paris: Les Éditions du Cerf, 1997). In what follows I am much indebted to Pinckaers.

25. For an attempt to classify contemporary interpreters of Aquinas as either intellectualists or voluntarists, see Jeffrey Hause, "Thomas Aquinas and the Voluntarists," *Medieval Philosophy and Theology* 6 (1997): 168. Hause is an intellectualist.

26. The proper interpretation of Aquinas's position is muddied by a debate about whether his own position evolved in a more voluntaristic direction over the course of his life. My own view, which I cannot argue for here, is that while there is some evolution and a marked change in terminology, Aquinas nonetheless had a consistent view on freedom as an interplay of both intellect and will. For a balanced treatment of the major texts in chronological order and a bibliographical guide, see David M. Gallagher, "Free Choice and Free Judgment in Thomas Aquinas," *Archiv für Geschichte der Philosophie* 76 (1994): 247–77. I am going to concentrate on texts from the later period of Aquinas's life.

tion of its ultimate end is a causal explanatory factor in every choice of what conduces to the end, even if not consciously adverted to; the intention of the end shapes all choosing for its sake.[27] Choice is an act of the will informed by rational deliberation and judgment regarding how best to attain what conduces to happiness in the concrete choice here and now of some non-ultimate good that is not necessarily connected with happiness. It is precisely the rational recognition of the contingent connection of any choice with the will's natural desire for happiness that makes it free. In circumstances such as these, the will's choice is not determined to one option and genuinely could be otherwise. As we shall see, when it comes to choice in the strict sense, the PAP generally holds for Aquinas, albeit in a qualified way.

It is customary in describing Aquinas's theory of human action to put correlative acts of intellect and will opposite each other in matching columns of the "acts of the mind."[28] When it comes to choice, the relevant intellectual acts are (1) deliberation *(consilio)* and (3) judgement *(iudicium)*, while the corresponding will acts are (2) consent *(consensus)* and (4) election *(electio)*. Looking at the columns, one is naturally inclined to think that the acts are sequential: 1-2-3-4. To focus on the last two moments in this way is to conceive the mind as independently judging one action to be rationally preferable and then "presenting" it to the will for an up or down vote that is either an inevitable *fait accompli* (intellectual determinism) or an arbitrary roll of the dice (voluntarism). To separate intellect and will in this way, however, is to engender a whole series of false problems. It is rather the case that for Aquinas, the practical judgment of the intellect and the choice of the will are separable conceptually but not according to time or being. The so-called last judgment of the practical intellect is last because it is chosen and it is chosen because it is last. It is the same act looked at from two different vantage points, not two different acts.[29]

In the formal discussion of *electio* in the *prima secundae*, Aquinas de-

27. "Alio modo potest considerari secundum quod voluntas fertur in id quod est ad finem, propter finem. Et sic unus et idem subiecto motus voluntatis est tendens ad finem, et in id quod est ad finem. Cum enim dico: Volo medicinam propter sanitatem, non designo nisi unum motum voluntatis. Cuius ratio est quia finis ratio est volendi ea quae sunt ad finem. . . Sic igitur inquantum motus voluntatis fertur in id quod est ad finem, prout ordinatur ad finem, est electio. Motus autem voluntatis qui fertur in finem, secundum quod acquiritur per ea quae sunt ad finem, vocatur intentio." ST I-II, 12, 4c and ad 3.

28. See Thomas Gilby's chart on p. 211 in *Summa theologiae*, vol. 17, *Psychology of Human Acts* (1a2ae. 6–17), trans. Gilby (Great Britain: Eyre and Spottiswoode Limited, 1970). For another (and less reliable) chart, see Alan Donagan, "Thomas Aquinas on Human Action," in *The Cambridge History of Later Medieval Philosophy*, ed. Norman Kretzmann, Anthony Kenny, and Jan Pinborg (Cambridge: Cambridge University Press, 1982), 653.

29. On the unity of intellect and will in the act of choice see Pinckaers, *Les actes humains*, 352–57, and Gallagher, "Free Choice and Free Judgment," 276.

scribes the intellect-will relationship as forming a unity in the act of *electio*. Aquinas tends to conceive metaphysical unities in terms of the form-matter and act-potency distinctions. Here he gives a kind of priority to reason as forming or shaping the will in choice:

It must be said that in the term "election" is implied both something pertaining to reason or intellect and something pertaining to will. . . . It is clear that in one sense reason precedes will and orders its act insofar as the will tends to its object according to the ordering of reason which presents to the appetitive power its object. Accordingly this act by which the will tends to something proposed as good, in the sense of being judged to be ordered to the end, is materially an act of the will but formally one of reason. In such a case the substance of the act is related as matter to the order which is imposed by the superior power. Hence, election is in its substance not an act of reason but an act of will, because it is perfected in the movement of the soul towards the good that is elected; hence it is clearly an act of the appetitive power.[30]

Without going into the complexities of the analogies implied by Aquinas, what is to be noted here is that he is trying to find a way to unify intellect and will in the act of choice. The practical intellect's role is to shape and order human desiring. *Nihil volitum nisi praecognitum*—the will cannot desire blindly or wildly; it depends upon the intellect to provide intelligible order to its pursuit of the human good as good. Yet choice is fundamentally an appetitive act rather than an intellectual act because it involves the soul's movements towards a good to be done.

If this account seems to give the intellect pride of formal place, Aquinas makes it abundantly clear in his account of the mutual causal relationship of intellect and will that the latter is an active and directive power also. In his mature treatments of the intellect-will relationship, Aquinas distinguishes two different ways in which a power of the soul can be in potency to multiple actualizations.[31] The first is with respect to act or not to act—to see or not to see, to will or not to will—this kind of potency is with respect to the exercise of the act. The second potency is with respect to what kind of action to perform—to see white or black, to will to run or to eat—this is a potency to different species or kinds of actions. In order to explain the complete actualization of a power, one must assign a cause to both aspects of the action. The principle explaining the very exercise of the act comes from the subject, while the formal specification of the act derives from the object. When it comes to human choices, the exercise of the act is explained by the will itself.

---

30. ST I-II, 13, 1.
31. The key treatment of the distinction between exercise and specification is *De malo* 6, 1.

The will is naturally ordered to the *bonum commune* as its end and so all movements toward the good fall under the will's domain of action. In this sense the will directs all the powers of the human person, including the intellect, in the exercise of their activities with respect to their own proper goods. So it belongs to the will to originate all action for the good as the free origin of the exercise of the act. Yet every act originating from the will with respect to its exercise requires some intelligible object which specifies and shapes its character. This formal specification comes from the intellect's apprehension of a good. The intellect provides the formal cause of the voluntary action. So in the analysis of any human choice, the efficient causality of the will originates the exercise of the act with respect to any good as end, while the intellect provides the formal cause of the will's act with respect to the kind of activity. In reply to an objection that it is not possible for the will to both move and be moved by the intellect, Thomas explains:

> The will moves the intellect with respect to the exercise of its act because truth itself, which is the perfection of the intellect, is contained within the universal good as a sort of particular good. But with respect to the determination of the act, which comes from the object, the intellect moves the will because the good itself is apprehended as a particular aspect comprehended by the universal notion of truth. Hence it is clear that one power is not moved and moving in the same respect.[32]

It is important to note that while these distinct kinds of causation can be pried apart intellectually, they cannot be pulled apart really. Exercise and specification are not two distinct acts or two distinct moments in an act, but rather are united in a single act of choice seen as originating in the reciprocal causality of two powers.

So in talking about the freedom of human action, it is necessary to distinguish between the exercise of the act and the specification of the act. When it comes to exercise, the will is always free and never necessitated.[33] The will determines whether to set itself into motion with respect to any of its own acts. Because the will controls the exercise of all the other powers, it can shut them off or activate them at any time in a self-determining way. When it comes to specification, however, the will's freedom is not absolute. As we have already noted, because the will is created for the perfect universal good, it would will such a good of necessity if it were to have an adequate intellectual insight into its nature. If the intellect were to specify the will with the vision of God in his es-

---

32. ST I-II, 9, 1 ad 3.

33. "Quantum ergo ad exercitium actus, primo quidem manifestum est quod uoluntas mouetur a seipsa: sicut enim mouet alias potentias, ita et se ipsam mouet." *De malo* 6, 1.

sence, then the will would not be able to refuse. So the will can only be related in one way to its ultimate end. But when it comes to any finite good specifying the will's act, nothing can necessitate an affirmative response. This is true even of God on this side of the beatific vision. An agent can think about God as the perfect good, but this intellectual grasp cannot necessitate the will because it cannot result in a presentation of God as infinite good. Any thought we can have of God is finite and refusable. One could think about God qua ultimate good and still choose something else or even stop thinking about God at all.

In the presence of any finite good, the will's response will be explained by the perspective under which the particular good is considered here and now in relation to a concrete agent.[34] The evaluation of the good will be influenced by such factors as the agent's conception of the ultimate good, his ability to discriminate particular goods in its light, the state of his appetites, and the history of his choices as settled into character. In considering any particular good, the agent's rational consideration is free to focus on many different features of the object in their varying relations of suitableness to any particular power of the agent or to the good of the agent as a whole. For example, the same object could appear as good under one aspect while bad under another.[35] I can consider a piece of cheesecake as good qua pleasant to my taste buds or bad qua fattening for my body as a whole. I can evaluate a situation according to different reasons and with respect to different aspects of the object. Which aspect is decisive will be partially explained by the agent's character: is he moved by reason or passion, virtue or vice?[36] As noted earlier, one of the ways in which Aquinas differs from some forms of libertarianism is by locating freedom in intellect *and* will. But it would

34. "Cum autem consilia et electiones sint circa particularia, quorum est actus, requiritur quod id quod apprehenditur ut bonum et conveniens in particulari et non uniuersali tantum." Ibid.

35. "Si autem tale bonum quod non inueniatur esse bonum secundum omni particularia que considerari possunt, non ex necessitate mouebit, etiam quantum ad determinationem actus: poterit enim aliquis uelle eius oppositum, etiam de eo cogitans, quia forte est bonum uel conueniens secundum aliquod aliud particulare consideratum; sicut quod est bonum sanitati non est bonum delectioni, et sic de aliis." Ibid.

36. "Et quod uoluntas feratur in id quod sibi offertur, magis secundum hanc particularem conditionem quam secundum aliam, potest contingere tripliciter. Vno quidem modo in quantum una preponderat, et tunc mouetur uoluntas secundum rationem: puta cum homo preeligit id quod est utile sanitati ei quod est utile uoluptati. Alio vero modo in quantum cogitat de una particulari circumstantia et non de alia, et hoc contingit plerumque per aliquam occasionem, exhibitam uel ab interiori uel ab exteriori, ut ei talis cogitatio occurrat. Tertio uero modo contingit ex dispositione hominis: quia secundum Philosophum 'qualis unusquisque est, talis finis uidetur ei'; unde aliter mouetur ad aliquid uoluntas irati et uoluntas quieti, quia non idem est conueniens utrique, sicut etiam aliter acceptatur cibus a sano et egro." Ibid.

be still more accurate to see freedom as the property of the person as a whole and conceived diachronically. In other words, freedom of choice originates in the interplay of intellect and will and character. Freedom is not explicable in terms of factors operative at atomic moments of will acts, but rather is the residue of past choices and a tendency towards future choices. When all of the causal factors required to account for a choice have been enumerated, what ultimately determines which aspect of the object is determinative for the agent is the judgment operative in the act of *electio* itself.

The role of character in choice raises a further complication for some kinds of libertarian readings of Aquinas. It has already been noted that the will's necessary relationship to ultimate beatitude and inability to will otherwise in the face of the beatitific vision means that Aquinas cannot be a libertarian if libertarianism requires the PAP or ability to do otherwise. This kind of necessitation is a function of the will's natural orientation to the good. Yet this very ordination to the ultimate good also causes another complication for libertarian freedom on this side of the beatific vision. For while we are free with respect to all created goods, it is not integral to that freedom that we be poised indifferently between good and evil. In other words, the ability to do otherwise that we possess in this life does not entail the ability to do evil or sin. Ideally, it is a freedom to choose between genuine goods as *ea quae sunt ad finem*. In a discussion of whether beatified angels can sin or not, Aquinas replies to the objection that freedom of choice involves the possibility of choosing both good and evil as follows:

It must be said that freedom of choice is related to choosing what is in relation to the end as the intellect's power of grasping principles is related to drawing conclusions. It is obvious that it pertains to the power of the intellect that it can procede to diverse conclusions from the given principles, but that it draw a conclusion by neglecting the order imposed by the principles is a defect. Hence that freedom of choice can elect diverse goods ordered to the end pertains to the perfection of liberty, while the choice of something deviating from the end, which is sin, is a defect in liberty. So there is greater freedom of choice in angels who cannot sin than in we who can sin.[37]

Human freedom is related to the alternative possibility of evil only insofar as it is imperfect. Perfect freedom is exercised within the range of goods that are truly consonant with the ultimate good. Hence it is no part of the freedom of a virtuous agent that he or she possesses the ability to do otherwise than choose the good, in the sense of choose evil.

---

37. ST I, 62, 8, ad 3. See also II *Sent.* 25, 1, 1 ad 2; *De veritate* 22, 6; and *De malo* 16, 5.

On this point Aquinas is consonant with contemporary libertarians like Stump who argue that the inconceivability of evil and irresistability of good to a virtuous agent is not an impediment to freedom but rather its perfection.[38] It is precisely in a case where it is morally impossible for the agent to do anything but the good that perfect freedom is manifested, rather than in the cases where the agent is poised neutrally between good and evil with both alternatives as live and open.[39]

At this point it is important to note that the paradigm perfected case of human freedom for Aquinas is Jesus Christ. Aquinas argues that Jesus had *liberum arbitrium* in its perfect form without the ability to sin at all.[40] The root of Christ's freedom is his possession of the beatific vision; precisely because he was immovably fixed in his orientation to God, in the face of all other goods he was perfectly free. As confirmed in the beatific vision, he was supremely free to consider all other goods in its light. Here lies something of a paradox to us: the closer a human will comes to being joined to divine goodness, the more free it becomes.

Indeed the ultimate paradigm of *liberum arbitrium* precisely is God. Like human beings, God's will is necessitated with respect to its proper object.[41] God cannot not will his own goodness; in this sense, God's will is determined by a necessity of nature just as we are. Yet unlike us, God's will is by nature united with its end and so does not experience any striving. Thus it is not a necessary feature of will that it experience striving or desire for a good to be obtained. Rather, what is essential to the will is love of the good. When the will has achieved its good, it rests in it; when it does not possess it, it strives for it. This entails also that freedom of choice is likewise a contingent feature of will as such. Because God is perfectly completed in his own nature, there is no necessity for him to will anything else and hence no necessity to exercise *liberum arbitrium*. God's will is only contingently related to the choice to create at all and to the choice to create a particular world. There need not have been any freedom of choice at all in reality and reality would have nonetheless been perfect.[42] God freely chooses to create, and this freedom of choice

---

38. Stump, "Intellect, Will, and the Principle of Alternative Possibilities."

39. Contrast this view with Peter Van Inwagen's "When Is the Will Free?" in *Philosophical Perspectives* 3 (1989): 399–422. Van Inwagen argues that if the ability to do otherwise is central to incompatibilist freedom, then we can only be confident about freedom in cases where there is real moral struggle or incommensurable values. Aquinas would have more sympathy with Susan Wolf's "Asymmetrical Freedom," *Journal of Philosophy* 77 (1980): 151–66. For Wolf, freedom does not entail the alternative possibility of doing evil, but rather is perfected when the agent is determined by the Good that is the goal of freedom.

40. ST III, 18, 4.   41. ST I, 19, 3.

42. "Dicendum quod licet Deus ex necessitate velit bonitatem suam, non tamen ex necessitate vult ea quae vult propter bonitatem suam, quia bonitas eius potest esse sine aliis." Ibid., ad 2.

provides not only for the possibility of choice but also its paradigm: freedom of choice is ordered to goods compatible with an ultimate good that will eliminate the need for choice by satisfying the will's desire for the good. The world is created out of choice but not for choice; it is rather created for a love beyond choice.

III. DIVINE CAUSALITY AND HUMAN FREEDOM

Thus far I have been identifying ways in which Aquinas's account of human freedom strains at the bounds of libertarianism. If this were all there were to Aquinas's account, we might still conclude that he is merely a peculiar kind of libertarian. But Aquinas's God does more than model and create freedom. He also causes it. Here is where Aquinas collides with a feature that seems necessary to any kind of libertarianism: As Stump puts it, "the causal chain resulting in any voluntary act on an agent's part has to originate in the system of the agent's own intellect and will [because] if it originates in some cause external to the agent which acts with efficient causation on the agent's will, what results will not be an act of will at all."[43] If Stump is right about this, then Aquinas cannot be a libertarian at all and indeed all of the previous discussion of will acts has really not been about will at all. For Aquinas believes that God the Creator has to be the ultimate efficient cause of every act of the will. Now this seems to make him into some kind of compatibilist, but what I want to maintain in this section is that while Aquinas's doctrine of the causal relationship between the divine will and human freedom puts him beyond the parameters of libertarianism, it does not make him a compatibilist by default.

There is a complex story to be told about the relationship between divine causation and human freedom that I can only outline here.[44] The first point to be made is that Aquinas's treatment of God's causal influence on the human will is a corollary to his treatment of God's causal influence on *all* created causes.[45] In other words, Aquinas's claims about God's causal influence on the human will are occasioned not by some peculiar feature of human action requiring an appeal to divine causality, but rather by the application to the human will of a larger metaphysical story about God's involvement in the causing of all causes. What motivates the appeal to divine causality is not some kind of introspective

---

43. "Aquinas's Account of Freedom," 586.
44. I discuss this matter at length in "Divine Causation and Human Freedom in Aquinas," *American Catholic Philosophical Quarterly* 72 (1998): 99–122.
45. The classic texts on God's causal involvement in all created causes are *De potentia* 3, 7 and ST I, 105, 5.

or psychological approach, but rather the metaphysics of creation. In Aquinas's account of God's causal immanence in creation, God is understood to be the origin and ongoing ground of the being of creatures in creation and conservation. God is the final cause of all action as the ultimate good, the formal-exemplar cause of the essential-natural sources of action, and the efficient cause of all created activity. This latter kind of causality is what is most relevant and problematic here. Aquinas describes God as moving and applying *(ut movens et applicans)* all created causes in their very actions as the *primum movens non motum*. Because all finite causes are characterized by potentiality with respect to their proper operations, and so are moved movers, their motions require the invocation of a higher-order cause of actuality—an unmoved mover—in order to account for their own activity. The kind of reasoning at work here is what powers the first two ways of arguing for the existence of God in *Summa Theologiae* I, 2, 3, and it presupposes the Aristotelian axiom that whatever is moved is moved by another.

In discussing God's causal involvement with the human will, Aquinas simply applies to it the logic of the foregoing analysis.[46] First, God can be said to be the cause of the acts of the human will insofar as he creates and conserves in being the human person. Second, God is the final cause of the human will insofar as it is created for the infinite good. Third, and most importantly here, God moves the will through efficient causation by inclining it interiorly *(interius eam inclinando)*. Whenever the will moves from potentiality to actuality, it is required that some exterior efficient cause be invoked as the ultimate cause. Aquinas links this vertical-metaphysical argument for divine causality with the horizontal problem of the infinite regress of deliberation and volition in choice: it is necessary to hold that there is a cause transcending intellect and will that gives the will its first motion toward the good prior to any intellectual deliberation.[47]

When Aquinas describes God's causality as "exterior," he means this in the sense of originating in a principle outside the human agent. But he stresses that God's movement of the will is rooted in God's creative causal immanence. God does not act on the human will through intermediaries, but rather directly out of God's ongoing creative causality of the *esse* of all things. He argues that God alone can move the will without coercion precisely because he is its Creator; if any other cause were to move the will in an efficient way, it would violate its freedom.[48] Aquinas

---

46. ST I, 105, 5.   47. ST I-II, 9, 4.

48. "Amplius. Violentum, ut dicitur in III *Ethic.*, est *cuius principium est extra nil conferente vim passo. Si igitur voluntas moveatur ab aliquo exteriori principio, erit violentus motus:*

consistently asserts that the divine motion does not determine the will to choose any particular good and he studiously avoids the term *praedeterminatio* precisely to avoid the overtones of divine determinism.[49] He claims instead that God moves the will so that it acts in accord with its own nature as a self-determining power:

> It ought to be noted that, as Dionysius says, "it does not pertain to providence to destroy the nature of things but rather to preserve them." Hence providence moves all things in accord with their natures in such a way that by the divine motion necessary effects follow from necessary causes and contingent effects follow from contingent causes. Accordingly, because the will is an active principle not determined to one thing but rather related non-determinately to many things, God so moves the will that it is not determined to one thing but rather its motion remains contingent and not necessary, except regarding those things to which it is moved by its own nature.[50]

The motion by which God moves the will is interior, non-coercive, and non-determining because it is of the nature of the Creator to preserve the modality of what he creates in divine providence. Aquinas is rather spare in his account; he asserts what is metaphysically required without purporting to give a detailed explanation of how God causes freedom.

What sets Aquinas apart from modern libertarianism then is that he does not think causal independence from God is a necessary condition for human freedom. Indeed, it is rather the case that human freedom precisely as created freedom requires divine causality as a necessary condition. Only God's freedom is absolutely originative and independent. Created freedom need not and cannot be utterly originative, as if it were its own first cause, in order for it to be genuinely self-determinative. Aquinas writes:

> It should be said that freedom of choice is the cause of its own motion because a person moves himself into action by freedom of choice. But it is not neces-

---

dico autem moveri a principio extrinsico quod moveat per modum agentis, non per modum finis. Violentum autem voluntario repugnat. Impossibile est ergo quod voluntas moveatur a principio extrinsico quasi ab agente, sed oportet quod omnis motus voluntatis ab interiori procedat. Nulla autem substantia creata coniungitur animae intellectuali quantum ad sua interiora nisi solus Deus, qui solus est causa esse ipsius, et sustinens eam in esse. A solo Deo potest autem motus voluntarius causari. . . . Illud autem solum agens potest causare motum voluntatis absque violentia, quod causat principium intrinsecum huius motus, quod est potentia ipsa voluntatis. Hoc autem est Deus, qui animam solus creat, ut in Secundo ostensum est [c.87]. Solus igitur Deus potest movere voluntatem, per modum agentis, absque violentia." *Summa contra gentiles* III, 88 (Rome: Editio Leonina Manualis, 1934). See also *De malo* 3, 3.

49. M.-J. Congar, "*Praedeterminare* et *praedeterminatio* chez S. Thomas," *Revue des sciences philosophique et théologique* 23 (1934): 363–71.

50. ST I-II, 10, 4.

sary for freedom that what is free be its own first cause, just as it is not required that whatever causes another be its first cause. Accordingly, God is the first cause moving both natural and voluntary causes. And just as in moving natural causes God does not destroy their natural abilities, so by moving voluntary causes God does not destroy their voluntary actions *but rather makes them to be such.* For God works in each thing in accord with its own nature.[51]

From this text emerges the fundamental complaint that one might imagine Aquinas lodging against libertarianism: that its claims about the kind of causal origination and independence which the human will must have is incompatible with the doctrine of creation. Roderick Chisholm puts his finger on the nerve of the problem when he argues regarding libertarian agent causation:

If we are responsible, and if what I have been trying to say is true, then we have a prerogative which some would attribute only to God: each of us, when we act, is a prime mover unmoved. In doing what we do, we cause certain events to happen, and nothing—or no one—causes us to cause those events to happen.[52]

It is precisely this presupposition of the human will as a kind of *causa prima* that makes libertarianism incompatible with Aquinas's view of created freedom.

Yet this fundamental complaint against libertarianism does not make Aquinas into a compatibilist by default. Aquinas would agree with the libertarian that in order for a choice to be free, it cannot be causally determined by temporally antecedent causal factors. For any agent A at time T, A chooses freely if and only if A's choice is not determined by any temporally antecedent causal chain originating outside of A. In this sense Aquinas would make common cause with the libertarian against the compatibilist. For this reason it is misleading to label him as a compatibilist. Insofar as compatibilism is a claim about the compatibility of human freedom with causal determinism originating in the physical world antecedent in choice, Aquinas emphatically denies compatibilism and sides with the libertarian. But, against the libertarian, Aquinas does want to argue that human freedom is consistent with a causation that originates in the Creator at a metaphysically prior moment, indeed the moment of eternity. This is a kind of causation that neither libertarianism nor compatibilism is designed to deny or affirm because it is not part of the problematic generating the libertarian-compatibilist debate. It is for this reason that I do not think it appropriate to label Aquinas's

---

51. ST I, 83, 1 ad 3. Emphasis added.
52. "Human Freedom and the Self," in *Free Will*, ed. Gary Watson (Oxford: Oxford University Press, 1982), 32.

doctrine a form of "theological compatibilism," since such a species-genus formulation seems to imply that it is really some version of compatibilism after all. What I have been arguing for all along is that Aquinas does not fit into either category, even as a special case.

IV. BEYOND LIBERTARIANISM AND COMPATIBILISM

Between Aquinas and the contemporary problematic there is a lot of philosophical water under the bridge, beginning with the voluntaristic versions of freedom in Scotus and Ockham that are the medieval precursors of modern libertarianism. What I want to stress in this conclusion, however, is that the most significant divide between Aquinas and the present problematic are the assumptions about creation that inform Aquinas's account of human freedom. For in the background of his discussion of human freedom lies a theological anthropology that is grounded in the claim that human beings are created in the image of God precisely in order to share in God's own life.[53] As Aquinas notes in the prologue of the *secunda pars*, our freedom of choice is a reflection of the divine image.[54] Precisely as created in the image of God for union with God, our freedom is designed, not for God-independent autonomy, but rather for deeper union with God by action in conformity with the ultimate exemplar of created freedom.[55] Precisely because we are created to find rest and completion in God in the beatific vision, no other good can compel the will's assent. Here is the Augustinian side of Aquinas: "You have made us for yourself, O Lord, and our hearts are restless until they rest in thee."[56] We are free precisely because we are *capax dei*. And that restless freedom of choice is not the end of the will, but rather the peace and joy that comes from love's rest in its fulfilling good. It is for love, not choice, that the will is created.

Because we are created to find fulfillment in God, human freedom is inherently relational for Aquinas. In contrast to modern notions of autonomy as the absolute independence and self-creativity of sover-

---

53. ST I, 93.

54. "Quia, sicut Damascenus dicit, homo factus est ad imaginem Dei dicitur, secundum quod per imaginem significatur intellectuale et arbitrio liberum et per se postestativum ... restat ut consideremus de eius imagine, idest de homine, secundum quod et ipse est suorum operum principium, quasi liberum arbitrium habens et suorum operum potestatem."

55. Servais Pinckaers comments on the prologue: "... dans l'idée de S. Thomas, le thème de l'image indique que l'homme est appelé à coordoner son action à celle de Dieu, de telle sorte que sa maîtrise sur ses actes puisse grandir dans la mesure même où il participera à la maîtrise de Dieu, grâce à l'accord des volontés réalisé par l'amour." *La Béatitude*, 1a-2ae, Questions 1–5 (Paris: Les Éditions du Cerf, 2001), 210.

56. *Confessiones* I, 1.

eign individuals, Aquinas paradoxically sees human beings as most free when they are most dependent upon and responsive to God.[57] In order to explain this paradoxical truth, it would be necessary to tell a larger metaphysical story about creation that would emphasize God's transcendence.[58] Aquinas does not see God as a rival to human freedom along the lines of the biggest being in the universe throwing his metaphysical weight around by overpowering all other sources of action; God is not a being like any other being, sharing the same metaphysical space as a potential rival. God utterly transcends all creation and stands related to it as creative source. We are free because God creates and sustains us in freedom, not despite God. And though we are compelled to use language drawn from our experience of causation in the physical world, it must be remembered here that we are talking about the action of Creative Spirit upon spirit which finds its consummation in the peculiar kind of causality originating in the love between two persons in grace. The action of God on the human will is not like the evil genius of Frankfurt-style counterexamples manipulating neurons in the brain, but rather something altogether different that cannot be pictured by any kind of physical interaction.

If I am right about Aquinas, then any attempt to claim him for either libertarianism or compatibilism will end up falsifying his position. If he is to be of any more than historical value to us today, it is not because he confirms our prejudices and paradigms about freedom, but rather because he challenges them and offers us an alternative. To the theist or theologian looking for an account of human freedom outside the box of the libertarian-compatibilist debate and inside the doctrine of creation, Aquinas offers a different way of thinking about human freedom in relationship to God. It has been the burden of this paper to outline that different way of thinking. I know that I have not offered argumentation to show that it is true, only how and why it is different. The reader is free to believe it or not.

57. See David Burrell's "Freedom and Creation in the Abrahamic Traditions," *International Philosophical Quarterly* 40 (2000): 161–71. It is a common feature of medieval Abrahamic notions of created freedom that "the glory of the human being is to respond rather than to originate; responding is the creativity proper to creatures" (170).

58. This is done admirably by Robert Sokolowski in *The God of Faith and Reason* (Washington, D.C.: The Catholic University of America Press, 1995). See also David Burrell, *Freedom and Creation in Three Traditions* (Notre Dame: University of Notre Dame Press, 1993).

6   JUSTIFYING FAITH, FREE WILL, AND THE ATONEMENT

ELEONORE STUMP

INTRODUCTION

That we are justified by faith is one of the fundamental claims of Christian doctrine, variously understood but equally accepted by all traditional Christian theologians, including Aquinas. On the traditional understanding, all human beings are marred by original sin, which means, among other things, that a post-fall person has a will which tends to will what he ought not to will, and that that inborn defect of will results sooner or later in sinful actions, with consequent moral deterioration. In such a state a person cannot be united with God in heaven but is rather bound to be left to himself in hell. God in his goodness, however, has provided salvation from this state, which is available for all, though not all avail themselves of it.

What is the nature of this salvation? Either of two answers to this question is equally appropriate, and Aquinas subscribes to both of them. On the one hand, there is the doctrine of justification by faith, which explains that a person is rescued from the evil in himself not because of any successful moral struggles on his part but rather by faith, which justifies him when he believes. On the other hand, there is the doctrine of the atonement, which explains that salvation is won for us by Christ's passion and death. The connection between these two answers is not apparent at first glance.

Generally speaking, Aquinas understands justification by faith as necessary and sufficient for salvation. It involves acceptance by God apart from any moral virtue on the part of the person being justified, but it is also the beginning of the process by which a person is made righteous and acquires the virtues; that is, on Aquinas's understanding of the doctrine, justification by faith initiates the process by which real change for the better is effected in the character of the person being justified.

Understood in this way, there is something puzzling about the doctrine that faith justifies. Aquinas takes faith to be the intellect's assenting to the propositions of faith at the direction of the will. But if faith is understood in this way, the problem is that a person's being committed to religious beliefs seems compatible with a persistent lack of the virtues, as witness some of the unsavory characters who have undoubtedly been sincere adherents to Christianity. And it hardly seems consonant with divine goodness to make God's acceptance of a person dependent on that person's holding certain beliefs, as distinct from a person's moral state.

On the other hand, the doctrine of the atonement, that we are saved from sin by Christ's passion and death, is problematic in part because it is a second answer to the question about the nature of salvation. If faith can justify a person, and if justification is sufficient for salvation, what is the role of the atonement in salvation? But there are other puzzles as well. If Christ's passion and death save post–Fall human beings, how do they do so?[1] What is the nature of the benefit which his passion and death produce? In particular, how is that benefit appropriated to the person justified by faith in order for that person to be saved? And how is this benefit related to the beneficial effects of justifying faith?

GRACE AND FAITH

In order to show what I take to be Aquinas's answers to these questions, I want to begin by delineating the rudiments of Aquinas's account of justification by faith in order to bring out one interesting and complicated idea of his that seems to me sufficient to solve the puzzles raised by an initial consideration of faith.

For justification, Aquinas says, the following three things are required: (1) an infusion of grace, (2) an act of free will on the part of the person being justified, and (3) the remission of sins. These elements can be understood as (1) the motion of the mover (God's infusion of grace), (2) the motion of what is moved (the mind's act of free will) and (3) the consummation of the motion or the attainment of the end (the process of remission or removal of sins).[2] So to understand Aquinas's account of justification by faith, we need to consider each of these three elements of justification.

It is easiest to begin with (3), the attainment of the end of justification. By 'justification', according to Aquinas, we mean movement toward justice, and justice in this case consists in rectitude or right order

---

1. For a fuller treatment of issues connected with Aquinas's views of the doctrine of the atonement, see the chapter on the atonement in my *Aquinas* (London: Routledge, 2003). This paper is taken largely from material in this book.

2. *ST* IaIIae q. 113, a. 6.

in a person's mind and will, so that his passions are subject to his rational faculties, and his rational faculties are subject to God. Justification is the process by which someone who was previously an unrepentant sinner changes direction and has his intellect and will directed to God. In this process his habits of sinning are gradually removed as a result of the changes wrought in his intellect and will by God's grace.

To understand element (1) of justification, God's infusion of grace, we need to be clearer about one of Aquinas's several divisions of grace, namely, the division between operating and cooperating grace. Operating and cooperating grace are the same grace, Aquinas says, but distinguished on the basis of the effects produced in the mind of the believer.[3] Grace that is the source of meritorious acts a person performs is cooperating grace, but grace that justifies or heals a person's soul is operating grace. In other words, God is responsible for all that is good in us. Sometimes, however, what is good in us is also to be attributed to us, not because we could do any good without God, but simply because our will cooperates with God, who moves us to a good work by his *cooperating* grace.[4] But the process of justification is different. In this case all the work is done by God alone, and so the grace of God which justifies a person is *operating* grace.

Nonetheless, echoing Augustine's famous line that God who made us without our consent will not justify us without it,[5] Aquinas says that God does not justify us "without ourselves": simultaneous with God's justifying us, he says, we consent to God's justice in an act of free will, which constitutes element (2) in the process of justification.[6] Operating grace comes to a person suddenly, Aquinas says. The preparation for operating grace may take a period of time (during which God may be working providentially in a person's life), but the actual infusion of operating grace is instantaneous.[7] And the act of free will which is part of justification is simultaneous with the infusion of operating grace.[8] The infusion of grace is prior in nature, or logically prior, to the act of free will, in the sense that the willing is dependent on the grace rather than the other way around; but temporally they occur together and at once. While grace is being infused into a person, that person assents to the process in an act of free will,[9] Aquinas says, so that the infusion of grace and the

---

3. *ST* IaIIae q. 111, a. 2, ad 4.

4. For some philosophical explanation of cooperating grace and the way in which it is compatible even with libertarian freedom, see my "Augustine on Free Will," in *The Cambridge Companion to Augustine*, ed. Eleonore Stump and Norman Kretzmann (Cambridge: Cambridge University Press, 2001).

5. *Sermo* 169.11.13.

6. *ST* IaIIae q. 111, a. 2, ad 2.

7. *ST* IaIIae q. 113, a. 7.

8. Ibid., a. 8.

9. *ST* IaIIae q. 111, a. 2.

act of free will occur simultaneously.[10] Aquinas says, for example, "the motion of the free will, which occurs in the justification of an impious person, is the ultimate disposition to grace. For this reason, in one and the same instant there is the infusion of grace together with this motion of the free will."[11]

On Aquinas's account, this act of will always has two parts. The entire process of justification, which only begins with the infusion of operating grace, is a movement in which God brings a person from a state of sin to a state of justice; and so, Aquinas holds, a person who is being justified must consider both ends of this motion and form an act of will regarding both. By an act of free will a person being justified must want to withdraw from his sins and draw near to God's goodness. Consequently, the act of will concomitant with operating grace must have one part in which a person detests his sins and another part in which he longs for divine goodness or righteousness.[12]

Aquinas's example of a person being justified by operating grace is Paul on the road to Damascus. Aquinas recognizes that this case is an example of a rare method of justification, but it nonetheless elucidates the elements he thinks essential to the process. Paul was converted suddenly because of a vision he had while traveling to Damascus; but his assent to Christianity in consequence of his vision still constitutes the twofold act of will in faith which accompanies operating grace. We can contrast this twofold act of will with, for example, the decision Paul makes to continue his missionary activity after being stoned in Lystra. That Paul wills to continue preaching instead of becoming discouraged or frightened and so withdrawing from the work shows him to be virtuous; this act of will on Paul's part can be attributed to Paul as a good work and increases Paul's merit. Consequently, on Aquinas's account, it must have as its source God's cooperating grace, which had as its aim Paul's continuing to preach the gospel. On the other hand, the very act of will in which Paul adopts Christianity is not something Paul labors at in any way, so that it is not attributable to Paul as a good *work*. Rather all the work in this case is on God's part, and attributable to his providence and grace; Paul's only contribution is not to refuse the grace God is infusing in him. For that reason it also does not increase Paul's merit.[13]

10. *ST* IaIIae q. 113, a. 7.

11. *ST* III q. 89, a. 2.

12. *ST* IaIIae q. 113, a. 5; cf. also aa. 6–7. A person does not have to remember and detest each sin he has ever committed in order to be justified, Aquinas says; rather he has to detest those sins of which he is conscious and be disposed to detest any other sin of his if he should remember it.

13. When the faith which Paul is adopting in this act of will becomes habitual and

JUSTIFICATION BY MEANS OF FAITH

On Aquinas's account of faith and grace, then, a human being Nathan is justified when God operates on Nathan in such a way as to bring Nathan to faith with its twofold act of will. In consequence of God's operating grace, Nathan desires God's goodness and hates his own sins, and (among the other things he believes in faith) Nathan believes that God fulfills such desires as Nathan's desire for goodness because God justifies believers. But by 'believers' here is meant just those who have the faith which justifies, or more specifically, those who believe what Nathan believes and will as he does. If we spell out the implications of what Nathan believes, then, we will say that, as regards belief, Nathan is justified by believing (implicitly or explicitly) that God justifies those who believe that God justifies them. If we now also include Aquinas's understanding of justification as God's bringing a person to righteousness, then, on Aquinas's view, as regards the intellectual component of justification by faith, the process of making Nathan righteous is begun by Nathan's believing that God will make him righteous, and it continues so long as Nathan maintains this belief, until the culmination of the process when Nathan is made perfectly righteous. The act of will which accompanies this belief in the process of justification is one in which the will draws near to goodness by longing for it and hating its sin.[14] In other words, the act of will accompanying Nathan's justifying belief that God will justify him is in effect Nathan's desire for God's doing so.

Consequently, Nathan's part in the process of coming to righteousness is to believe that God will make him righteous and to want God to do so.[15] And God's undertaking to justify those who have faith is a com-

---

eventuates in other physical and mental acts, it becomes a virtue; as such, it is nurtured by cooperating grace and is a source of merit.

14. *ST* IaIIae q. 113, a. 5.

15. There is something at least mildly puzzling about the initial description of the act of will at issue as the believer's volition that God bring him to righteousness, since the proper objects of our volitions are only those things which are in our power to do. Lydgate in Eliot's *Middlemarch* may wish or desire that Bulstrode make up his mind to lend him money; but it would be odd to say Lydgate *wills* that Bulstrode give him a loan, because what Bulstrode chooses to do can be an object only of Bulstrode's will and not of Lydgate's. Furthermore, this way of describing the second-order volition seems to violate the definition of a second-order volition, as the will's commanding itself. But there are occasions when it does seem appropriate to say something somewhat similar to "Lydgate wills that Bulstrode lend him money," and reflections on these help to solve both problems. To take just one sort of example, if Lydgate needed medical attention (rather than money) and at last consented to an operation, we might be inclined to describe his situation by saying that Lydgate wills the doctor to operate on him. But what we are describing here is not a situation in which the doctor's action is the object of Lydgate's volition. In this example, the doctor is urging medical treatment which Lydgate is reluctant to undergo. In saying that Lydgate wills the doctor to operate, we mean that Lydgate has both ceased to

mitment to bring to righteousness those who believe he will do so and who want him to do so.

This account of justification by faith may seem to savor of the notion that wishes are horses and therefore beggars ride, but in this particular case there is something to be said for that notion. The act of will concomitant with the infusion of operating grace is equivalent, logically and perhaps also psychologically, to willing that God make the believer's will righteous. To desire God's goodness, in the sense intended here, is to want righteousness, and the righteousness of any person depends first of all on his will's willing what it ought to will. Similarly, to repudiate one's sins is to want not to engage in those sins any longer and so to have a will which wills what it should. So the act of will involved in justification is a will to will what one ought to will. In contemporary philosophy, such a will is what has been called 'a second-order volition', a volition in which the will operates reflexively to command itself.[16]

If Nathan has a second-order volition of this sort, then God can bring about changes in Nathan's first-order desires and volitions to bring them into accord with that second-order volition, thereby removing Nathan's sin and making him righteous, a process of moral improvement which culminates (after death) in a state of perfect righteousness. If God were simply to alter a first-order volition of Nathan's without Nathan's having such a second-order volition, it seems clear that God would be violating Nathan's free will, since, as Aquinas holds, a person's volition is not free if it is altered as a direct result of the exercise of efficient causality on the part of some external agent.[17] But if God brings about a volition in Nathan when Nathan has a second-order volition that God do so, then

---

offer resistance to the doctor's proposal and made up his mind to consent to the operation. The object of Lydgate's volition, then, is not an action on the doctor's part, but rather his own first-order volitions. In willing the doctor to operate, he wills not to have a will that resists the doctor's urging and to have instead a will that permits the operation; that is, he wills to have a will that wills all those things necessary on his part before the doctor is able (legally and morally) to operate.

16. The terminology has been made familiar by the work of Harry Frankfurt. See his "Freedom of the Will and the Concept of a Person," *Journal of Philosophy* 68 (1971): 5–20; reprinted in Harry Frankfurt, *The Importance of What We Care About* (Cambridge: Cambridge University Press, 1988), pp. 11–25. A large literature has been generated by this original paper of Frankfurt's. For use of his work in connection with issues of grace and free will, see my "Sanctification, Hardening of the Heart, and Frankfurt's Concept of Free Will," *Journal of Philosophy* 85 (1988): 395–420 [reprinted in *Moral Responsibility*, ed. John Martin Fischer and Mark Ravizza (Ithaca, N.Y.: Cornell University Press, 1993), pp. 211–34] and "Augustine on Free Will," in *The Cambridge Companion to Augustine*, ed. Eleonore Stump and Norman Kretzmann (Cambridge: Cambridge University Press, 2001).

17. See the chapter on Aquinas's account of free will in Stump, *Aquinas* (2003). Cf. also, e.g., *SCG* III, chap. 148 and *ST* IaIIae q. 111, a. 2, ad 1, in which Aquinas says that grace operates on the will in the manner of a formal cause, rather than in the manner of an efficient cause.

in altering some first-order volition in Nathan God does not undermine Nathan's free will but instead enhances or evokes it.[18]

Nathan's own second-order volition thus cooperates with grace in bringing it about that Nathan has the first-order volition he does, not in the sense that it is the strength or even the agency of Nathan's second-order volition that produces the desired first-order volition in him, but rather in the sense that unless Nathan had had such a second-order volition God would not have acted on his first-order volitions to strengthen them in good by grace. If Nathan's second-order volition had been different, his first-order volition would have been different also, because to produce in Nathan a first-order volition discordant with his second-order desires would be to undermine his freedom of will; and that is something which God, who does not undermine the nature of his creatures, would not do.

Making a sinner righteous, then, will be a process in which a believer's specific volitions are brought into harmony with the governing second-order volition assenting to God's bringing him to righteousness, with the consequent gradual alteration in first-order volitions.[19] Unlike the act of free will simultaneous with the infusion of operating grace, which occurs at an instant, this part of the process takes time.

Aquinas's theory of justification by faith thus gives a helpful insight into Paul's claim that God quickens the dead and calls those things that are not as though they were,[20] and it also gives a consistent and interesting reading of various other well-known Pauline passages about faith. On Aquinas's theory, for example, God is just and a justifier of those who believe.[21] He is a justifier of those who believe because he brings believers to righteousness, and he is just himself because in the process of justification he really does eradicate sin. Those people God takes to himself are those who have been made righteous, in a process extending through this life and culminating in the next. Furthermore, it is clear why "the works of the law" can justify no one. On Aquinas's theory, justification is the process whereby a person who was not righteous is changed and brought to righteousness.[22] But to do the works of the law is to do what is righteous. Anyone who does the works of the law is

---

18. Cf. my "Augustine on Free Will," which gives detailed argument for a similar position held by Augustine.

19. I do not mean to suggest that the changes occurring in the process of justification will take place only in the will on Aquinas's views. Insofar as the intellect and the will are connected as Aquinas takes them to be, changes in one faculty or power will result in changes in the other as well. My focus here, however, is on justification and atonement, and so Aquinas's views on changes in the will are more important for my purposes.

20. Rom. 4:17.   21. Rom. 3:26.

22. ST IaIIae q. 113, a. 1.

not thereby being changed from unrighteousness to righteousness but is already at the end or at least in the middle of the transformation. Justification involves getting a will which was bent on evil to turn to what is good. It is not that the will of a person before justification is constrained in some way toward evil; the problem is rather that such a will does not want the good. Any person who did the works of the law, however, would have a will which already willed the good. Even a person who is only beginning a struggle to do the works of the law, a person, that is, who is trying, often unsuccessfully, to do those things that satisfy the law, is a person whose will is bent on good, at least to the extent of wanting to *try* to do the works of the law. Therefore, the works of the law, that is, righteous actions, cannot accomplish the transformation of an evil will into a good one. That is why even the initial assent to grace, which constitutes the volitional part of faith, must be a result of God's work on the believer. Since that initial willing is a hungering for goodness and to that extent a righteous willing, a will which forms that volition has already been turned to righteousness to some extent.

FAITH: THE RESOLUTION OF SOME PUZZLES

With this much understanding of Aquinas's account of justification by faith, we are in a position to resolve some of the puzzles with which I began. For example, it is easy to see why, on Aquinas's account, a person's having faith has an impact on her moral character. Insofar as a desire for a good will is morally preferable to the absence of that desire, to the state in which a person does not recognize her moral shortcomings or is indifferent to them, a person who comes to faith undergoes a moral improvement simply in virtue of acquiring faith. Furthermore, once a believer has the second-order volition at issue in justification by faith, God can work on the believer's first-order desires and volitions to bring her to righteousness without violating her freedom of will. On the other hand, it is also easy to see why having faith is compatible with the perpetration of evil. The second-order volition involved in faith is a volition whose content is vague and which is thus compatible with specific volitions to do what is evil. That is why the movement toward righteousness which is begun with the believer's second-order volition in faith is carried out in a process which takes time, a process in which more and more of a believer's will and intellect are brought into harmony with the general second-order volition desiring goodness and detesting sin. Finally, Aquinas's theory also explains why a person who is justified finds acceptance with God, because the nature of the volitional component of faith is such that it enables God to unite a believer with himself, insofar as that volition allows God to make the believer morally good without violating his freedom of will.

ATONEMENT AND THE WILL

The way in which Aquinas's account solves these puzzles about faith may, however, leave the puzzle about the atonement's role looking only more intractable. On Aquinas's account, faith justifies because it includes a second-order volition assenting to God's doing the work of justification in the believer. There seems no need, in fact no room, in this process for the atonement. If God can do the work of making a believer righteous in virtue of the believer's assent to God's work, then what is the role of the atonement in salvation? Why shouldn't God have done the entire work of justification without the suffering and death of the incarnate Christ? On the other hand, if we can describe the atonement in such a way as to make it an integral part of salvation, what is its relation to the process of justification by faith? How does the atonement contribute to justification if justification consists in God's producing and responding to the believer's second-order volition assenting to God's justification of him?[23]

To see how the doctrine of the atonement and the doctrine of justification by faith fit together for Aquinas, it helps to reflect on the nature of the problem to which the atonement is a solution. Consider, for example, Rosamond Lydgate in Eliot's *Middlemarch*. Her prodigality, social climbing, and selfish manipulation of her husband bring him to ruin, forcing him to give up his aspirations to do medical research and causing him to lead a life he despises. Insofar as she gives religion any thought at all, Rosamond might fairly be said to be vaguely theistic, but no one would ever say of her that she has a will which desires God's goodness and detests her own sin. How is Rosamond to be brought to such a will, the will of faith, on Aquinas's view?

We could, of course, suppose that God simply produces such a will in her, moving her directly from the evil state in which her will refuses grace to a state in which it assents to grace, because free will, like everything else, is in the control of an omnipotent God; that is, we might suppose that God could simply compel her to will otherwise.[24] But this re-

---

23. It should be understood at the outset that the atonement has several functions in the plan of salvation, according to Aquinas, and that its role in the process of justification by faith is only one of them. Aquinas in fact lists five major effects of Christ's passion and death, including liberation from punishment and reconciliation with God. Here my focus is solely on the atonement in its relationship to justifying faith. For detailed discussion of Aquinas's account of the atonement, see the chapter in Stump, *Aquinas* (2003) on atonement.

24. For a good representative of an interpreter of Aquinas who understands Aquinas's

sponse would be incompatible with Aquinas's view that grace acts on the will with formal and not with efficient causality. It would also increase, not lessen, the puzzle over the atonement. If with a single act of will God could compel the volitions he wants in human beings, the volitions necessary for salvation, why would he instead save people by submitting Christ to the pain of crucifixion? And why would he not compel this volition in everybody, so that all people are saved?

We might suppose, alternatively, that Rosamond can herself produce the act of will necessary to salvation. The act of will in question, however, is one which begins a whole moral rebirth. And it seems clear that Rosamond alone cannot effect such a change in herself. Just in wanting such a change, Rosamond would already be exercising a changed will.

But if we are not to account for the act of will necessary for justification by attributing it to Rosamond's reforming herself or to God's compelling Rosamond's will to be reformed, how are we to account for it? To answer that question, it is helpful to consider in some detail what changes there would have to be in Rosamond in order for her to form the act of will involved in faith.

First, Rosamond would have to recognize at least that some of what she has done is seriously wrong, and then she would have to care about that fact. She would have to come to understand further that the evil she has done is symptomatic of a much deeper disorder in her will, a disorder which has alienated her from God, and she would have to have some desire that that disorder be remedied. She would need to suppose that she is capable of moral rebirth, so that she does not despair of herself, but she would also need to recognize that she needs help in order to effect such a moral change. Finally, she would have to come to see that God can work the desired moral transformation in her even if she can't do so herself. This belief will itself depend on other beliefs, perhaps most importantly on the belief that her past evil has not left her permanently separated from God and that God is willing to renew her. Finally, she would have to have some desire that God change her in this way; what she sees of God must inspire her with some desire to draw nearer.

No doubt many things in a person's life can contribute to readying her for and inviting her to this transformation. Rosamond's one stirring of genuine altruism is a result of the self-disregarding compassion shown her by Dorothea Casaubon. Such stirrings or softenings of the

---

view differently from the interpretation I am arguing for in this section, see R. Garrigou-Lagrange, *God, His Existence and Nature*, 5th ed., trans. Dom Bede Rose (St. Louis: Herder, 1955), p. 546. My reasons for thinking Garrigou-Lagrange's position mistaken are found in Stump, *Aquinas* (2003) in the chapter on divine simplicity.

heart are the harbingers of a moral rebirth; and, except for cases such as that of Paul on the road to Damascus, perhaps all instances of moral renewal are preceded by such experiences. But in order for their promise to be fulfilled, the heart of a person such as Rosamund must not only stir or soften but crack and melt. The cold, proud self-will and self-love which have animated her must break and give way to a new understanding of goodness and a new desire to follow it.

When the providentially ordered circumstances and the choices of her life have left her ready, reflection on the passion and death of Christ will be the wedge that cracks her heart. Christ's willingness to die for the spiritually poor and lost sets a standard by which Rosamond can measure herself and see the petty egotism which has been the basis of her character and actions. The same events also show her God's great love for her. God, who sees Rosamond's failings clearly, responds to her evil not by abandoning her in anger and disgust but by coming to draw her to himself. If Dorothea's generous and compassionate move towards Rosamond can soften her heart, Christ's passion and death will crack it, if anything can do so at all.

So besides the role it has in making satisfaction to God for sin, liberating sinners from punishment, and the other benefits Aquinas attributes to it, the atonement figures significantly in justification because of its role in working with divine grace to elicit the assent to moral rebirth requisite for justification.

These considerations help us see why Aquinas holds that, although the grace Christ merited by his passion is sufficient for undoing bad habits acquired in the past and preventing further sin in the future, it is efficacious to cure the sinful tendencies only of those united to him; and the uniting is effected by faith and love.[25] So, for example, Aquinas says, "the power of Christ is joined to us by means of faith. Now the power of remitting sins in a certain special way belongs to Christ's passion. And therefore by means of faith in his passion human beings are specially freed from sins. . . ."[26] But this faith is faith informed by charity. And, Aquinas holds, although charity can be stimulated by other examples of God's love for his creatures, it is stirred especially by reflection on Christ's passion.[27] That is why, in one of the many passages in which he makes the point, Aquinas claims that the passion of Christ frees us from our sinful nature in three ways, the first of which is "by means of

25. See, e.g., *ST* III q. 73, a. 3.
26. *ST* III q. 62, a. 5, ad 2.
27. *In Sent.*, Bk. III, d. 19, q. 1, a. 1, q. 2. Cf. also *ST* III q. 1, a. 2, where Aquinas is discussing the benefits of the incarnation and points especially to charity in human beings, which (he says) "is stimulated to the highest degree by this."

stimulating us to charity, because, as the Apostle says in Romans 5, 'God commends his charity to us since when we were enemies, Christ died for us.'"[28] And in another place, Aquinas remarks, speaking of Christ's passion, "by this human beings know how much God loves them, and by this they are stimulated to love God [in return]; and the perfection of human salvation consists in this."[29]

GRACE AND FREE WILL: ONE SUGGESTION

At this point, it is no doubt necessary to say something about the vexed question of the relation of grace and free will. According to Aquinas, though God's grace and the sinner's act of will in justifying faith are simultaneous, the act of will is both free and also the result of God's grace. My account of the connection between the atonement and that volition has presupposed the freedom of the will, but it may seem to have neglected the claim that the willing in question is produced by God's grace. The problem of the relation of grace to free will is, of course, at the center of the longstanding conflict between Molina and Bañez and their intellectual descendants, and the conflict has seemed to many to be irresoluble. In a spirit of altogether appropriate diffidence, however, I want to suggest that it is not impossible to see a way in which to maintain compatibly both Aquinas's claim that divine grace produces the act of will necessary for justification and that God produces that act in the willer as a response to something in her. Seeing how to reconcile these claims also helps illuminate the role of the atonement in bringing about that act of will. Whether Aquinas himself actually held the position I am about to suggest or whether he would even have liked this position if he had not held it but could have seen it with all its implications and ramifications will no doubt always be controversial.

It helps in this connection to remember Aquinas's view of the nature of the will. According to Aquinas, the will can assent to something or reject it, but it can also simply do nothing at all. It can just be turned off.[30] Sometimes the will is determined to want something by the nature of the will's object, Aquinas says, but the exercise of the will—whether the will is turned off or not—is always in the power of the will itself.[31] Furthermore, in principle, the will can move directly from any one of these positions to another. That is, it can move from rejecting to quiescence, from quiescence to assenting, from assenting to rejecting, and so on.

28. *ST* III q. 49, a. 1.   29. *ST* III q. 46, a. 3.
30. See, for example, *ST* IaIIae q. 9, a. 1.
31. See, for example, *ST* IaIIae q. 10, a. 2.

If this view of the will is right, then there are at least three possibilities for the will as regards grace: the will can assent to grace; it can refuse grace; or it can be quiescent. When it is quiescent, it doesn't refuse grace, but it doesn't accept it either. It is thus possible to hold that a human person has it in her power to refuse grace or to fail to refuse grace without also holding that she has it in her power to form the good act of will which is the assent to grace.

This view of the will allows one to attribute any good act of will to God's action on the will and yet to maintain that God's grace is responsive to something free, something uncaused, in human beings. It is possible to hold, that is, that divine grace produces any good act of a human will, including the act of will in justifying faith, and that God does not give grace to a will that refuses it, without also supposing that God alone is the controller of the wills of human beings. So, for example, in a section of *SCG* in which Aquinas argues that grace is necessary for faith, he also has a chapter in which he explains why, in his view, a person who doesn't come to faith is nonetheless responsible for his unregenerate condition. Aquinas says,[32] "One must consider that although a person cannot merit or produce grace by a motion of free will, he can nonetheless impede himself from receiving grace. . . . And so this is in the power of free will: to impede the reception of the divine grace or not to impede it. For this reason the person who provides an obstacle to the reception of divine grace merits the blame imputed to him. For insofar as it lies in him himself, God is prepared to give grace to everyone. . . . But the only people deprived of grace are the ones who provide in themselves an obstacle to grace."[33]

This position is manifestly not Pelagian. A will that simply fails to impede the reception of grace, that is, a will that is simply quiescent as regards the act of will in justifying faith, is not a good will. The will of faith is the will to have God bring the will to righteousness; it is a will to have a

---

32. I will have it pointed out to me that in the chapter following the one from which I am quoting, Aquinas qualifies his position by saying that after a person has once sinned, it is not in his power to fail to provide an impediment for grace unless he is first helped to do so by grace. Nonetheless, in that very chapter (*SCG* III, 160), Aquinas also says this: "Although it is not possible for those who are in sin to avoid, by their own power, providing an impediment to grace . . . unless they are first helped by grace, nonetheless this is imputed to them as fault, because this defect is left in them as a result of the preceding fault. . . . Furthermore, although the person who is in sin does not have it in his power to avoid sin altogether, he nonetheless has it in his power now to avoid this or that sin, and so whatever he commits, he commits voluntarily." The position Aquinas is concerned to rule out here is the position of the Pelagians, that a sinful person can do good without grace (see his discussion of the Pelagians in this same chapter, *SCG* III, 161). But the will's ceasing to act isn't itself an act of will of any kind; a fortiori, the will's quiescing isn't a good act of will.

33. *SCG* III, 159.

will that wills the good. And a will which is quiescent with regard to this volition can hardly count as good. It is consequently open to a person to move from the rejection of grace to quiescence in the will without thereby forming a good state in the will which would have to be attributed to the workings of grace. It is true that quiescence in the will with regard to grace is better than the rejection of grace, but comparatives don't presuppose positives; A can be taller than B without A's being tall. If God fails to give grace to a will that rejects grace but does give it to a will that is quiescent with respect to grace, then God's giving of grace can be responsive to something in a human person's will without its being the case that something good in a human person initiates the process of justification.

As the quotation from *SCG* above makes clear, on Aquinas's view, God is constantly offering grace to every human being in such a way that if a person doesn't refuse that grace, she receives it and it produces in her the will of faith. So, for Aquinas, normal adult human beings[34] in a post-Fall condition who are not converted or in the process of being converted refuse grace continually, even if they are not aware of doing so; and it is solely up to a human person whether or not she refuses grace.[35] But a person can cease to refuse grace without assenting to God's infusion of grace; instead, she can just be quiescent in will.

Insofar as it is open to a human person to be simply quiescent in will, there are alternative possibilities for a human person's will—rejecting and quiescent—neither of which is a good act of will. The will of faith is consequently a gift of God's, but a human person's will is still ultimately in the control of that person, because it is up to her either to refuse grace or to fail to refuse grace, and God's giving of grace depends on what the will of a human person does.[36] Nonetheless, this position steers clear of even semi-Pelagianism, because what God is responsive to in a human will does not count as a good act of will. Any good act on the part of a human will is thus still a result of grace. Consequently, without danger of any form of Pelagianism, it is possible to hold that a post-Fall human being who cannot form a good act of will apart from grace can

---

34. Children and adult human beings in non-normal conditions pose special problems which complicate the case, and so I am simply leaving those cases to one side here.

35. By saying that it is solely up to her, I do not mean to rule out all the influences for good which Augustine sometimes also describes as grace, such as the influence of good preaching or good friends. I mean only that it is up to the human willer alone whether such good influences are persuasive with her; rejecting the influence of graces of this sort remains possible for her.

36. I am presenting this position as one which allows Aquinas to have both of the apparently incompatible claims he wants, but I am not proposing this position as problem-free.

nonetheless control whether or not his will refuses grace. In ceasing to refuse grace, he does not make an act of will, but he nonetheless moves into a condition to which God responds by giving him the grace that produces in him the will of faith.

As I said above, my point here is to show one possible way in which Aquinas's account of human psychology, and especially his view of the nature of the will, enables him to combine consistently the claims he holds as regards grace and free will. I am strongly inclined to think that this possible way is the way Aquinas himself took, but the subject has been so controversial and so divisive in the history of interpretations of Aquinas that it is better perhaps simply to show the consistency of this position and to leave open whether Aquinas availed himself of it or not.

There is one other advantage of the position I have sketched that is worth pointing out. It enables us to give a plausible explanation of the kind of connection Aquinas makes between the atonement and the will of faith. In explaining the role of the atonement in justification on Aquinas's view, I showed the way in which the passion and death of Christ might crack and melt a heart already prepared by providentially ordered circumstances. But the notion of a heart's cracking or melting is, of course, a metaphor. To speak of something's cracking or melting is to describe something's giving way to an external force after (or in spite of) some internal resistance or disinclination. To say that a heart cracks or melts, then, is another way of saying that a will which previously was resistant or disinclined toward something urged on it by some one (or something) else gives over its dissent and leaves off its resistance, or goes contrary to its earlier disinclination.[37]

On the position I have outlined, we can explain the connection between the atonement and justification by faith in this way. Before he is justified, a person has a resistance or disinclination toward the second-order volition in which sinners detest their sin and long for God's goodness, a volition toward which the providence of God urges him. When a person has been readied (or perhaps as in the case of Paul does not need to be readied) by past experience and grace, the passion and death of Christ are the means for subduing the sinner's final resistance to such a volition. The internal opposition to undergoing the wholesale changes and the humbling entailed by such a volition is broken by the suffering of Christ and the love it shows. But the quelling of dissent need not be

37. I have described the will's state in such a case as if it consisted in ceasing to do an action, rather than as performing the action of ceasing, both because the description of the will as passive seems to me truer to the phenomena and because Aquinas's philosophical psychology allows for this possibility, which is the basis for the position I am arguing for.

equivalent to freely willed assent, as I have been at pains to show here. If we can distinguish the breaking down of refusal from the positive good of assent—and Aquinas's philosophical psychology makes it plain that we can—then God can avail himself of the absence of refusal to infuse the previously refused grace, in order to move the will from quiescence all the way to assent. On this view, God's grace is what produces the second-order volition requisite for justification, as Aquinas's theory of justification claims; and yet, because God does so only in the absence of the refusal of grace, he does not coerce the will or undermine its freedom, but is instead responsive to it. Nonetheless, all forms of Pelagianism are avoided since there is nothing good in a human person's will that is not produced in it by God's grace. Consequently, in addition to the many other benefits the atonement works for human beings, there is this very important one: the atonement cracks the will's resistence to grace so that God may reform it without violating it.[38]

In this way, Aquinas's theory of justification by faith, together with his view of the nature of the will, can be shown to have the resources for a solution to the puzzles which I raised earlier. Using Aquinas's theory of justification, then, we can show both why faith justifies and how the atonement is related to that faith.

38. I have discussed the way in which God might bring about such a volition in the case of a person whose religious beliefs I described as vaguely theistic. We could, however, tell a similar story, although one bound to be longer and more complicated, about the way in which God might bring an atheist to the same sort of volition.

7   SOVEREIGN STATES AND SOVEREIGN INDIVIDUALS
The Question of Political Theory

MICHAEL ALLEN GILLESPIE

On a beautiful day in the spring of 146 B.C., Publius Cornelius Scipio Aemilianus, who was just approaching his fortieth birthday, stood on a low hill in northern Africa, looking out over the still blue waters of the Mediterranean toward the peninsular city of Carthage. For three years this great city had been besieged by his legions, but now it had fallen and was being burned to the ground and all of its surviving inhabitants slaughtered or enslaved. The vicious war between the two greatest powers of the Western Mediterranean that had raged for more than 118 years had finally come to an end. Scipio, however, did not relish this moment of triumph. His eyes did not glitter with victory nor did they reflect the glory of this great accomplishment. In fact, they were filled with tears as he turned to his companion, the Greek historian Polybius, and repeated Hector's most melancholy line from the *Iliad,* "The day shall come when Troy shall fall and Priam, lord of spears, and the people of Priam." At the peak of his success, Scipio could only think that his city too would one day suffer a similar fate, that it too like all the great states and empires before it—like the Assyrians, the Medes, the Persians, and the Macedonians—would be brutally destroyed, that one bright and beautiful day another commander would watch as Rome and its people, Scipio's people, were obliterated.[1]

In a manner surprisingly similar to that of Rome, we too recently achieved a great and final victory over a mortal enemy and watched as that "evil empire" crumbled and fell into ruin. It is perhaps a measure of the distance between us and the ancients that we were not struck with the sense of transience and fragility that overcame Scipio, but assumed instead that we had won a final victory, that history was at an end, and

---

1. Polybius, *Histories,* bk. 39.

that our way of life would now be triumphant everywhere and last forever.

The difference between these two cases is instructive, for it is only out of the recognition of the finitude and mortality of our political institutions that *political* theory and a realistic political practice arise. The belief that one is invulnerable leads to the feeling that politics is onerous and unnecessary, and that political theory is superfluous. It is only when we recognize the mortality of our institutions and come to fear for their existence, or recognize the need for new institutions to avoid slipping into anarchy and civil war, that political theory becomes necessary. Fortunately and unfortunately, the new millennium has brought with it a renewed sense of our own vulnerability and with it a renewed understanding of the need for political theory.

But what can political theory mean for us today? In what sense is it necessary? Political theory has a provenance that stretches back in one form or another more than three thousand years. Originally, it was not clearly distinguished from other forms of thinking about things human and divine. Sometimes in poetry, sometimes in prose, sometimes in public debate, and sometimes in proverbs or songs, human beings reflected on political life. Such reflections, however, were not strictly speaking "theoretical."

The theoretical element of political theory has a Greek origin. The term itself derives from the Greek term *theoria*, which originally meant not the contemplation of the unchanging but the "beholding of the gods." The gods, as Homer portrays them, do not contemplate the eternal shapes or motions of nature; rather they view and concern themselves with the ever-changing social and political activities of human beings. Not only do they watch these events, they seek to influence their outcome. Political theory, I want to argue, follows a similar path. It is not content to be merely a spectator, but seeks to reach into the affairs of men and affect social and political action and institutions. Political theory is thus not a transcendent "theoretical" enterprise, but a form of human praxis. It thus has no standpoint above the world, but is constantly engaged with shifting events in an effort to master those that can be mastered and to learn how to live with those that cannot. Political theory thus can never be complete and is always confronted with new tasks.

Twentieth-century political theory from the end of the First World War until the end of the Cold War was dominated by the question of free versus unfree government, or as it came to be understood, the confrontation of liberalism and totalitarianism. The question behind this debate, however, disappeared with the collapse of the Soviet Union, in large measure because liberalism seemed to have triumphed, consigning all other forms of political life to the ash heap of world history.[2] Throughout the 1990s, however, an increasing number of thinkers began to challenge the hegemony of liberalism both from democratic and theological directions. Questions also arose concerning both individual and national identity. These questions reflected a growing sense of drift in post–Cold War liberalism. Were we essentially individuals or members of a community or set of communities? Were we a secular nation or a religious people or peoples? These questions were related to questions of race and gender, of ethnicity and sexuality, all of which were bound up with identity politics and multiculturalism.

These questions were complicated by the growing globalization of economic life. The decline in the sense of a distinctive American identity as the leader of the free world, and the growing sense that politics and the state were becoming less important for our social existence seemed to indicate the end of political theory and the rise of economic and social thought.

Then came September 11th. Suddenly, all of the certainties about the inevitable triumph of our way of life vanished. As a result, our view of the world and our place in it had to be rethought. One group of scholars has interpreted our current predicament on the model of the Cold War as a clash of civilizations.[3] A second group has portrayed it as an international version of the American struggle between secularism and religion that had played such an important role in the 1990s. A third group has characterized the conflict as a multicultural encounter brought about by globalization. I suggest in what follows that all of these are inadequate because they rest an understanding of human being and the state that is inadequate to today's world.

I want to begin with a brief discussion not of political theory but of political philosophy. I take political philosophy to be a fundamental questioning that grows out of the way in which we are constituted as beings. Each human being is an individual and is also a member of a species. No one is an absolute particular and yet no one is simply a reflection or instance of the universal. This ontological condition is the source of the abiding question that guides all of our thinking about political life. It is abiding and perennial because it has no final or definitive answer. There is thus no escape from this question. It shapes all of our thinking about politics. We can never become absolutely independent self-

2. This liberal triumphalism was reflected in Francis Fukuyama's *The End of History and the Last Man* (New York: Free Press, 1992) and other similar works.

3. Samuel Huntington, *The Clash of Civilizations and the Remaking of the World Order* (New York: Simon and Schuster, 1996).

creating and self-sustaining beings nor can we ever be reduced to mere moments of some species-being.

This question is a manifestation of *the* fundamental philosophical question—whether being itself is one or many. As Plato demonstrated in his *Parmenides*, this ontological question is fundamental because it cannot be answered, and it cannot be answered because it is itself the presupposition of all thinking, and therefore of all questioning and answering. We thus cannot think about things without thinking those things as being *both* one and many. As a result, there can be no final theoretical vision of the whole that can serve as the absolute, fundamental, and unshakable truth.

Political theory—as opposed to political philosophy—is concerned not with this fundamental question as a question, but with how we might answer it, i.e., with how we might reconcile or explain the relationship between the one and the many that we are in this time and place. Political theory seeks to construct an answer that is both theoretically sound (which is to say, consistent, coherent, and complete) and practically feasible or workable, and thus to articulate structures that allow us to survive and thrive in the circumstances in which we find ourselves. This dual goal poses a problem for political theory, since the demand for theoretical rigor often comes into competition with efforts to frame practical solutions. Thus, while the general question that guides political philosophy remains the same, the answers to it that political theory develops must satisfy not merely the abstract needs of human beings as such, but the needs of human beings dwelling in specific times and places with particular customs and institutions. All political theory thus may have some universal characteristics that are derived from our basic character as human beings, but the specific solutions that political theory proposes will always be conditioned by the idiosyncratic factors of our particular situations.

In order to understand the need for political theory in our time and place we need to examine the conditions of modern life that political theory is meant to address. Modern political theory originated in the seventeenth century as an attempt to resolve the tremendous political-theological problems that characterized early modernity and that erupted in the wars of religion surrounding the Reformation. The solution that modern political theory found to this problem was the notion of "sovereignty." This term refers not merely to state sovereignty but also and perhaps primarily to the sovereignty of the individual. Modern political theory in this sense is both individualistic and statist. Let's examine this claim more carefully.

Modern thought sees individuals as sovereign over themselves. The core of their being and the source of their dignity are not in their reason or in the fact that they were created by God, but in their freedom and ability to govern themselves. What is preeminent in this notion of individuality is not rationality but will. Individuals are conceived as willing and thus desiring beings. This is not to say that reason plays no role in the notion of the sovereign individual, but only that it plays a subordinate role. It is the spy and scout of the passions.[4] Individuals, so conceived, have no natural ends and correspondingly no natural duties. What is good for them is their freedom and the use of this freedom to attain what they desire.

Sovereign states are similarly free, masters over their domestic affairs, powers deserving recognition by other states. This idea of sovereign states has roots in earlier thought, but is actually quite different from the feudal notion of a principality, or the Roman idea of a republic, or the Greek vision of the polis, to name only a few other possibilities. Each state is imagined to be absolutely independent of all other states and not subordinate to them in any way—indeed, related to other states only by explicit contracts or treaties. Although we today tend to think of states as individuals writ large, it would be a mistake to believe that the sovereign state is merely an analogue to the truly real sovereign individual.

Both the notion of the sovereign individual and the notion of the sovereign state were responses to the chaos that resulted from the collapse of the medieval world. Formalized and frozen by a series of measures introduced at the end of the wars of religion in the seventeenth century, they have remained determinative for us ever since. Their origin is thus wrapped up with the origin of the modern age.

Modernity, as Hans Blumenberg and others have shown, originates in the nominalist revolution of the thirteenth and fourteenth centuries. This revolution overturned scholastic efforts to reconcile pagan philosophy and Christian theology. Scholasticism had suggested that divine omnipotence had to be understood within the context of divine omniscience, i.e., that in his creation of the world out of nothing God had acted rationally and structured the world categorically. According to this view, what is ultimately real is not the individual but the species or universal. The world so understood can then be grasped by a syllogistic logic that explains the relations of all universals to one another. Against this view, a group of theologians and thinkers, drawing on the work of William of Ockham and typically referred to as nominalists, argued that such a view of God undermines his divinity because it subjects divine

4. Hobbes, *Leviathan*, ed. Edwin Curley (Indianapolis: Hackett, 1994), 41.

freedom and power to human reason. From the nominalist point of view, if God is to be God, he must be truly omnipotent and thus able to will and do anything that is not contradictory. God thus could not have created species because in so doing he would have limited his own omnipotence. Consequently, God must have created all beings individually. If there are no species, then syllogistic logic is an illusion. Words do not correspond to universals but are merely signs or tools with which we try to understand the confusing totality of radically individual beings that we confront in experience. Moreover, if God is radically omnipotent in the way nominalism suggests, neither he nor his purposes can be rationally understood.

Nominalism thus presents a new answer to the question of the one and the many that lays great weight upon the manyness of existence. In this sense it was called a *via moderna* in contrast to the *via antiqua* of scholasticism. At its core is an unsettling view of God that undermines long-established ways of conceiving of man's relationship to God, nature, and other human beings. The nominalist God is no longer a rational or just God. He is no man's debtor and is not bound by reason or even by his own promises. Today he may save the saints and damn the sinners, but tomorrow he may do exactly the reverse. Humans thus have no way of knowing what God wants from them or how they can gain salvation. The conjunction of this new view of God with various disasters of the thirteenth and fourteenth centuries—including the Black Death, the schism in the papacy, and the Hundred Years War—undermined medieval Christianity and gave rise to a more anxious and more terrifying view of life. At the end of the Middle Ages, man was thus confronted by a chaotic and frightening world ruled by an irrational and unpredictable God.

Modernity was a series of attempts to come to terms with this problematic God and the very uncertain world he seemed to have created. We cannot go into detail about all the elements of this process, but I will briefly discuss the idea of sovereignty that is essential to the development of modern political theory.

The notion of individual sovereignty originated in the earliest humanist efforts to come to terms with the problem of radical individuality opened up by the nominalist revolution. The first to point in this direction was Francesco Petrarch. In scholastic doctrine, individual humans were considered members of a species. Each in this sense had a natural end corresponding to his universal nature. Nominalism exploded this notion, suggesting that each human being had a unique destiny determined by God alone. Petrarch accepted this notion, but argued that man is dependent not on God but on himself to realize his own unique character. Man, in other words, can form himself. Petrarch's followers developed this idea into a full-fledged notion of individuality. Pico argued, for example, that God had given man the capacity to choose his own nature, and artists and thinkers such as Alberti, Bruni, and Michelangelo exemplified and articulated this notion in their own lives and practice. While they believed that man was created in the image of God, they saw God not as a supremely rational being but as a creative force. Consequently, the best life for them was not that of the philosopher or scholar but that of the creative artist who sought to reshape himself and his world.

Humanism thus accepted the ontological and anthropological conclusions of nominalism but sought to show that they did not necessarily lead to despair and indeed might be the basis for a renewed human magnificence. While such a view was not hostile to religion, it seemed to some to call into question the sovereignty of God and to vastly exaggerate human power. Foremost among these was Luther, who, in a remarkable debate with Erasmus on the freedom of the will, disputed the central humanist claim, arguing that human pride was simply a tool of the devil and that humans themselves were always subject to either God or Satan. Luther in this sense accepted the nominalist notion of the divine omnipotence and sovereignty of God, but mitigated the terrifying consequences of this doctrine by showing that God was not something transcendent and independent of the individual. In his view, God always acts through human beings. Divine omnipotence is thus not a distant power but a power in the heart of each Christian. One of the unintended consequences of Luther's attack on humanism was thus to further divinize the notion of individuality that humanism had first established.

Building on this notion in a more secular framework, Descartes argued that even an omnipotent God could not deceive us about our own existence. Descartes believed that human beings can establish a position independent of God and shape their own destiny, making themselves masters and possessors of nature. However, this claim rests on Descartes' belief that man has within him the same infinite will that is found in God. The sovereign self that Descartes defines and that becomes so central to modernity is thus derived from the nominalist notion of an omnipotent and sovereign God.[5]

It would be an exaggeration to suggest that all modern thought accepts this Cartesian notion of the self. An alternative strain of modern thought that begins with Hobbes and Locke develops a notion of an in-

---

5. For a fuller explanation of this point see my *Nihilism before Nietzsche* (Chicago: University of Chicago Press, 1995), 33–63.

dividual who is more limited in his capacities. However, while this strain of thought is less sanguine about what humans can do individually, it is perhaps more optimistic about what they can do collectively, either guided by the hidden hand in economic life, or in and as a sovereign state.

The development of the idea of state sovereignty follows a path parallel to that of individual sovereignty. When we think of the modern notion of state sovereignty, we often contrast it to the theological notions of political life that characterize the medieval world, assuming that the modern notion is essentially secular and rational. The actual origins of the idea of state sovereignty, however, belie this assumption. The modern notion of sovereignty is itself rooted in religion, but in the religion of a God reconceived in the struggles of the Reformation. We see this in the work of the thinker who first articulated the theory of sovereignty, Jean Bodin.

Bodin was educated in both the scholastic and the humanist traditions by the Carmelites, but he left the order at an early age, perhaps because of his attraction to Calvinism, and devoted himself to humanist learning and particularly the study of linguistics and history. Like many of his humanist predecessors, however, his interest in history was deeply theological, aimed at understanding the hidden harmony in all of the world's religions and philosophies. He thus came to favor religious toleration, not because he sought to wean man from religion (he hated atheism), but because he believed we have no way of definitively answering fundamental religious questions. As a corollary to this insight, he recognized that there could be no theological answer to the religious violence spawned by the Reformation. He thus concluded that the only solution to this conflict was the recognition of the absolute authority of the state as the image and voice of God on earth. Peace, he believed, would be possible only if everyone recognized the state's absolute sovereignty. While he came to this understanding through the study of Roman institutions, he also drew heavily on revelation. Like Calvin he believed that the state was made necessary by the Fall, but while Calvin saw sin as a rebellion against God and the state as a kind of punishment, Bodin saw sin as injustice toward one's fellow man and the state as the fulfillment of divine and natural law. On the surface this claim sounds very Thomistic, but Bodin did not see the state as an embodiment of divine reason. He saw it rather as an emanation of divine will or power. In his view it is thus a *puissance souveraine*, a sovereign power. It is perpetual and absolute, greater even than any king, who is merely the momentary person within which sovereignty resides. Moreover, the sovereign is characterized not by his superior knowledge, but by the unqualified right to command, independent of all consent. Like God, he is an absolute and independent power. This does not mean that he is God. Rather he is the agent of God on earth and thus answerable to him. The sovereign is not therefore a law unto himself, but the instrument of divine will.[6] While Bodin's notion of the sovereign state thus has a humanist origin akin to that of the sovereign individual, his state, like Luther's individual, is not only independent but a manifestation of divine power.

A similar argument is made by Hobbes who claims that the sovereign is a mortal god.[7] In contrast to Bodin, however, Hobbes argues that this mortal god (or Leviathan) is formed by the consent or will of individuals following their natural passions and aided by their natural reason. Once formed, however, the sovereign is no longer subordinate to their will, but is an independent force that they must obey. Moreover, his power is unchecked in any realm. He is the arbiter of all public notions of good and evil, and thus the final judge in all matters of morality. He is likewise the head of the church and has the right to regulate all other social groups within his domain. The Leviathan is thus a collective human creation but a creation that transcends the limits of all mortal human beings. Thus, while Hobbes does not believe that individuals can be gods, he does believe that they can create a godlike being, absolute in his power to rule over them.

These speculations about a political order that could resolve the problem of religious conflict were paralleled by the development of such an order following the treaty of Westphalia. This order has come increasingly to dominate the modern world. The principle that underlay this Westphalian notion of sovereignty was that each prince should be sovereign over all affairs within his borders, and that his subjects consequently had to conform to his faith and obey the laws that he established. Spheres of overlapping authority that had played such a disastrous role in the preceding period were thereby eliminated. Individuals no longer owed obedience to the emperor or the pope or anyone else inside or outside their state. In this way, peace was obtained. But at what a price! Political power, which hitherto was understood as one of a number of forces governing human beings, henceforth became (at least in principal and often in fact) absolute. The state thereby became sovereign over all internal affairs, the entire life of civil society and the family, and also came to regulate all relations with those outside the state.

---

6. "BECAUSE there are none on earth, after God, greater than sovereign princes, whom God establishes as His lieutenants to command the rest of mankind, we must enquire carefully into their estate, that we may respect and revere their majesty in all due obedience, speak and think of them with all due honour. He who contemns his sovereign prince, contemns God whose image he is." Jean Bodin, *Six Books of the Commonwealth*, abridged and trans. M. J. Tooley (Oxford: Blackwell, 1955), 40.

7. Hobbes, *Leviathan*, ed. Curley, 109.

The early modern period was thus characterized by the development of both sovereign individuals and sovereign states. While these new constructions solved a number of problems, it was not clear how such individuals and states could peacefully co-exist. How was this problem to be solved? Certainly not by a return to a rational order or great chain of being as the basis for all reciprocal relations and obligations. The nominalist revolution had overturned such notions. The individual and the state could be reconciled only by the utter subordination of the individual to the state (that is, by absolutism) or by the utter subordination of the state to the will or consent of the individuals (that is, by liberal democracy).

Both of these solutions have had their day. While absolutism gained sway in some states, in others it was mitigated by the development of popular sovereignty. We see this development first in the thought Locke and Rousseau, but it soon plays a role in practice as well. Sovereign states thus came to be identified with the people rather than with the ruler or rulers. The success of popular sovereignty, however, did not entail the rejection of the idea of the state as a quasi-divine entity. In fact, this notion was further strengthened by democratization. The French Revolution, for example, propagated the notion that *vox populi, vox dei,* that the voice of the people is the voice of God. Following in this same tradition, Hegel suggested that the development of the state was nothing other than the march of God through the world.[8] Nationalism in this respect was thus only the culmination of a long process that ended in the apotheosis of state sovereignty in both its absolutist and its democratic forms.

Given the events of the first half of the twentieth century, it would be easy to believe that the state was a great evil and to opt for either anarchism or a radical libertarianism that seeks to reduce our collective existence to freely chosen interactions between sovereign individuals. Those who hold such views are quite reasonably dismayed with the overwhelming power of the state and its obvious disdain on many occasions for individual rights, but they see only the manifest danger of the state in front of them and not the distant dangers that arise in its absence. They too believe in sovereignty, but they believe that it inheres only in the individual. They place great weight upon the belief that sovereign individuals acting merely in their self-interest under free market conditions will produce human well-being. This view, however, is one-sided. Human beings are certainly individuals but they are also part of a community, connected not merely by choice but in their very being. Their

8. Hegel, *Philosophy of Right*, §258.

happiness and utility cannot be calculated simply one person at a time. They are not simply self-interested in a narrow economic sense, for the good of others matters to them. The notion of the sovereignty of the individual obscures this fact, but it does not obliterate it. Individuals cannot live without some collective institutions, and the attempt to do so almost invariably leads to a situation that calls forth more repressive collective institutions.

It is also necessary to recognize that, whatever its shortcomings, state sovereignty has produced great benefits. It has provided a workable solution to the problem of sectarian violence, which in seventeenth-century Germany, for example, claimed the lives of more than a third of the population. Second, it has made possible the development of an internal market free from tariffs and other barriers to trade, which in turn fostered economic development and prosperity. Third, at least in its democratic form, it has generally helped to protect the lives and rights of individuals and groups from non-governmental actors. Finally, it has enabled states not merely to preserve themselves but to expand their reach around the world both economically and militarily. The sovereign state in short has supplied security, freedom, prosperity, and power.

As successful as sovereignty has been, its success has been limited to particular goods. Neither the notion nor the institution of sovereignty aims at virtue, justice, piety, harmony, or even substantive rationality. Rather, on the model of the nominalist God, it aims at power. The questions that underlie the notion of sovereignty, as well as the dangers that it poses thus reprise the troubling questions that underlay the nominalist idea of an omnipotent God. In reflecting on the problems of sovereignty at the end of modernity, we thus come face to face with the troubling question that in a variety of ways gave birth to modernity.

The notion of sovereignty is at its core a counterfactual, theomorphic notion that is grounded not in knowledge but in belief. It imagines an entity that is absolutely independent and all-powerful, bound in no way by any other entity or force. While this might make sense as the description of a transcendent God, it does not make much sense as a way of describing entities within the world, where all beings interact and are dependent upon other beings and forces. The idea of individual and state sovereignty thus enormously exaggerates human potentiality. Its profound hubris leads to the belief, for example, that man can make himself master and possessor of nature. It also suggests that all human activity is a striving for power, and that there is no intrinsic good or evil, i.e., that good is only what increases my power and evil only what diminishes it. It leads to the further view that the only end of power is self-satisfaction understood as the maximal satisfaction of our desires. Or, to sum matters up, the modern notion of individual and state sovereignty leads human beings to believe that either individually or collectively they can become gods.

This critique of the modern notion of sovereignty, however, needs to be spelled out more fully. I will speak first about the idea of individual sovereignty and then about the notion of state sovereignty.

As a number of communitarian thinkers have argued, the idea of individual sovereignty is a radically one-sided answer to the philosophical question of the one and the many. Each individual is imagined to be radically separate in his essence from all other human beings, self-governing because self-creating and/or self-sustaining. This notion thus imagines humans to be godlike beings, independent of all other beings. It is thus akin to Oedipus's titanic claim to be "fortune's child." None of us, however, are born out of nothing. None of us forms ourselves as the beings we are. We are individuals in some sense, but much of what we take to be our individuality is produced by others around us. Modern individuals thus constantly stand Oedipus-like on the verge of a horrifying discovery that in proclaiming their independence they are sinning against their own mysterious beginnings.

We are also determined by psychological factors in ways that we cannot understand. A sovereign self must be self-transparent and in control of itself. For humans, however, this is just not the case. Consciousness is only the tip of the iceberg; a great deal of what we are is hidden beneath the surface. As conscious beings, we help to shape our own character and actions, but our conscious will is only a moment of a larger matrix of forces. What we are is thus something complex that is entangled with many other human and natural beings.

For these and other reasons, we need to acknowledge that the idea of the sovereign individual is inadequate to capture the full reality of our being. It is, however, so central to our self-understanding and so embedded in our practices and institutions that it is difficult to think our way beyond it. This difficulty is exacerbated by the absence of any alternative to this reigning paradigm.

For similar reasons the idea of state sovereignty is inadequate as a tool for coming to terms with our contemporary circumstances. The idea of sovereign states was originally intended to solve the problem of religious warfare by separating the combatants into separate units, allowing them to live at peace with others of their same confession. This was a radical but not unreasonable solution in a world that was largely agrarian and in which trade was generally local and limited. The phenomenon of globalization has now rendered this solution impossible. Individuals are entangled with one another in many different ways that transcend states.

Moreover, corporations, religions, and other groups operate on a transnational scale and are thus difficult for sovereign states to regulate or control. Indeed, in some instances their resources and powers exceed those of many states.

One solution to this problem would be to reverse globalization and retreat back within our borders. Such a possibility is alluring to those who long for a simpler time. Moreover, it has the virtue of being possible. Globalization is not a new or unique phenomenon. The first great age of modern globalization occurred at the end of the nineteenth and the beginning of the twentieth centuries. This age came to a crashing end with World War I and the widespread imposition of trade restrictions in the 1930s. The costs of retreat from globalization were tremendous, and it is hard to imagine anyone choosing to pay such costs today. Absent such a retreat, we have to recognize the inadequacy of the notion of sovereignty in dealing with our current and future affairs.

We have also come to recognize that the concept of state sovereignty cannot explain or control the force that the subliminal factors of mass psychology exercise on state behavior. Just as we have come to understand that individuals often are motivated by hidden psychological factors, we have come to see that such factors play an important role in state action. States thus cannot be realistically conceived merely as conscious beings that rationally choose how to maximize their preferences. They are often motivated by factors such as ethnic hatred or religious zeal or the longing for a lost homeland, or any number of other factors that they themselves do not understand. The concept of sovereignty, which imagines the absolute independence of the state, thus does not recognize and cannot accommodate these deep-seated sources of state activity.

I am not the first to question the notion of individual sovereignty. Communitarians and postmodernists have already raised questions about the sovereign individual in decisive ways. Neither, however, provides a satisfying answer. Communitarians all too often assume that human beings can adequately be described as a product of community practices. They thus provide an answer to the question of the one and the many that gives great weight to the one as the source of the many. As a result, they find it difficult to explain human individuality as anything other than a peculiar locus of group affiliations. But what can groups be beyond the practices and beliefs of the individuals that make them up? It seems undeniable that they need to give a more convincing account of the origin and nature of individuality and face more forthrightly the question of the one and the many.

Postmodernism is on even more difficult ground. For postmodernism, there is no one at all, no identity, even to the many things that are. At the core of things is not identity but pure difference that deconstructs every individual thing into a manyness that is constantly at odds with itself. Such a notion leads to a view of politics as sheer conflict without providing the grounds for a community of any sort. Indeed, each community, in this account, is merely a form of discipline, an imposition of a particular ideological view or will to power that strives for dominance. This view leads to a notion that political action must be constant struggle, a kind of permanent revolution to liberate ourselves from linguistic and political tyrannies that are continually reimposed by our very efforts at liberation. There can be no ultimate goal because in rejecting all identity we abandon any effort to distinguish a good or rational order from a bad or irrational one.

The problem for political theory today is to put the individual and community back together in the context of the world in which we live. This is the world of globalization, the world in which we are increasingly connected to others both in our own countries and around the world in multiple and unavoidable ways. We cannot retreat within ourselves or within the borders of states with others who are essentially like us. Ours is a time of collision, and a time that consequently confronts us with great danger of conflict. How can such conflict be avoided or mitigated?

Traditionally human beings have found two different solutions to this problem. The first is the simple use of force to eliminate or dominate those with whom we are at odds. This is sometimes successful but almost always provokes retaliation. Even much weaker parties have recourse to guerrilla or terroristic tactics that have a tremendous impact upon the dominant power. Such a solution thus requires not just one forceful act, but the repeated, continual, and in many cases increasing use of force. It may be supplemented by persuasive efforts to establish legitimacy, but these are seldom sufficient to free one from the repeated need to use force. A second solution is to emphasize what is common and promote the toleration of alternative views. This solution too requires a willingness to use force, especially against groups that teach and practice intolerance, but force is seen here as a last resort. Such toleration is more likely when the potentially antagonistic parties are facing a common enemy. Fear is a glue that holds them together. In a similar way, a common market unites people to one another. Self-interest promotes steady cooperation even among those who disagree about many other matters. Such commercial intercourse can succeed, however, only if there is a common law and an impartial judge, and the success of such a system of adjudication depends upon the existence of a hegemonic power that is willing to enforce rules and prevent or eliminate criminal activity.

The first of these alternatives is typified by Rome. The triumph of Rome over Carthage, with which we began, was the triumph of a militaristic power. The ensuing period saw the expansion of this power through conquest, and the consolidation of power through the imposition of Roman law and a centralized system of bureaucratic administration backed up by overwhelming military force. Rome was constantly under threat from those outside its reach and thus lasted as long as, but no longer than, Roman courage. Scipio rightly feared for his city. The survival and expansion of Rome for 600 years after the conquest of Carthage was a testimony to Roman success in devising a legal system, a bureaucratic apparatus, and a political philosophy to meet the needs of their time.

Their time and our own, however, are vastly different. Indeed, one might say by analogy that what differentiates us from them is that this time it was not Rome but Carthage that won, not the militaristic power but the commercial power. This in itself has tremendous consequences.

Commercial powers succeed not by enslaving others but by selling them things they need and want. Their goal is not to conquer, plunder, and enslave others but to trade with them. It is undoubtedly true that they take advantage of their hegemonic position to gain marginal advantages, but both sides benefit in any trade, even if one side has a larger relative gain. Successful commercial relations also depend upon adherence to contractual obligations, a practice that fosters a habit of law-abidingness on both sides. Successful trading regimes also depend upon the acceptance of transnational standards of value and adjudication. Furthermore, commercial powers are less likely to go to war because war disrupts trade. Finally, successful commercial partners need detailed knowledge of their customers, need to think about the needs of those to whom they hope to sell their goods. As a result, commerce leads people to put themselves in the place of others and this promotes mutual understanding.

The continued dominance of the notion of sovereignty poses a real danger for two reasons. First, it makes us reluctant to intervene in the internal affairs of other states when intervention for humanitarian reasons is necessary. We thus almost always appear late on the scene and as a result must use greater force to resolve the problems. Second and perhaps even more importantly, the notion of sovereignty gives a hegemonic power a false sense of what it can and should do. As I argued earlier, a hubristic self-understanding leaves the hegemon prone to overreach its abilities. A hegemon needs to recognize its limits and work with other states. It also needs to teach toleration and insist that others do so as well or at least that they not teach intolerance and hatred. In a similar fashion, it needs to act to meet humanitarian challenges and to oppose or at least not to support local oligarchies and tyrannies. It should act in concert with others if possible, but it must act even if they are not willing to do so in crucial or difficult cases.

Any political theory that seeks to deal forthrightly with our current situation must recognize the crucial role that America as the sole surviving superpower has to play in the world system. Such a theory must, however, also help us to understand how America can operate as a hegemonic force without succumbing to the temptation to act in a supersovereign manner and thereby become an imperial power.

However, such restraint will not be possible unless we also are able to reconceptualize our notion of the individual and the relation of the individual to the larger community. The emphasis on the sovereign individual has led to a belief that human well-being consists in the maximization of individual preferences. Measured in monetary terms, the aggregate utility of a society of sovereign individuals may be quite high and yet its real well-being quite low. To paraphrase Hobbes, the lives of individuals in such a society may not be poor, brutish, or short, but they will almost certainly be solitary and nasty. A happy human life requires not only accepting but also transcending our individuality.

Hegel suggested a hundred and seventy-five years ago that humans need to conceive of themselves not merely as self-interested individuals and moral agents, but also as family members, as parts of corporations, as members of congregations, and above all as citizens. He believed, however, that the successful integration of all of these depended upon the existence of a generally accepted philosophical system that made sense out of the ways in which these different selves or "identities" were related to one another. In our globalized world, we clearly need to be able to conceive of ourselves in even more interrelated and overlapping ways. Formulating a theory that allows us to understand the connections between these various roles or identities is the chief task of political theory today. Without it we will remain divided beings struggling to make sense of our multiple personalities in an increasingly complex, mystifying, and dangerous world.

8 FREEDOM, REPUBLICS, AND PEOPLES IN MACHIAVELLI'S *PRINCE*

NATHAN TARCOV

This essay considers three interwoven subjects in Machiavelli's *Prince* that are usually considered rather in relation to his *Discourses on Livy:* freedom, republics, and peoples. Machiavelli implies or announces early in *The Prince* that he will not discuss two of these subjects. In the dedicatory letter he writes that he will discuss and give rules for the governments of princes because as one of the people he can know the nature of princes, whereas to know the nature of peoples one needs to be a prince. In Chapter II he writes that he will leave out reasoning on republics and confine himself to considering only principalities. And since we will see that by freedom he means primarily republican freedom, it would seem that freedom too would be omitted from *The Prince*. Nonetheless, freedom, republics, and peoples play a surprisingly crucial role in *The Prince* alongside princes and principalities.

Machiavelli's *Discourses* advises the peoples, leaders, reformers, and founders of republics on how to order republics to preserve their freedom. It not only reasons about republics, but recommends them over principalities and praises peoples over princes. Machiavelli writes there that "a people is more prudent, more stable, and of better judgment than a prince," that "governments of peoples are better than those of princes," and that "the people will be seen to be by far superior [to princes] in goodness and in glory." He argues there that "the common good is not observed if not in republics," whereas "the contrary happens when there is a prince." He concludes that "a republic has greater life and has good fortune longer than a principality."[1] It has often been wondered how the author of the *Discourses* could at about the same time

---

1. Niccolò Machiavelli, *Discourses on Livy,* trans. Harvey C. Mansfield and Nathan Tarcov (Chicago: University of Chicago Press, 1996), I 58.3, II 2.1, III 9.2. All citation to this work are by book, chapter, and paragraph numbers in this edition.

also write *The Prince*, which is notorious for advising princes to destroy republics and deprive their peoples of freedom.

The Prince, however, does not explicitly endorse principalities over republics, as the *Discourses* explicitly recommends republics over principalities. Indeed republican political philosophers such as Spinoza and Rousseau claimed that *The Prince* is a republican book addressed to free peoples. Spinoza wrote in his *Political Treatise:*

> But what means a prince, whose sole motive is lust of mastery, should use to establish and maintain his dominion, the most ingenious Machiavelli has set forth at large in his book called *Il Principe* or *The Prince*, but with what design one can hardly be sure. . . . [H]e perhaps wished to show how cautious a free multitude should be of entrusting its welfare absolutely to one man, who, unless in his vanity he thinks he can please everybody, must be in daily fear of plots, and so is forced to look chiefly after his own interest, and, as for the multitude, rather to plot against it than consult its good. And I am the more led to this opinion concerning that most far-seeing man, because it is known that he was favorable to freedom, for the maintenance of which he has besides given the most wholesome advice.[2]

Similarly, Rousseau in *The Social Contract* writes of Machiavelli that "while pretending to give lessons to Kings, he gave great ones to the people. Machiavelli's *The Prince* is the book of republicans." To those remarks he adds the following explanation in a footnote: "Machiavelli was a decent man and a good citizen; but being attached to the Medici household, he was forced, during the oppression of his fatherland, to disguise his love for freedom."[3] My reading of *The Prince* may help to explain how Spinoza and Rousseau could say such things about that book, even if it will not vindicate everything they say about it.

The dedicatory letter of *The Prince* addresses young Lorenzo de Medici as a prince. Lorenzo was the grandson of Lorenzo the Magnificent, who had dominated the Florentine republic from 1469 to his death in 1492, the year of the younger Lorenzo's birth, and he was the son of Piero II, who was overthrown in 1494, since which time the family had been in exile. Machiavelli, born in 1469, the year of the beginning of the elder Lorenzo's rule, had served in various diplomatic and bureaucratic posts in the Florentine republic from 1498 to 1512, when a Spanish and papal army restored Medici rule, and he had been dismissed, arrested, imprisoned, and tortured the next year as a suspected conspirator against the Medici regime. Shortly after the Medici family's return

---

2. *The Chief Works of Benedict De Spinoza*, trans. R. H. M. Elwes (New York: Dover, 1955), *Political Treatise*, Chapter V end, p. 315.

3. Jean-Jacques Rousseau, *Collected Writings*, ed. Roger D. Masters and Christopher Kelly (Hanover, NH: University Press of New England, 1994), vol. 4, p. 177, *Social Contract* III 6.

to power in Florence, the twenty-year-old Lorenzo had been installed by his uncle Pope Leo X as the effectual ruler of what was still nominally a republic in Florence. Machiavelli's addressing Lorenzo as a prince is in part a gesture of respect to the pretensions of the Medici family. Leo X arranged for his brother Giuliano to marry a French princess and obtain the title of Duke of Nemours in 1516 when Machiavelli had still planned to dedicate the book to Giuliano; henceforth the family considered themselves royalty and never married below that level.[4] Nonetheless, Leo prudently shrank from offending the republican passion of the Florentines by giving Lorenzo the title of Duke of Florence and left Florence formally a republic.[5] Machiavelli's addressing Lorenzo as a prince is therefore also an exposure of the effectual princely truth behind the imaginary Florentine republic.

The dedicatory letter declares that the book is intended to convey Machiavelli's "knowledge of the actions of great men" and to "discuss and give rules for the governments of princes."[6] The book thus not only is addressed to a prince (albeit that of a nominal republic), but has princes for its primary subject matter, though "great men" may be a wider category than princes, including captains, prophets, and even the leaders of republics. Machiavelli writes that his daring to discuss and give rules for the government of princes should not be reputed presumption on his part as a man of low and mean estate because to know well "the nature of princes" one needs to be of the people, just as to know well "the nature of peoples" one needs to be a prince. This claim suggests that princes and peoples are fundamentally different by nature, that to be a prince one has to have a princely nature lacking among the people, but that both natures naturally lack self-knowledge, which can be supplied only artificially through those possessing the opposite nature. One would expect Machiavelli therefore as a professed man of low estate to be lacking in knowledge of the nature of peoples.

This view of the kinds of knowledge possessed by princes and peoples hardly goes without saying. It might have been thought on the contrary that princes come to know other princes with whom they deal but lack knowledge of the people from whom they are distant and who may misrepresent themselves to their princes (IX 42, XVII 66), and that members of the people know other members of the people with whom they

---

4. Ferdinand Schevill, *The Medici* (Harper: New York, 1960), 189.
5. Ibid., pp. 190–91.
6. All quotations and parenthetical citations from *The Prince* are from the translation by Harvey C. Mansfield (Chicago: University of Chicago Press 1985, 1998), 2d ed., giving chapter and where necessary page numbers.

deal but lack knowledge of princes from whom they are distant and who may misrepresent themselves to their peoples (XVIII 70–71).

This picture of princes and peoples as possessing different natures and kinds of knowledge is complicated rather than simply illustrated by the analogy Machiavelli gives to explain it: those who sketch landscapes place themselves in the plain to consider the nature of mountains and place themselves atop mountains to consider the nature of low places. In this analogy there are not two kinds of sketchers possessing different natures that limit their subjects but one sort who descend and ascend to understand both subjects, as if Lorenzo could descend to the popular perspective to view the nature of princes and Machiavelli could ascend to the princely perspective to view that of peoples. Such descent and ascent is not always purely in thought: some princes lose their states, and some men of low and mean estate climb high; the first example in Chapter I is Francesco Sforza, who became a prince from being a private individual (explicitly said in Chapter VII), and Chapter II refers to unnamed hereditary princes who may be deprived of their states. Princes and peoples might not be of such different natures after all, or if there are such distinct natures, they may not correspond to those individuals who happen to be princes or members of the people at any given time. Lorenzo's having been made a prince by his uncle does not necessarily mean he has the nature of a prince, and Machiavelli's low birth does not necessarily mean he lacks that nature. There might also be a third nature that understands both princes and peoples and differs from them both almost as much as sketchers differ from mountains and valleys.

Chapter I starts with a distinction of kinds among all the states and dominions that have held and do hold empire over men: between republics and principalities. The most fundamental political distinction appears to be between rule by one man and rule by more than one, overshadowing the distinction between rule by few and rule by many stressed by such writers as Aristotle. Machiavelli may take this position here only because he is addressing a prince and focusing on principalities, writing, that is, from a perspective in which the differences among republics do not figure greatly. Or he may do so because he thinks the distinction between few and many is simply less important than that between one and more or that the many never really rule.[7] In any case, he could have simply proceeded to his subdivisions of principalities without first drawing attention as he does to the republican alternative to princely rule. It is not clear how this fundamental distinction applies to

7. See *Discourses* I 16.6.

Florence. Since Machiavelli referred to Lorenzo in the dedicatory letter as a prince, Florence might really be a principality rather than the republic it formally pretended to be under the restored rule of the Medici. Alternatively, even republics might have princes, and the apparently simple distinction between principalities and republics may be more complex than it seems.

The answer to the first question raised by the title of Chapter I (how many kinds of principalities there are) at first appears to be that there are two kinds (hereditary and new) or rather three (hereditary, altogether new, and new additions to hereditary states). Machiavelli offers Francesco Sforza's rule over Milan as the example of an altogether new principality and the king of Spain's acquisition of the kingdom of Naples in 1504 as that of a member added to a hereditary principality. Sforza stands in relation to the distinction between republics and principalities much as the landscape sketchers in the dedicatory letter do in relation to the distinction between princes and peoples. Sforza became Duke of Milan in 1450 by overthrowing the republic that ruled there after the death of Duke Filippo Visconti in 1447:[8] states are not necessarily permanently republics or principalities.

Machiavelli turns to the second question raised by the title of Chapter I, the modes by which principalities are acquired. The first distinction he makes is between dominions accustomed to living under a prince and those used to being free, a distinction already implied by the examples of Naples and Milan and highly relevant to the case of Lorenzo's Florence. Machiavelli's choice of terms indicates that dominions living under princes are not free; only republics are free. This is the first mention of freedom in the book. It indicates that being free means not living under a prince. The distinction seems equivalent to the initial distinction between republics and principalities.

Machiavelli begins Chapter II, "Of Hereditary Principalities," by saying he will "leave out reasoning on republics" because he has "reasoned on them at length another time" (in the *Discourses*) and will address himself instead "only to the principality." We have just seen, however, that republics play at least the background role of one kind of state acquired by some principalities. And in this very chapter, when Machiavelli illustrates the ease with which hereditary principalities resist external attacks owing to the love and good will of their subjects, he gives as his example the ability of the Duke of Ferrara to withstand the attacks of the Venetians and of Pope Julius II. "The Venetians" are of course the Vene-

8. See Chapter XII and Niccolò Machiavelli, *Florentine Histories*, trans. Laura A. Banfield and Harvey C. Mansfield (Princeton: Princeton University Press, 1988), VI 17–24. References to this work are by book and chapter numbers in this edition.

tian republic. (Machiavelli's use of such plurals as "the Venetians," "the Florentines," and "the Romans" rather than "Venice," "Florence," and "Rome" throughout the work indicates when he is writing about republics.) The first mention in the book of a particular republic is as a force attacking and resisted by a hereditary prince. Machiavelli says here that a hereditary prince of ordinary industry may, however, be deprived of his state by "an extraordinary and excessive force," but he does not yet give an example of such a force.

Chapter III, "Of Mixed Principalities," opens with "a natural difficulty that is in all new principalities," that the belief that they will do better makes men take up arms against their lords only to find by experience that they have done worse owing to "another natural and ordinary necessity," that a new prince must always offend his subjects with infinite injuries. (Although Machiavelli writes here of "men" rather than peoples, he seems to be telling princes about the variability of peoples, despite his claim that to know the nature of peoples one needs to be a prince.) The result of this situation for a new prince is that he has as enemies those whom he offended in seizing the principality and he cannot keep his supporters as friends because he can neither satisfy them nor "use strong medicines" against them since he is obligated to them.

Machiavelli explains that acquisitions of the same province and language as the prince's old state may be held "with great ease," especially if they are not used to "living free." This is the second mention in the book of a city's being "free," and it too means being a republic rather than a principality. Whereas holding acquisitions that were previously republics is more difficult, all that needs to be done to hold conquered principalities of the same province and language is eliminate their princely bloodlines and not alter their laws or taxes, for when their old conditions are maintained, "men live quietly." Although Machiavelli again writes of "men," he again seems to mean peoples and indicates they care more about the continuity of their laws and taxes than about that of the bloodlines of their princely rulers. Peoples seem to love hereditary princes only passively: as long as they are around, peoples may recur to them, but once they have been eliminated, so long as the old laws and taxes are maintained peoples have no desire for revenge against whoever eliminated them.

Machiavelli offers five remedies to the prince who has acquired additions of different language, customs, and orders from his ancient state: (1) inhabiting the acquired state personally; (2) sending colonies; (3) defending the less powerful; (4) weakening the powerful; and (5) preventing another powerful foreigner from entering the province. He discusses the entrance of a powerful foreigner into a province in such a way that the reader cannot tell whether he is discussing the entrance of the foreign prince he is advising or that of a potential competitor. He offers the example of the Aetolians' bringing "the Romans" into Greece. It is not clear, therefore, whether this first introduction of the Romans is as an example of a foreign competitor or of the prince being advised, in which case the prince he is advising is a republic.[9] After discussing how a powerful foreigner who enters a province attracts and limits the lesser powers and uses them to put down the more powerful, Machiavelli returns to the example of the Romans, who "observed these policies well in the provinces they took" and did "what all wise princes should do." Machiavelli began Chapter II by saying he would leave out reasoning about republics, but by Chapter III he offers the ancient Roman republic as the model for "wise princes."

As model wise princes, the leaders of the Roman republic used all their industry to remedy not only present but future troubles. In affairs of state, as in medicine, evils are easy to cure early when they are difficult to know (which is possible only for someone prudent), but difficult to cure later when they are easy for everyone to know. The superiority of a "prudent one" over "everyone" would be at odds with the praise of a republic over a principality unless well-ordered republics like Rome are so ordered as to have everyone follow the leadership of a prudent one. The Romans remedied evils in advance since they knew war is deferred only to the advantage of others: they fought Philip and Antiochus in Greece so as not to have to fight them later in Italy. They recognized that the best defense is a good offense, and this policy taken to its logical conclusion leads to world conquest, as the example of the Roman republic shows.

Having put forward the Roman republic or its leaders as the model of doing "what all wise princes should do" in acquiring and maintaining additions to their country, Machiavelli puts forward a monarch, Louis XII of France, as the model of error and failure. Machiavelli examines the causes of Louis's second loss of Milan in the light of the available remedies and the Romans' wise application of them. Machiavelli begins surprisingly, however, by defending Louis's sharing Lombardy with the Venetians, an apparent violation of the rule to weaken rather than strengthen the powerful, an action he says should not be blamed since it was necessary so as to enter Italy. Unlike the ancient Romans, the modern Venetian republic can be safely strengthened by another prince. Not all re-

9. The Aetolians brought the Romans into Greece in 211 B.C., when Rome was a republic; see Livy XXVI 24. Machiavelli adds here that the Romans were brought in by the inhabitants of every province they entered; for more details see *Discourses* II 1.3, which explicitly refers back to *The Prince*.

publics are equally dangerous to monarchs or equally deserving of being models for wise princes.[10]

In Chapter IV Machiavelli distinguishes between principalities governed by a prince and his servants, which are difficult to acquire but easy to hold, and principalities governed by a prince and hereditary barons with their own states and subjects, which are easy to acquire but difficult to hold. He puts forward "the Romans" as the model of those who succeeded not only in acquiring but eventually in securely possessing states with many hereditary lords such as Spain, France, and Greece.[11] Again he means the leaders of the Roman republic, at least as regards the initial acquisition of Spain, France, and Greece, though the Romans may have become "secure possessors of them" as Machiavelli says only "with the power and long duration of the empire," i.e., only after the republic gave way to the empire.[12] The ancient Roman republic, which succeeded in eliminating the bloodlines and even the memory of many hereditary princes and lords, appears to be the prime example of an "extraordinary and excessive force" that deprives hereditary princes of their states invoked but not yet exemplified in Chapter II.[13] By saying that "when they later fought among themselves, each took for himself a part of those provinces in accordance with the authority he had got within it," Machiavelli alludes to the civil wars that ended the Roman republic and occasionally disturbed the empire.[14] A republic of the Roman model excels in acquiring an empire that in turn threatens its republican character: Machiavelli prepares the reader for the eventual abandonment of the Roman republic as the model for princes in *The Prince.*

The republican meaning of freedom implied by the distinction in Chapter I between dominions accustomed to living under a prince and those used to being free is confirmed in the exploration of that distinction in Chapter V. The title explicitly mentions only "cities or principalities which lived by their own laws," not republics or free cities, but

10. For a fuller interpretation of Chapter III see my "Machiavelli and the Foundations of Modernity: A Reading of Chapter 3 of *The Prince,*" in *Educating the Prince: Essays in Honor of Harvey Mansfield,* ed. Mark Blitz and William Kristol (Lanham, Md.: Rowman & Littlefield, 2000), pp. 30–44.

11. The example of Greece implicitly raises the issue of republics in another way since it consists mainly in republics rather than hereditary principalities, as is admitted in the next chapter.

12. Sulla put down the last major rebellion in Greece during the Mithridatic War; Caesar put down the last great rebellion of "France," as Machiavelli calls ancient Gaul.

13. In Chapter III Machiavelli did not yet say that the Romans eliminated the bloodlines of the previous rulers. That policy was recommended explicitly only in the case of additions of the same language and customs, whereas the Romans were held up as models in connection with additions of different language, customs, and orders.

14. See *Discourses* II 4.1, III 24.

the first sentence refers to them as states "accustomed to living by their own laws and in freedom." (The presence of principalities in the title obscures the chapter's republican subject.) The title's use of "living by their own laws" without mention of being free may suggest that living by their own laws is equivalent to being free or not living under a prince or being a republic. But the pairing of "living by their own laws and in freedom" in the first sentence suggests that these two are distinct, that the meaning of freedom is not exhausted by living under their own laws, though they may be so closely connected that they are not likely to be found separately. The contrast between living by their own laws and living under a prince could mean either (a) that the laws states under a prince live by are not truly their own (made by them) but the laws of their prince or (b) that states under a prince do not truly live by laws but rather by the arbitrary will of their prince. In other words, it is not clear whether the emphasis is on "their own" or on "laws," whether republican freedom is being connected with autonomy or with rule by law. (The ambiguity is, so to speak, clearer in the original: English translations can hardly avoid emphasizing alternative (a) above by rendering the *suis* of the Latin in the title or the *loro* of the Italian in the chapter as "their own" rather than simply as "their.")

One mode by which a prince may seek to hold states accustomed to living by their own laws and in freedom is to "let them live by their own laws, taking tribute from them and creating within them an oligarchical state." This is shortly afterward referred to, in the cases of Spartan and Roman efforts to hold Greece, as "making it free and leaving it its own laws." Being free and living under a prince seem therefore not to be incompatible after all. The republican meaning of freedom as not living under a prince might be preserved, however, not by pointing to the curious fact that the acquiring "princes" in this case were the Spartan and Roman republics, but by distinguishing between a state's being subject to a foreign power while retaining its internal republican government and therefore remaining in this crucial sense "free," and a state's being subject to internal princely government and therefore in this sense ceasing to be free. Being free in this republican sense would then be compatible with submitting to foreign rule in certain respects, including paying tribute and presumably accepting direction in foreign policy (being "friendly" to the foreign prince and "doing everything to maintain" him), so long as the state is administered by its own citizens and lives by its own laws. Being free in this republican sense does not seem to require internal *democratic* rule; internal oligarchical rule is also free; only internal princely rule seems excluded.

This distinction between internal republican freedom and independence from foreign direction proves, however, to be slippery. The chief point stressed in Chapter V turns out to be that leaving it internally free is not a secure mode of holding a state accustomed to being free. Republican freedom spurs a city also to reject foreign servitude. The inhabitants of republics never forget the name of freedom or their ancient orders "either through length of time or because of benefits received." The appeal of freedom does not rest simply on a comparison of the benefits received under it and under servitude. States used to living under their own princes are thereby also prepared to obey a foreign ruler because they do not "know how to live free." Freedom seems to depend on a kind of knowledge gained through experience of freedom in a sort of virtuous circle.

Machiavelli writes here that a city accustomed to living free has as a refuge the "name" of freedom, which is never forgotten unless the inhabitants are dispersed. His putting this point in terms of the "name" of freedom leads us to ask whether this unforgettable freedom so beloved of republican cities is a mere name. The only uses of the word "name" *(nome)* in the book besides these two here connected with "freedom" are the eight mentions of a name for liberality (4), or for meanness (3), or for rapacity (1) in Chapter XVI, and the four mentions of a name for cruelty in Chapter XVII, all of which mean merely a reputation for these virtues or vices as distinguished from their reality, and most of which assert that princes should not care about such names. We may wonder similarly whether the name of freedom that animates republics is distinct from the reality, or even whether freedom possesses a reality for Machiavelli. Republican peoples may imagine that they are free, failing to realize that they are always commanded by princes one way or another; they may imagine that they love freedom for its own sake rather than as a means to dominion and riches.[15]

Chapter V advises conquerors of republics not to leave them under their own laws (to do so would have amounted to in some sense a pro-republican policy), but instead to destroy such cities (in an obvious sense a severely anti-republican policy) or expect to be destroyed by them, so powerful is their memory of their ancient liberty and orders, so strong are their hatred of those who deprive them of liberty, their desire for revenge, and their propensity for rebellion. The most eloquent passage in the book prior to the closing "Exhortation," this compelling tribute to the allure of republican liberty and the vitality of republican peoples only makes the accompanying advice more disturbing: how could a man who so powerfully appreciates the appeal of liberty advocate the destruc-

15. See *Discourses* II 2.1, 2.3.

tion of republics? This incongruity is mitigated insofar as the warning that republics are acquired only to be destroyed should persuade would-be conquerors to try to acquire other principalities instead, in a sense a pro-republican policy, but such warnings are not always effective.[16] It cannot be completely excused on the grounds that any conqueror who disregards this implicit warning and conquers a republic anyway would also disregard this advice to destroy them, or that conquerors willing to destroy the republics they conquer would do so without this advice.[17] Machiavelli's praise here of the longevity of republican orders might, however, suggest to a prince who wanted to hold his state after his death that he turn it into a republic, and Chapter V finally concludes that the most secure way to hold republics is to eliminate them *or live in them*. By recommending the destruction of republics, Machiavelli may have re-assured Lorenzo that his literary adviser is free from republican parti-sanship as well as from moral scruple, while frightening him with the prospect of having to destroy the only state he possesses, but Machiavelli now lets him breathe a sigh of relief on learning that a prince who in-habits such a city does not have to destroy it.[18]

Chapter V violates Machiavelli's announced exclusion of reasoning about republics not only by discussing how to hold conquered repub-lics but also, like the two preceding chapters, by putting forward the Ro-man republic as the model of success in holding onto acquisitions, in this case other republics. All the examples of conquering princes in the chapter are republics: the Spartans, the Romans, and the Florentines. The superior longevity of republics was no match for the extraordinari-ly powerful and long-lasting Roman republic. Whereas a prince who is only one man can go to live in only one city, as the Turkish sultan went to live in Greece, a republic can send colonies of its citizens to many oth-er cities (III 10–12). The tension between the Roman republic and the liberty of other republics is indicated by the asymmetry between "a city" accustomed to living free and "cities or provinces" used to living under a prince, which suggests that republican freedom belongs not to whole provinces as such but only to single cities; republican cities under the sway of another republican city in their province are not free but in "ser-

16. In his *Florentine Histories* Machiavelli has some of the Florentine signori beg Wal-ter of Brienne, the Duke of Athens, not to try to enslave Florence. They warn him about the power of the desire for and memory of freedom, but these warnings do not dissuade the duke from making himself tyrant, though they are amply vindicated by his being over-thrown in a general revolt ten months later (II 34–36).

17. Cf. Leo Strauss, *Thoughts on Machiavelli* (Glencoe, Ill.: Free Press, 1958), p. 82.

18. When I served on the Policy Planning Staff of the Department of State in 1981–82, I heard it said jocularly that the typical policy memo proposed three options: full-scale nu-clear attack, immediate surrender, or the continuation of present policies.

vitude," as Pisa was to the Florentines.[19] The subjection of Greece, the test case in ancient times for the different modes of holding republics, to the absolute rule of the Turk in modern times (III 10, IV 17–18) suggests the weakness of republican liberty after the elimination of its memory under the Roman Empire. The memory of the liberty and orders of the ancient Greek republics was not, of course, literally eliminated, but rather preserved by the Greek and even the Roman writers, whom Machiavelli has continuously read, and his own praise of ancient liberty helps to revive that memory.

Despite the claim in the dedicatory letter that only princes can know the nature of peoples, Machiavelli in Chapter V seems to discuss the nature of peoples or rather the different natures of republican and monarchical peoples. He does not, however, present these differences as natural but writes repeatedly here (as in Chapters I and III) of a city's being "accustomed to" or "used to" living free or under a prince, indicating the power of habit or historical experience.[20] He does not say how long an experience of republican government is required to attach a city so strongly to liberty or how long an experience of princely rule is required to make it incapable of freedom, but he gives the impression that no experience of princely rule would be sufficient to erase the effects of republican government. It may therefore be possible to revive the memory of ancient liberty in cities or provinces that once were free but have become used to living under a prince and no longer know how to live free.[21]

Chapter VI, "Of New Principalities That Are Acquired through One's Own Arms and Virtue," recommends the imitation especially of "new princes," who introduce new orders and modes to found their new states, of whom the most excellent are Moses, Cyrus, Romulus, Theseus, and the like. According to the *Discourses*, even though Romulus' end was to found a kingdom not a republic, he made many and good laws conforming to free life, his orders were more conformable to a civil and free than to an absolute and tyrannical way of life, and his actions and orders were necessary to maintain or create a republic or a free way of living.[22] In short, one of the top models held up for princes to imitate in *The Prince* is the founder of a republic or at least of a proto-republic, indeed of that very republic itself held up in the previous three chapters

19. Servitude to a republic is the hardest, most durable, and most weakening (*Discourses* II 2.4).

20. See Niccolò Machiavelli, *Il Principe,* ed. Manfredo Vanni (Milano: Signorelli, 1968), pp. 31 n. 8 and 33 n. 7.

21. See *Discourses* I 16–18.

22. *Discourses* I 2.7, 9.2, 18.5, 49.1, III 1.2

as the model for wise princes to imitate. Theseus' Athens similarly became the conquering republic mentioned in Chapter V, whereas Cyrus turned a quasi-republican monarchy into an absolute one, and Moses founded a republic with ecclesiastical and theocratic elements that later became a hereditary human monarchy.

In the course of Chapter VI's discussion of the difficulties new princes have in acquiring their principalities, Machiavelli emphasizes the difficulty posed by "the incredulity of men, who do not truly believe in new things unless they come to have a firm experience of them." New princes must therefore be able to use force because, Machiavelli writes, "the nature of peoples is variable; and it is easy to persuade them of something, but difficult to keep them in that persuasion." Although in the dedicatory letter Machiavelli wrote that to know the nature of peoples one needs to be a prince, now he writes precisely and explicitly (just as earlier he did vaguely or implicitly) about "the nature of peoples" as if he were a prince. What sort of prince could he be? I believe it is no accident that he writes explicitly of "the nature of peoples" for the first time in this chapter about "new princes," suggesting that he may be a kind of founder who introduces new orders and modes.[23]

My suggestion that princes are urged by Machiavelli in *The Prince* to imitate a republic or the founder of a republic differs from the suggestions of Spinoza and Rousseau that peoples are urged by Machiavelli's *Prince* to institute republics rather than principalities, in that it accepts the surface appearance that *The Prince* is addressed to a prince. It is easy enough to see why peoples might want to live in republics rather than principalities, especially if princes are the way Machiavelli describes them in *The Prince*. But it is more difficult to see why princes should want to imitate republics or the founders of republics, especially if princes are the way Machiavelli describes them in *The Prince*.

Machiavelli advises princes how to maintain their states and their glory not only during the long life they hope for but also after their death. In Chapter II it seems as if this is best ensured by a hereditary principality, which a prince can maintain merely by following the order of his ancestors without any need for extraordinary virtue as long as he also does not have any extraordinary vices. Even if he is deprived of it by an extraordinary force, he can reacquire it if the new acquirer slips up. The reacquisition may not necessarily be by the prince himself but may be by his family after his death, as is indicated by the advice Machiavelli gives in the next chapter to those who acquire such a hereditary principality to eliminate the prince's bloodline. Hereditary principalities have that

23. Compare *Discourses* I Preface.

advantage in serving the prince's goal of maintaining his state and glory after his death: his bloodline can continue in the principality after his death or even reacquire it if he has lost it so that others have to kill not only him but his whole family to deprive him of his state and glory. In Chapter IV, a prince's sharing the government with a hereditary nobility that can rebel and restore his old state even when his bloodline is eliminated by a new acquirer seems to offer a greater advantage in maintaining his state and glory, though as we saw, even this advantage was overcome by the Roman republic, which wiped out all the noble families. In Chapter V we finally saw that the durability and vitality of republics offer the princes who found them the greatest advantage of all in preserving their state and glory, though even this advantage was canceled by the super republic of Rome, which conquered, destroyed, and securely held many other republics.

This review of the first chapters of *The Prince* reveals that the book is not exclusively about principalities but reasons about republics too, albeit from the perspective of princes; that it explicitly advises princes to imitate a republic, the Roman one, in acquiring and holding other states; and that it implicitly advises princes to found republics to perpetuate their states and glory. It further suggests that the success of the Roman republic in wiping out not only principalities and princely families but also other republics, which eventually undermined its own republican freedom, may be part of the reason why it is necessary for Machiavelli both to revive the memory of ancient freedom and to move beyond the Roman republican model. I will treat more briefly some of the passages in later chapters dealing with freedom, republics, and peoples.

Whereas Chapters VI and VII treat new principalities acquired respectively by one's own arms and virtue and by others' arms and fortune, Chapters VIII and IX deal with two additional modes by which private individuals become princes: either through crime or through the support of their fellow citizens. Machiavelli says these modes should not be left out even though "one of them can be reasoned about more amply where republics are treated" (referring again to the *Discourses*). Becoming prince through the support of one's fellow citizens is the obvious but not the only one of these modes that pertains to republics: the examples in Chapter VIII of private individuals who became princes through crime—Agathocles and Oliverotto da Fermo—indicate that the crime Machiavelli has in mind is that of violently destroying a republic or taking away "the freedom of their fatherland" (36). Perhaps that is what makes it a crime for Machiavelli, and part of what distinguishes cruelty badly used from cruelty well used.

The destruction of the liberty of Fermo was accomplished through a combination of Oliverotto's own sense that it was "servile to be at the level of others" and the sense of certain citizens of Fermo who aided him that "servitude was dearer than the freedom of their fatherland." Freedom is threatened both by those who want something more than freedom (to rule as prince), for whom equal freedom seems like servitude, and by those who prefer something less than freedom (servitude to a prince who allows them to acquire favor). The preservation of freedom requires citizens for whom the freedom of their fatherland is most dear and for whom equality does not appear servile. It requires as well ways to deal with those whose aspirations are too high or too low.

Chapter IX is entitled "Of the Civil Principality": this ambiguous term for the rule of a prince who comes to power through the support of his fellow citizens seems to indicate a kind of state in between a republic and a principality, an elective principality despite the first sentence of Chapter I, which indicates that all states have been or are either republics or principalities. Toward the end of this chapter Machiavelli further distinguishes a "civil order" from an "absolute" one on the basis of whether the princes command by means of magistrates or by themselves. Most of the chapter concerns the distinction between coming to power with the support of the people and with the support of the great, "two diverse humors" found in every city. Machiavelli explains that "one cannot satisfy the great with decency [or honesty, *onestà*] and without injury to others, but one can satisfy the people; for the end of the people is more decent [or honest] than that of the great, since the great want to oppress and the people want not to be oppressed." Unlike the great, the people love freedom. In calling this end more decent, Machiavelli seems to side with, and urge would-be "civil princes" to side with, the people as opposed to the great. And since the aim of the great (to command and oppress the people) would seem to be shared by princes, he seems also to side implicitly with the people as opposed to princes. But from the pen of Machiavelli writing as an adviser to a prince, a declaration of the greater decency or honesty of the aim of the people is not necessarily a judgment of their superiority. He may mean primarily instead that the people themselves consider their aim more decent or honest than that of the great: the people make a claim to a kind of superiority, moral superiority.

Machiavelli says here that from "these two diverse appetites" of the people and of the great arise one of three effects: "principality, freedom, or license." He explains how principality is caused by their various interactions, but he does not explain how freedom or license arises or how those two effects are distinguished. The simplest (and most democratic) interpretation would be to say that freedom results when the people succeed in not being commanded or oppressed by the great, whereas license results when the great succeed in commanding and oppressing the people.[24] There may, however, be a significant distinction between being commanded and being oppressed: freedom may be the result when the people are commanded but not oppressed by the great (a compromise or mixture of the appetites of the two humors), whereas democratic or oligarchic license results when the people are neither commanded nor oppressed or both commanded and oppressed by the great. Machiavelli does not say whether peoples want not to be commanded or oppressed for the sake of freedom or for other goods, but in Chapter XXV he writes of "the end that each has before him, that is glories and riches," omitting freedom. The people may love freedom only for the sake of dominion or riches.[25]

In Chapter X the free cities of modern Germany, republics again, are presented as the model. They are free even though they are nominally subject to the German emperor because in fact they obey him only when they want to.[26] Unlike the ancient Roman republic in Chapters III–V, however, they are presented as the model for princes who are under the necessity of taking refuge behind walls because they cannot put together an army to fight a battle in the field against an enemy who comes to attack them. Modern republics are weaker than ancient ones, above all the Roman republic.

Chapter XI discusses ecclesiastical principalities, which like "civil principalities" are elective but seem to differ from "civil principalities" not only in being ecclesiastical rather than civil but also in being absolute rather than civil.

After discussing in the first eleven chapters all the kinds of principalities, including some that emerge from or even still resemble republics, Machiavelli turns to offense and defense starting in Chapter XII. He explains there that "because there cannot be good laws where there are not good arms, and where there are good arms there must be good laws, I shall leave out the reasoning on laws and shall speak of arms." This gives the reader the impression that good arms are the necessary and sufficient condition of good laws, but these correlations could just as easily result were good laws the necessary and sufficient condition of good arms. Machiavelli sticks to this avowal that he will leave out the reasoning on laws about as well as he did to those that he would leave out discussing the nature of peoples and reasoning about republics. He condemns the sin of reliance on mercenary arms and warns that virtu-

---

24. The other non-metaphorical uses of "license" in the book all concern the soldiers' oppression of the people (XVII 68, XIX 77, 80; the metaphorical use applies to Fortune as a river, XXV 98).

25. See *Discourses* II 2.1, 2.3.   26. See *Discourses* II 19.2.

ous mercenary captains either oppress you or oppress others contrary to your intention, whereas nonvirtuous mercenary captains ruin you "in the ordinary way" (by losing). He replies to the objection that all captains do this by explaining the following: "Arms have to be employed either by a prince or by a republic. The prince should go in person, and perform himself the office of captain. The republic has to send its citizens, and when it sends one who does not turn out to be a worthy man, it must change him; and if he is, it must check him with laws so that he does not step out of bounds." This is the only time in *The Prince* an issue is explicitly considered from the perspective of republics. Machiavelli considers the issue therefore with an eye not only to a republic's military success but also to the preservation of its internal freedom, its not being brought to obey one of its citizens (as he here delicately puts its becoming a principality). The key to good arms for a republic turns out to be good laws, checking its worthy captains with laws so they do not step out of bounds and threaten its freedom.[27] The examples Machiavelli gives in Chapter XII are all of republics: Rome, Sparta, the Swiss, the Carthaginians, the Thebans, and the Milanese (during the brief period of republican rule between the Visconti and Sforzas).[28] He uses republics to exemplify both disastrous reliance on mercenaries and successful combination of freedom and military strength: no example is given of a prince who serves as his own captain, as if princes were expected rather to imitate the example of armed republics.

Perhaps the most famous passage in *The Prince* is the statement in Chapter XV that "Many have imagined republics and principalities that have never been seen or known to exist in truth," whereas "it is necessary to a prince, if he wants to maintain himself, to learn to be able not to be good, and to use and not use it according to necessity." Machiavelli does not explain why he mentions imaginary *republics* here if his concern is only with what it is necessary for a prince in a principality to learn and to do, but in earlier chapters he has held up the Roman republic as a model for princes. This mention of imagined republics is the last explicit use of the term "republic" in the book, and the final chapter invokes freedom only in the non-republican sense of freedom from foreign domination.[29]

27. On the role of law and arms in *The Prince* see my "Law and Innovation in Machiavelli's *Prince*," in *Enlightening Revolutions*, ed. Stéphane Douard and Svetozar Minkov (Lanham, Md.: Lexington Books, 2005), pp. 75–88, and "Arms and Politics in Machiavelli's *Prince*," in *Entre Kant et Kosovo: Études offertes à Pierre Hassner*, ed. Anne-Marie Le Gloannec and Aleksander Smolar (Paris: Presses de Sciences Po, 2003), pp. 109–21.

28. See also XIII 57.

29. Most of the subsequent references to Rome and the Romans are non-republican: XVI 64 (Caesar); XIX (the emperors); XXV (papal Rome). Only XXI 89–90 and XXIV 97 refer to the republic's actions in Greece as in III–V, but here they are no longer held up as

Machiavelli gives princes advice in Chapters XV to XIX on how to deal with subjects and friends. Chapter XVI, "Of Liberality and Parsimony," recommends that a prince employ what is usually considered stinginess rather than what is usually considered liberality, because by this means "he comes to use liberality with all those from whom he does not take, who are infinite, and meanness with all those to whom he does not give, who are few." Similarly Chapter XVII, "Of Cruelty and Mercy, and Whether It Is Better to Be Loved Than Feared, or the Contrary," recommends that a prince use well what is usually held to be cruelty "because with very few examples [of cruel punishments] he will be more merciful than those who for the sake of too much mercy allow disorders to continue, from which come killings or robberies; for these customarily hurt a whole community but the executions that come from the prince hurt one particular person." In both cases Machiavelli recommends that princes use virtues or vices that are good for the many or the people though harmful to the few. Though Machiavelli no longer holds up the model of the Roman republic or even mentions republics, he recommends to princes quasi-republican or populist policies resembling the policy recommended to the would-be civil prince of Chapter IX, that he seek the support of the people rather than the great. There seems to be a coincidence of interests between princes and peoples.

Chapter XVIII, "In What Mode Faith Should Be Kept by Princes," casts further light on the meaning of the claim in the dedicatory letter that to know well the nature of princes one needs to be of the people. "Everyone sees how you appear, few touch what you are," and "the vulgar are taken in by the appearance and the outcome of a thing." The people seem to be deceived by and about princes. The people see how princes appear rather than how they are, but that may be precisely the knowledge princes lack and need to learn from one of the people, the knowledge of how they appear or need to appear to the people: as "all mercy [or piety], all faith, all honesty, all humanity, all religion. And nothing is more necessary to appear to have than this last quality." The need to have this appearance in such contrast to their true natures is a crucial component of the conjunction of the nature of princes with the nature of peoples. To return to the dedicatory letter's analogy of those who sketch landscapes, what one sees by looking at princes from the

---

the model: XXI shows that despite the Roman efforts described in III, the Aetolians who invited them into Greece later invited Antiochus; XXIV holds up as a model instead the Philip of Macedon who fought against them in Greece. The weaker modern republics of the Venetians and the Florentines continue to appear negatively: the Venetians in XX 84–85, XXI 90, XXV 100; the Florentines in XVII 65 and XIX 91. Freedom ceases to be used in its republican sense: XIX 74, XXIII 94, XXVI title.

perspective of peoples is how high they appear, like mountains viewed from plains. The necessary apparent lofty elevation of princes is derived from the high standards of the people, their demands for an appearance of mercy, faith, honesty, humanity, and above all religion. In this respect, peoples appear to be higher than princes. Conversely, one sees how low peoples are or appear from the perspective of princes, especially those in need. In quiet times a prince sees everyone promising that they would die for him, but he finds it otherwise in adverse times (IX 42). From the perspective of Machiavelli, who climbs up and down to look at both parties from both perspectives, who sees how they misrepresent themselves to each other and how they really are, they may both appear low in their selfishness and high in their aspirations, princes for glory and peoples for morality.

The quasi-republican or populist recommendations in Chapters XVI and XVII that princes side with the people or the many rather than with the few are substantially qualified in Chapter XIX, "Of Avoiding Contempt and Hatred." Machiavelli here praises France as "among the well-ordered and governed kingdoms in our times," with "infinite good institutions on which the liberty and security of the king depend," including the parlement, which beats down the great and favors the popular side (74–75). The king thereby satisfies the people's hatred for the great but secures only his own liberty. The general rule, however, turns out not to be to side with people rather than with the great but to side with whatever group is most powerful: the example is the Roman Empire (not the republic) when the soldiers were more powerful than the people and so the emperors had to let the soldiers, once corrupted, vent their avarice and cruelty on the people (76–81). There is no necessary coincidence of interests between princes and peoples. But this shocking development does not last long. In Chapter XX, "Whether Fortresses and Many Other Things Which Are Made Every Day Are Useful or Useless," Machiavelli advises princes to arm their subjects and do without fortresses, in effect leaving the prince at the mercy of the people. This is not, however, a trap to overthrow the prince and replace him with a republic but a way of compelling him or advising him to compel himself to act in a quasi-republican way. While Chapter XIX teaches princes to side with the most powerful group in their circumstances, even if it is corrupt and its satisfaction requires injuring the people, Chapter XX teaches them to create circumstances in which the people is the most powerful group, a quasi-republic, so that their interests coincide with those of the people.

Why does Machiavelli indicate he will not discuss the nature of peoples and say he will not reason about republics in *The Prince* but then do both so often? The answers in the two cases are quite different. He says only that to discuss the nature of princes one needs to be a prince, leaving it to Lorenzo or the reader to infer that therefore he will not do so, on the assumption that he is not a prince. This preliminary concession allows him to discuss and regulate the government of princes without the appearance of presumption, but it turns out instead, once he goes on to discuss the nature of peoples, to be an indication of his own princely nature. He offers Lorenzo a division of labor in which each party has its expertise, the high party about the low subject and the low party about the high subject, but the reader able to discern what others understand discovers Machiavelli's superiority.[30] The promise not to discuss republics, in contrast, is designed to conceal Machiavelli's republican leanings at least until the diligent reader comes to see how founding a republic, quasi-republic, or proto-republic may be conducive to princely glory.

I cannot leave the subject of freedom in *The Prince* having spoken only of political freedom without having said anything about two other kinds of freedom. The first is the freedom a prudent prince gives to wise men to speak the truth to him (XXIII), perhaps best exemplified by the republican prince Philipoemen, who reasoned with his friends, listened to their opinions, gave his own, and supported it with reasons (XIV). This is the freedom masterfully enjoyed by Machiavelli himself,[31] though exercised only with restraint in writing *The Prince*. The second is the freedom of human beings from Fortune, God, or nature. Machiavelli starts Chapter XXV, "How Much Fortune Can Do in Human Affairs, and in What Mode It May Be Opposed," by saying that he knows "many have held and hold the opinion that worldly things are so governed by fortune and by God that men cannot correct them with their prudence, indeed that they have no remedy at all." But to preserve what he calls "our free will," he insists that Fortune (and presumably God too) leaves half our actions for us to govern. He explains this by his famous metaphor of building dikes and dams against the river of Fortune. But which half of our actions does this leave to Fortune and which half to us? One might say that the actions of men who neglect to build dikes and dams (to prepare in quiet times for stormy times) are governed by Fortune, whereas the actions of men who do so are free or governed by themselves. Though Machiavelli goes on to argue that men are so constrained by their natures that they cannot so conform their actions to

30. See Chapter XXII.

31. See, e.g., his famous letter to Francesco Vettori of December 10, 1513, in *The Prince*, ed. Mansfield, pp. 109–10.

the times, he equivocates on whether humans can change their natures: he leaves open whether they fail to do so because they simply "cannot deviate from what nature inclines them to" or because "when one has always flourished by walking on one path, he cannot be persuaded to depart from it." The latter alternative would be not nature but stupid habit, unless it is our nature to be the slaves of stupid habit. Machiavelli thereby suggests the possibility of the most radical kind of human freedom, freedom from our own natures. Such an aspiration seems limited for Machiavelli, however, to freedom to change our modes of procedure in pursuit of our ends, not freedom to choose the end each has before him, that is, glories and riches.

JOHN LOCKE
Toward a Politics of Liberty

MICHAEL P. ZUCKERT,
JESSE COVINGTON, JAMES THOMPSON

Many years ago Robert Goldwin opened his fine essay on John Locke by calling attention to Locke's identification of the two chief propositions put forward by Sir Robert Filmer: "[Filmer's] system . . . is no more than this: *That all government is absolute monarchy*. And the ground he builds on is this: *That no man is born free*" (I2). Goldwin then astutely observed: "Locke's own political teaching may be stated in opposite terms but with similar brevity, in this way: *All government is limited in its powers and exists only by consent of the governed*. And the ground Locke builds on is this: *All men are born free*."[1] One could even go farther than Goldwin does in identifying Locke with freedom; not only is the "ground" "free birth," but the "true end" of politics is the preservation of rights, among which, of course, is the right to liberty. So, for Locke the origin is free, the end is freedom, the means (limited government by consent of the governed) are free institutions.

In order to establish the true ground, means, and end as freedom, Locke felt compelled to preface his statement on free politics with a critique of the "false ground" on which Filmer built his unfree political order. Locke's widely read *Second Treatise* is thus preceded by his widely ignored *First Treatise*, a detailed examination of Filmer's *Patriarcha* and other writings. Filmer had lived through the political turmoil of the first half of the seventeenth century in England and in response had, like Hobbes, attempted to generate a theory of politics that would decisively settle the conflict over the organization of church and state. As he said in one place, he much approved of the structure Hobbes built— the absolute sovereign—but he did greatly "mislike [Hobbes's] founda-

---

1. Robert Goldwin, "John Locke," in *History of Political Philosophy*, ed. Joseph Cropsey and Leo Strauss (Chicago: University of Chicago Press, 1963), 476.

tion," the right of nature, with its accompanying doctrines of the state of nature and the social contract.[2] He has many, often astute, objections to these central Hobbesean doctrines about the initial human situation and the origin of political authority.

Hobbes goes astray, thinks Filmer, in not taking seriously enough what Scripture teaches about the origins of humanity and of political authority. Scripture does not endorse Hobbes's view of "a company of men at the very first to have been all created together without any dependency one of another, or as 'mushrooms' (fungorum more) they all on a sudden were sprung out of the earth without any obligations one to another."[3] "The Scripture teaches us otherwise," insists Filmer. "All men came by succession and generation from one man. We must not deny the truth of the history of the creation."[4]

Filmer's authority is Scripture, and the lesson it teaches is that men are not born free. What Locke considers Filmer's false ground is presented by Filmer as the scriptural ground. If Filmer is correct in his reliance on Scripture, then the real enemy Locke is facing is the authority standing behind Filmer: the Bible, especially its account of creation. Of course, Locke denies that Filmer reads the sacred texts correctly, and he thereby denies the latter's right to rely on them to ground his idea "that no man is born free." Yet fairness to Sir Robert requires that we at least attempt to understand his argument.

I. FILMER

Filmer believed he had recaptured the true scriptural doctrine about politics, a doctrine long lost in the years of Roman Catholic domination, and not even properly recovered by the Protestant Reformers.[5] A contentious fellow, he wrote against many of his contemporaries, including the counter-Reformation thinker Robert Bellarmine, who, according to Filmer, made the strongest argument he (Filmer) had ever seen for the wrong position, i.e., for the "natural liberty of the people." Filmer stated Bellarmine's argument in short compass in a passage which well may have stood as the pattern for Locke's equally brief recapitulation of Filmer: "that God hath given or ordained power is evident by Scripture; but God hath given it to no particular man, because by nature all men are equal; therefore he hath given power to the people or mul-

---

2. Sir Robert Filmer, *Patriarcha and Other Writings*, ed. Johann P. Sommerville (Cambridge: Cambridge University Press, 1991), 185.
3. Filmer, *Patriarcha and Other Writings*, 186, citing Hobbes, *De Cive*, 8.1.
4. Ibid.
5. Filmer, *Patriarcha and Other Writings*, 23.

titude."[6] Filmer agrees perfectly with the major premise of the syllogism he attributes to Bellarmine: it is evident from the Bible that God has ordained political power. However, he does not accept the minor premise that men are equal, or that "God hath given [political power] to no particular man." Bellarmine and Filmer, like most Christian political thinkers before them, are agreed that the divine ordination of political power is "evident," apparently because of the very clear statement in Paul's Letter to the Romans: "Let every person be subject to the governing authorities. For there is no authority except from God, and those that exist have been instituted by God. Therefore he who resists the authorities resists what God has appointed."[7]

The uniqueness of Filmer's political theology derives from his minor premise, or from the way he understands God's "institution of political power." That institution is contained in the "history of creation." God ordained political authority by the way he ordered the creation. The creation of man was different from that of every other living creature. "Swarms" of aquatic creatures were "brought forth"; "birds" in the plural, were created; and "living creatures after their kind" were "brought forth" and "made."[8] But man was emphatically created in the singular: one first man. Even his mate derived from him. This is "the truth of creation" that Filmer believes Hobbes, Bellarmine, and most others have denied or ignored.

Filmer sees an intention in the details of creation: just as God is the source of all creation and, as source, is superior to and rightful ruler over creation, so Adam is made the source of all humans who succeed him. God "appointed" Adam ruler by creating him alone and generating all later humans from him. Men are not equal, for from the first the later-born were subject to their living source, Adam. God, in other words, did give political power to "a particular man."[9]

Filmer's argument from the creation of Adam alone at best establishes Adam's dominion or authority over other human beings. It does not establish any claim over the rest of creation; indeed it seems to preclude

---

6. Filmer, *Patriarcha and Other Writings*, 6.
7. Romans 13:1–2, RSV; Filmer, *Patriarcha and Other Writings*, 147, 238–39.
8. Genesis 2.
9. W. M. Spellman seriously overstates the case when he asserts that "Filmer believed that Scripture and reason were in harmony, but . . . one was on safer ground in turning to the inspired word for direction" on politics (W. M. Spellman, *John Locke* [New York: St. Martin's Press, 1997]). Filmer's position is that the fundamental truths about politics are available only through the revealed account of creation. Thus the rationalist pagan authors, who had no knowledge of creation, do not supply reliable bases for understanding political authority (Filmer, *Patriarcha and Other Writings*, 14–15; *Observations upon Aristotle's Politiques*, 236).

such a claim, for if his dominion over his offspring derives from being their source, he can raise no such claim to the earth or the creatures who live upon it. To what is in effect a natural appointment to be ruler of all humans descended from him God has therefore added a positive grant to Adam of dominion over the rest of creation. Filmer finds that grant in Genesis 1:28: "And God blessed them, and God said unto them, be fruitful and multiply and replenish the earth and subdue it, and have dominion over the fish of the sea, and over the fowl of the air, and over every living thing that moveth on the earth." With this positive grant Adam becomes, in effect, owner of the earth and all that is on it. He takes dominion (under God) over the whole of creation.

Filmer's best expression of his central thought on Adam's ground of authority comes not in *Patriarcha* but in his critique of Hobbes:

[1] If God created only Adam and of a piece of him made the woman, and if by generation from them two as parts of them all mankind be propagated; [2] if *also* God gave to Adam not only the dominion over the woman and children that should issue from them [as in [1] above] but also over the whole earth to subdue it, and over all creatures on it, so that as long as Adam lived no man could claim or enjoy anything but by donation, assignation, or permission from him; [3] I wonder how the right of nature can be imagined by Mr. Hobbes, which, he saith is a liberty for "each man to use his own power as he will for preservation of his own life"; "a condition" of war of everyone against everyone, a right of every man to everything, even to one another's body.[10]

We can restate Filmer's position more formally:

Major premise: Authority is ordained by God (Romans 13);
Minor premise: Authority and property are given to Adam as progenitor and donee (Genesis 1–2);
Conclusion: Political authority naturally belongs to whoever rightly exercises the natural and donated authority of Adam, hence no man is born free of obligation to existing authority.

In relying heavily on Romans 13 Filmer's argument clearly flows in the mainstream of Christian political theology, especially Reformation theology. But that fact should not obscure the great novelties, or at least divergences, from most Christian political theology in his complete abstraction from the doctrine of the Fall. At least since Augustine's *City of God* the Fall had figured centrally in most versions of Christian political thought, but it has absolutely no role in Filmer's version: "For by appointment of God, as soon as Adam was created he was monarch of the

---

10. Filmer, *Patriarcha and Other Writings*, 187.

world . . . Adam was a King from his creation, and in the state of inno-
cency he had been governor of his children . . . Eve was subject to Adam
before he sinned."[11]

For Filmer, then, the authority relations at the core of politics are
dependent solely on creation and donation. Thus many scholars (like
W. M. Spellman or Ian Harris)[12] are quite offbase when they claim that
"original sin" was "central to Filmer's politics."[13] This, of course, is not
to say that Filmer denies original sin or the Fall, but only that it plays
no essential role in his politics. It is difficult not to speculate that the
omission of the Fall was central to Filmer's attempt to settle political life
on solid, if not unbreakable, ground. With the Reformation and the renewed emphasis on the Pauline theme of Christ's redemptive sacrifice,
the question of the ongoing significance of the Fall had become a con-
troverted one. If, as was frequently argued, politics was one consequence
of the Fall, what follows from the fact that Jesus Christ came to undo the
effects of what Adam had done?[14] By finding the ground of political authority entirely in the pre-lapsarian order, Filmer was able to deny that
the coming of Christ made any fundamental political difference, and
thus could avoid the controversies that had arisen over the significance
for politics of Christ's redemptive act. In particular, he could resist any
pressure in an antinomian direction, such as was strongly felt on the left
wing of the Reformation.

II. OUR ONLY STAR AND COMPASS

Locke will spend much of the *First Treatise* contesting the accuracy
and validity of Filmer's attempt to ground his denial of human freedom
in Scriptures, but he does concede part of Filmer's claim—that he (Filmer) attempts to build his political doctrine on Scriptures, a claim Locke
repeats many times in the *Treatise*. Although Locke has been criticized
by some for focusing exclusively on Filmer's proof-texts and thereby ig-
noring many of the latter's historical, practical, or logical arguments,
Locke is on solid ground, for the central issue is Filmer's basis for denying human freedom. It is the biblical arguments which serve that function in Filmer's system.[15]

Locke concedes that Filmer tries to rest his case on Scriptures, but he

11. Filmer, *Patriarcha and Other Writings*, 144–45.
12. Ian Harris, "The Politics of Christianity," in *Locke's Philosophy: Content and Context,*
ed. G. A. J. Rogers (Oxford/New York: Oxford University Press, 1994), 198–205.
13. Spellman, *John Locke*, 75.
14. Romans 5:17–20.
15. See Michael Zuckert, *Launching Liberalism* (Lawrence: University Press of Kansas,
2002), 137.

finds him extraordinarily unsuccessful in that attempt. Locke will show that the biblical text does not support Filmer's own conclusions; that leaves open the possibility that Locke finds the true ground for his competing claims—that man is born free, retains the right to be free, and ought to be governed in a free polity—in the Scriptures properly understood.

Locke gives us advance reason to wonder about that possibility, however. Reason, he tells us, is man's "only star and compass," i.e., the only reliable means of navigation or guidance through life.[16] Thus, we must "steer by" reason. Locke does not mention revelation as an alternative mode of steering. The alternatives to reason are "fancy and passion," which "must needs run him [man] into strange courses." Without the guidance of reason, "the imagination is always restless and suggests variety of thoughts, and the will, reason being laid aside, is ready for every extravagant project."[17] Revelation is not, then, an independent source of guidance, is not the "ground" for Locke's affirmation of freedom. Revelation either agrees with reason or it does not. If not, it is to be treated, Locke suggests, as the product of imagination and passion. Locke seems to have a view rather the reverse of the fabled stance of the Muslims who attacked Greek philosophy: if the philosophy differs from the Koran it is false, and should be suppressed as error. If it agrees with the Koran it is true, but should be suppressed as otiose.[18]

Locke seems much friendlier to revelation and religion in general than this parallel suggests, however. There is, indeed, a widespread and perhaps growing consensus today that Locke is above all a religious thinker, that his orientation (his "star and compass") is derived from theology, his "grounds" to be found in his religious beliefs.[19] But much of what is said today about Locke and religion suffers from and then produces confusion. The confusion in the first instance follows from a tendency to identify and translate categories and dualities from our day into Locke's thinking. We in the twenty-first century tend to think in terms of the opposition between religious and secular thinking; Locke thought in terms of the distinction between revealed religion (a matter of faith) and natural or rational religion (in principle, part of philosophy and rational). When scholars see Locke deploying religious con-

16. John Locke, *First Treatise*, in *Two Treatises of Government*, ed. Peter Laslett (Cambridge: Cambridge University Press, 1988), 58, hereafter I.

17. Ibid.

18. For a somewhat parallel discussion, see John Marshall, *John Locke: Resistance, Religion and Responsibility* (Cambridge: Cambridge University Press, 1994), 146–47.

19. Cf. Jeremy Waldron, *God, Locke, and Equality: Christian Foundations in Locke's Political Thought* (Cambridge: Cambridge University Press, 2002); Marshall, *John Locke;* Spellman, in *John Locke*, writes: "Locke's was a doctrinal Christian politics" (98).

cepts and categories they tend to transpose them into our twenty-first–century category of the religious, contraposed with the category of the secular and the rational. Thus scholars tend to blur the religious and the Christian, to assume that Locke's "God-talk" is *ipso facto* Christian and scriptural. We will argue this is not the case, at least not in his *Two Treaties*.

For Locke, "God-talk" can belong to both modes of discourse, secular and religious—a position he held to from his earliest days.[20] So when Locke identifies reason as our "only star and compass," he rules out revelation as a source of truths different from those of reason, but he does not necessarily rule out truths of natural or rational religion. Indeed, many of the arguments of the *Second Treatise* depend absolutely on claims rooted or said to be rooted in natural theology.

The question remains, however, how does the Bible stack up against the teachings of reason. Is the Bible as such and as a whole "reasonable," as Locke famously pronounced Christianity to be? Locke gives us to think that this is so: he often asserts that reason and revelation say the same true things.[21]

And yet Locke leads us to wonder how candid he feels he can be in speaking of the Bible. In the section where he affirms reason as "our only star and compass" he points out that unguided by reason "the busie mind of man" will run into "strange courses" and "extravagant projects."[22] "Strangeness" and "extravagance" are no barriers to widespread acceptance, however. "Reason being laid aside . . . he that goes farthest out of the way, is thought fittest to lead, and is sure of most followers."[23] Locke is not here referring to primitive, uncivilized peoples; the "inhabitants" of "the woods and forests where the irrational, untaught inhabitants keep right by following nature, are fitter to give us rules."[24] It is of the so-called civilized nations, it is of Christendom that Locke speaks. They are the ones formed around "strange" ideas and "extravagant projects."

"Out of the way" ideas become "sacred" via "custom," and when that happens "'twill be thought impudence or madness, to contradict or question" them.[25] Candid challenge to "sacred" views is thus imprudent,

---

20. *Locke: Political Essays*, ed. Mark Goldie (Cambridge: Cambridge University Press, 1997).

21. John Locke, "Second Treatise," in *Two Treatises of Government*, ed. Peter Laslett (Cambridge: Cambridge University Press, 1988), 25 hereafter II; cf. John Locke, *An Essay Concerning Human Understanding*, ed. Peter H. Nidditch (Oxford: Clarendon Press, 1979), IV, xviii, hereafter ECHU.

22. I, 58.

23. Ibid.

24. Ibid.

25. Ibid.

to say the least. Although the views and practices of the civilized nations (like Locke's England?) may deserve "little reverence," nonetheless only a man willing to be thought impudent or mad would candidly speak of them as they deserve. A man who understands the prevailing order as Locke does may not blare forth his true views about the strange and extravagant foundations of that order.

It thus seems possible that the Bible may indeed be the "ground" for the extravagant claim that man is unfree and the critique of the Bible the prerequisite for grounding Locke's competing claim that man is free. But it would be more than hasty to draw such a conclusion. More conservatively, what we have seen so far of Locke's argument requires that we keep three, in principle different, positions in view: Filmer's own, allegedly grounded on Scripture; the doctrine of reason, which Locke unequivocally champions; and the Bible itself, according to Locke certainly different from Filmer. But we are not yet able to see whether the Bible is entirely or at least more or less congruent with the conclusions of reason or not. We must be open to the possibility, suggested by Locke's ruminations in I 58, that the Bible, even if correctly interpreted, does not contain (in Locke's view) the true doctrine about politics and human freedom.

III. LOCKE'S FILMER

Becoming self-conscious about the need to identify three potentially different claims to truth (Filmer's version of the Bible, the Bible itself, and Lockean reason) allows us to make sense of several otherwise puzzling features of the *First Treatise*. Let us work our way to those puzzling things by starting with the most surface feature of Locke's text, its structure. The *First Treatise* is constructed in a straightforward and clear manner. Its eleven chapters divide naturally into three parts: a brief introductory section (ch. 1) in which Locke introduces his task (to refute Filmer's contentions about absolute government and his denials of human freedom); a second, longer section (chs. 2–7) in which Locke hunts for and then considers in turn the various "titles" to authority Filmer invokes on behalf of Adam; finally, there is a third section, consisting of fewer chapters (chs. 8–11), but longer in pages and numbered paragraphs than the "titles section." This last part of the book is dedicated to the general theme of "the conveyance of Adam's sovereign monarchical power."[26] Long as it is, this last section is apparently incomplete. As Locke famously said in the preface to the work, we have here

---

26. See I, ch. 8, title.

"the beginning and the end of a discourse concerning government." He means by that the *First Treatise* (the beginning) and the *Second Treatise* (the end). "What fate has otherwise disposed of the papers that should have filled up the middle, and were more than all the rest, 'tis not worth while to tell thee."[27] The middle is something between the existing *First* and *Second Treatises* and there are many indications it is a continuation of the *First Treatise*. In the first chapter of the "conveyance section" Locke identifies four Filmerian modes of conveyance of Adam's alleged power (inheritance, grant, usurpation, or election), which he promises "a little more particularly to consider."[28] In point of fact, however, he covers only one of the four promised topics, inheritance, and it is not even clear that he finishes that topic. Since the treatment of inheritance consumed eighty-nine numbered paragraphs (out of 169 total in the *First Treatise* as we have it), it is quite believable that a completed version of the "conveyance section" would be "more than all the rest."

Locke apparently concluded on second thought that the missing papers were not necessary; what remains is "sufficient." "If these papers have that evidence, I flatter myself is to be found in them, there will be no great miss of those which are lost, and my reader may be satisfied without them."[29]

Locke's procedure in promising us text and then apologizing for not supplying it is odd, if not unintelligible, but each of the two substantive sections has more striking oddities than this. Both sections have a very similar internal structure: the one opens with a chapter seeking out Filmer's grounds for attributing sovereign authority to Adam, the other with a chapter seeking the various means that Filmer affirms as modes of conveyance to others of Adam's original authority.[30] In the first case, Locke professes a difficult time finding any grounds for Filmer's affirmation-in-chief, but finally he comes to settle on the passage from Filmer's critique of Hobbes that we quoted earlier. Locke astutely privileges this passage as containing "the sum of all his [Filmer's] arguments, for Adam's sovereignty, and against natural freedom." Locke rightly pounces on this passage, for it does indeed contain in a nutshell the core of Filmer's doctrine on the power of Adam. Immediately on quoting the Filmerian passage, however, Locke restates it in such a way as to miss its point: "and they [the arguments for Adam's sovereignty] are the following: God's creation of Adam, the dominion he gave him over Eve; and

---

27. John Locke, *Two Treatises of Government*, Preface.
28. I 80.
29. John Locke, *Two Treatises of Government*, Preface.
30. I, chs. 2, 8.

the dominion he had as father over his children." Locke promises to "particularly consider" all of these.[31] Locke at least partly lives up to his promise. His chapter 3 is on the creation of Adam, his chapter 5 is on the "subjection of Eve," his chapter 6 on "Adam's title by fatherhood." Chapter 4, however, is mostly about the alleged donation in Genesis 1:28 of the world and what is on it to Adam as his exclusive property; and chapter 7 considers fatherhood and property together as potential sources of Adam's power.

In the mode of "what's wrong with this picture," let us take explicit note of Locke's important distortions of Filmer's position. First, in his restatement Locke has severed three elements, which for Filmer are indissolubly united—creation of Adam, sovereignty over Eve, sovereignty over his children. Adam's creation is not a separate item, as Locke makes it, but the crux of his sovereignty over both Eve and his descendents. A related distinction appears when we look to Locke's way of treating the theme of the "subjection of Eve." He treats that subjection as a result of the Fall, a position we have seen Filmer very explicitly reject. Locke, however, nowhere explicitly notes Filmer's refusal to ground political life on the Fall.

A third oddity in Locke's use of Filmer's Hobbes-critique as his program is his failure to adhere to his own restatement of Filmer's point in I 14 in his execution of the promise to examine the titles identified there. The restatement of Filmer's "arguments" in I 14 does not prepare us for the (very Lockean) theme of chapters 4 and 7: property. That omission in the I 14 restatement is odd, for in the very passage Locke is restating Filmer quite explicitly emphasizes the property theme.

So, to summarize some of the oddities: Locke deconstructs Filmer's position in his restatement and then examination of it so as to guarantee a failure to consider it on its own terms; Locke in his restatement omits some topics clearly present in Filmer's statement; finally, Locke's deconstruction of Filmer not only leads him to lose the sense of the latter's argument, but leads him to consider topics Filmer never invoked, and to consider those he did in contexts quite foreign to Filmer.

Does Locke know what he is doing? Has he merely misread and misunderstood Filmer? Or, has he misrepresented Filmer intentionally in order, say, to set up a straw man of whom he can take rhetorical advantage? Locke's misrepresentation of Filmer cannot flow from mere misunderstanding, for from chapter 7 of the *First Treatise* onward, i.e., from the point where Locke has completed his individual examination of "Filmer's" presentation of Adam's "titles," Locke shows that he un-

31. I 14.

derstands the true character of Filmer's argument perfectly well. In I 73 (the first paragraph of chapter 7) Locke tells us that "the foundations which he [Filmer] lays the chief stress on . . . are two, viz., Fatherhood and Property." When he returns (in passing) to the theme a few paragraphs later, Locke even more unequivocally states his view of Filmer's argument:

This sovereignty he erects, as has been said upon a double Foundation, viz., that of Property, and that of Fatherhood. One was the right he was supposed to have in all Creatures, a right to possess the Earth with the Beasts, and other inferior Ranks of things in it for his Private use, exclusive of all other men. The other was the Right he was supposed to have to Rule and Govern men, all the rest of mankind.[32]

Now, that is a perfect restatement of Filmer's position, especially when his explanation from the next paragraph is added to it. Adam's property right, "our A. [Filmer] supposes to arise from God's immediate declaration, *Genesis* 1:28, and that of Fatherhood from the Act of Begetting."[33] From this point forward, Locke never misstates Filmer's position on Adam's "titles," never, for example, attributes to him any argument depending on the Fall, never attributes to him an argument for the independent significance of creation (as presented in Locke's third chapter), but always understands that the creation issue and the fatherhood issue are for Filmer one and the same.

Some of the misrepresentation does seem inspired by the effort to take rhetorical advantage of poor Sir Robert. So, for example, in chapter 4 of the *First Treatise*, Locke takes up "Adam's title to sovereignty by Donation, *Genesis* 1:28" As we have seen, Filmer puts great weight on the donation theme, but he always means it as a supplement to his "sourcist" arguments (if we might be allowed this neologism). Being the source of all humans who came after him was the basis for Adam's sovereignty over them; the donation was the basis for his dominion over the nonhuman world. But Locke treats the donation argument as though Filmer means by it that God included human beings in the grant of dominion.[34] This misrepresentation gives Locke an opportunity to heap ridicule on Filmer. For example, he points out that the same "dominion" given to Adam in Genesis 1:28 was "renewed" to Noah and his sons, but with a crucial addition: to Adam's "dominion" is added Noah's right to eat the creatures.

32. I 84.   33. I 85.
34. I 24–28.

And if God made all Mankind slaves to Adam and his Heirs, by giving Adam Dominion over every living thing that moveth on the Earth . . . as our A—[Filmer]
would have it, methinks Sir Robert should have carried his Monarchical Power
one step higher, and satisfied the World, that Princes might eat their Subjects
too, since God gave as full Power to Noah and his heirs . . . to eat every living
thing that moveth, as he did to Adam to have Dominion over them . . .[35]

Here Locke clearly is using his shameless distortions of Filmer's argument for rhetorical advantage.

But we can discern no such great rhetorical gain from many of Locke's
other misrepresentations. A more comprehensive insight into Locke's
procedure results from noticing that his most egregious distortion of
Filmer consists of his reading the Fall into Filmer's theory. Although the
Fall plays no role in Filmer's derivation of political authority, it does, as
we have already observed, play a significant role in most Christian political thinking, and it certainly plays a major role in all Christian theology, to say nothing of its prominent place in the Bible itself. By distort-
ing Filmer, Locke is enabled to bring into his text a doctrine irrelevant
to Filmer but extremely relevant to the broader context of Christian political thought, Christian theology, and the Bible itself. The same, in one
way or another, is true of the other topics that flow into Locke's text from
his misrepresentations of Filmer. He generates separate discussions of
creation, donation, and Fall—topics central to the Bible's presentation
of the human situation. This observation returns us to the conclusion we
drew in an earlier discussion. Locke calls attention to three potentially
separate and different sources of political understanding: Filmer's (false)
biblicism, Locke's rationalism, and the Bible itself. Locke's distortion of
Filmer allows him to put the third on the table, in such a way as to allow
us to judge whether the biblical and the rational views concur.

The conveyance section, too, has its oddities. If one approaches it
systematically, it is difficult not to wonder about it from the very outset.
The "titles section" has—certainly to Locke's satisfaction—already de-
molished Adam's "titles" to sovereignty as alleged by Filmer. Yet in the
"conveyance section" Locke is going to prove that whatever titles Adam
had cannot have been conveyed to others, in particular not to rulers
of seventeenth-century Europe.[36] But this seems superfluous, given that
Locke has already demonstrated that Adam lacks any title to begin with.
It seems even more superfluous when one notices again that the conveyance section is actually much longer than the titles section. What, if anything, is the added value of the conveyance section?

35. I 27.
36. See esp. I 124.

The opening chapter of this section—chapter 8—is brief (three paragraphs), concise, and to the point compared to the opening chapter of the titles section (I 6–14). An even more significant difference between the two chapters is the reversal in argumentation from chapter 2 to chapter 8: in chapter 2 Locke seeks Filmer's arguments for Adam's titles and professes a very hard time finding any; in chapter 8 Locke seeks out Filmer's argument for the modes of conveyance of Adam's power, but this time he has no trouble finding them. Indeed it is not the paucity of such means but their fecundity that arouses Locke's notice.[37] Whereas Locke conceals and distorts Filmer's argument on titles in chapter 2, he incisively and correctly identifies the main features of the argument on conveyance in chapter 8. He brings out three points of particular importance. (1) Filmer identifies a large number of modes of conveyance, some of them mutually inconsistent or even contradictory. (2) At bottom, Filmer's doctrine of conveyance amounts to a version of *de factoism*—the belief that the present holder of political power holds that power legitimately.[38] Locke quotes Filmer to this very effect: "It skills not which way Kings come by their power."[39] And Locke quotes Filmer's really decisive point: "All Kings that now are, or ever were, are or were Fathers of their people, or Heirs of such Fathers, or Usurpers of the Right of such Fathers" (3). Despite his *de factoism*, however, Filmer does grant a certain priority to inheritance as a means of conveyance, for all those who are not heirs "are to be reputed, as the next heirs of those progenitors who were at first the natural parents of the whole people."[40] Locke exposes the nerve of Filmer's position—his *de factoism*—and shows the deep subordination if not quite irrelevance of inheritance as a mode of conveyance. Indeed, he shows here the near irrelevance of the question of conveyance—which is why Filmer handles it so casually and (from a point of view that takes conveyance seriously), so inadequately.

Yet, having exposed the relative irrelevance of inheritance to Filmer's argument, Locke instantly sets off on an inquiry into inheritance as a mode of conveyance of Adam's original authority. Why is Locke giving so much time and space to the doubly irrelevant topic of the conveyance of Adam's non-existent powers via inheritance? Again, it helps to consider Filmer's doctrine in his own terms. As we have already noticed, Filmer is not overly concerned about the gaping chasm separating Adam and all reigning monarchs over which Filmer's critics gleefully held him. Sir

---

37. Cf. I 13–14, with I 79, 81.
38. I 78, cf. I 121.
39. I 78.
40. Filmer, *Patriarcha and Other Writings*, 10; quoted in Locke, I 78.

Robert admitted to it easily enough. Contrary to what one would expect on the basis of a superficial grasp of Filmer's scheme, he did not believe it made any difference whether the prince actually possesses the Adamic paternal power or is merely "reputed" to do so:

> In all kingdoms or commonwealths in the world, whether the Prince be the supreme Father of the people or but the true heir of such a Father, or whether he come to the crown by usurpation, or by election of the nobles or of the people, or by any other way whatsoever, or whether some few or a multitude govern the commonwealth, yet still the authority that is in any one, or in many, or in all these, is the only right and natural authority of a supreme Father.[41]

In other words, no matter who possesses authority, and no matter how it is acquired, that authority is the authority of the fatherhood of Adam; all human authority is ultimately derived from the authority of Adam. Filmer is even willing to defend the legitimacy of authority in the hardest case, the usurper: "If it please God, for the correction of the Prince or punishment of the people, to suffer Princes to be removed and others to be placed in their rooms . . . in all such cases, the judgment of God, who hath power to give and take away kingdoms, is most just."[42]

Filmer is untroubled by the inability of any princes to trace their authority back to Adam, for three reasons. In the first place, he means to say that the Pauline affirmation that all authority is of God finds its explication in Genesis in the creation of Adam. This is where and how God has "appointed" rule; all rightful authority is nothing but the subjection owed to the original source, God, and derivatively to the derivative source, Adam. God could have provided for human beings to come into being in some other way, but he did not. The most common fact of nature, generation, when understood in the light of the revealed creation, proves fathers to have sovereign authority in the human world. The objections of Locke and others to the contrary, this "fatherly" authority can be transferred, or held by others, for it is the original of all authority. Certainly no authority can arise from individual consent, for no individual is free; no man has the moral authority to subject himself, because he is already caught within a web of subjection.

Secondly, according to Filmer, rulers can exercise the power of fathers and of the heirs of Adam, even if they are usurpers of that power. From the point of view of the subject, it matters much less who possesses the power than that it is recognized and obeyed; the relevant fact is the same whether the ruler he faces is Adam or Richard III: the king is he to

---

41. Filmer, *Patriarcha and Other Writings*, 60–61.
42. Filmer, *Patriarcha and Other Writings*, 62.

whom he can render his obedience. John Calvin made more or less the same point:

It belongeth not to us to be inquisitive by what right and title a prince reigneth . . . and whether he have it by God and lawful inheritance. . . . To us it ought to suffice that they do rule. For they have not ascended unto this estate by their own strength, but they are placed by the hand of God.[43]

For the subject, it is enough to know he lies under the obligation to obey those he finds in positions of authority. The subject is concerned only with his own duties, not with the duties of the authorities to God. What is common to all such authority relations is precisely the obligation of obedience. For Filmer, this is the decisive matter, and it makes possible his acceptance of the apparent absurdities his Whig critics denounced.

Third, it is indeed possible, Filmer concludes, that the true heir to Adam no longer exercises power, or even that great criminals do so, but this is thoroughly compatible with God's ways. God is not bound even by his own ordinations. If he chooses to use evil men to rebuke Princes or peoples, that "is most just." "God doth but use and turn men's unrighteous acts to the performance of His righteous decrees."[44] Not only is the power that rulers possess an embodiment or reflection of God's creative power, but so is their loss of power. The other side of human subjection is the supervening sovereignty of God, uncontained and uncontainable. The authority of the usurper does not contradict Filmer's system but completes it.[45]

Filmer's doctrine of conveyance amounts to the imperative: "Be subject unto the higher powers, for the powers that be are of God." They are "of God" in the first instance, for God has "appointed rule" via his mode of creating mankind and then donating dominion over the rest of creation to the first man. The powers are "of God" in the second instance because whether the true and proper heir of Adam or not, they fill the role of authority God appointed in creating only Adam, and in the third instance they hold their place due to the inscrutable will and direct action of God himself. The lesson of creation is that men are not born free, but are subjected to the "powers."

---

43. John Calvin, Sermons on the *Epistles of St. Paul to Timothy and Titus* (1579), a commentary upon the Epistles of St. Paul to the Romans (1583), quoted in Michael Walzer, *Revolution of the Saints* (Cambridge, Mass.: Harvard University Press, 1965), 38. Also see 57–59.
44. Filmer, *Patriarcha and Other Writings*, 60–61.
45. For a very interesting account of Filmerian conveyance, see Harris, "Politics of Christianity," 201.

Filmer's doctrine of conveyance represents, then, a radical version of the major premise of his own main syllogism, i.e., it presents an explication of Romans 13. The "conveyance section" thus gives Locke the opportunity to consider the decisive biblical (New Testament) text of politics. Just as the "titles section" gives him independent access to (some of) the chief Old Testament texts on politics, so the conveyance section allows him to consider the chief New Testament political thesis. We may draw a conclusion: Locke's structural oddities are the means by which he subtly brings into his book for examination the biblical texts themselves, independent of Filmer's misuse of them.

IV. CREATION

Locke has good fun with what he presents as Filmer's argument for the creation of Adam. The lion, he points out, was as much created as Adam, and if being created is the source of title to rule, then the "king of beasts" has as much a claim as Adam—more really, having been created earlier—to being king of creation. This "refutation" of Filmer is, of course, a huge parody, for here is a place where Locke's failure to bring out Filmer's sourcist argument is particularly relevant: Adam has a title to rule other humans *as their source* that the lion lacks. For Filmer, it is not creation *per se*, but the singular human creation of Adam that counts.

From that conception of creation, Filmer draws his very strong conclusion: no succeeding man is free; all are subject to a lawful ruler from birth. The father has what amounts to sovereign power—Adam's progenitive power is indeed for Filmer the one and only source of legitimate authority. This power extends even to the power of life and death.[46] This does not mean that every father in every society retains that power, for the authority of the "Supreme Father," the sovereign ruler in the society, supersedes the authority of each individual father, and that authority may be exercised to limit and restrain the powers private fathers may exercise. But Filmer insists that the inherent primal right of fatherhood carries with it something like ownership rights. Thus Filmer recognizes no fundamental distinction between the various human relations Locke is at great pains to distinguish in the *Second Treatise*. The power of the father, king, master, and owner are indistinguishable for Filmer. When seen in its full scope, it is easy to grasp what Filmer has done: Adam and his "heirs," or those who possess the Adamic power are in effect wielders on earth of the kind of power God exercises over his whole creation.

46. I 50 and citations to Filmer therein.

As Filmer once said, "even the power which God himself exercises over mankind is by right of fatherhood."[47]

It is that parallel that provides the ingress for Locke's most telling criticism of Filmer's doctrine of Adamic power. The nerve of this argument is in I 52:

The Argument, I have heard others make use of, to prove that Fathers, by begetting them, come by an absolute Power over their Children, is this; That *Fathers have a Power over the Lives of their Children, because they give them Life and Being,* which is the only proof it is capable of, since there can be no reason, why naturally one Man should have any claim or pretence of Right over that in another, which was never his, which he bestowed not, but was received from the bounty of another.

Locke clearly captures the sourcist character of Filmer's argument. Locke has two replies. First, "every one who gives another any thing, has not always thereby a right to take it away again." We can recognize immediately the strength of Locke's point. Suppose we give someone a gift; we normally do not retain the right to reclaim it. When Locke affirms self-ownership, as he does so prominently in the *Second Treatise,* he is registering his conviction that who or whatever is the source of life does not retain the right to reclaim it from its possessor.

That first objection is very far reaching, but Locke develops it very little in this place—failing explicitly to raise the question, for example, of whether the limitation on the right of reclamation applies to God or not. Locke's second objection is better developed and in the context of his attempt to deny the scriptural foundations of Filmer's doctrine, has more traction:

Those who say the *Father* gives Life to his Children, are so dazzled with the thoughts of Monarchy, that they do not, as they ought, remember God, who is *the Author and Giver of Life: 'Tis in him alone we live, move, and have our Being.*[48]

Contrary to what Filmer believes, the relation of Adam to his successors is not the same as the relation between God and his creatures. God transcends his creation in a way that Adam (and fathers in general) do not transcend their offspring. Adam is created in the image of God, but that is nonetheless a much lesser thing than being God. One consequence of that difference is that God produced the world through creation: Adam, says Locke, "was created, or began to exist, by God's immediate power, without the intervention of parents or the pre-existence

---

47. Filmer, "Directions for Obedience in Dangerous or Doubtful Times," in *Patriarcha and Other Writings,* 284.
48. I 52.

of any of the same species to beget him."[49] Or, as Locke expands the thought in his *Essay Concerning Human Understanding,* "when a thing is wholly made new, so that no part thereof did exist before; as when a new particle of matter doth begin to exist, in *rerum natura,* which had before no being, and this we call creation."[50] Creation is thus quite different, and much greater than generation, which merely produces something out of "particles which did all of them before exist."[51]

This difference between creation and generation is so immense, thinks Locke, that it makes all the difference with respect to the powers Filmer claims for fatherhood.

> To give Life to that which has yet no being, is to frame and make a living Creature, fashion the parts, and mould and suit them to their uses, and then having proportion'd and fitted them together, to put into them a living Soul. He that could do this, might indeed have some pretence to destroy his own Workmanship. (I 53)

Note that in this case Locke hesitates to conclude that the genuine creator has a right to destroy what he has made; such a creator "might indeed" raise such a claim—that is the outer bound to which Locke goes in this place. The mere progenitor has "no pretense" whatever to such a power, however:

> But is there any one so bold, that dares thus far Arrogate to himself the Incomprehensible Works of the Almighty? Who alone did at first, and continues still to make a living Soul, He alone can breathe in the breath of Life. If any one thinks himself an Artist at this, let him number up the parts of his Childs Body which he hath made, tell me their Uses and Operations, and when the living and rational Soul began to inhabit this curious Structure, when Sense began, and how this Engine which he has framed Thinks and Reasons: If he made it, let him, when it is out of order, mend it, at least tell wherein the defects lie. *Shall he that made the Eye not see?* Says the Psalmist, *Psalm* 94.9. See these Mens Vanities: The Structure of that one part is sufficient to convince us of an All-wise Contriver, and he has so visible a claim to us as his Workmanship, that one of the ordinary Appellations of God in Scripture is, *God our Maker,* and *the Lord our Maker.* And therefore though our *A.* for the magnifying his *Fatherhood,* be pleased to say, *That even the Power which God himself exerciseth over Mankind is by Right of Fatherhood,* yet this Fatherhood is such an one as utterly excludes all pretence of Title in Earthly Parents; for he is *King* because he is indeed Maker of us all, which no Parents can pretend to be of their Children.[52]

Filmer's argument for creation, claiming to be biblically grounded, fails precisely because it fails to take seriously enough the very notions of the

---

49. I 15.
51. Ibid.
50. ECHU II.26.2.
52. I 53.

creature and the creator. That is to say, the biblical grounding that Filmer claims for his Adamic power is in fact lacking.

But what about the biblical view itself? Does it support the Lockean proposition that man is free? The place to begin consideration of this topic is by noticing a detail in Locke's text that might be surprising, given the set of arguments we have just examined. Shortly after drawing his conclusion that Filmer lacks scriptural warrant for attributing the power of life and death to fathers, Locke ostensibly changes the subject. Whatever power fathers have is equally had by mothers, as witnessed by the fact that Filmer cites only one-half of the Fifth Commandment ("honor thy father") in order to make his point about fatherly authority. The truth is the biblical text enjoins "honor" for "thy mother" as well.[53] Locke proceeds to quote at least thirteen passages from both Testaments joining mother to father. All these passages would repay detailed attention, but here let us only note some classic instances of Lockean "writing out of context." The question ostensibly is whether mother shares power with father under the biblical mandate. The evidence is overwhelmingly in favor of an affirmative answer, but what is truly interesting about this string of passages is the fact that nearly all of them involve the death penalty for the child who does not honor or who disobeys his parents. Locke quotes Zechariah 13:3, on which he comments: "Here not the Father only, but Father and Mother, jointly, *had Power in this Case of Life and Death.*"[54] In plain English, the Bible, as Locke here indicates, is much closer to Filmer than Locke had previously allowed. Indeed the mother is most often joined to the father, but the more important point that Locke makes is that the parents, according to the Bible, do possess the power of life and death. The scriptural position as Locke gives it is much closer to Filmer than to what Locke had only a little earlier presented as the biblical view. Most readers fail to notice Locke's strange citation of counter-evidence to his own ostensible position because they are fooled by his feinting definition of the context and point of his recital of the biblical passages. Locke proceeds here rather like the classic sleight-of-hand artist: he encourages the audience to watch his right hand while he performs his tricks with his left. The trick that he performs in this case is to demonstrate that Filmer is more or less correct about the power he attributes to fathers.

Locke's account of the authentic biblical doctrine does not go so far as Filmer does, but it does recognize the sort of power Filmer claimed the Bible did. The Bible recognizes subjection of children to parents,

53. I 61.
54. I 61, emphasis added.

extending even to life and death. The Bible does not then endorse the Lockean position on freedom. The distance between the Lockean vision of freedom and the biblical position becomes clear if one compares what Locke concludes about parental power in the *Second Treatise* with what he has shown us about the biblical position in the *First*. The natural law or rational doctrine of parental power, according to Locke, not only includes the mother equally with the father but, more to our present point, mandates a power at odds with the biblical doctrine. "Capital Punishment . . . is the proper power of the Magistrate, of which the Father has not so much as the shadow. His command over his children is but temporary, and reaches not their Life or Property . . . or to their Liberty neither . . ."[55] The obligation to honor their father and mother requires of children "an inward esteem and reverence to be shown by all outward Expressions, . . . but this is very far from giving Parents a power to command over their Children, or an Authority to make laws and dispose as they please of their lives and liberties."[56] There can be no question of a penalty of death for failing to honor father and mother as they wish to be. Rather, the rightful power parents have, which they may use to enforce the obligation of honor, "is the Power Men generally have to bestow their Estates on those, who please them best."[57] The Bible, then, is more "sourcist" than Locke had led us to believe, and the view contained in it of the implications of creation are not at all the same as the rational doctrine Locke presents in his own name.

That recognition propels us to look back to Locke's explicit and thematic discussion of creation in the third chapter of the *First Treatise*. In I 44, in the midst of his treatment of Filmer's alleged appeal to the Fall as one source of Adam's "title," Locke says that he will "consider the force of the text in hand" independently of the errors Locke finds in Filmer's interpretations.[58] This promise also describes Locke's procedure regarding the passages on creation and donation that he discusses.

Locke's initial reply to Filmer's alleged appeal to the creation of Adam is to remind Filmer of the lion, also created by God. Locke's retort has a much broader implication: not only man, not only the lion, but all that is, is presented in Genesis as created by God, who brought it into being out of his "omnipotency" by His "immediate power," when it "pleased" Him to do it.[59] The biblical doctrine of creation emphasizes that the world is the product of an omnipotent will and intelligence. The world is an order, embodying the design of its maker.

55. II 65.   56. II 66.
57. II, 72; cf. I 88–93 which is clarified by II 72.
58. I 44.   59. I 15.

In the guise of rebutting another of Filmer's alleged claims, Locke proceeds to bring out another important dimension of the biblical creation conception. Filmer claims God "appointed" Adam ruler, a claim Locke finds to be systematically ambiguous. The important point here, relevant to the biblical text itself more than to Filmer, is that God not only made but also rules the world. The created world is an order governed by God, in which all the creatures are subject to God. Locke identifies three different expressions of God's rulership: "What Providence orders, or the Law of Nature directs, or positive Revelation declares."[60] He finds Filmer's notion of "God's appointment" unclear as to which of these three is meant (this would be less of a problem if Locke presented Filmer's doctrine correctly) but the list captures a systematic ambiguity in the biblical text, or at least in theological reflections based on the biblical text. God is said to rule in all three of these ways: directly as the cause of everything (divine particular providence), normatively as the source of revealed commands, and finally through the law of nature as natural norms.

Locke makes no effort in this context to sort out which of these three is the authentic biblical doctrine. He does indicate that these are different, conflicting, and perhaps incompatible notions. He also makes clear the chief corollary of the idea of creation by the omnipotent, intelligent and willing God—the rule of God and the subjection of creation, including man, to Him. Vis-à-vis God, that is, essentially and fundamentally, man is a subject being. Man is not in the fundamental sense free.

The book of Genesis expresses this view in its accounts of the original situation of mankind and of the Fall. Humans are well cared for by the omnipotent Being who made them; they are placed in a garden requiring minimal effort on their parts to satisfy their needs. More than that, they are not in their initial nature condemned to die. "Paradise was a place of bliss, as well as immortality; without drudgery, and without sorrow."[61]

But in paradise human beings are also under strict obligations of obedience to God.[62] They are most especially, on pain of death, not to eat of the fruit of the tree of knowledge of good and evil. Possession of that knowledge would allow man to guide his own life, to be free. To deny access to that knowledge, Locke suggests, is to commit humanity to remaining obedient and dependent. The original biblical mandate may not be for subjection to Adam, as Filmer has it, but it is for subjection.

60. I 16.
61. John Locke, *The Reasonableness of Christianity: As Delivered in the Scriptures*, ed. John C. Higgins-Biddle (Oxford; New York: Clarendon Press, 1999), 7.
62. I 44–45; John Locke, *The Reasonableness of Christianity*, 6.

Just as Locke quietly shows us that the Bible is closer to Filmer on the power of fathers (and mothers) than Locke at first led us to believe, so he shows that the Bible's fundamental understanding of the human way of being in the world is far closer to what Filmer asserted, human un-freedom, than Locke has up to this point led us to believe. Of course, there remain many questions: does the Fall make a difference on the fundamental questions of knowledge of good and evil, of human self-governance, of human freedom? In paradise man's subjection is directly to God. To what are humans subjected after the expulsion from Eden? Is there, along the lines of Bellarmine, for example, a possible harmo-nization between the biblical attitude of human subjection and human freedom? Does Christianity make any difference?

Whatever may be the answer to these questions, Locke never suggest-ed that reason was suited only to a post-lapsarian condition.[63] In his own name Locke commits to the autonomous, rational guidance that the Bi-ble turns away from as sinful. This is not to say that the doctrine of cre-ation played no role in Locke's philosophy of politics. Indeed, in the form of the well-known "workmanship argument" it played a major role. "For men all being the workmanship of one omnipotent, and infinitely wise maker; all the servants of one sovereign master, sent into the world by his order and about his business, they are his property, whose work-manship they are, made to last during his, not one another's pleasure."[64] Locke presents this doctrine not as the deliverance of revelation, but as the conclusion of reason.[65] Interestingly, in the *Two Treatises* Locke make no effort to rationally prove the existence of the omnipotent cre-ator God, but in his *Essay Concerning Human Understanding* he devotes a whole chapter to such a proof.[66]

Locke does not conclude from the existence of the creator God that man is not to know good and evil, or to exercise his reason to direct his own life. It is only through reason that man can rightly come to know of God and of the law of nature. The law of nature teaches humans their rights and their duty to respect one another's rights. It teaches them their non-subjection to others. The law of nature, or rather "reason, which is that law, teaches all mankind, who will but consult it, that [they are] all equal and independent."[67] Each and every individual is obliged to respect the property claim God has to all humans, and therefore may not rightly interfere with the "life, health, liberty, or possessions" of others. The core of the law of nature is thus fairly minimal and, we might

---

63. Cf. Ian Harris, "Politics of Christianity," 205–12.
64. II 6.   65. Ibid.
66. IV10.   67. Ibid.

say, negative—respect the rights or the objects of the rights of others.

Such is the rational doctrine of creation and its implications. It has some resonances in common with the biblical doctrine of creation, resonances which Locke sometimes enhances through his rhetoric and his hesitation to trumpet too loudly the differences between his doctrine of rational theology and the biblical Revelation. Locke would not wish to be thought impudent or mad, and to that end he attempts to leave his readers with the impression that the biblical doctrine is in fact identical to the rational doctrine. The task of *Two Treatises,* and of several others of Locke's works, is thus rather complex: he wants, on the one hand, to indicate (quietly) the differences between rational doctrine and revelation, but on the other to interpret biblical doctrine in such a way as to make it converge with or come very close to rational doctrine.

Two Treatises trades heavily on Locke's blurring intention, for he makes no real effort to prove the existence of the creating God or the fact of creation there; he expects his normal reader to grant him these points on the basis of widely accepted revelatory teachings. He does attempt a rational proof in his *Essay,* but many (perhaps all) readers find that argument less than compelling. Some readers find that Locke merely went astray, as thinkers often do.[68] Others think Locke may have been aware of defects in his argument,[69] indeed, may have been intentionally forwarding an argument he knew to be a failure. We find ourselves between these two poles. We see reasons why Locke may have had less than full confidence in his argument for God, but incline more to the view that these doubts led him to a state of ambivalence or uncertainty about his argument rather than to outright skepticism or rejection of it.[70] One basis for inferring Locke's possible doubts about his rational derivation of the "workmanship argument" is the presence in the *Second Treatise* of an alternative to the workmanship argument as a ground for natural rights. We refer to the self-ownership thesis Locke invokes in many places in the *Second Treatise.* As the senior author of this essay has argued elsewhere, the self-ownership thesis is different from the workmanship argument (we belong to ourselves versus belonging to God), but strange to say, the practical implications—universal equal natural rights and the moral need to respect the rights of others—are nearly identical on both grounds. We suspect Locke of employing something like a "Locke's wager"—on the basis of either theistic or non-theistic premises he can

68. E.g., Michael Ayers, *Locke* (London: Routledge, 1991), II 198–99.

69. William T. Bluhm et al., "Locke's Idea of God: Rational Truth or Political Myth?" *Journal of Politics* 42.2 (1980): 414–38.

70. Michael Zuckert, *Launching Liberalism,* ch. 5; cf. Locke's essay "Atheism," in Goldie, ed., *Locke: Political Essays,* 245–46.

derive roughly the same results.[71] So far as Locke does appeal to self-ownership he is clearly moving firmly toward a theory of human freedom and autonomy.[72]

To summarize then: we can reconstruct three doctrines in Locke's presentation of the themes of creation: Filmer's, the authentic biblical doctrine, and Locke's own rational doctrine. The first two are far more different than Filmer claims, but the biblical is much closer to Filmer than Locke usually likes to admit, and it is much closer to Filmer than to Locke's rationalist position. On our question in chief—where does the Bible stand on freedom?—we see Locke locating the Bible nearer to Filmer than to his own position. Obedience and subjection are the initial, essential, and normative stances for man. Locke remarkably turns the biblical doctrine on its head and, using guidance from the self-ownership argument, shows that the implications of creation are more rightly seen as underwriting human liberty and equality.

V. DONATION

According to Locke, Filmer claims that in the donation passage (*Genesis* 1:28) God grants the entire created world, including other human beings, to Adam alone as his private property. Locke is only half correct in this reading of Filmer, for the latter does not trace "dominion" over other human beings to the donation. Filmer interprets the donation passage as he does because he sees that God's purpose is to elevate Adam to a pinnacle of singularity in order to establish and settle an unrivaled claim of authority and an unquestionable focus for obedience and allegiance among men. Thus the donation of the world to Adam alone as his private property supplements and completes his singular creation by giving him rightful claim on all resources of rule and sources of legitimacy. By treating the donation separately Locke loses the wholeness of Filmer's vision.

Locke has more good fun at Filmer's expense in "refuting" that part of the doctrine he falsely attributes to the author of *Patriarcha;* with the renewal and extension of the donation to Noah after the flood, Locke concludes that Filmerian sovereigns have the right to eat their subjects. Since Filmer does not look to the donation to establish rule over other humans, this point is no more than good fun, however. Locke also maintains that, even if the donation is to Adam alone, the ownership of the

---

71. Zuckert, *Launching Liberalism,* ch. 5.

72. See Michael Zuckert, *Natural Rights and New Republicanism* (Princeton: Princeton University Press, 1994), ch. 9.

world does not carry with it political authority, directly or indirectly.[73] Although Locke has much of interest to say on this topic, it too is irrelevant to Filmer's authentic position.

Only one of Locke's three responses or "corrections" to Filmer's alleged doctrine on the donation is telling against Filmer's actual position—but it is very telling. This is the central and longest response: the donation was not to Adam in particular, exclusive of all other men; whatever dominion he had thereby, it was not private dominion, but a dominion in common with the rest of mankind.[74] Locke has a powerful appeal to "the direct and plain meaning of the words" of the relevant texts to hold up against Filmer's interpretation.[75] In all places where the donation is spoken of, the text speaks of the donees as "them." This cannot mean Adam, or, later, Noah alone. Locke accuses Filmer of outright distortion in substituting singulars for the text's plurals. On the other hand, we might accuse Locke of the same, for he says that when renewing the donation to Noah and his sons, "God says . . . to Noah and his sons . . . into your *hands* they [the animals] are given." But the text actually says *hand*.

However that may be, Locke provides a more persuasive account than Filmer's of the meaning of the various donation passages. In the first instance, they are meant to "set . . . mankind above the other kinds of creatures, in this habitable earth of ours. 'Tis nothing but the giving of man, the whole species of man, as the chief inhabitants, who is the image of his maker, the dominion over the other creatures."[76] This "dominion" is not "private dominion" in any individuals at all. It is a donation to "mankind in common," and not to any members of the species as private property. The donation, Locke insists, creates no exclusive property claims in any human being relative to any other.[77] The donation expresses both the special dignity of mankind within the created order and the special care God took to provide for this being who is the crown of creation.[78] Locke thus brings out the way the biblical donation is of a piece with the doctrine of creation—a supremely wise, benevolent, and intelligent creator has provided for His favored creature.

Locke also brings out the limitations contained in the original donation in the context of discussing its renewal to Noah. Although at the beginning God gave mankind "dominion" over the earth, and over the different classes of living (animal) beings of earth, air and water, He gave men only "every plant yielding seed which is upon the face of all the

---

73. I 41–43.
75. I 36.
77. I 36; cf. II 26.

74. I 29.
76. I 40.
78. Cf. I 86.

earth, and every tree with seed in its fruit" for food. Neither men nor beasts are to eat meat, i.e., animal beings whose life must be given to be eaten. God takes special care to insure that the sustenance of the life of some parts of the created order need not come at the expense of other parts of that order. This is especially true for men; their limitation to seed-bearing plants and fruit-bearing trees seems to signal that they are not to feed themselves at the expense of the life even of plants.

The pre-lapsarian world is a world of order, harmony, and natural preservation. It is, as God pronounced it, "very good."[79] This is not the Darwinian world of "nature red in tooth and claw." It is the "peaceable kingdom" of William Hicks. Later, after the flood, the terms of the donation are much modified. The "dominion" of mankind is now expressed in very different terms. Rather than the complete terrestrial harmony of paradise, "the fear and the dread" of man is "upon every beast of the earth." The beasts are delivered into men's "hand" [sic]. Men are now allowed to eat everything, i.e., meat in addition to plants, so long as they do not eat it alive, or, perhaps, raw.[80] Only at this moment is an explicit prohibition of murder of human beings set forth, necessary now because only now is the taking of blood at all lawful. (Even the beasts are prohibited from killing humans, presumably because now they too are free to kill other animals in their struggle for survival.)

In depicting God's grants and withholdings as it does, the Bible is expressing the underlying idea that God gives and withholds because this created world is His; what rights men have to use it are due to His explicit grant; He may give and He may withhold as He wills. Man has no inherent claim on a world that belongs to and is rightly governed by God. Man is, at best, the steward of God's world.

Locke emphasizes the sense of God's ownership and freedom to grant or not in the biblical doctrine when he points out the immense differences between the grants to Adam and to Noah. Contrary to what Filmer thinks, Adam

has no absolute dominion over even the brutal part of the creatures, and the property he has in them is very narrow and scanty. . . . Should anyone who is absolute lord of a country have bidden [Filmer] "Subdue the earth," and given him dominion over the creatures in it, but not have permitted him to have taken a kid or a lamb out of the flock, to satisfy his hunger, I guess he would scarce have thought himself lord or proprietor of that land, or of the cattel on it: But would have found the difference between having dominion, which a shepherd may have and having full property as an owner.[81]

79. Gen. 1:31.   80. Gen. 9:1–8.
81. I 39.

The implication of Locke's explication of the various donation passages, then, is that God remains the true owner, and man's "propriety" is what God by positive grant allows.

The authentic biblical view, on Locke's showing, does share something with Filmer's rendition of it. God owns the world and may do with it what He will. But Locke also brings out ways in which Filmer greatly deviates from the scriptural understanding. The chief point is this: the doctrine is part of the Bible's demonstration of God's care for mankind as a species in the context of his loving care for the whole of creation. The granting of exclusive possession of the world to Adam and his heirs is not in harmony with that kind of divine care. Thus it is not merely Filmer's illicit substitution of singular for plural pronouns that damns his reading.

As sometimes happens in *Two Treatises,* Locke leads the reader to believe that reason and the Bible teach the same with regard to the donation and property.[82] Yet on closer look it is apparent that the two differ very substantially on these matters. Locke returns to the donation/property themes at least twice in the *Treatises,* the first in an important statement on rights, the second in his famous chapter on property in the *Second Treatise.*

The first and perhaps most striking feature of Locke's initial return to the donation is his reinterpretation of it from being a matter of positive revealed religion to being a deliverance of reason in the mode of natural theology. "And therefore I doubt not, but before these words were pronounced, 1 Gen. 28, 29 (if they must be understood literally to have been spoken) and without such verbal donation, man had a right to a use of the creatures, by the will and grant of God."[83] This is no longer a doctrine of positive revelation, but a natural inference, drawn by reason from the make of nature. Locke goes so far as to question whether there is any independent revelation, for he identifies reason with "the voice of God."[84]

It would seem that reason as the voice of God says the same as the voice of God as reported in Genesis, but there is in fact a major difference. "Reason, which was the voice of God in him, could not but teach him and assure him, that pursuing that natural inclination he had to preserve his being, he followed the will of his maker, and therefore had a right to make use of those creatures, which by his reason or senses he could discover would be serviceable thereunto."[85] The right discovered by reason is a right to all things that man could discover could serve as

82. E.g., II 25.
84. Ibid.

83. I 86.
85. Ibid.

food; by *natural* right man is not limited to the seed-bearing plants and the fruit-bearing trees.[86] Reason tells us that the taking of life for the sake of life is permissible. The world seen by reason is thus quite different from the world depicted in Scripture. The latter is a world of such harmony and order that no life must be sacrificed for any other. Reason apparently does not know of such a world as that.

The biblical account of how man and the other creatures came to have permission to eat other parts of the world emphasizes the theme of donation. The emphasis on donation in turn both highlights ownership of all by God—his positive permission is needed for use to be permissible—and his gracious kindness to his creatures. The Lockean rational account rests the claim to use the creatures on universal need, and on "the desire, the strong desire of preserving his life and being."[87] The Lockean account greatly shifts the focus to a claim based on need and a world marked, not by harmony and gracious divine care, but by the inharmonious drive for preservation.

From the beginning and by nature human beings have a right to "use the creatures," i.e., do with them what they need to in order to protect their life and even secure their comfort.[88] The original natural right is not merely a right to eat the animals but to kill whatever being—man or animal—that is, or even appears to be, threatening to him.[89] According to the Bible the right to kill another human, like the right to kill animals for food, does not arise until after the flood, i.e., after the original created order is washed away and God makes a fresh start with His creation. The right to kill is much more confined by the Bible's God than by the voice of Locke's God as delivered by reason.[90]

Contrary to what Locke tells us that he is telling us (that reason and revelation say much the same), in fact he tells us that they say quite different things. What was given to Adam was "very narrow and scanty," not only compared to what was added to the grant to Noah, but compared to what reason tells us is the true natural and divine dispensation.

Locke extends this argument in his chapter on property. He in effect establishes there a natural right to property, which means a right to free use, even to the point of destroying what one has property in. To own things is to have the right to use or dispose of them according to one's own will. One is free to disinherit one's children; one is free to amass or spend as one chooses.[91] None of these is true of the biblical conception

86. Cf. II 25.
88. I 92; II 26.
90. Gen. 9:5–6.

87. Ibid.
89. II 16.
91. II 194, I 92, I 115, II 72.

of property ultimately grounded in the notion of donation as portrayed by Locke. His premises for his development of the rational doctrine on property are quite contrary to the premise of the donation story. The Bible means to affirm God's providential care for man; God provides what men and the other creatures require. The beginning is a garden; only that is compatible with the nature of God. But Locke's rational doctrine tells him something quite different. The beginning is a situation of scarcity, of penury.[92] The true doctrine of property is a doctrine of free use, and the lesson for political life of the true doctrine of property is the need for "laws of liberty to secure protection and incouragement to the honest industry of mankind."[93] Human industry must be encouraged because the penury of the human condition can be overcome only by human labor, not by prayer. Property is grounded in human freedom, and the proper ordering relating to property—the encouragement of appropriation, labor, and security—requires a regime of political and economic freedom. Locke attempts to reorient the human attitude toward the world from one of gratitude toward the provident God to one of rational industry in response to the scarcity and near valuelessness of the given that is mankind's birthright.

VI. FALL

As we have seen, the Fall plays no part whatsoever in Filmer's political thinking. Hence, we way safely pass over whatever thoughts he had about it.

The Fall is, of course, a major part of the biblical understanding of the human situation and plays an especially strong role in Christianity, and thence in Christian political thought. To be brief: the Fall play a critical role in the biblical story because it reconciles its account of the omnipotent and loving God, who made the world and "saw that it was good," with the world as we experience it—shot through with mortality, need, scarcity, suffering. These harsh qualities cannot be His fault, but are instead the fault of the only other free being, man himself. The Fall results from man's (or woman's) unwillingness or inability to remain in the state of free dependence that God mandated.[94] The state of the world is man's doing, and to the gratitude owed a provident God must be added guilt for disobeying or falling away from the commands of that God.

---

92. Eg., II 32, 37.
93. II 42.
94. For a probing discussion, see Thomas Pangle, *Political Philosophy and the God of Abraham* (Baltimore: Johns Hopkins University Press, 2003).

Locke spends much time on the Fall in *First Treatise* and *The Reason-ableness of Christianity*, but the upshot of Locke's view is rather like Film-er's: the Fall plays no part to speak of in Locke's political philosophy.[95] When he speaks of the state of nature, the condition at the beginning, he does not mean paradise: the closest he comes to echoing Genesis lies in his proclamation: "in the beginning all the world was America," a place marked by penury and waste, despite its natural potential for wealth production.[96] The way the world is cannot be understood as pun-ishment—that would run counter to the goodness and justice of Locke's God of reason. It must be understood as the natural dispensation, which man is free or even propelled to improve via labor and sound political order.[97] Above all, Locke's rational philosophical theology replaces an orientation toward the world grounded in guilt (for the Fall), an orien-tation which renders normative in some sense the scarcity and imperfec-tions of the world. He would replace this guilt with the same rational at-titude of rational industry with which he would replace the attitude of gratitude. Locke thus urges humanity to a great improvement if not a conquest of nature. Men must be freed from the central doctrines of the book of Genesis—creation, donation, and Fall—in order to establish themselves on the footing of their own freedom. Or, perhaps more accu-rately, these doctrines must be judiciously reinterpreted to make them more compatible with the rational truth.

VII. THE HIGHER POWERS

In the first half of the *First Treatise* Locke addresses and refutes the mi-nor premise of Filmer's political patriarchalism: that God, in the mode of His creation of the world, has appointed political power in Adam and his successors. More significantly, however, he uses the occasion to ex-amine the biblical conceptions at the core of the Old Testament and to demonstrate their distance from the true doctrine of reason, "our only star and compass."

The second substantive section of the *First Treatise* turns to the ques-tion of the conveyance of Adam's (already shown to be nonexistent) power to others, chiefly via inheritance, which Filmer concedes is not in fact the normatively necessary or historically actual mode of convey-ance. Filmer's full doctrine of conveyance, as we have seen, amounts to a thoroughgoing *de factoism:* we are obliged to obey those who have au-

---

95. Cf. Marshall, *John Locke,* 145.
96. II 41–49. Cf. Waldron, *God, Locke, and Equality,* 169.
97. This, contra Waldron, *God, Locke, and Equality,* 163.

thority in their hands, for "all authority is of God." That is to say, the section on conveyance in effect takes up Filmer's major premise: that God has surely mandated political authority. It then takes up *the* Christian text on politics, Romans 13, given by Filmer an interpretation in line with certain Reformation views of God's active role in history. Locke approaches this topic even more cautiously than he had approached the Old Testament.

The general topic of the "conveyance section" is, of course, the conveyance of Adam's alleged power, but the more specific topic is inheritance as a means of conveyance, a topic spread over chs. 9–11, i.e., all but one chapter of the conveyance section, including by far the longest chapter of both *Treatises*, ch. 11, which addresses the question "who Heir?": who is *the* heir of Adam?

Whoever that person happened to be, as Locke points out, would thus enjoy the status of "King over all men," a veritable king of kings.[98] Locke shows Filmer to have a difficult time identifying the one true heir of Adam, but the New Testament gives a very clear answer to the question. In the first instance, all of us, but in the most important senses, Jesus. According to the genealogy presented in Luke 3:23–38 Jesus is *the* heir of Adam. The genealogy of Jesus in Matthew points to the same conclusion.[99]

The claim of Jesus' "heirdom" raises the central theological issue of Christianity, as developed, for example, in Paul's Letter to the Romans.[100] In Pauline theology, "heirdom" has a double meaning: on the one hand, all human beings are viewed as the inheritors of Adam's sinfulness, while at the same time Jesus is the "second Adam," who, by paying the inheritance tax, so to speak, for all humanity, overcomes the legacy of sin bequeathed us by Adam.

Although Jeremy Waldron, in his *God, Locke, and Equality*, is quite correct to notice that New Testament texts play a rather limited role in *First Treatise*, it is not quite true that they are entirely absent. By our count there is explicit, identified reference to only two New Testament texts in the *First Treatise*, Ephesians 6:1 and Matthew 15:4. The latter text is cited twice,[101] the former once.[102] All three citations are part of Locke's campaign to convict Filmer for omitting "honor thy mother." (The passage from Matthew, interestingly, reproduces the harsh Old Testament

---

98. I 108.
99. See Matt. 1:16; Gen. 5:1–32; 11:10–27.
100. See esp. Rom 5:12–17.   101. I 60, 61.
102. I, 61.

accounts of parental power.) There are several other places in the *First Treatise* where Locke seems to quote snatches of New Testament passages, but without attribution.[103] There are a number of other places where Locke strongly suggests a New Testament passage, but neither directly quotes nor cites it.[104]

Of the New Testament passages echoed in *First Treatise*, some seem to support unequivocally the notion of Jesus as King of Kings, i.e., the proper holder of political authority. The book of Revelation presents us with images of the victorious Christ. There, twenty-four elders ". . . fall down before him who sits on the throne, and worship him who lives for ever and ever. They lay their crowns before the throne and say: 'You are worthy, our Lord and God . . .'"[105] Locke picks up the theme and echoes this language when he draws out the implication of Filmer's idea of inheritance of Adamic authority. The logical implication of Filmer's claim requires the recognition of a single, Christ-like world monarch. If Filmer is correct, writes Locke, ". . . the first thing to be done, is to find out this true Heir of Adam, seat him in his Throne, and then all the Kings or Princes of the World ought to come and resign up their Crowns and Scepters to him, as things that belong no more to them, than to any of their subjects."[106]

Yet the idea that Jesus comes to wield actual political authority is far from uniformly held in the New Testament sources: "My kingdom is not of this world," he often says. Perhaps the most striking places where the New Testament shows Jesus' eschewal of temporal power is in the narratives of his temptations in the wilderness:

And the devil took him up and showed him all the kingdoms of the world in a moment of time, and said to him, "To you I will give all this authority and their glory; for it has been delivered to me, and I give it to whom I will." (Luke 4:1–6)

To that offer Jesus replied: "You shall worship the Lord your God and Him alone shall you serve" (Luke 4:8).

Moreover, even if Jesus is the true heir, even if He is the rightful King of Kings, this fact is of limited use in the seventeenth century, when Jesus is long gone from the earth. In nearly the very first paragraph of the conveyance section, Locke writes:

103. E.g., I 2 quoting from Heb. 8:5; I 40, quoting from I Tim 6:17; I, 67, quoting from Rom. 9:5; I 92, quoting from Rom. 13:5.
104. E.g., I 79 and I 103, suggesting Rev. 4:9–10; I, 110, 114, 120, 122, 125, weakly suggesting Rom. 13:6; I 128, suggesting Heb. 1:20.
105. 4:10–11a, also see Rev. 17:14, 19:16.
106. I 104.

Though it be never so plain that there ought to be Government in the World, nay should all men be of our A—'s mind, that Divine appointment had ordained it to be Monarchical, yet since Man cannot obey anything, that cannot command, and Ideas of Government in the Fancy, though never so perfect, though never so right, cannot give laws, nor prescribe Rules to the Actions of Men; it would be of no behoof in its Exercise and Use amongst Men, unless there were a way also taught how to know the Person, to whom it belonged to have this Power, and Exercise this Dominion over others. 'Tis in vain then to talk of subjection and obedience, without telling whom we are to obey. (I 81)

Locke repeats the point many times; for instance, in I 106:

The great Question which in all Ages has disturbed Mankind . . . has been Not whether there be Power in the world, nor whence it came, but who should have it. (I 106; also see 107)

Locke is calling attention to the following problem: even if Jesus as *the* heir of Adam or on some other basis (e.g. as the incarnated son of the living God) has rightful claim to temporal authority, the question remains, who actually can exercise this power in a world where Jesus is not present? In other words, who speaks for Jesus? Or, in the language of the conveyance section, who is the heir of Jesus' power?

The problem is brought out in a particularly striking passage in the "Who Heir?" chapter, when Locke asserts:

In the state the world now is, irreversibly ignorant who is Adam's heir, this Fatherhood, this Monarchical Power of Adam descending to his Heirs, would be of no more use to the Government of Mankind, than it would be to the quieting of Men's Consciences, or securing their Health, if our A. had assured them, that Adam had a Power to forgive sins, or cure Diseases, which by Divine Institution descended to his Heir, whilst his Heir is impossible to be known. (I 125)

The explicit target is Filmer, but the implicit reference is to Jesus, as is clear in Locke's recital of the "Adamic" powers he mentions: the power to forgive sins and the power to heal. These are, of course, not powers attributed to Adam, but they are powers of Jesus. That is to say, Locke is insinuating the question: assuming that Jesus had these powers, and has a claim to temporal authority, these claims do nothing to settle governance in the world until we know who now on this earth has the right to exercise these powers. Of course, it is not as though the world were lacking claimants to the heirdom of Jesus: Locke's Europe was replete with churches and sects claiming to be the true heirs of Jesus.

Locke is pointing to two apparent ambiguities in the New Testament view: (1) Does Jesus have any claims to temporal authority, or not? (2) Who now speaks for Jesus? Lying behind both is the broader question: Does the appearance of Jesus in the world, and his church(es) after him, have any implications for the endorsement and identification of "the higher powers" in Romans 13?

Locke indicates the presence of these questions early in the conveyance section when he goes on at length ridiculing Filmer's *de factoism*, suggesting it would lead to some ridiculous situations. He writes,

> By this notable way, our A. may make Oliver [Cromwell] as properly King, as any one else he could think of: And had he the Happiness to live under Massaniello's government, he could not by this his own Rule have forborne to have done Homage to him, with *O King live forever*, since the Manner of his Government by Supreme Power, made him properly King, who was but the Day before properly a Fisherman. And if Don Quixote had taught his Squire to govern with Supreme Authority our A. no doubt could have made a most Loyal Subject in Sancho Panza's Island. (I, 79)

Locke is here citing three rulers whose authority would be rendered legitimate by Filmer's principles, but who are, by ordinary standards, of questionable legitimacy. Two are leaders of rebellions, one of whom, Cromwell, was of very recent memory in Locke's England. Massaniello was the leader of a rebellion in Naples against the Spanish in 1647; he routed the Spanish rulers for a short while, but then became crazed with his own power and had Neapolitans killed more or less at random. He was in turn overthrown and killed. Sancho Panza, a character in Locke's favorite novel, *Don Quixote*, became ruler of an "island" when, as a joke, the real rulers set him to rule. All three of these individuals, furthermore, are examples of men who rose from common ranks to rulership, and whose regimes proved short lived. Cromwell's "republic" lasted less than a decade, and Massaniello's rulership came and went in one week. Sancho's governorship lasted only four days.[107] Most significantly, all have something to do with Jesus or his Christian successors. The Neapolitan, before becoming King, "was but the Day before [a] Fisherman." Like Jesus, Massaniello was raised up from a very lowly position to a very high one; like many of Jesus' immediate followers, including Peter, the first head of the church, Massaniello was a fisherman (Matthew 4:18–22; 16:13–20). Massaniello is the Jesus or apostle of Jesus who becomes a king.

Sancho Panza, governor of the island of Barataria, also echoes Jesus in important, but importantly different, ways. On being appointed by the Duke and Duchess to his governorship, Sancho replies: "Ever since I came down from the heavens and ever since I looked down from the

---

107. Miguel de Cervantes, *Don Quixote,* trans. John Rutherford (Middlesex, England: Penguin Books, 2000), II 42.

top of them at the earth and saw it so small, that great urge I had to be a governor has been cooling off a bit—what's so marvelous about ruling over a mustard seed, and what's so lordly or important about governing half a dozen men the size of hazelnuts?"[108] Sancho is directly echoing the claim of Jesus: "For I have come down from heaven," to which his listeners reply, "How does he now say, 'I have come down from heaven'?" (John 6:38, 42). Sancho seems to be running the thought of this passage together with Jesus' temptation to rulership in the wilderness. Like Jesus, Sancho prefers "a little bit of heaven, even if only a couple of miles of it[;] I'd be happier with that than with the biggest island in the world."[109]

Locke's third example in I 79—that of Cromwell—likewise has a connection to the ambiguities of Christian politics, for Cromwell led a revolution in order to bring England into closer conformity with the Kingdom of Christ. He led the faction, or an alliance of factions and sects, which claimed to have a truer vision of the proper governance of a Christian commonwealth than the faction led by the king and the established Christian church. That is, the English Civil War was in large part a battle over who was "heir to Jesus" and his claims to authority in seventeenth-century Britain.

Locke's three examples reproduce the ambiguities of the Christian dispensation for politics. Romans 13 tells all Christians to be subject to the higher powers "for conscience's sake," but, Locke shows, the Christian mandate for politics does not settle the issue of who the higher powers are to whom conscientious obedience is due.

Locke introduces the conveyance theme not only to reveal the difficulties in Filmer's doctrine, but to bring out the broader and more significant difficulties in Christian political thought. Christian doctrine can legitimate the politics of Oliver, Sancho, or Massaniello, and Locke shows that all are disruptive of free political life, and counter to the rational doctrine of politics. Sancho Panza in effect opts for the position that "my kingdom is not of this world." His choice for the Kingdom of Heaven over the kingdom of this earth implies and underwrites the version of the doctrine of passive obedience that Filmer and many Christian thinkers preached: Whoever is in authority must be obeyed, and resistance is illegitimate. Locke, however, has serious reservations against this doctrine. "Government," he tells us, "being for the Preservation of every Man's Right and Property, by preserving him from the Violence or Injury of Others, is for the Good of the Governed" (I 92). There is a standard against

108. Ibid. II 42.
109. Ibid.

which rulers must be judged. This, of course, is a preview of what Locke will present in the *Second Treatise*. Locke refuses to accept as the rational or true political doctrine this conservative reading of Romans 13. Such a doctrine imposes no standards of governance to which rulers ought to or must conform, and no practical mechanism by which standards could be enforced. In practice, this doctrine leaves subjects at the mercy of rulers, whom Locke describes in a very unflattering way:

He that would have been insolent and injurious in the Woods of America, would not probably be much better in a Throne; where perhaps Learning and Religion shall be found to justify all, that he shall do to his subjects, and the sword presently silence all those that dare question it. (I 92)

On the one side, then, the Romans 13 doctrine encourages a kind of passivity and quiescence in the populace that leads to abusive rulers, because the rulers are too secure in their position and too independent of those over whom they rule. The conservative reading of the Christian political dispensation has the paradoxical result that "there would be no distinction between Pirates and Lawful Princes, he that has Force is without any more ado to be oblig'd and Crowns and Scepters would become the Inheritances only of Violence and Rapine" (I 81). (The reference to the pirates and lawful princes, of course, connects Locke's discussion to one of the classic texts of Christian political theology, Augustine's *City of God*.)

Locke maintains that the conservative interpretation of Christian doctrine (all possessors of political power are *ipso facto* the "higher powers" to whom obedience is due) has the paradoxically opposite effects of encouraging tyranny by rendering rulers too secure and too immune from the judgment of their subjects, and also of encouraging unrest and rebellion by legitimating whoever can emerge victorious in the struggle for authority. If it "remains disputable" who has the actual right to power, the Christian doctrine

will seem only to give a greater edge to Man's Natural Ambition, which of itself is but too keen. What can this do but set men on the more eagerly to scramble, and so lay a sure and lasting Foundation of endless Contention and Disorder, instead of that Peace and Tranquility, which is the business of Government, and the end of Humane Society. (I 106)

Massaniello and Cromwell, usurpers both, are equally empowered by Christian political theology. Whoever can seize power and become "the higher powers" is justified in doing so, if he is successful. But, of course, one cannot know if one has the "mandate of Heaven" until one makes the attempt.

Moreover, as the example of Cromwell makes clear, Christianity can give incentives beyond mere ambition to the struggle for power. The true heir of Christ has the true claim to secular power, or at least to supervising the secular order. So long as it is contestable who the true heir of Christ is, that is an open invitation to political struggle.

No matter how one takes the chief guiding principle of Christian politics, the result, Locke suggests, is unsettling and dangerous. As Locke says of Filmer, Paul does not sufficiently specify who or on what grounds are the true "governing authorities."

The various consequences of the attempt to determine who should rule according to peculiarly Christian criteria then are either tyranny, usurpation and political adventurism, or struggle fired by conscience and the sacredness of rule because of its divine institution. None of these options is good, or comports with what reason teaches about the true end of politics, "the preservation of every man's rights and property, by preserving him from the violence or injury of others" (I 92). As much or more than Filmer's doctrine, Pauline theology "leaves no room for humane prudence, or consent. . . . And thus this doctrine cuts up all government by the Roots" (I 126). This passage may therefore be taken to point toward an alternative kind of politics that Locke is attempting to institute in place of the various versions of Christian politics; Locke's politics would leave full scope for human prudence and consent.

Given the potential political difficulties of the Romans 13 text, Locke, not surprisingly, reinterprets it into a version of the rational political truth, i.e., of his own political philosophy.

Government being for the Preservation of every Man's Right and Property, by preserving him from the Violence or Injury of others, is for the good of the Governed. For the magistrates' sword being for a Terror to Evil Doers, and by that Terror to enforce them to observe the positive Laws of Society, made conformable to the Laws of Nature, for the public good, i.e. the good of every particular Member of that Society, as far as by common Rulers, it can be provided for. (I 92)

Although Locke has mingled some of the text of Romans 13 into this passage, the substance of it derives from his rational account of politics. He discerns the rational teaching and then interprets the biblical text to conform to it (as far as he is able).

Locke's "Lockean" reading of Romans 13 harmonizes biblical doctrine with the rational political doctrine he adumbrates in the *Second Treatise*, a doctrine with three elements lacking from Locke's interpretation of the Christian doctrine as laid out in Romans. First, it rests political authority clearly on the "consent of the governed," i.e., on the free agreement of the citizens to the authority they are under. This requirement both grows out of and preserves the natural freedom of humanity. Second, the Lockean doctrine has a clear criterion of rightful governance: as the Lockean Thomas Jefferson put it, "to preserve these [natural] rights governments are instituted among men." Finally, there are clear mechanisms established by which the consent and rights securing requirements may be enforced. The property owners (i.e., everyone, as a self-owner) or their representatives must consent to taxation and perhaps legislation; beyond that, the people have "the right to alter or abolish" governments which, in their judgment, do not fulfill the requirements for legitimacy. Those requirements, in turn, are the requirements for a free politics, one consistently recognizing and serving human freedom. The prerequisite to that achievement was Locke's critique cum reinterpretation of the biblical understanding of man, God, and politics, for the Bible, almost to the same degree as Filmer himself, fails to lay the groundwork for a free politics.

10   FREEDOM AND FAITH WITHIN THE BOUNDARIES OF BARE REASON

SUSAN MELD SHELL

Religion within the Boundaries of Bare Reason has been the object of new and growing interest in recent years. Henry Allison, for example, finds in it Kant's fullest and most detailed treatment of the executive power, or "autocracy," of the will whereby we determine ourselves decisively for good or evil. Felicitas Munzel has mined it for Kant's understanding of moral "character" as a crucial link between his critical philosophy and his anthropology. And a number of scholars, including Allen Wood, Philip J. Rossi, and Sharon Anderson-Gold, have used it as a springboard in their respective efforts to uncover a less "individualistic," more attractively "communitarian" Kant than he is generally taken to be. Mark Lilla, on the other hand, finds in these same communitarian tendencies ominous anticipations of the anti-liberal, quasi-religious German nationalism that was to have such tragic consequences for the twentieth century. Each of these broadly conceived approaches to Kant's work draws valuable attention to neglected aspects of Kant's thought. At the same time, each, taken in itself, risks simplifying a text that is complicated, even by Kantian standards. Interpreting a text in which interpretation is itself a major theme is no simple task, and I will be happy if the following remarks go some way toward clarifying Kant's central argument.

I

That *Religion* is a particularly difficult work in which to gain one's footing is evident from the variety of responses it has provoked among serious readers from its inception. Is it an unworthy concession to religious orthodoxy (as Goethe famously accused) or merely a prudent restatement of his thought in Christian guise (as Herman Cohen, among others, has urged). Or, finally, does it represent a new insight into the character of authentic (and authentically German) religious faith (as Schleiermacher and other Romantics claimed)?

The dove-like yet serpentine elusiveness[1] of *Religion* partly results from the new political circumstances that both called it forth and famously threatened its arrival. The ascension to the throne of the Frederick William II, in 1789, and the subsequent installment of the Johann Christoph Wöllner as minister of education and religious affairs, had placed new obstacles in the way of public enlightenment of the sort that Frederick the Great had tolerated and even encouraged. In *What is Enlightenment* and other works of the early 1780s, Kant had, it seems, made his peace with a monarchy that allowed "public" discourse to flourish in return for "private" obedience. Hope of juridical and moral progress, through the gradual transformation of "enlightened" despotism, was not, for him, unthinkable, as is born out by Kant's 1784 *Idea for a Universal History*. The French Revolution transformed those hopes, even as German reaction threatened to upend them. For Wöllner and his conservative allies, continuing political stability demanded a strengthening of popular belief in divine punishment for civil disobedience. Wöllner's consequent policies challenged Kant's critical project of enlightenment on *four* distinct, yet related, fronts. *First,* by requiring of candidates in theology a formal profession of faith, they threatened to make the principle teachers (and potential enlighteners) of the people into tools of spiritual and moral despotism. *Second,* by reactivating the previously dead letter of the religious censorship laws, Wöllner threatened Kant himself (and his immediate followers) with public silence. The difficulties, culminating in formal censorship, that dogged Kant's effort to publish *Religion*, without violating his own principles of civic obedience and (outward) honesty, are well known, and constitute one of the work's more obvious rhetorical challenges. *Third,* the challenge faced by Kant was not only to *immediate* prospects for enlightenment—though that was serious enough; beyond the clumsy maneuverings of the new government lay a deeper challenge to Kant's fundamental conception of the rational life. Behind Wöllner's edicts lies a real question (raised by critic August Wilhelm Rehberg and others) as to the adequacy of the moral law alone as an incentive to right action. That question raises doubts, in turn, as to the sufficiency of conscience, as Kant understands it, to govern the human soul.[2] As we shall see, such doubts, and a related "hesitancy [*Bedenklichkeit*]" in human beings ("even the best") to obey the moral law, guide Kant's discussion of the source of human evil and the conditions that must be met if man is ever to improve. *Fourth,* and finally, by threatening pros-

---

1. Cf. *Perpetual Peace* [8:370].
2. See editor's Introduction, Kant, *Religion and Rational Theology*, ed. Allen Wood and George di Giovanni (Cambridge: Cambridge University Press, 1996), xiii.

pects for "progress" on this triple front (among the masses, among the educated, and philosophically), Wöllner's edicts call into question the predominance of good over evil in the human soul; they thus pose a potentially disabling challenge, both theoretical and practical, to moral resoluteness as Kant conceives it. Indeed, Kant's later "historical" essays are taken up with meeting precisely this challenge. A similar resort to "history," is, as I hope to show, at once the most urgent and the deepest goal of *Religion within the Boundaries of Bare Reason*.

Before turning directly to Kant's text, two preliminary considerations may prove helpful.

1. Kant's understanding of "true religion" follows in the revolutionary path, blazed by Rousseau, which subordinates religious faith to sincerity before the voice of human conscience.[3] Like Rousseau, Kant treats religion as a mere means, albeit an "exalted" one, to the fulfillment of demands "written on the human heart." Such demands, in this view, are known directly, by all normal human beings, without reliance on the authority of others. In this, Kant departs both from the classical philosophic tradition and from traditional Christian theology, for each of which authority serves as an essential human remedy.

According to this new understanding, man's conscience, taken in itself, is unambiguous and incorruptible. Conscience represents what we cannot help believing (or, in Kantian terms, "holding to be true"). The foundation of virtue, on this view, is neither theoretical wisdom nor loving obedience to God (and his chosen representatives), but a kind of inner candor or "sincerity" in acknowledging what we actually hold to be true—a conscientiousness that is always in our power and for which we can therefore be held accountable.

Kant also follows Rousseau (or his Savoyard Vicar) in seeing in the primacy of conscience so understood a resolution to the conflict, in which human reason otherwise entangles itself, between dogmatic assurance and skeptical despair.[4] For both Rousseau's Vicar and Kant the primacy of conscience follows upon recognition of the limits of human reason insofar as it lays claim to ultimate metaphysical knowledge. Kant and Rousseau seem to draw different conclusions, however, from these lim-

---

3. Sincerity is already a potent vehicle for Hobbes and Locke, each of whom appeals to it (in different ways) as a means to the preservation of civil peace. The view that we should not be held to account for the doctrine in which we were raised (which, for Rousseau, vindicates decent women, who quite properly assume the religion of their parents and then of their husbands), is, for Kant, itself a snare that justifies moral "passivity" [6:132n.]. On Rousseau and sincerity see also Arthur Melzer, "Rousseau and the Modern Cult of Sincerity," in *The Legacy of Rousseau*, ed. Clifford Orwin and Nathan Tarcov (Chicago: University of Chicago Press, 1997).

4. See *Critique of Pure Reason*, A/710=B/738.

its. Whereas conscience competes in the Rousseauian corpus with other (non-moral) expressions of longing for an irrecoverable, pre-rational state, Kant makes conscience the ultimate basis for what Richard Velkley has described as the self-rectifying "unity of reason."[5] Conscience becomes the court in which reason lays down for itself its own inner law. Finally, and perhaps most importantly, Kant goes further than Rousseau in insisting on the *sufficiency* of conscience, or the moral law, to motivate the human heart. Where otherworldly reward and punishment remains, for Rousseau, a necessary *ressort* of virtue, Kant urges the sufficiency of practical reason, or the moral law, as its own incentive. Reconciling that sufficiency with our subjective *experience* of duty as an unremitting debt constitutes, as we shall see, the crucial task of his *Religion*.

2. A second preliminary note: In locating the foundation of morality in the certitude of conscience, Kant practices what has been called a sort of ethical Cartesianism. Although one's judgments as to what is right in a given instance can be wrong, "I absolutely cannot be mistaken as to whether or not I believe something to be right." (I may be wrong in saying that the earth is flat; I cannot be wrong about whether or not I genuinely believe it.) Such a foundation suits Kant's identification of personality with the capacity for imputable agency. (A person, according to the *Metaphysics of Morals*, is a being who can get moral credit for its acts [6: 223].)

And yet, if inner candor is always possible (and hence imputable to us) it is also, for Kant, strangely difficult: As he puts it in his essay on *Theodicy* (which appeared two years before *Religion*), though "I absolutely cannot be mistaken" as to whether or not I believe something to be right, I can lack conscientiousness [*Gewissenhaftigkeit*] about becoming conscious of this belief. "The human being knows how to distort even inner declarations before his own conscience" [8:270]. Where the Savoyard Vicar had only to consult his interest "in the silence of the prejudices" [E269], Kant confronts a wilier enemy in *self*-interest [cf. E 267]. Something in the human soul *resists* becoming aware of that which we cannot help "holding to be true." The highest human virtue is thus not perfect candor (or "openheartedness [*Offenherzigkeit*] ") but only sincerity [*Aufrichtigkeit*], understood as "[constant] care [Sorghaft]" in "becoming conscious" of our belief (or lack thereof), "and asserting no holding-to-be-true [*Fürwahrhalten*] of which one is not conscious" [8:268].[6]

---

5. Richard L. Velkley, *Freedom and the End of Reason* (Chicago: University of Chicago Press, 1989).
6. Cf. Kant's own declaration of "full conscientiousness" in his letter of response to the Royal edict of censorship; Kant published both the edict and his letter of response in the Preface to the *Conflict of the Faculties* [7:10].

Frederick William II's recently imposed "profession of faith" on candidates in theology—the immediate context and impetus for both of Kant's essays—thus posed an immediate threat to public enlightenment. A people accustomed to using external professions of faith "as *means of gain* [Erwerbmittel]"—acquires a kind of falsehood in its "communal way of thinking [*Falschheit in die Denkungsart selbst des gemeinen Wesens*]." And yet, given current policy, Kant says, all efforts to purify the public way of thinking must be deferred to the indefinite future, when they can be undertaken under the "protection of free thinking [*unter dem Schutze der Denkfreiheit*]."

In the meantime, Kant expends [*verwenden*] "a few lines" on consideration of the fact that "sincerity" is at once the "least that can possibly be required of a good character" and "the property farthest removed from human nature" [8.267–69; 270]. We need good character to become sincere, and we need sincerity to acquire good character. How, then, are we to avoid becoming (like Rousseau himself)[7] a "contemplative" (and morally dispirited) "misanthrope?"

II

Religion within the Boundaries of Bare Reason takes up the problem of "contemplative" misanthropy anew with a question of its own: Why do we need religion at all? For:

So far as morality is grounded on the concept of man as a free being, who thus binds himself through his reason to unconditioned laws, it needs neither the idea of a being above man for him recognize his duties, nor an incentive [*Triebfeder*] other than the law itself in order for him to observe it. At least it is man's own fault [*Schuld*] if such a need is found in him, though in this case too the need could not be relieved by anything else; for what does not originate from himself and his freedom provides no substitute [*Ersatz*] for a lack in his morality. [6: 3][8]

Man does not require religion to provide morality with an incentive (as Kant's current enemies insisted);[9] we require religion, instead, to satisfy a "natural need" that would otherwise constitute a moral "hindrance [*Hindering*]" [6:5].

Kant's argument is immediately perplexing. The difference between

---

7. On Rousseau's "gloomy hypochondria" concerning the human species, see *Anthropology* [7:326–32].

8. All translations are my own unless otherwise indicated.

9. And Kant himself had once allowed. On Kant's early struggles over the question of moral motivation, see Dieter Henrich, *The Unity of Reason: Essays on Kant's Philosophy*, ed. Richard Velkley (Cambridge: Harvard University Press, 1994), chapter 2.

claiming (with Rehberg and his allies) that man needs religion because the incentives of the law are "not enough" and claiming that we need religion to overcome a natural hindrance to morality, seems fine indeed. And yet the importance of the difference to Kant can hardly be overstated, given that a profession of reverence for the moral law that does not grant its self-sufficiency as an incentive, amounts to "hypocrisy" and "inner falsity" [6:42n.].

There is a further difficulty: If our religious need arises from a limitation intrinsic to our nature, how can it be our fault, as Kant insists?

Kant's answer to this second question is relatively clear. If we were, morally speaking, what we ought to be—if our virtue were unshakable—nothing could interfere with our adherence to the moral law, whose incentives are per se "enough." Our religious need is thus our fault in the same way that moral imperfection is our fault.

An answer to the first question is harder to work out, though it will prove essential to Kant's argument. As embodied rational, i.e., human, beings, we cannot act without entertaining some purpose: without an end "no determination of the will can take place in human beings at all." Hence, although the law suffices [*genug ist*] for morality, a will intent on acting in obedience to the moral law still needs to know the "whither," without which the will itself wouldn't "do enough [*Gnüge*]" [6:4].[10] Thus, if we are to be adequate to the law's incentives, we need an end "determined by the law." Accordingly, morality itself gives rise to the idea—the highest good possible in the world—of what a will with principles would aim at. This idea is said to "meet our natural need, which would otherwise be a hindrance to moral resolve [*Entschließung*]," to "think [*denken*] for all our doings and nondoings taken as a whole some sort of ultimate end [*Endzweck*] that reason can justify." Such an end gives practical reality to the for us indispensable combination of the purposiveness of nature with a purposiveness arising out of freedom [6:5]. But this idea requires, in turn, the idea of a divine author, without whom the possibility of realizing that end remains unthinkable.

The idea of the highest good possible in the world is, as idea, not a possible object of experience, and yet, as "possible in the world," not experientially vacant either, at least insofar as we actively *make* it our end.

---

10. "Although on its own behalf morality needs no representation of an end . . . it may well be that it has a necessary reference to such an end. . . . For without any relation to an end no determination of the will can take place in a human being . . . who must [at least] be able to represent an end as the consequence [*Folge*] of the determination of his will. Without this, a power of choice [*Willkür*], unable to add in thought [*hin zu denkt*] . . . a determinate object to an action before it, is instructed, to be sure, as to how but not *whither* [wohin] it is to have an effect [zu *wirken habe*], [and thus] cannot satisfy/do enough [*nicht Gnüge thun kann*]" [6:4].

The *Endzweck* is at once within our power (for otherwise it could not overcome impediments to our resolve) and beyond our power (for only the idea of a divine highest cause of such an end allows us to think of it as possible). Kant's "authentic" interpretation of biblical religion (as a "reading" of the intention of God made manifest in history) will join these opposing claims in a single allegorizing narrative.

III

We can better understand how religion meets what Kant calls man's "natural need" by examining his treatment of radical evil. "The thesis of innate evil," Kant says, "is of no use in moral *dogmatics*" (it doesn't affect our knowledge of what the law demands); it is of use only in moral "discipline" [6:50–51; cf. *Metaphysics of Morals* (6:484, 485)]. Discipline, according to the *Critique of Pure Reason,* is the "compulsion through which the constant propensity [*beständige Hang*] to stray from certain rules is limited and finally eradicated [*vertilgt*]."[11] *The Critique of Judgment* calls discipline a "negative liberation [*Befreiung*]" of the will from a despotism through which "we become made incapable of choosing for ourselves." Discipline, then, constitutes a kind of negative culture, which counters the propensities (or *Hangen*) that would otherwise obstruct development of our natural dispositions (or *Anlagen*).

Wherein, then, lies that obstruction to the (natural) development of our moral dispositions (or "active opposition to the good" [6:23n.]) which *moral* discipline must counter? The original disposition, or *Anlage,* to the good, according to Kant [6:26], is threefold, consisting in:

1. the *Anlage* to animality (insofar as we are living beings);

2. the *Anlage* to humanity (insofar as we are living and also rational beings); and

3. the *Anlage* to personality (insofar as we are rational and also responsible beings).

Kant here insists upon the difference between embodied rationality as such, and embodied rationality endowed with personality. "So far as we can see," "the most rational being in the world" might not be able to determine [*bestimmen*] his power of choice [*Willkür*] without incentives coming from the objects of inclination. He might apply to those objects the most rationalizing [*vernünftigste*] reflection, concerning both the

---

11. As such, it differs from culture, which produces one readiness [*Fertigkeit*] without canceling [*aufzuheben*] another [A/709=B/737]. In the *Critique of Judgment,* discipline is called a branch of culture, whose other branch is skill [5:42].

greatest sum of incentives and the means of achieving the end thereby determined, without suspecting even the possibility of moral, absolutely binding law. The *announcement* of that law—what Kant elsewhere calls the "sole *factum* of reason"—on the other hand, is no mere ratiocination.[12] "If the law, which makes us conscious both of our freedom and of the accountability of our actions, were not given to us from *within*, no amount of reasoning would cleverly reveal it [*durch keine Vernunft herausklügeln*] nor persuade our power of choice" [6: 26n.].

Whereas the animal drives associated with the *Anlage* to animality are concerned with immediate enjoyment, the inclinations associated with humanity (i.e., with reason with or without personality) exhibit themselves in a concern for "happiness" in general. These inclinations presuppose a timely rational capacity to defer present enjoyment with a view to maximizing the future total.

Now reason, so understood, implies not only an ability to compare relative goods, but also a concern with what Kant calls "external freedom" as "the highest formal good of our natural condition."[13] As Kant puts it in the *Anthropology*, a man whose happiness depends on *another* man's choice (no matter how benevolent the other may be) "rightly considers himself unhappy," because he lacks a guarantee that his and his powerful neighbor's judgment concerning his well-being will agree now and in the future.[14]

As an embodied rational being, who seeks to maximize the satisfaction of my desires, I cannot help placing a supreme formal value on my external freedom from dependence on another's arbitrary will. And yet I cannot *feel* this freedom, Kant says, other than by measuring my freedom against the external freedom (and hence happiness) of others. I abhor others' contempt, in other words, because I thereby *feel* myself diminished in a good that I necessarily cherish.

Such considerations best explain, I think, Kant's elliptical claim, in

12. "*Vernünftelei*" is elsewhere defined as "a use of reason that ignores its final end." "Vain *Vernünfteleien*," though not "untrue," constitute "an unprofitable expenditure of understanding." *Vernünftelei* in its proper form is called *Scharfsinnigkeit* or "acumen," in that it consists in the "talent of noticing even the slightest similarities and dissimilarities" [7:200–201].

13. See Kant's *Anthropology* lectures of 1788/9: "Freedom is fundamentally a *negative* condition of the satisfaction of our desires and consists in the distancing of all opposition to determining oneself according to one's own inclination. It is the greatest formal inclination and is held by everyone to be the greatest good. It permits itself to be felt [*empfinden*] only through comparison with the condition of others or through diminishment [*Beraubung*] of the latter. Crude nations therefore have great contempt for *subalterns*. They cannot think as having any worth [*Werth*] a human being who is *at the behest* [befehligt] of another" [25.2:1520].

14. *Anthropology* [9:68].

Religion, that "one judges oneself happy or unhappy only in comparison with others" [6: 27]. Accordingly, *rational* self-love (which seeks satisfaction in one's total life condition, rather than mere animal pleasures of the moment) necessarily gives rise to "the inclination *to gain value in the opinion of others*" as a way of feeling provided against a loss of external freedom, a loss one cannot help but find painful. Originally, this inclination will take the form of an insistence on *equal worth,* or not allowing anyone superiority over oneself. And yet "constant anxiety" that others might be striving for superiority over us gradually gives rise to an "unjust desire" for preemptive domination [6: 27]. What Kant calls the "vices of civilization" "do not [then] . . . issue from nature as their root." As expressions of our desire for external freedom, "jealousy" and "rivalry" "make room for" vice without requiring it. Moral evil arises not out of rational self-love per se, nor the ensuing competition (which ought to be a spur to culture),[15] but only (as we shall see) by an elevation of external freedom, or the "highest formal good of our natural condition," to the highest value simply.

Against what, then, is moral discipline to direct its forces? The propensity to evil must be rooted in the will (for otherwise we would not be responsible for extirpating it), yet without touching on personality (for otherwise we would not be capable of doing so). The propensity to evil must thus involve the will's fundamental choice, without implying the insufficiency of law as an incentive. There are, Kant finds, three ways in which that condition can be met. We can "take up" the incentive of the law into our fundamental maxim and yet neglect to apply it (frailty); or we can "take up" that incentive without taking care to distinguish it from others (impurity); or, finally, we can actively invert the order of incentives, so that we make our obedience to the law conditional on *first* satisfying incentives of happiness (perversity). Evil, so conceived, does not involve a repudiation of the law (which would be inconsistent with man's incorruptible *Anlage* to personality), but only its deferral, so

---

15. Competition [*Wetteifers*] is literally a kind of bet or wager, in which we risk failure in an attempt to prove ourselves. In the *Anthropology,* Kant highlights "competition" as the site of passion "of the most intense and enduring kind"—a passion attached to what Kant calls "the inclination to illusion." This inclination has the natural purpose of "stimulating the vital force" to "make us more active" and "prevent our losing the feeling of life completely in mere enjoyment." This tendency to take objects of imagination for real ends is a ploy on nature's part to arouse the lazy to healthy exertion. The ensuing sense of bodily wellbeing makes illusional passions (such as that for gambling) especially intractable. The related tendency to "mistake the subjective for the objective, and to take the voice of inner sense for knowledge of things themselves" explains men's susceptibility to superstition, or "the inclination to expect interesting results" (something to be hoped for or feared) from circumstances that "cannot be natural causes"—a susceptibility especially common in gamblers. (Kant was himself in his early years an avid billiards player.)

that instead of morality trumping happiness, here and now, happiness trumps morality.

How, then, are we to account for this inversion (as we must try to do if we are to counter it adequately)?[16] The inversion must be both inextirpable (for it involves a corruption of the ground of maxims) and overcomable (for it is culpable—the result of human beings acting freely). Kant associates the inversion with the same "competitiveness" that, for good and ill, marks the *Anlage* to humanity. Evil, he says, springs from frailty and dishonesty in not screening one intentions "even in the case of well-intentioned actions"—in short, a certain perfidy [*Tücke*] and "self deceit" in which one fails to trouble oneself [*zu beunruhigen*] about one's own way of thinking, and instead holds oneself justified to the extent that one compares favorably with others [6:38]. (He ran the light. I stopped; hence, I'm justified.)

Our lazy failure to inquire, as we should, into our own inner way of thinking—an inquiry that might put us on the road to self-improvement—is ultimately rooted in a self-satisfaction we take in our own outward conformity to law (in comparison with others). That false self-satisfaction, or lack of inner conscientiousness, as Kant insists, "puts out of tune [*verstimmt*] moral judgment as to what one should take a person [*einen Menschen*] for," by making "imputation [or moral accounting] [*Zurechnung*] entirely uncertain [*ungewiß*]" [6:38].[17] And it thus prevents the inner disposition to goodness from developing as it should. Moral judgment is like a moneychanger's scale, which—if sound—instantaneously registers the infinite superiority of the law's incentive to anything else that makes life worth choosing.

Elucidation of the source of evil (the *Verstimmung* of the scale) is complicated, however, by the fact that the origin of evil, as an act of freedom, cannot be located in some past moment of time. Nothing can obviate my duty *now* to better myself, which, therefore, must always still be possible. One can, however, inquire into the "inner possibility" of falling into evil, i.e., "the subjective universal ground of the taking up of a transgression

16. Since man is in a morally dangerous state through his own fault, he is obliged to expend as much force as he can to work himself out of it. But how? "That is the question" [6:93].

17. Kant goes on to cite Walpole (and, indirectly, Hobbes) to the effect that "every man has his price, for which he sells himself," If this is so—and here each may "add things up [*ausmachen*]" for himself—if no virtue is to be found that has the wealth/means [*Vermögen*] to cast down [*stürzen*] every vitiation/contamination [*Versuchung*] (*stürzen* also means "count the cash"), if the victory of the good or evil principle depends only on "which bids the most and pays off most quickly,"—then, "as the Apostle says," we are all under sin [6:38–39]. Kant's refutation of original sin in the traditional sense rests on "finding" in man a moral capital sufficient to offset the values by which calculative reason necessarily reckons.

into our maxim" [6:41]. Kant pursues that inquiry through an allegorical interpretation of Genesis that represents the origin of evil in time without literally implying its inheritability or temporal transmission.

Accordingly, the origin of evil arises from an act, in which the human being (Adam), does not follow the law immediately as a sufficient incentive ("which alone is unconditionally good, and about which there can be no hesitation [*Bedenken*]").[18] Instead he

looked around [*umsehen*] for other incentives, which could only be conditionally good (i.e., insofar as they do not infringe upon the law). And he made it his maxim—if one thinks of the action as originating consciously from freedom—to follow the law of duty not out of duty but—just in case [*allenfalls*]—with a view to other aims. With this, he began to doubt [*bezweifeln*] the strength/rigor [*Strenge*] of the command, which excludes the influence of any other incentive, and thereupon to rationalize [*zu vernünfteln*] obedience to that of a bare, conditioned means (under the principle of self-love); so that finally the preponderance of sensible impulses over the incentive of the law was taken up into the maxim of action, and thus he became sinful/unsound [*gesündigt*]. [6:42]

The human being hedges his bets, looking—just in case the law should not itself suffice (as if the law could fail to suffice!)—for another reason to obey it.[19] He thus begins to doubt the strength/rigor of the law, which excludes all other incentives, and, in so doing, gradually "takes up" into his maxim, incentives foreign to the law.[20] In his unwillingness to wager everything upon the law, he undermines its force, giving sensual impulses [*Antrieben*] preponderant weight [*Übergewicht*] against its *Triebfeder*. The radical corruption of the human will lies in its pursuit of incentives to obey beyond the law, its failure to incorporate the moral law into its maxims literally "without bethinking itself" *(unbedenklich)* [6: 42–43; 58n.].[21]

But the human being, in this regard, confronts a difficulty he cannot get round: our need to see, in any practically contemplated action, what it is good for. Religion, indeed, is (as we earlier saw) the concession that morality in general makes to the human "limitation" that leads

18. Compare Kant's insistence that we are "certainly and immediately conscious" of a capacity [*Vermögens*] of being able to overcome, by firm resolve [*Vorsatz*], every possible incentive to transgression, and that, nevertheless, we are all uncertain whether we might not, in a given situation, waver in our resolve [6:49n.–50n.]. Certitude as to our capacity and incertitude as to our performance are the necessary concomitants of conscience as man experiences it.

19. See note 14.

20. Moral faith, on the other hand, is registered in one's willingness to stake everything upon it. Cf. *Critique of Pure Reason* A/824=B/852 ff.

21. I am indebted to Peter Fenves for calling my attention to the importance of this term in Kant's late writings.

us to seek, in every action, something that might serve us as an end, if only that of proving our own inner purity [6:7n.]. (It is this very limitation, intrinsic to our experience of ourselves as worldly actors, that makes possible the synthetic "extension" of the moral law, as a "duty" to make "the highest good possible in the world our ultimate end"—a duty beyond "the concept of all duties in the world" and arising "sui generis" in the human species.) Religion thus answers to the weakness that gets the procrastinating Adam in all of us in trouble—our dissatisfaction with a law whose unconditional goodness does not immediately attract us. Beyond the respect that motivates obedience to the law, we "seek something [we] can love."[22] True religion will thus have the character of love, or unforced veneration—a veneration that can be "truthful" only if (contrary to Wöllner's edicts) it is given freely.[23]

To be sure, the formation [*Bildung*] of a character must begin with a transformation [*Umwandlung*] in the way of thinking [*Denkungsart*], a transformation that lies outside of time. Still, in no human being is moral judgment entirely uncorrupted: in "even the most limited [*eingeschränkteste*] human beings," including children, the slightest admixture of impure incentive destroys, "in a twinkling of an eye [*augenblicklich*]," all the moral value of an action. The *Anlage* to the good is thus initially cultivated "in no better way," Kant says, than by inviting students to ferret out the impurity in the apparently good deeds of others.[24] The engrafted vices of civilization can be combatted, at least initially, through the same inclination to competitiveness and ratiocination that invites them.

Kant here takes explicit issue with the classical ethical view according to which admiration of noble deeds is the appropriate starting point for moral education. To teach pupils to admire [*bewundern*] virtuous activity, however great the sacrifice that it may cost, does not produce the "correct balance/attunement [*rechte Stimmung*]" that sustains the disposition to the good. On the contrary, such admiration [*bewundern*] puts "out of tune"/unbalances [as in *Abstimmung*] our feeling for duty, for it suggests that obedience to duty deserves "special merit" [6:49]. What truly arouses wonder [*Bewunderung*] is not any particular human actor (who never, after all, can do more than what he owes), nor even duty as such, which does not lie outside "the common moral order"—but rather, reason's inexplicable capacity to override "reasoning," i.e., its own calculus of finite value.

---

22. [6:7n.]

23. This requirement is the main theme of Kant's later essay *The End of All Things*.

24. In this way, duty for its own sake begins to acquire, in the novice's heart, a "noticeable weight [*Gewicht*]" [6:48].

What is it in us (one can ask oneself) through which we, as beings ever dependent on nature through so many needs, are at the same time lifted up so far above it in the idea of an original predisposition (in us) that we would hold the whole of nature to be nothing [*nichts*], and ourselves to be unworthy of existence, were we to pursue [*nachhängen*] an *enjoyment of nature that can alone make life worth wishing for* [*wünchenswerth*], against a moral law that reason commands without promising or threatening anything. [6:49; emphasis added]

In the sublime unanswerability of this question—which Kant repeatedly puts to his readers—"worthiness" immediately trumps the collective value of *everything* that might make life worth wishing for. Hence, its peculiarly attuning "weight," as Kant has it, "for every man of the least capacity who has been instructed in the holiness of the idea of duty." We can best counter the perversion of incentives that obstructs cultivation of our *Anlage* to the good only by bearing witness, over and over again, to reason's sublime failure to comprehend how its own determination [or *Bestimmung*] is possible [6:50].

In the sublime experience of that necessary failure, *pure* religion enters the picture: the incomprehensibility [*Unbegreiflichkeit*] of our predisposition "to overcome with firm resolve" every incentive contrary to the moral law—a predisposition to which no concept (of reason) can be adequate—"announces the divinity of its origin," and affects the mind [*Gemüth*] "to the point of exhaltation [*Begeisterung*]". Unable either to deny or to comprehend the possibility of human goodness, reason registers a divinity within itself (or "enthusiasm" in the true and literal sense, and as distinguished from mere *Schwärmerei*) that (almost) makes law lovable.

And yet, the effort to better oneself morally cannot stop here. The transformation [*Umwandlung*] of an evil into a good human being must be "posited" as an alteration of the will's "highest inner ground" in such a way that the new ground (or heart) is now unchangeable [*unwandelbar*]. Of such a transformation, man can have no "immediate consciousness," nor can he attain conviction [*Überzeugung*] of it by any natural means, including the evidence furnished by his past life-conduct/exchange [*Lebenswandel*].

Given the incomprehensibility, in subjectively rational terms, of moral worth, we are prone to find our own powers wanting when we compare them with the infinite expenditure of moral force that is required of us. To be sure, "practical conviction as to the fact that one is judged morally good only on the basis of what can be imputed [*zugerechnet*] to one," *ought* to suffice to support the hope that "by the expenditure of [our] own forces [*Kraftanwendung*]" we can set ourselves on the right road [*Weg*] [6:51]. And yet reason "naturally" finds moral labor vexing/

disheartening [*verdrossene*]; it thus "summons up," against the aforementioned moral "presumption [*Zumuthung*]", and under the pretext of incapacity/bankruptcy [*Unvermögens*], "all sorts of impure religious ideas." These impure ideas seem to absolve us, in one way or another, from the hard labor of attending to our own self-improvement.

On the one hand, our "self-incurred perversity" can be overcome only through the idea of the moral good "in its absolute purity," along with "consciousness that it belongs to our original *Anlage*." Hence the crucial role of moral/religious exaltation in overcoming that contemplative misanthropy which puts possession of this *Anlage* in doubt.

And yet, the very need that leads to pure moral religion bespeaks a fundamental human vulnerability. The people, especially, "seek a more vivid way of representing things" than pure moral religion can furnish. They are thus tempted to make good their lack of moral confidence, with superstition, faith in false expiations, and *Schwärmerei* (inner illuminations) [6:83; 6:53].

From this weakness, particularly associated with the people, arises the need for a church faith, which provides pure moral religion with greater allegorical vividness, without thereby mystically corrupting it. Accordingly, Kant divides all religion between "that seeking to acquire [divine] favor (bare cult)," and religion of good life conduct. In the first case:

> the human being flatters himself [*schmeichelt sich*] either that God can make him eternally happy without his having to do anything to become a better human being (through the remission of his debts), or, if this does not seem possible . . . that God can make him a better human being without his having to do more than ask for it, which, since to an all-seeing being such asking is no more than *wishing*, amounts to doing nothing. [6:51]

In the case of moral religion, on the other hand (a religion, according to Kant, of which Christianity is the only known public example):

> It is a fundamental principle [*Grundsatz*] that each must do as much as lies in his forces, and only then, if he has not buried his inborn capital/talent [*Pfund*] (Luke 19:12–16), [i.e.] if he has used the original deposit [*Anlage*] to the good in order to become a better human being, could he hope that what is not in his means [*Vermögen*] will be completed through higher cooperation [*Mitwirkung*]. [6:52][25]

Kant's allegorical interpretation of Jesus' parable of the talents [Luke 19:12–27 and Matthew 25:14–30] points to the crucial difference that

---

25. One should keep in mind that *"Anlage"* in German also means "capital, or money put out at interest."

divides a cultic "bondservice [*Lohndienst*]" to God (or spiritual serfdom) from a service under what Kant calls "the dominion of the good." According to that parable, a master entrusted money to his servants, rewarding those who invested it profitably. The master punishes the servant who, for fear of the "hardness" of a master who "takes out what he didn't put in [*hinlegen*]," buries his talents instead of investing them [Luke 19:20–26]. That servant's wickedness, on Kant's account, consists in a counterpurposive rejection of the entire system of spiritual interest in which the master and his household are invested. Thus, the servant is upbraided by the master for his failure to put the master's money on interest-bearing loan. (In Luther's words, "warum hast du denn mein Geld nicht in die Wechselbank gegeben? [Why then did you not put my money into the bank?]") If he feared that the master would demand more back of him than he was given, he had only, if he genuinely wished to please his master, to make his deposit grow by his own efforts. But that would take a spiritual/economic revolution—an overturning of that moral arithmetic in which we can only passively return what we receive. The evil servant's unwillingness to expend his means, even with an interest-bearing guarantee, is an expression of the same Adamic "hesitation" that subjectively impedes our recognition of the objective sufficiency of the law's incentive. Worthiness—as that which alone gives worth to everything that makes life worth wishing for—trumps anything whose value must be measured in the currency of happiness. Religion, in its evil form, plays on our reluctance to expend the moral forces that have been deposited in us. Cultivation of our *Anlagen* to the good means expending those forces, not for an immediate return in the medium of happiness, but at an interest that will accrue to us in the higher currency of dignity (i.e., moral worthiness). For this, however, one's inner scale of judgment must be "rightly adjusted" or "in tune"—so that what is objectively of infinite worth (i.e., what gives value to one's very existence) subjectively receives its proper weight. Religion in its evil (gloomily penitential) form exacerbates the mood that puts out of tune the scale by which objective value is properly weighed—so that one looks about, with Adam, for an incentive to obey beyond that which is objectively sufficient. False religion does this, above all, by playing on the very sense of debt, or something owed, by which moral obligation registers subjectively. For if what is morally owed always overrides the incentives of human happiness, should they conflict, it can only be (to one who does not think rightly) because that debt is unremitting—a conclusion which furnishes a pretext for holding that one altogether lacks the means to satisfy it. The direct opposite of such a morally disabling, penitential attitude lies in the good mood of fortitude and cheer, i.e., in the presumption [*vermuthen*] of self-improvement in the future—such a good mood furnishing, indeed, the only available inner sign of moral genuineness [*Ächtheit*] [6:24n.].[26] For only the cheerful heart resists dissuasion from the expenditure that the moral law demands, on the "self-swindling" pretext that it lacks the capital [*Pfund*] to fund it.

In the *Metaphysics of Morals*, Kant identifies the rules of moral self-improvement with the attainment of two "attunements of the soul/mood [*Gemüthsstimmungen*]": cheerfulness and valor [*wacker*].[27] Valor, which follows from the Stoic maxim of renouncing and enduring, constitutes a kind of "mental health," which, like bodily soundness, can't, as such, be felt. To this merely negative well-being there must be added, then, that which, though only moral, *positively* contributes to the "agreeableness of life," namely the always [*jederzeit*] cheerful heart proposed by Epicurus.

According to the *Metaphysics of Morals*, no one has more cause to cheer than him for whom it is "no longer even a duty" to put himself in an habitually cheerful mood, i.e., one who is both "conscious of no resolved-upon transgressions," *and* "secured against the occasion for such." In lieu of absolute security on this account (an absolute security of which, as we have seen, our status as embodied rational beings [or "humanity"] necessarily deprives us), our only resort is a "gymnastics" through which one "combats natural drives sufficiently so as to be able, should the moral need arise, to master them." This "formal" awareness of one's means, and the cheer to which that awareness gives rise, is the closest one can come to actual "consciousness of one's recovered freedom."

To such gymnastic exercise, and a related moral mental health (or as close as we can knowingly come to it), Kant contrasts (a falsely Christian) penance, as a self-inflicted pain that serves no moral purpose. Penance cannot be what it is usually taken for, i.e., self-punishment (for to will to contradict one's will [as punishment must do] is itself self-contradictory); hence, it can only be a "serfdom [*Frohndeinst*]", in which one seeks to please through an expenditure of bodily force that leaves one's own moral capital untouched. The "discipline" that a human being perpetrates [*verübt*] upon himself can become deserving [*verdienstlich*] and exemplary only through the sense of cheer [*Frohsinn*] accompanying it [6:485].

In light of these considerations, "true" Christianity, in the Kantian sense, becomes Christianity without penance—that is to say, without an expenditure of one's own forces in whose end reason cannot share. A

26. In Kant's spelling, *Achtung* and *Echtheit* are verbally related.
27. According to Grimm, "*wacker*" derives from an old root (related to the English word "awake") meaning to stand watch; "*wacker*" conveys a sense, not just of general courage, but one of aroused and militant alertness against an enemy.

human being so enslaved to the dominion of the evil principle is, as we have seen, a spiritual bondsman, who serves God only with his body [*Frohn*], because he refuses to undertake that moral change of heart by which God's final purpose in creation would become his own. True service to God, by way of contrast, is an exercise in spiritual freedom, because any action whose end one immediately shares—however difficult and painful it may be—is uncoerced, and hence free by definition. The true servant of God is not a serf, passively dependent on his master, but (as in Kant's version of the parable of the talents) a fellow spiritual capitalist. The spiritual bondsman mistakes the dignity invested in his own moral *Anlagen* for an external fund on which he can infinitely draw, allowing him to postpone applying his own forces indefinitely. The true servant, on the other hand, earns interest on that deposit through an expenditure for which he can himself take credit, Kant here proposing what could be called a "labor" theory of moral value.[28]

True Christianity, so understood, becomes both a positive and a negative vehicle of cheer—a means, however "exalted," whose end (as Kant's Latin references make clear) resembles that of "virtuous" Epicurus. The difference between Epicurean and Christian approaches to cheer lies largely in Christianity's complex relation to the Judaism with which it is historically and institutionally entangled.[29] Paganism, with its many

28. *Religion's* supplementary "sideworks," or *parerga,* on the other hand, specifically address reason's consciousness of its own lack of means (i.e., its impotence or bankruptcy) to "do enough for" [*ein Genüge zu thun*] or satisfy, its moral needs, and its consequent resort to extravagant [*überschwenglichen*] ideas that it cannot take up into its maxims of "thought and action," and hence can make no proper moral use of. And yet, since such ideas "make up for" that bankruptcy, however unknowably, reason "reckons them available to its good will." Reason thus supplements its lack, without self-swindling, by consciously drawing against the same *unerforschlich* ground in which its own inner disposition lies hidden. (For who is to say how, in this inscrutable region, good will might or might not be aided?) Such a mode of dealing with reason's "difficulties" with respect to that which in itself "stands fast" (namely, reason's ultimate moral sufficiency) can remain "sincere" only by expelling itself beyond the boundaries of reason's proper work, as a merely secondary occupation [*Nebengeschäfte*] or parergon. (Without that acknowledgment, such moral borrowing is just another way of slipping off the hook—another version of the human propensity to "subtle self-deception" [see 6:52].)

29. Judaism in its purity "entails absolutely no religious faith." Thus the sublimity of the Jewish law against idolatry (as famously celebrated in *The Critique of Judgment*) must be radically discounted: "we should not place too much weight on the fact that [the Jews] set up . . . a God that could not be represented by any visible image. For we find in most other peoples that their doctrine of faith equally tended in that direction" [6:126]. Kant also plays with the notion of a non-epigenetic (re)birth of the human species, in which Greece and Rome play the role of sole (masculine) progenitor, to the exclusion of the (merely female) Jews [see 6:79–82; 102]. Judaism is the womb from whose fetters humanity (or the true church) must completely free itself, and/or to which it remains attached only by a common written word or scripture—i.e., the "Leitband" of holy tradition [6:121]. On the other hand, scripture, which "hinders the church's unity and universality," is pure religion's "still indispensable *Hülle*." And yet, a people with a sacred text "never assimi-

gods—the faith with which Epicurus grappled—was ethically far superior, Kant says, to the monotheism of the Jews, which represented slavish
service in the extreme, and whose only contribution to world history was
the commission of its laws to scripture. Christianity as a vehicle of cheer
(good news) is thus Christianity born by a scripture that has been liberated from its Mosaic-Messianic Jewish remnants—from everything that
encourages an attitude of passive "waiting," as if anything other than
the goodness of one's own deed could ground hope in ultimate salvation.[30] The negative purpose of *true* Christianity is to aid recovery from
the false one.

The recovery from false religion begins with the allowance that a human being need not know in what the "divine cooperation" (of which
good conduct gives us hope) itself consists [6:52]. In this morally ad-
missible ignorance lies an opening for "religion within the boundaries
of bare reason," i.e., for harmonizing true religion with religion as it
had been "handed down" historically.[31]

Accordingly, the figure of Jesus (never mentioned by name) is to be
interpreted, not as an historical redeemer (or "vicarious substitute" in
the traditional sense)[32] but only as "an unequalled moral example"; for
human beings, who cannot experience the transcendental without sensible clothing, cannot conceive of the force of their own moral *Anlage*—infinite as it is—other than by representing it as surrounded by ob-

---

lates" with a people [like the Roman Empire] that has "nothing of the kind" [6:135n.].
The most potent sensible exhibition of true religion is wordless or ineffable: the "letter . . .
should finally fall away" [6:197–98]. Judaism is the letter or shell from which humanity absolutely must free itself and yet with which it can still absolutely not do without.

30. To be sure, the superiority of Christianity over all other known public religions is
itself merely historical. Nothing gives Christianity authority to assume that it is the only
route to personal or collective salvation: indeed, given our rational ignorance of how God
cooperates to make us better human beings, it is "perhaps unavoidable that, were the way
revealed at a given time, different people would, at some other time, form different conceptions of it, and that in all sincerity"—an ecumenicism on Kant's part from which only
Judaism (in the strict sense) is excluded [6:52].

31. For who can be certain, as Kant adds, that the moral truths taught by Jesus, which
are fully available to human reason, where not also delivered as a timely revelation, aimed
at hastening human improvement? See also *Metaphysics of Morals* [6:488]: religion within
the boundaries of bare reason is not derived from alone, but "is also based on the teachings of history and revelation," and "it considers only the *harmony* [Übereinstimmung] of
pure practical reason with these (shows that there is no conflict between them). But in
that case . . . religion is not *pure*" but rather "religion applied to a handed down [*vorlieg-
ende*] history."

32. Accordingly, the figure of "vicarious substitute" becomes a personification of the
death of the old man "that each of us ought to endure," so that what, from the point of
view of the "old man" would be punishment, becomes, from the new point of view, "self-
discipline." Such a personification specifically addresses the assault on moral confidence
[*Vertrauen*] that arises from our awareness of the impossibility, in temporal terms, of wiping out the debt incurred by our previous moral inadequacy [6:75–76].

stacles and yet—amidst the greatest temptations—victorious. The main positive role of Christianity, in other words, lies in the historically un-equalled pedagogic power of the story of Christ's passion. Jesus, so un-derstood, is an "ideal" in the precise Kantian sense—a concrete exhibi-tion of the "idea of humanity" as a moral maximum [6:61].[33] Unlike the presumed supererogatory virtue of ordinary human beings (represen-tation of which puts moral judgment out of tune), the holiness of Jesus (whether or not he actually lived or was sent by God) evokes true won-der. Christianity, rightly understood, might thus serve as an historically unequaled teacher of the people, even as, wrongly understood, it threat-ens to become (as Judaism scripturally universalized) an historically un-equalled vehicle of popular corruption.

The remaining sections of the work will sketch out the schema of an evolving human organism (the "kingdom of God on earth") as the idea of humanity transposed over time, that is to say, as mankind itself, pro-gressively victorious over the greatest inner obstacles. The vehicle of that schema is scriptural Christianity (and its public institutions), gradually freeing itself from its own "Jewish" remnants, i.e., its "tendency" (his-torically rooted in its birth among the Jews, and continuing as "Pfaffer-tum [popery]") to take the letter for the spirit (or the clothing for the man).[34]

The visible church as Kant newly conceives it, is the (mystic) "shell [*Hülle*]" out of which the species as a collective organism can develop.[35] From this point of view the proper translation of Kant's title is "Religion within the limits of Bare Naked Reason," "bare-naked" rendering with a peculiar precision the meaning of the German "blöße." (To be sure, it is ultimately difficult to tell what is *Hülle* [or clothing] from what isn't.) Removing Judaism from Christianity (distinguishing the clothing from the man) proves in several ways defining (as a reading of *The Conflict of the Faculties* would show)[36] of the human problem simply. In any case,

---

33. Cf. *Critique of Pure Reason* [A/568–9=B/596–7]. Christianity, rightly understood, seems to accomplish what would be "preposterous" [*unthunlich*] in a novel: realization of "the ideal in an example, i.e., in appearance."

34. See also Kant's *Reflexionen zur Religionsphilosophie* [IXX: 652]. Among the few hand-written notations in Kant's personal Bible, the editors of the Akademie edition note the following: "old clothing" [alt Kleid] (at Matthew 9:16) is underlined in black, over which is written "Judenthum." [IX: 652] (Luther's text reads: "Niemand flickt ein altes Kleid mit einem Lappen von neuem Tuch; denn der Lappen reißt doch wieder vom Kleid, und der Riß wird ärger." [No one puts a patch of new cloth on an old garment for the patch tears away from the garment and the tear is more vexing]).

35. See [6:121].

36. For an anticipation of that task, see [6:41n.]; see also Shell, "Kant as Educator: Rea-son and Religion in the *Conflict of the Faculties*, Part One," in *Kant's Legacy: Essays in Honor of Lewis White Beck*, ed. Predag Cicovacki (Rochester: University of Rochester Press, 2001).

the historical appearance of Christianity is both genuinely "fortunate," as Kant puts it, and—to the extent that the church does not desist from promising a "vicarious substitute" for man's own deed—human reason's "salto mortale."[37]

IV

Religion within the Boundaries is a response, not only to Kant's immediate political difficulties, but also to a problem intrinsic to the moral life as Kant conceives it: how reconcile the injunction to put duty first with the acknowledged human "limitation" that forces us to seek, in every action, some end that reason can justify. This limitation exposes us both to a perpetual temptation to insist upon a justifying reason, beyond the law itself, for our obeying it and to the perpetual danger (so far as we can tell) of our succumbing. We ought to, and hence can, act *now* to make the moral law our overriding incentive, and yet—since such an act of transcendental freedom is timeless—we cannot (in this life at least) ever be *aware* of doing so. What Rousseau called "the science of simple souls" is thus anything but easy. If sincerity, which is always in our power (and hence justly imputable to us), is that for which, in the last analysis, we can alone take credit, insincerity is an inner enemy—an insinuating temptation—that cannot be consciously vanquished. What gives insincerity its power over us is our resistance to the spiritual labor that the moral law imposes on us—an unhesitating choice that goes against the naturally crooked grain of human reason, which cannot help but think discursively and hence in a timely fashion. Man's moral disposition [*Gesinnung*] must make up for the deficiency "which is in principle inseparable from the existence of a temporal being"—namely, "never to be able to become quite fully what one is *im Begriffe* [according to the concept]" [6: 67n.]. But that means that we can never make our own moral capital fully present to ourselves. To think is to be tempted to hesitate or to "bethink" ourselves. Investment of our talents[38] requires an immediate expenditure of moral capital that defies ordinary calculations of profit and loss. Hence, our positive incentive toward the "self-swindling" that prefers the lesser good.

In the face of our self-doubt (Kant's own version of original sin), we must strive to cultivate receptivity to the law's incentive, in ourselves and others—above all, by contemplating the idea of the moral good "in its absolute purity," and becoming "conscious that it belongs to our origi-

37. [6:121]
38. On "talents" as our moral capital (or *Anlage*), see also *Critique of Practical Reason* [5:160].

nal *Anlage*." Wöllner's edicts (and the political and spiritual movement behind them) threatened Kant's central and nearly lifelong effort to promote such cultivation. A new task thus historically emerges: moral cultivation cannot go forward until certain newly resurgent obstacles— Wöllner's school of insincerity—are dealt with. That task must proceed within the letter of the law—hence, not by defying the statutory authority of the church directly, but through resistance to the *Afterdienst* (the counterfeit service which is publicly authorized in what has been handed down to us) that mistakes the letter of religion for the spirit.

Recent communitarian interpretations are thus right to stress the importance of community for Kant, but wrong to link it with a "progressive" agenda in the simple sense that it is usually taken. It is, for example, misleading to imply, as do some recent commentators, that "Kant does not think [one] can achieve [the] inner revolution toward goodness entirely on [one's] own," but only with the help of others.[39] It is true that the *thought* of our collective struggle (and its always endangered success) is, on Kant's account, morally empowering. It would be going too far, however, to suggest that our personal effort to improve depends, for him, upon the historical transformation of society, not only because we are obligated *now* to make ourselves better human beings, but also because the precariousness of human progress is itself—as Kant indicates again and again—a necessary condition of our freedom.

It is thus, I think, a mistake to overstate Kant's confidence in organized religion (however liberal), or to insist that individuals are ethically obliged to form or join one.[40] The only clear-cut "duty" *Religion* imposes upon individuals at large is one of interpretive resistance to a penitential (or "judaizing") understanding of the true end of Christianity.[41] Un-

39. See Wood, *Kant's Ethical Thought*, 314; the dependence of moral self-transformation on a prior transformation of society at large is asserted even more strikingly by Sharon Anderson-Gold: "Kant implies that our hope to effect a revolution 'within' rests upon the transformation of the social conditions of our existence" [*Unnecessary Evil*, 46].

40. The true church is "an idea of reason, whose representation in an adequate intuition is impossible for us, but which has objective reality as a practical regulative principle in working toward this end of unity of the pure religion of reason." Human nature, on the other hand, furnishes little hope of bringing about such unity "in a visible church" [6:123n.]. Still, a personal duty to partake of rituals, church going, etc., follows only if one finds it "morally enlivening" [6:196], and only if the church in question "does not contain formalities that might lead to idolatry" [6:199]—a proviso that excludes all churches other than the (invisibly) true one. Kant's general suspicion of prayerful language as a means of spiritual enlivening is relaxed in the sole case of communal "hymn singing." Such singing, which represents the wish of each united with the wish of all toward one and the same end, "not only can elevate emotion to the point of exhaltation . . . , but also possesses a stronger rational basis [than does private prayer] for clothing the moral wish" [6:196].

41. See, for example, [6:3n.–44n.]. With the exception of the duty not to hold any merely historical faith for salvational, *Religion* does not add (to the duties sketched out in *The Metaphysics of Morals*) a single injunction on which individuals are necessarily obliged

til that penitential understanding is completely rectified (the inner cir-
cumcision by which the true spirit of Christianity is separated from its
skin), the injunction to "leave the ethical state of nature" can have no
other definite meaning.[42] As for rulers and others in a position to influence the people's way of thinking—they must resist their own evil propensity to make hypocrisy pay (via false professions of faith), i.e., to use
man's moral capital as a mere means.[43] In Catholics, such resistance will
especially involve a rejection of "probabilism" (Pascal's "just in case,"
and its morally perverse calculus of safety) [6:186]; in Protestants, it will
especially involve a rejection of false pride [6:188–89].

In thus resisting the evil propensity, rulers would, in turn, make pur-
posive the human tendency, otherwise *counterpurposive*, to make conscience a tool of politics and policy. *Perpetual Peace* will sketch out in
greater detail this essential "anthropological" perspective, by which
(false) honor, or the human inclination "to gain value in the opinion
of others," can be turned, finally, to moral account.[44] It will do so, however, in an ironic register that acknowledges that war—and, indeed, total war—will remain an ever-present danger, "constantly threatening to
break out."

In the meantime, and whatever his political success, Kant's represen-
tation of the deliverance of the true church out of and against its own
historical integuments,[45] bears immediate, sublime witness to man's in-

---

to act. Thus, it is left entirely to the individual to judge for himself how much of the historical faith, rightly interpreted, "he finds beneficial" to the vitality of his religious [i.e.,
moral] disposition [6:182]. And any moral duty of churchgoing applies only if and when
it does not involve formalities which *could* lead to idolatry (emphasis added)—a proviso
that, given the human proclivities Kant has just laid out, furnishes what amounts to a general escape clause [6:199]. Even the "duty" to find the right meaning in scripture—a duty
that seems to inform Kant's own effort—is conditional on the judgment that lack of moral
confidence would otherwise give rise belief in superstition, miracles, false expiation and
enthusiasm [*Schwärmerei*] [6:83, 53]. From Kant's own point of view, publishing *Religion* is
less a duty than an exercise in what he elsewhere calls moral prudence in attending to the
"call of nature." *Perpetual Peace* [8:373n.].* (I am indebted to Corey Dyck for calling my attention to this phrase.)

42. To be sure, Kant also speaks of historical Christianity as a "fact," without which the
"special duty" of humanity to form a visible church would remain inoperative [6:158].

43. See here especially Kant's preference for the "pure doctrine of virtue," which is "already contained in the human soul in full, though undeveloped," to the religious "doctrine of divine blessedness," which requires "ratiocination [*herausvernünfteln*] through
Schlüsse" [6:182–83]. Kant's emphasis on the unhesitating or immediate character of moral resolve should be contrasted with the "Bedenklichkeit" he urges upon hypocritical authorities [6:187].

44. Cf. [6:35n.; 97n.]. The distinction between false religion and true turns on the
"immediate pleasure" "human beings take in attestations of honor"—an immediate pleasure that leads them to believe that God, too, is vainglorious [6:104]. Religious education
is thus inseparable from an education in the true meaning of (human) honor.

45. Cf. [6:64n.–65n.]: "it is plainly a limitation of human reason, not any time separable from it, that we cannot think of any significant moral worth in the actions of a per-

nate goodness and hence to our own moral adequacy. Human nature, as Kant elsewhere puts it, does not of itself harmonize with [the] good [5:271]. Our very *in*ability to represent the idea of humanity as a completed organism purposefully exhibits (in the catastrophic exposure of human history represented in that very intellectual failure) the sublime *in*adequacy of consequential, or timely reasoning to reason's "done deed" or moral *factum*. In the ineluctable tension (itself defining of the "boundaries" of reason) between temporal reasoning (reason as contained in our *Anlage* to humanity) and the timeless ground of the idea (reason as contained in our *Anlage* to personality), human reason registers its own sublimity, and thus wordlessly answers the misanthropic question that the essay on *Theodicy* left hanging.[46]

The sublime is "a presentation that determines [*bestimmt*] the mind to think [*denken*] of nature's inability to attain to an exhibition of ideas" [5:268]. In this capacity, the sublime calls to mind the archaic sense of *Stimmung*, as an attunement of the scales by which votes (or sums of money) are tallied.[47] Where the historicized figure of humanity (man as "species being") itself evokes a feeling for the sublime, we are moved by the discrepancy between *human* purposelessness—the recalcitrance of *human* nature to moral purposes—and some higher purpose served, however perplexingly, by that very recalcitrance. The historical sublime determines us to think the *in*adequacy of human reason (i.e., of thought itself) to the idea of personality. The aesthetic force of Kant's educational project depends as much upon our common exposure to despair as upon the reach of our collective hope.

If this reading is correct, *Religion* belongs to that peculiar Kantian genre of which *Observations on the Feeling of the Beautiful and the Sublime* provides perhaps the earliest example: a beautiful portrayal of the sub-

---

son without at the same time portraying this person or his expression in a human way . . . for we always need a certain analogy with natural being in order to make supersensible characteristics comprehensible to us." To transform such a "schematism of analogy" into a schematism of "object determination" has, however, "most injurious consequences." Compare, too, his elusive definition of the "true (visible) church" as "that which exhibits the kingdom of God on earth to the extent that it can be realized by human beings" [6:101].

46. Compare the apostrophe, at [6:190n.], to "Astraea [*Aufrichtigkeit*]" brought down to earth as *Wahrhaftigkeit* (not saying anything that isn't true), with *Theodicy* [8:270]. Honesty is reconcilable with humanity only as a resistance to lying (as distinguished from full candor or "openheartedness"). Kant's history of the church is meant to overcome doubts as to the existence of a capacity for truth telling (in this sense) without which "the human race would have to be in its own eyes the most contemptible." It thus overcomes misanthropy—provided, as Kant immediately adds, that one can count upon reversal of our "way of education," in which "one attributes one's own moral condemnation to an all-powerful God" [6:190]. Overcoming misanthropy and facilitation of Kant's critical pedagogy more generally, are thus interdependent.

47. See Grimm and Grimm, v. 18, p. 3091. "Stimmen" in this sense is synonymous with "Bestimmen."

limity of human nature.[48] Such a portrayal is neither a direct cause of moral self-improvement (which would contradict human freedom) nor simply its effect,[49] but a morally empowering exhibition of reason's self-affected pathos.[50]

This reading, I could add, helps answer some of the charges of moral inconsistency (or "unfairness") with which Kant's treatment of history is sometimes taxed.[51] Kant's sketch of the realization of the kingdom of God on earth is aimed primarily at overcoming moral hesitation—first by providing a great, offsetting goal, and second by dissolving a "contemplative misanthropy" that raises doubts as to the adequacy of man's (and hence our own) moral capital.[52] History, as Kant conceives it, is no more unfair than life itself, which not only kills infants in the cradle, but may also doom whole races (and the entire female sex) to a perpetual moral childhood.[53] Only God knows the hidden disposition that lies beneath appearances, and the obstacles it has or hasn't vanquished.[54] In any event, nothing prevents us from enjoying, here and now, the "good fortune" of those who may come after us. We have only to make the highest good possible in the world our own to belong *already* to the true church or ethical commonwealth. Indeed, if one trusts the *Anthropology*, we have only to make that goal our own to attain already all the happiness that lies in our (human) nature.[55]

Still, there is a dangerous tendency unleashed by such an understanding of the dignity of man, which men like Henrich Steffens and

48. Cf. Kant's reply to Schiller at [6:23n.]: the "glorious picture of humanity, as portrayed in the figure of virtue, does allow the attendance of the graces," but only "at a respectful distance."

49. See [6:170n.]: the mutual influence of the sensuous and intellectual principles "must never be thought as *direct*." It is only in "deed" [*in der That*], i.e., "in the determination of our physical forces through free *Willkür* as relates to actions," that cause and effect are represented as "of like kind." It is thus, precisely, in the resolve to expend those forces that the effect of the intelligible upon the sensible, and vice versa, become homogenous, or are necessarily so represented.

50. *Critique of Judgment* [5:267]: If the beautiful "prepares us" to love something without interest, as Kant says elsewhere, the sublime "prepares us to esteem it against our interest."

51. See, for example, Paul Stern, "The Problem of History and Temporality in Kantian Ethics," *Review of Metaphysics* 39 (March 1986): 505–45.

52. "The ethical communion of [true] believers" constitutes "the essence of the true church" [6:133n.].

53. Cf. [6:121n.]: thus man can at least be comparatively deserving, i.e., in relation to another.

54. Those who lack the opportunity to acquire a character (e.g., children who die in infancy) can (or are presumed to) have personality, albeit of a sort that does not express itself in timely (worldly) terms. Why some (but not other) noumenal beings should be in a position to "acquire a character for themselves" seems to be, for Kant, an unfathomable mystery to us.

55. See *Anthropology* [7:234–35].

Houston Stewart Chamberlain would later seize on. If what gives each of us dignity is, in the last analysis, the racial germ we bear (the role we play in the historical development of man as a species-being or a pan-human organism), then groups whose relation to history can be portrayed as nil, or even parasitic, may well come to seem sub-human.[56] It is thus especially important to insist upon the altogether secondary role, for Kant, of church history as a self-organizing human construct.

Religion within the Boundaries of Bare Reason has had enduring political and spiritual effect, and not only in today's liberated theological schools. Both Martin Heidegger's attempt to wholly temporalize the "call of conscience" and Walter Benjamin's attempted reprisal of the messianic (over and against the pagan) are—each in its own way—deeply marked by Kant's "historical" elaboration of the fundamental question: what is law and why obey it? If we are dissatisfied with Kant's answer (and those that follow in its wake), it may be time to revisit the Socratic question of whether and how virtue is its own incentive.

56. Cf., in this regard, Kant's restriction of religious "history" to "that portion of the human race in which the *Anlage* to the unity of the universal church has been brought close to development. . . . We can, for this purpose [*Absicht*] deal only with the history of that church that from its beginning bore the germ [*Keim*] and principles of the objective unity of the true and *universal* religious faith to which it is gradually being brought nearer.—And this shows, first of all, that the *Jewish* faith stands entirely in no essential connection [*Verbindung*] with that church faith, i.e., in no unity from concepts, through the latter immediately arose from it, which gave physical occasion [*Veranlassung*] for its grounding" [6:125]. The problem of human development, out of and against nature, is reenacted in the relation between Christianity and Judaism. Judaism is, at best, the historical occasion for a human development in which it does not participate and, at worst, the historical expression of mankind's propensity toward self-subversion.

11   ON GIVING ONESELF THE LAW

ROBERT B. PIPPIN

I

Kant's claim that morality is a matter of rationality clearly counts as a legacy to contemporary Anglophone philosophy. Thanks largely to the influence of John Rawls and his legions of Kant scholar students, this Kantian position has again become a contemporary option in debates about moral theory. It was also a great living legacy to Kant's German Idealist successors, although the nature of that linkage is still not well understood. So before addressing what I want to claim is the central issue in the contemporary appropriation of Idealist moral theory (the idea of "self-legislation"), I would like to begin with a brief comment about Hegel, the relevance of which will, I hope, become clear by the end of this discussion of Kant.

A common and understandable view of Hegel's ethical theory has it that Hegel has a "social role" theory of right human conduct. What it is "right" to do is supposed to be accounted for by appeal to the social role one occupies. Since Hegel also regularly describes modern ethical life as rational, this last point must mean that appealing to such ethical roles is for him a normative or justificatory appeal, that such an appeal can function as a practical reason, a justification.[1] "Because I am a father," "because that is what a good business man should do," or "because I am

---

This essay appeared in Nalin Ranasinghe, ed., *Logos and Eros: Essays Honoring Stanley Rosen* (South Bend, Ind.: St. Augustine's Press, 2007).

1. Since Hegel denies philosophy any prescriptive role, many assume that any such account is a purely descriptive or an explanatory, not a normative, account. But that would be the wrong inference to draw, since Hegel also clearly insists that occupying such modern roles *is* rational, that the roles in some way manifest the work of reason, even while denying that this means "what a purely rational agent would will." See "Hegel's Ethical Rationalism," in my *Idealism as Modernism: Hegelian Variations* (Cambridge: Cambridge University Press, 1997), and "The Realization of Freedom: Hegel's Practical Philosophy," in *The Cambridge Companion to German Idealism*, edited by Karl Ameriks (Cambridge: Cambridge University Press, 2000).

a citizen" would be the obvious sorts of candidates for what Hegel must regard as "practical reasons."

On the face of it, this is unsatisfying. Any practical argument which concludes with this sort of justification appears clearly incomplete, to require another, final step in which the justifiability and goodness of occupying these roles at all is defended universally and objectively. Only such a final step, it would seem, could complete the invoking of this consideration to someone who demands a justification. We might up the stakes by adding that such roles have become "essential" to a person's identity, that I couldn't even begin to reflect on what to do were I not to begin reflecting qua something or other—family member, producer/worker/professional, or citizen. But that move only adds to the suspicion that such considerations are not really playing a normative role, that they instead describe some psychological or social necessity that delimits the possibility of practical reasoning. There might be something interesting to say about someone's social identity, but without the further step we are looking for there is no clear reason to think that "what my social identity requires" could be the sort of practical reason whose binding force others ought also to acknowledge. Likewise, trying to make this next move—to complete the argument by claiming that such social functions are indispensable elements of any good or flourishing life, or that they should be seen as the outcome of a rational historical process—has come to look hopeless to most modern philosophers, almost all of whom have come to accept a "plurality" of equally legitimate and incommensurable claims about ultimate human ends or goods, and who, after the twentieth century, would view any notion of historical progress as Panglossean.

This is a natural and plausible way to think about the limitations of what is traditionally taken to be the Hegelian position. Assertions about the normative dimensions of social roles, especially if they are understood to involve rights or entitlement claims, must be able to survive, we think, a full "*reflective* endorsement" by an individual, a reasoned defense that does not presuppose our social roles, but concludes in affirming them (if it does); only thereby can such claims be said to count as binding practical reasons for any reflective individual.

This line of thinking seems natural and unavoidable. It is however, already quite theoretically "thick," and leads fairly directly to a Kantian position on obligation, or on the binding "source of normativity."[2] If ev-

---

2. Indeed, another initial way to stress the differences between Kant's and Hegel's approaches is to note that Hegel must be striking out in some very different direction because he appears to have no interest at all in any refutation of moral or normative skepticism; he appears to think it is wholly unnecessary.

ery sort of consideration can count as a justifiable practical reason only if it survives some sort of reflective endorsement test, and there are such tests, and some considerations do survive them, and we can accept or reject such proposals *because* they pass or fail, then we have claimed that reason can be practical in some way, that passing this reflective endorsement test is, at some basic, fundamental level, what most matters, is the crucial component in the rational source of normativity, and that all this can motivate agents. And we have at least opened a clear path to the claim that the question of what we ought to do (especially the question of what we may never do) is finally a matter of *pure* reason being practical, that there is a form of reflective reason not already tied to some pursuit of contingent, material ends (and it too "can be practical"), and that all our actions can be judged permissible or not by appeal to such an a priori endorsement test. On such an account, *being* in a certain social role could never of itself count as a reason to do anything. I must reflectively *adopt* the requirements of such a role as a principle of action, actively require of myself a course of action, and determine that what I find myself engaged in ought to be engaged in or not.

And therewith the other, now very familiar, side of the Kant-Hegel dialectic on this issue begins to come into view as well. The list of counter-questions is well known: in what sense can we be said to be normatively bound to, committed to, what a purely practically rational agent would legislate as required? In what sense am I, just qua agent, "committed" to the requirements of reflective endorsement? Is there any such test? That is, does anything action-guiding really follow from such a commitment, and is there any coherent theory of human motivation that could account for the motivational efficacy of such an always over-riding commitment? On the Hegelian picture, our claims on each other, our normative rules, arise out of and are grounded in already ongoing ways of life, attachments, institutions, and dependencies. Some such attachments and dependencies are said to be constitutive of being an individual human agent (at some historical period). Any reflective abstraction from such involvements creates an artificial construct, whose putative endorsements (if any determinate ones can be made out) amount to a philosophical fantasy world and bear no relation to the requirements of a concretely human life.[3]

And so the familiar back-and-forth. According to Hegel's theory, such social commitments and dependencies do not merely reflect *beliefs* about value held by individuals for various reasons. They are much

---

3. Most obviously for the Hegelian side, the long period of childhood dependency in a particular community counts as one of the un-abstractable features at issue.

"deeper" than that: they are in some sense forms of life or, in Hegel's terms, "shapes [*Gestalten*] of spirit." On the Kantian picture, this all ignores how radically we certainly *can*, in concreto, detach ourselves from, reflect on, and possibly reject such inheritances and   thereby determine—in some purely rational (or impersonal or agent-neutral or not at all self-regarding) way—what ought to be done. (In Korsgaard's very apt words: "A good soldier obeys orders, but a good human being doesn't massacre the innocent.")[4]

However, we should also immediately note that, for *both* Kant and Hegel, to understand each other as *merely* passively shaped by, and in our practical lives merely expressing, the influences of socialization and habituation, communal mores and roles, is to fail to accord each other the appropriate respect, dignity, and worth as the kinds of creatures we are. We are entitled to such respect because the lives we lead *are* up to us, are actively *led* by us.[5] Whatever social roles we inhabit or conventions we act out, we have somehow made them our own; they function as norms and ideals for us that we must actively and with some justification to ourselves and others sustain, and which, like any ideal, we can hold and yet fail to live up to. They are certainly not, according to Hegel, just regularities and dispositions. The worth of our lives is tied to their being free lives, and their being free lives is tied to a capacity for some sort of reflection, and such reflection *is* reflection only if genuinely reasoned, not merely a re-enactment of an inheritance. The disagreement at issue turns on the nature of this act of "making them our own" or "acknowledging their authority" and so on Hegel's disagreement with equating such a dimension (which Hegel calls simply "subjectivity") with individual "reflective endorsement," especially when that is understood as the *practicality of pure reason*. And this finally brings me back to my main topic: Kant on the self-imposed norms of reason.

II

The clearest way to state the radicality of the Kantian claim about the only possible origin of normative commitments is to repeat his claim that we are always obligated only to what we, from our own first-person

4. Christine Korsgaard, *The Sources of Normativity* (SN hereafter) (Cambridge: Cambridge University Press), p. 102.

5. On the importance of reflective, subjective allegiance in Hegel's theory of objective spirit, see my "Hegel, Freedom, the Will: *The Philosophy of Right*, #1-33," in *Hegel: Grundlinien der Philosophie des Rechts,* ed. Ludwig Siep (Berlin: Akademie Verlag, 1997); "Hegel on the Rationality and Priority of Ethical Life," in *Idealism as Modernism;* and "Hegel on Institutional Rationality," in *The Southern Journal of Philosophy,* Vol. XXXIX, Supplement, "The Contemporary Relevance of Hegel's Philosophy of Right" (2001).

perspective, rationally obligate *ourselves* to.[6] That is Kant's solution to the problem of obligation descended from the dead ends created by the divine command and natural law traditions.[7] If human beings can be duty-bound, that is, can be subject to a universal law, then we must be able to explain how this is consistent with another indispensable premise in Kant's Protestant enterprise: that human beings are full *subjects of* their own lives, not *subject to* any normative authority they cannot, from their first-person perspective, reflectively endorse. And the only way this is possible is if they are *both* legislators of and subject to the laws they obey. Nothing about the state of things, history, my social role, nature, or even God can function as a practical reason unless I count such a consideration as a reason to act, and in doing so, in Kant's language, I am "giving myself the law." And I can be said to be genuinely conferring such value (as opposed to, say, just expressing an inherited, socialized attitude) only if I do so with reason.[8] It is a big and controversial step to go on to say, as an extension of this claim, that, since reflective reasoning is the "source of value" in this way, we are, therefore, as a result of some sort of "regress" argument, unconditionally bound to reason itself and its pure, universal requirements, all with a kind of moral necessity and in a way that can guide a life. It is an understandable step, though, and we shall examine it in due course. As Korsgaard rightly put it, engaging in such reflective endorsement "is not for Kant a way of justifying morality; it [subjecting myself only to what I can reflectively endorse] is morality itself."[9] (From here on, I will be making use of Korsgaard's version of Kant as representative of contemporary Kantian approaches. There are of course other approaches, but several aspects of her project seem to me to capture best the appeal of this reflective endorsement and self-constitution ideal.)

So, in sum, both the attractiveness of the Kantian position against the supposedly Hegelian, and its potential paradoxes, are evident in this famous, densely dialectical claim from the *Groundwork*.

---

6. On what it means to occupy, necessarily, such a first-person perspective, see Christine Korsgaard, "Morality as Freedom," in *Creating the Kingdom of Ends* (CKE hereafter) (Cambridge: Cambridge University Press, 1996), pp. 159–87, or the opening remarks in the first lecture of her forthcoming Locke lectures, "Self-Constitution: Action, Identity and Integrity," available at: http://www.people.fas.harvard.edu/~korsgaar/#Locke%20Lectures.

7. A solution many now understand as descended from Pufendorf. See especially Chapter 7 of J. B. Schneewind, *The Invention of Autonomy: A History of Modern Moral Philosophy* (Cambridge: Cambridge University Press, 1998), pp. 118–40.

8. Cf. Korsgaard's account in "Kant's Formula of Humanity," CKE: "in our actions we view ourselves as having a value-conferring status in virtue of our rational nature. We act as if our own choice were the sufficient condition of the goodness of its object: this attitude is built into [a subjective principle of] rational action" (p. 123).

9. SN, p. 89. Clearly this claim will then also in a different way push the question back a step and raise again the question of the justification of morality so construed.

The will is thus not solely subject to the law [*dem Gesetze unterworfen*] but is subject in such a way that it must be regarded also as legislating to itself [*selbtsgesetzgebend*] and precisely for this reason as subject to the law (of which it can consider itself as the author [*Urheber*]).[10]

Surely the first point to make about Kant's claim is that it is *metaphorical*. The image of some sort of putatively lawless person making or originating or legislating a principle and "only" thereby being bound to it—otherwise not bound at all—makes it very hard to imagine on what sort of "basis" such a law-less subject could decide what to legislate. Unless you are *already* bound to the constraint of reason, on what basis could you "subject yourself" to such constraints? If rational reflection and ultimately reflective rationality itself are the source of all human value, then the whole idea of authoring or legislating *that* principle looks groundless, and the picture coming into focus looks more like a melancholy Dane ready to "leap" or an anguished, near-sighted Frenchman "condemned to be free" than the dutiful sage of Königsberg.[11]

Of course, some aspects of the metaphorical dimension of "authoring the law" are not that obscure. "Reason legislates" when *we* simply determine what to do *on the basis* of reasons, and when we do so, *we* are determining what will count as decisive; it cannot be anyone else or any other authority unless *we* also so determine a possibility rationally defensible. And in so determining, we are always relying on a principle of some generality. "Because I felt like it" cannot ever be our legislated norm, even if we think it is. But "Always to do what I feel inclined to at the moment" can be. But this still leaves the basis of such determination—"ourselves as authors"—obscure and so does not help explain Kant's paradoxically

10. *Groundwork of the Metaphysics of Morals*, ed. and trans. by Allen Wood (GW hereafter) (New Haven: Yale University Press, 2002), p. 49; Kant, *Gesammelte Schriften*. Edited by the Prussian Academy of Sciences (Berlin: de Gruyter, 1902–), Bd. 4, *Grundlegung zur Metaphysik der Sitten* (GL hereafter), p. 431. See also SN, p. 100.

11. Perhaps the clearest contemporary expression of the principle Kant is assuming can be found, not surprisingly, in Rawls, *A Theory of Justice* (Cambridge: Harvard University Press, 1971): "(T)he self is prior to the ends which are affirmed by it" (p. 560). The spirit of my response to that claim is similar to Nagel's concluding objections to Korsgaard in SN. He is objecting to Korsgaard's account of *why* someone might sacrifice his life for others. Korsgaard says it is because his very "identity" is at stake and he could not live with himself if he betrayed the others. Nagel says, quite rightly I think, "The real explanation is whatever would *make* it impossible for him to live with himself and that is the non-first-personal reason against the betrayal" (p. 206). This can be the right response without, I think, any necessary commitment to what Nagel calls "realism." In her forthcoming Locke lectures, Korsgaard presses hard on the radical notion of self-constitution and tries to minimize the paradox with analogies to animals who are "making themselves" (sustaining their lives) even though they already are. But this latter notion trades on Aristotelian notions of possibility, actuality, and actualization that are not relevant to a person's self-constitution and so represents a slide from self-maintenance according to one's nature to self-constitution and autonomy.

reflexive formulations—that reason has itself for its object, that the will "wills itself," and so forth.

Of course, again, at a sufficient level of generality, even very unKantian predecessors like Christian Wolff could adopt such rhetoric. "Because we know through reason what the law of nature prescribes [*haben will*], a rational person needs no further law; he is rather by reason a law unto himself."[12] And

> Since a rational person is a law unto himself and besides natural obligation needs no other, so neither rewards nor punishment are for him motives for good action and for the avoidance of bad ones. . . . And hence someone rational performs the good because it is good and omits the bad because it is bad, in which case he becomes like a god, as one who has no superior who can obligate him to do the good and omit the bad . . . but rather by the perfection of his nature, does this and omits that.[13]

Wolff's autonomy language is of course quite restricted by his rationalist perfectionism (reason has an intelligible object in such legislation, not, as in Kant, itself) and by his helping himself to the notion of "intrinsically motivating by nature"—a dodge that Kant cannot afford—but the emphasis on a kind of autonomy and the flexible interpretability of being a law unto oneself are still quite striking. But the contrast with Kant's version is also striking. Kant is not just claiming that we exclude empirical considerations and rely on what pure reason and no other consideration can determine we ought to do. He is claiming something like *"pure practical reason determines that its law should be the constraint of pure practical reason, and it thereby submits to the authority of this law."* This separation of pure practical reason from itself and then this re-union is what is so metaphorically puzzling. (For one thing, without some nonmetaphorical gloss, the situation looks like one Nietzsche might describe, where self-rule or self-mastery is simultaneously, and perhaps indistinguishably, self-enslavement.)

Using some of the passages from Kant's *Religion* book, we might also make more plausible the idea of someone's responsibility for "legislating" a life-plan in which she determines that the moral law and not self-love is to be the always superordinate principle in all her decisions. That would be a way of "electing" to subject oneself to the law.[14] But that would not be an explanation of her *being* duty-bound in the first place

---

12. Christian Wolff, *Gesammelte Schriften* (New York: Olms, 1976), Abteilung 3. *Deutsche Ethik* (DE hereafter), §24.
13. DE, §38.
14. Cf. Korsgaard's "Morality as Freedom," CKE, pp. 164–67, and what she calls the "Argument from Spontaneity."

(which is the problem), only of the *extent* to which she acknowledges and obeys the already binding law over the course of a whole life. We surely do not want to be in the position of saying that the moral law is obligatory only for those *who have actually made it binding*, and *not* binding otherwise. The passage surely cannot be opening that door, but it obviously forces on us the question of the compatibility between Kant's emphasis on autonomy as the human source of value with his emphasis on unconditional, or, let us say, unavoidable obligation.

Later in the *Groundwork* it is at least clearer what Kant means to *exclude* by his author or *"Urheber"* principle, and that points in a clearer direction. He says that accepting the authority of any "external" command, or accepting a course of action necessary to satisfy a sensible impulse, is an evasion of our very status as actors at all, of what is involved in inhabiting the unavoidable first-person viewpoint from which we must direct the course of our lives. It is a little unclear how to state this, since it is quite obviously important to Kant that the appearance of just *being* commanded or *being* determined is itself a delusion, in many cases a willful self-delusion. By "letting ourselves" be commanded or determined we are actually *not* passive at all, but are determining ourselves to act on such a principle, and this claim gets us closer to the "inescapability" that Kant's *Urheber* principle must involve. A representative passage:

> Now one cannot possibly think a reason that, in its own consciousness [*mit ihrem eigenen Bewußsein*] would receive steering from elsewhere [*eine Lenkung empfinge*] in regards to its judgments; for then the subject would ascribe the determination of its faculty of judgment not to his reason, but to an impulse. It [reason] must regard itself as the author [*die Urherberin*] of its principles independently of alien influences; consequently it must, as practical reason or as the will of a rational being, be regarded by itself as free.[15]

Various possible ways of rendering Kant's "authorship of the moral law" claim less metaphorical can now suggest themselves. As we have already begun to intimate, most such ways are, paradoxically, ways of denying what the metaphor itself suggests is possible: some state of not-being-obligated, which then becomes, by an act of authorship and subjection, a state of being obligated. The arguments amount to such a denial, and the strategy is already evident in the passage just quoted, with its denial that it is even "possible to think" that reason *could* receive direction from elsewhere than reason, and with its claim about the practical necessity of acting *always* "under the idea of freedom," and so the necessity of acting on reflectively considered reasons. Such a strategy must accomplish this

15. GW, p. 65; GL, p. 448.

goal while also showing that it is nevertheless in *some* sense (if not the obvious one) "up to us" whether we are guided by reason or not. That is to say, for Kant what is wrong in immoral or unjust actions consists in a violation of the minimal, formal constraints of rationality, and it is only by being subject to such constraints that we can be said to be actors at all. It must also be said that it is in some way up to us whether we subject ourselves to such constraints or not, even though attempting to avoid such requirements must also manifest that we are nonetheless already so subject. A simpler way to put the point would be to say that for Kant, despite the surface grammar, "person" is in no sense a substantive or metaphysical category, but rather is, in some way or other, a practical achievement, and the attribution of the notion to an other is an ascription not a description. As Fichte would say, the I posits itself; as Hegel would say, *Geist* is a "result of itself." But that is a digression.

III

One way to show this (that there really can be no such literal "act" or that the act of self-subjection must always already have gone on) is to show that we have somehow always already undertaken the basic obligation in whatever we do, and to be able to show that somehow that "already," and the claim of unavoidability and necessity, do not cancel out the self-legislation demanded by the active language of "authorship." (One wants to say that we are not bound to reason because we bind ourselves to it, but that reason is "constitutive" of the "binding" legislation without which there are no norms, and so without which there is no way to lead a life.)[16] This has been called a "regress" argument and has received a well-known formulation by Korsgaard, although a somewhat different version has also been proposed recently by Allen Wood.[17]

I'll return to the moral dimensions of this sort of case later. But first, before we reach the issues of practical unavoidability and implicit, undeniable commitments, we need to make less metaphorical the whole idea of *our* legislating rules or norms to ourselves, and our being bound

16. Korsgaard uses this phrase at SN, p. 234, and it is the basis of the idea of self-constitution in her Locke lectures.

17. Cf. Korsgaard's "Kant's Formula of Humanity," CKE, and her analysis of Kant's *Groundwork* on the practical version of reason's "regress to the unconditioned" (pp. 119–31). Wood's account in his *Kant's Ethical Theory* (Cambridge: Cambridge University Press, 1999) depends on a strong claim about the "objective" goodness which his version of Kant maintains must be claimed by anyone willing rationally in setting that end (any end). His regress then turns on the value of the "source" of this *goodness*. I have presented some objections to this approach in "Kant's Theory of Value: On Allen Wood's *Kant's Ethical Thought*," *Inquiry* 43 (summer 2000).

to them by "binding ourselves." And Korsgaard and others have argued that ordinary cases of hypothetical imperatives can show this rather easily, and so can help demystify or "de-metaphorize" the self-legislation language. This is important because the instrumental form is usually taken as an unproblematic application of practical reasoning, and so it allows a clear view, one would assume, of what practical reason can be said to require of us (what the so-called "normativity of instrumental reason" amounts to),[18] and thereby whether this language of self-legislation and authorship makes any sense in that context.

The basic idea in such an approach is not complicated. When I set an end, or do not merely "wish" (in Kant's sense) to pursue an end, but "will"—actually resolve—to pursue it, I can also be said thereby "to have committed myself" to achieving the means necessary to attain it. By "authoring" one rule for myself (to pursue an end) I have authored another and bound myself to it (to obtain the means), *whether I explicitly realize this or not.* I set the rules for the game I decide to play, and so can be said to have bound myself to play by them. If I am "rationally bound" to obtaining such means then "I *have* bound myself" just by setting the end, and reason will have been shown *already* to be practical, to have satisfied the "internalism" requirement, or will have been shown really to motivate an action. Not everyone, for example, must take organic chemistry to succeed in college, but if I resolve to go to medical school, when I learn how important for admission a good grade in "o-chem" is, I must either give up the end, or follow through on my commitment by attaining the relevant means. And the important point here, from a Kantian perspective, is not at all the predictive point that someone who resolves to go to medical school will very probably, almost certainly, sign up for that chemistry class. That would be a kind of third-person viewpoint which treats beliefs about means as a kind of gate or shunt for desire, such that beliefs about means merely direct the flow of motivational desire, which desire for the end is still doing all the real motivational work. In this case, it seems quite artificial to say, with the Humeans, that my desire to be a doctor remains the motivating force in this way, and that it has been "guided through o-chem," so that I somehow also "pick up a desire for it" on the way. Something more than that is clearly going on here, since, speaking from the first-person perspective, I can genuinely have that belief about the usefulness of o-chem, genuinely want to go to medical school, and still *not* "automatically" head for the regis-

---

18. Christine Korsgaard, "The Normativity of Instrumental Reason" (NIR hereafter), in *Ethics and Practical Reason*, ed. Garrett Cullity and Berys Gaut (Oxford: Clarendon Press, 1997), pp. 215–54.

trar's office. I can fail to live up to what I know *it is rational for me to do,* even while I really do commit myself to the end in question and the relevant means. (At least on the model we are considering. I will discuss in a moment the counter-intuition: that if we do not take the relevant means, we reveal either something about the depth [i.e. the thinness] of our commitment to the end, or could even plausibly be said to reveal that we have not in fact willed the end.) And if this is so then we must admit something that Hume, in effect, never did: that there is such a thing as *practical reason,* that there is a "normativity of instrumental reason" as Korsgaard has put it, or there is a question, as Kant put it, about the rational "necessitation" (or constraint, *Nötigung*) of the will in instrumental cases.[19] The ultimate point of seeing things this way is quite important (and one Hegel would agree with): that "to be rational just *is* to be autonomous" (my emphasis), or "to be governed by reason and to govern yourself, are one and the same thing."[20] There are no laws out there which we need to see and adopt our behavior to. There are only laws we give ourselves, to which we are bound because we have committed ourselves to them, such that, if we don't follow through, we won't have decided anything at all; we won't be rational, *that is:* subjects, persons, agents.[21] (The somewhat confusing but very important point here is that being a subject *means being able to fail to be one,* something that already tells us a lot about the uniquely practical, not metaphysical, status of subjectivity in the post-Kantian tradition.)

IV

There is an awful lot packed into this last claim. The difficulties come when we try to state in this case as well as the more ambitious case about moral commitment or self-legislation, what all of this amounts to in detail, how to gloss what it means to "govern ourselves" in cases like these. And, I want to show, the model of individual agents "detaching" or disengaging themselves from their concerns and lives, and then reflectively committing to or endorsing very general principles of action by reliance on some "pre-commitment" form of practical reasoning, will lead into one paradoxical situation after another. As we have seen, the question is a very large one; it goes to the meaning of this quintessentially modern insistence that some consideration can count as a genuine reason for action only if we "make it our own," adopt it in a way that we can defend (even

19. GW, p. 34; GL, p. 417.   20. NIR, p. 219.

21. Cf. the indispensable article by Dieter Henrich, "The Concept of Moral Insight and Kant's Doctrine of the Fact of Reason," in *The Unity of Reason: Essays on Kant's Philosophy,* ed. Richard Velkley, trans. Jeffrey Edwards (Cambridge: Harvard University Press, 1994).

just to ourselves), and when we can be said to have adopted it because of such a recognition of these justificatory considerations. On Korsgaard's account, this means that a person is not being *instrumentally rational* and so not "governing herself" (her life is not her own), if she merely wants an end, has a certain belief about the right means, and is in fact pursuing those means. For Korsgaard, she must also be pursuing the means *because* she believes she ought, that that is the rational thing to do, that that rational identification of the means is a norm she can live up to or not—all in order for her to count as self-governing and not "accidentally rational."

This is quite a controversial way to put the matter, because there is already an ambiguity in such an account between being "guided" by reason and being "motivated" by it (terms that Korsgaard tends to treat as synonymous). Again, a Humean could certainly accept the former. As just noted, this is precisely what practical reason does in Hume: guide us to the means that in fact themselves lead to an end. Insofar as we are being rational at all, we follow that guidance, where here being ideally rational at all just means that nothing has gone causally haywire. But in *that* sense of guidance (as Korsgaard points out), *not* going where such guiding reason leads is nothing like a failure of rationality. It has to be a mistake, a breakdown, or ignorance, or failure of memory etc., or a change of heart about the end. To show *rational failure* we have to show that we are motivated by what reason requires when we act rationally, and that we can fail to heed this claim, even though we acknowledge and accept it. That is a much different and more controversial matter, and I don't think that anything Korsgaard says supports that claim. At least at this point, the whole notion of "committing oneself" to an instrumental norm and "following through" or "failing" even while still committed, is still vague and metaphorical and needs to be clarified.

A major problem with all of this stems from Kant's complicated claim that

> Whoever wills the end, also wills (insofar as reason has decisive influence on his action) the means that are indispensably necessary to it that are in his control. As far as volition is concerned, this proposition is analytic; for, in the volition of an object, as my effect, is already thought my causality as an acting cause; i.e. the use of means. and the imperative extracts the concept of actions necessary for this end out of a concept of a volition of this end.[22]

But if it is *analytic* that "whoever wills the end, *wills* the means," then we have not *imposed* a normative law on ourselves *with respect to these means*, and the direction we were just following is irrelevant; we should u-turn

---

22. GW, p. 34; GL, p. 417.

back to Hume. According to Kant's strong analyticity claim, someone who does not pursue the means necessary to the end that he has committed to is not being irrational, is not failing to conform to a norm that he has imposed on himself. He simply reveals that he had not "really" willed such an end after all; he merely wished it. The criterion, the test, for having "really" willed it *is* willing the means.[23] You may tell yourself and everyone else that you are working to dismantle capitalist class inequalities, and you may give away a certain amount of money, but your Lexus and your Brioni suits and your Tuscany villa tell us much more about your genuine ends than about your weak will.

But there is an escape clause in this passage; the clause "so far as reason has decisive influence on his action." And it is a good thing too, because besides making this claim about analyticity, Kant also claims that hypothetical imperatives are *imperatives,* and that must mean "norms that we adopt and can fail to observe." Perhaps we can admit, in other words, that there may be self-deceived or hypocritical cases like our limousine socialist. But there are also cases where the right analysis of what happens when the means to an end are not sought is more directly a failure of rationality; we are being irrational, and that just means: not abiding by the norms we have legislated for ourselves, bound ourselves to. Surely this can happen too. We want to go to medical school with every fiber of our being, but math anxiety takes over when we face o-chem, and we sign up for art history classes instead. That is, we can genuinely will an end, but fail to will the means simply because the normative claim of reason fails. In such cases we should state the analyticity principle more carefully: anyone *who has reasons* to pursue an end *has reasons* to pursue the means relevant to it. Or whoever *ought* to pursue an end (setting a goal is a normative matter too, after all) *ought* to pursue the means. We have to state it this way because what is crucial about instrumental reason being reason (and therefore normative) is that it must be able to fail—to be adopted and held, but avoided and ignored at the relevant moment. Otherwise the language of norms and hypothetical imperatives is inappropriate, and we should be talking about what people are very likely going to do, given what else they are doing.

And Korsgaard gives a few plausible examples. A man who believes that an injection will spare him from a deadly disease, and who wants to be spared, nevertheless refuses the injection because he is terrified of needles. He does not give up the end of survival and adopt as a priority the end of avoiding being stuck by needles. And there is the clas-

---

23. Cf. the "already thought" above, and the "extracts the concept of actions necessary for this end."

sic Western or civil war movie scenario. Tex has been shot in the leg and will die if the leg is not amputated. As his comrades prepare to amputate, Tex begs them, in agony and fear, not to amputate. But we, and his comrades, do not take such protestations as what he genuinely wills. We (presumably) know that what he must really will is to stay alive, and we know that his protestations are the irrational irruption of anxiety and fear, that he doesn't *really* prefer avoiding amputation at all costs—prefer even death—to undergoing an operation like that without anesthetic.

This last case seems right, but we should be careful about concluding too much from it. There are three problems.

In the first place, it simply is not easy to tell when a person has "really" willed an end and is just irrationally "failing" to pursue the means he has normatively committed himself to. Unless we want to beg all questions from the outset and just require as a condition of agency always being prudentially concerned with long-term benefit over short-term gains (as Nagel ultimately does), we don't have any clear right, certainly not a priori, to tell what a person's "true end" really is in cases like the above. In the case of our limousine socialist, it seems much more appropriate to say that he hasn't really set any end of abolishing the class structure, even when he sincerely reports that belief, and the best evidence for such a denial is that his actions show no serious intention of attaining the means to do so. What distinguishes this from other cases, where we might want to say: he *has* set the end but is "weak," and cannot muster the resolve to seek the means? Why not say (in effect with Anscombe): his not seeking the means is very good evidence indeed that he has not really set, willed, the end? We need only add the plausible qualification that no one wills an end come what may, no matter what; rather, one wills an end only with a number of *ceteris paribus* hedges and subject to unforeseen difficulties not now known. In the case of Tex and our needle-avoider, we rely on the assumption that the end of staying alive is an obvious one to impute, and so we go the "weakness" route. But is it so outrageous to suppose that someone might reckon a distant probability not as important as avoidance of an immanent pain? There is certainly nothing that *requires* us to say that he is "weak" (whatever that means), or to reject a priori that someone might rather die than undergo a procedure that, to him, might be worse than death itself. And nothing requires us to reject the idea that someone might have no idea what is most important to him and can argue himself into either position. (Korsgaard wants to claim that "obligation in general is a reality of human life."[24] But what is going on here hardly seems like Tex is

24. SN, p. 113.

"avoiding an obligation." It would certainly be odd if one of his buddies pointed out to him, "But Tex, just by being alive and wanting to live you have rationally obligated yourself to have your leg amputated.") I would venture the bet that in most cases like this, where people profess (even to themselves) to have set an end but then do not seek the necessary means, it is much more likely that they either have not really set such an end, have changed their mind about the end when confronted by difficult means, or—what is most likely—have set the end in some qualified manner, as in, "so long as it doesn't cost me something else I value very highly." (This seems exactly how most people adopt the end of staying married "'till death do [them] part.")[25]

Secondly, it is not at all clear just how, from a Kantian point of view, we are supposed to state the elements in our irrational failure to live up to a norm to which we have supposedly committed ourselves. When Korsgaard mentions factors that might explain how people can be said to become "irrational and weak-willed," she mentions such things as "terror, idleness, shyness or depression," and she goes so far as to call these "forces" that "block" "susceptibility to reason."[26] With respect to Tex, we hear: "The right thing to say is that fear is making Tex irrational" (238). And in a similar passage, we read that "timidity, idleness and depression . . . will attempt to control or overrule my will" (246). For me to be leading my life, she insists I must actively seize control of my own destiny, "consciously pick up the reins, and make myself the cause of the end." When I don't do this, "I, considered as an agent, do not exist"; therefore, "Conformity to the instrumental principle is thus constitutive of having a will, in a sense it is even what gives you a will."

Surely the first thing to say here is that Korsgaard has let her Kantian admiration for autonomy get out of control. If, in not conforming to an instrumental principle, I have *ceased to be an agent*, then surely what we have here is not *my* failure of rationality. It sounds like: *I* haven't failed to realize a commitment; something has happened *to me*, in all these examples, that prevents this realization. Something *"blocks"* the motivating power of reason; fear *"makes"* me irrational," and so forth, all exactly as our Humean wanted to say earlier. This may be a breakdown in the power of reason to motivate, but it all here sounds like a disease or exogenous interference, not *my* failure or weakness. (As in many criticisms

25. There is a passage in SN where Korsgaard seems to make just this point. She points to cases where "rules and principles are *constitutive of, and therefore internal to,* the activities themselves. If I am to walk I must put one foot in front of the other: this is not a rule that externally constrains my walking, or boxes me in like the walls of a labyrinth, or that I can with much coherence rebel against" (p. 234, my emphasis). Or: if you want X and Y is in this way internal to it, not pursuing Y just means you have not really willed X.

26. NIR, p. 229.

of defenders of an akrasia explanation, a confusion between third-person perspectives on myself and first-person avowals is going on.) What has happened to the Kantian "incorporation" principle (which Korsgaard accepts),[27] according to which fears and desires and inclinations, while they may incline me to do something, can never be counted, just by their occurrence, as motives to act? What happened to the requirement that they must be incorporated in a maxim, taken as good reasons by an agent, for them to count as my motives? If we take this incorporation principle to heart, it becomes even less plausible to appeal to Korsgaard's "failure" or "weakness" account since I must be counting some present anxiety, aversion, or anticipation as worth acting on, and if I am doing so, then I am diverting *myself* from my original end, not failing to follow through on a commitment.[28] It makes a great deal of difference, in other words, whether these emotional factors are said to "control" *or* to "overrule" my will, to use the two terms Korsgaard uses synonymously.[29] They are not synonymous. If the former, "control," which Korsgaard's examples suggest, then we have, not an irrational action, but no action at all—a breakdown in agency, not its failure; if the latter, "overruling," we have a case of counting something as worth more than something else, and so perhaps a case of ignorance or foolishness, but not one of weakness or wantonness.

27. Cf. especially her "Kant's Formula of Humanity," in CKE, pp. 110–14, and her citation of passages from the *Metaphysics of Morals* and especially also from the *Conjectural Beginnings* essay, and the *Religion* book.

28. What is going wrong here, I think, originates in the Christian language of "weakness," and so the corresponding appeal to "strength" of resolve. The common-sense description of this as a case of irrationality is a good place to start. It would say that Tex's refusal is "irrational" because the urgency of the situation and the sheer lack of time and crisis conditions require Tex to make a decision in such unusual circumstances that he does not decide what he very likely *would*, were he to be able to reflect calmly and in full awareness of the facts and consequences. (His action is "impulsive.") We might (and usually do) add that he would like to identify as the "Real Tex" that calmly reflective agent. But this is a bit of a fantasy as well. In resisting the amputation, Tex is not "too weak" to be the "Real Tex." He expresses and discovers something about this real Tex in such resistance, something about the nature of his commitment to life, the weight of his fear of pain, his ability (or lack of it) to invoke and rely on an ideal picture of himself, and so on. (There are many people, perhaps the vast majority, to whom it would never even occur that they should risk their lives in fear of pain.) He is not, in resisting, "weakly" the Real Tex. *He is just Tex.*

29. Cf. also, in her "Morality as Freedom," CKE, "The person who acts from self-love is not actively willing at all, but simply allowing herself to be controlled by the passive part of her nature, which is in turn controlled by all of nature. From the perspective of the noumenal world, ends we adopt under the influence of inclination rather than morality do not even seem to be our own" (p. 168). Something is clearly going wrong here because *most* of our sensible ends are adopted "under the influence of inclination," and, strictly speaking, the idea that someone can "allow" themselves to be controlled, but is *not* thereby "actively willing" is incoherent. Not much is gained, I would argue, when one simply bites the bullet on this one and claims that, therefore, on the basis of these considerations, "evil is unintelligible" (p. 171).

Moreover, if we try to take a few steps back and argue that I am originally responsible for the kind of character that would produce these emotional storms (that I have "chosen" it and so must live with the current consequences as my fault, even if I can't do anything about it now), we will not only introduce all sorts of "moral luck" problems involving the social conditions and opportunities (or lack of them) under which such a character was formed (and so will have undermined any strong "responsibility for my character" view), we will thereby also introduce again the implausible picture of some characterless agent choosing a character as if a suit of clothes.[30] Indeed, that implausible picture is already suggested by Korsgaard's unusual language: that by committing yourself to some instrumental norm, you "give yourself" *a will* in the first place. While we couldn't ask for a better contemporary evocation of the route from Kant to Fichte (and his *Ich* that posits itself), I'm not sure we want to open up that Pandora's box.[31]

Finally, third, while it is important to stress that we cannot be living norm-governed lives unless we can both acknowledge the authority of, and yet fail to live up to, such norms, there are other ways of expressing and accounting for such failure than by the problematic (and in Kant paradoxical) appeal to weakness, or any other such Christian notion of a frailty usually tied to sensibility (or any such notion of sin). When we find that we do not seize an opportunity to acquire means to an end we had believed was an end of ours, something we had willed to pursue, we simply could be said to fail to live up to an ideal we had of ourselves. Someone simply finds out that she wasn't who she thought she was: all these years she was firmly convinced that she was seeking A, but it turns out she wasn't. We could of course put this by saying that finds she did not have the "will power" or strength of resolve, even though she had

30. For Korsgaard's attempt to make the notion plausible, see "Morality as Freedom," CKE, p. 181.

31. What Korsgaard wants to say (very clearly in the second of her recent Locke lectures) is that it cannot just be *tautologous* that someone who wills the end wills the means (and so: someone who doesn't will the means must not have willed the end), because then the clear normative force of claims like "You really should see the dentist about that tooth" would be hard to explain. But the Humean has no problem denying there is such a thing as practical reason at all, so it is no objection to point that out to him. (That is, he accepts that it cannot be said to be more irrational to prefer the continuing toothache to a speedy resolution at the feared dentist's office.) More broadly, I think Korsgaard is right to criticize the Humean for explaining how the motivational efficacy of some end pursued works causally, but I do not agree that this means hypothetical practical principles are norms in her sense. An "expressivist" account of action, and an account of a revisable-over-time, provisional theory of motivations (we very rarely *know* whether we have really opted for an end or not, until we see what we actually are willing *to do*) could fill out such a picture of a non-causal account. See my *Hegel's Practical Philosophy: Rational Agency as Ethical Life,* forthcoming.

committed to A, but we have already seen the paradoxes of that view. It seems more appropriate to invoke the language of self-knowledge and self-assessment, and to concentrate on what her actions reveal about the ends she really does care about.[32]

V

However, at this point, it may be that our search for some de-metaphorized account of the strong "authorship" interpretation of autonomy needs to take into fuller account an aspect of the issue mentioned briefly earlier. We seem to be getting into some trouble taking too literally some pre-law situation, whereas we might want to try harder to undermine the possibility of such a putative option, even while still trying to retain the authorship and self-subjection issues. Entertaining such an option in order to show its normative impossibility, would be the required argument. This gets us more directly to the "what we must be taken to have obligated ourselves to" position.

Indeed, even in the instrumental case, we have not addressed all of what it means to have "failed to live up to" a norm of instrumental rationality. As we saw, in Korsgaard's account that involves somehow failing to be an agent: not to have set the course of my life, but to have allowed it *to be set* exogenously. (We have also seen that it is unclear on a Kantian account how we should describe our doing that, since, despite the hedge words "letting" or "allowing," it *is* a doing and one must be an agent in order to "fail" to be one.) But the point at the moment is that we should describe the stake we have in our commitment to observing the claims of reason a bit more fully. We don't just "come that way," susceptible and responsive to such claims automatically. The point is that we must commit and hold to the commitment or else we will not be subjects of our lives; or the point concerns what the commitment *means* to us. Since, according to Korsgaard's Kant, when I don't hold to such commitments, "I, considered as an agent, do not exist," then this stake in reason "issue(s) in a deep way from our sense of who we are."[33] Our very "practical identity" is at stake.

Practical identity in general "is better understood as a description under which you value yourself, under which you find your life worth living and your actions to be worth undertaking."[34] There will be many contin-

---

32. That is, the idea would be: those who pursue an end that a full or fuller use of reason would not endorse are being "irrational," even if that pursuit cannot be traced to a weak act of "will."

33. SN, p. 18.

34. SN, p. 101.

gent versions of these—professor, husband, friend, American—so, even though in all of them I can be said to have a practical identity only by maintaining a commitment to the norms which constitute each, I could be said to "adopt" one, "abandon" another, and nothing about my commitment need have any claim on you.[35] But it is the next step in the development of this line of thought that returns us to Kantian moral theory. Are there "particular ways in which we *must* think of our identities"? If there are, will these be the sought-after "moral identities" the loss of which would be "worse than death"?[36]

We might first say that being a human being at all, or some universal feature of being human, can function like this inescapable identity, such that "losing" it would mean losing a recognizable human life, losing any course of existence that could have value to a human being. Or at least we might say it as long as we keep faith with Kant's "authorship" principle here too. We cannot *lead* a life at all without authoring, and without commitments to, such practical identities, but therefore the "value" of having any practical identity itself, and also the necessary conditions for any such identity, *does not have the same status as such particular roles or identities.* The value of reflective reasoning itself—the condition for anything mattering to us in a distinctly human way—doesn't arise out of contingent attachments and dependencies; it is what we must keep faith with if we are to sustain *any* identity at all. We have value as human beings because we value ourselves as human beings, and the introduction of this notion of practical identity is supposed to make more transparent, by means of this sort of regress, *why we could not but "value" our humanity.*[37] The direction suggested by the authorship principle is supposed to lead to this argument form. To value anything and hold one-

35. Cf also SN, pp. 239–41. Korsgaard often appeals to a claim like "at the moment of action, I must identify with my principle of choice if I am to regard myself as the *agent* of the action at all" (p. 241).

36. Clearly these claims about practical identity have put us somewhere in the neighborhood of the "social role" considerations that we noted at the outset. The differences are also becoming clearer. On this view of Kant, such roles, if they are to function as normative constraints, must be seen as products of reflective endorsement by each individual. An individual must be able to see himself as the author, *Urheber,* of the role and its relationships. For Hegel on the other hand, the practical roles are the prior conditions for any reflective content, and this not as a matter of fact limitation but as expressing the objective normative structure of modern ethical life itself. But more famously, on Kant's account there is an ultimate moral identity, and its attendant obligation trumps any other contingent obligation; his case for that will return us to the most important manifestation of the self-legislative metaphor.

37. SN, p. 121. Wood's version of this move is similar, but, because it involves quite a substantive commitment, it is considerably more controversial: I reveal "an esteem for myself which . . . is what holds me to my rational plan" (*Kant's Ethical Theory,* p. 119). I should think that I hold to my plan simply because I still want the end, even when my desire has turned into a calm passion, barely noticed as such.

self to the commitments necessary to attain it, is already to have valued this capacity itself, to have acknowledged that we cannot be human just *by being;* we must posit ends and hold ourselves to norms, and so valuing above all that capacity to do so is inescapable.[38]

In this way all value depends on the value of humanity; other forms of practical identity matter in part because humanity requires them. This "human" identity and the obligations it carries with it are therefore *inescapable and pervasive,* even though, given the kind of feature of human life it is, it is not an identity one can be said simply to have, like a substance's identity through time. This claim—that our human identity is a kind of result, a posit that we make and sustain over time—would be taken up eagerly and would provoke much speculative gymnastics by later Idealists, especially since, now that the very identity of a subject is at issue, the dialectical dimension of a subject as an unusual "result of itself" is clearly on view. And it is the source of some of Kant's own most speculative moments. (The second *Critique's* invocation of a "fact" of reason in what appears to be an unusual "exposition/demonstration" of the reality of human freedom already appeals to this notion of making in the root, *facere,* or "making," of *Faktum.* In this sense "acknowledging" the normative claims of reason is exactly not what the ordinary meaning of fact, or knowing a fact, would imply; it is much more like the "authoring" or self-legislation and self-subjection to such a norm. Or, a commitment to practical reason is a deed, a *"Faktum,"* something we do, not something we passively notice or accept; it is effected.)[39]

But all of this gets us only so far, and not yet to any *necessary moral identity.* In the first, and most well known place, this argument shows only that, in order to preserve any basic coherence in acting, you must be presumed to value humanity in *your own person,* must value *your* reflective capacity. To argue for some inescapable moral identity would be to argue that you cannot so legislate such a value without valuing humanity—respecting such a reflective, life-leading capacity in everyone. To show this, some try to demonstrate that we can start with our own private, unavoidable, normative commitment to our own humanity, and then reason in some "transcendental-argument" way that we are thereby committed to acknowledging the value of humanity in another, in anyone at all. But even if successful, this argument appears to show at most

38. "If we do not treat our humanity as normative, none of our other identities can be normative, and then we can have no reason to act at all" (SN, p. 129).

39. Or at least, that would be one, rather adventurous, way of reading the *Faktum* claim, in the spirit of Korsgaard's rather Fichtean Kantianism. For a general discussion of the *Faktum* passage, see Karl Ameriks, "Pure Reason of Itself Alone Suffices to Determine the Will," in *Kants Kritik der praktischen Vernunft,* ed. Otfried Hoeffe (Berlin: Akademie-Verlag, 2002).

that I must acknowledge the value of each person's humanity *to* him or her, and not that *I* must value *your* humanity. More ambitious attempts, like Korsgaard's and Nagel's, start by attempting to deny that my valuing my own humanity can really be understood as just *my* valuing *my own* humanity. They argue in different ways that whatever reasons I have, originally, from the outset, must be reasons to value humanity itself, and such reasons mean that I must be committed to the value of humanity anywhere there are human beings. I *can't* value it in just my case alone, goes the argument; there couldn't be any *"reasons"* to value it *like that.* And since I must value humanity itself in order to value my instantiation of it, I am committed to respecting humanity as an end it itself, and we would thus have shown a moral identity.

The question of whether this argument establishes such a moral commitment to a universal value is one that would obviously require at least another paper. But it is also unclear exactly what is being established by the claim, what "the value of our own humanity," and so the inherent value of humanity itself, involves. Korsgaard makes extraordinarily generous use of the argument form, so generous as to render it immediately suspicious. She claims, for example, that our valuing, taking care of and pleasure in, our animal nature presumes a commitment to the value of animal sentience wherever we find it, and so gives us a way of thinking about our duties to non-human animals. This seems to me like a quite a stretch, and the source of the discomfort resides in how much is being deduced from the observation that we must value our animal nature in some sense. I don't think I have any views about whether *animality* is a valuable thing, even if I take some pleasure in *mine,* and I can't see that I am expressing such a view when I avoid cold and pain and so forth. And this question points to the larger, similar issue at stake in the universal value of humanity. Any such moral identity—that view of ourselves as merely one among many—is, in the Rawlsean terms that Korsgaard adopts, merely a "concept," a statement of the problem, and not yet a "conception," a specification of the substantive answer. That is, let us assume that taking the source of value to be this capacity for reflective endorsement commits me to that value itself, and that I can't be holding such a commitment, and so cannot be an agent, have an identity, if I do not respect that capacity in others. But this too is still a concept, not a conception, a statement of the problem and not the solution. We don't for one thing, know *how* important that value should be. If it is automatically a trump against all other values, it would be hard to understand the kinds of real conflicts (not just resistance to duty) that emerge in the conflicts between our contingent practical identities and such a putative moral identity. And if it is so important as to be of inestimable value, then, when I take risks for my own amusement, and so value the pleasure of driving fast over safely maintaining my reflective endorsing capacities, am I being immoral?

But more importantly, we cannot derive from a deductive analysis of a rational agent alone any content for such a commitment, any sense of what makes up this value of humanity, or the essence of freedom as reflective endorsement. Given a "general" concept of ourselves as one-among-many, and as not relying on any consideration in my evaluating that I am not also willing to grant you entitlement to (which is all the regress argument allows us to say), the various "conceptions" that could manifest such a commitment are far broader than the specific "post-Enlightenment" ones that Korsgaard cites. As she often points out, which conception satisfies such a concept does so "by way of practical identity." We need to understand the distinctly human way in which persons acknowledge and hold themselves to values before we can understand what in particular they may not rationally ignore in others. As she points out,

> . . . human identity has been differently constituted in different social worlds. Sin, dishonour, and moral wrongness all represent conceptions of what one cannot do without being diminished or disfigured, without loss of identity, and therefore conceptions of what one must not do.[40]

And,

> The concept of moral wrongness as we now understand it belongs to the world we live in, the one brought about by the Enlightenment, where one's identity is one's relation to humanity itself.[41]

VI

Exactly right, say we card-carrying Hegelians, but such a sweeping admission *concedes the whole match between Kant and Hegel* and brings us round full circle to the alternatives with which we began. If the distinctly moral realization of the requirement of reciprocity inherent in any reflective end-setting is a matter of "history" in this way, and there is *nothing more* we can say about the normative authority of this historical epoch, then the formal requirements everywhere in force are nowhere near as important as the fact that the realization of these requirements is socio-historically specific. This makes it unlikely that there could be any deductive account of someone's core practical or moral identity and

40. SN, p. 117.
41. Ibid.

that whatever legitimating account there might be will probably be developmental, not deductive.

In this respect, Hegel may prove to be more Kantian than Kant understood in this way. As we have seen several times, the obvious Kantian thing to say here is that there is no particular reason to grant our historical location in "late modernity" any normative authority unless that form of life can be itself reflectively endorsed. But given the road we have traveled, just trying to fulfill such a criterion in the way "we" would understand such an attempt would be merely, and in a question-begging way, *manifesting again the form of life we wanted to authorize*. In Hegel's language, the rational status of Enlightenment modernity can be established, but not by means of a deductive methodology, nor by an analysis of the concept of agency. We still need some alternative way of accounting for how we can be said to make these historically specific attachments, dependencies, social roles, and social ideals "our own," some alternate way of accounting for their legislated character and our submission to such legislated results. Hegel's intuition is here quite a useful one. He focuses our attention on the experience of normative insufficiency, on a breakdown in a form of life (a situation wherein we can no longer make norms "our own"); through such a *via negativa*, he tries to provide a general theory of positive normative authority.

But that is of course another topic, and it would take a good deal of work to show that everything changes when we regard norms as collectively legislated over time rather than as elected by individual rational endorsement. I have only tried to suggest here that it is unlikely that an account of the subjectivity of moral life could rely on an appeal to something like such an individual endorsement test.

12   SLAVES, MASTERS, TYRANTS
Nietzsche's Concept of Freedom

ROBERT RETHY

In a note, parts of which were later incorporated into aphorism 289 of *Beyond Good and Evil*, Nietzsche spoke of "aphorism books like mine" in which "many lengthy, forbidden things and chains of thought stand between and behind short aphorisms."[1] Two years before the publication of *Toward the Genealogy of Morality* and its three essays he asserted that he did not write essays—"these are for asses and journal readers." A solitary like him, living in his cave which could just as well be a "labyrinth as a gold mine" and "whose very concepts finally retain a peculiar twilight color, a smell as much of the depths as of mold, something incommunicable and reluctant which blows coldly upon all the merely curious," writes as much to conceal as to reveal his thoughts, whether he will or no, as the note lets us know at the end. "A hermit's philosophy, even if it was written with a lion's claw [*wenn sie selbst mit einer Löwen Klaue geschrieben wäre*], would still always look like a philosophy of goose feet—a philosophy of quotation marks" [*eine Philosophie der 'Gansfüschen'*].[2]

This note warns us of the treacherousness of reading and interpreting Nietzsche's aphorism books.[3] The spaces between the aphorisms and the gaps between the works are not empty but filled with unexpressed thoughts which themselves must be reconstituted by the reader.[4] But

---

1. VII, 3, 37[5] (June–July 1885). All references, unless otherwise noted, are to the *Kritischer Gesamtausgabe, Werke (KGW)* of Nietzsche, ed. G. Colli and M. Montinari (Berlin-New York: de Gruyter, 1967ff.), and all translations are my own.

2. Eckhard Heftrich calls attention to this note in *Nietzsches Philosophie: Identität von Welt und Nichts* (Frankfurt a.M.: Vittorio Klostermann, 1962), pp. 5f.

3. See *Zur Genealogie der Moral [GM]* "Vorrede," §8 (VI, 2, 267f.).

4. "An aphorism is a link in a chain of thoughts. It demands that the reader reconstitute this chain with his own means. An aphorism is a presumption.—Or it is a precaution, as Heraclitus knew. An aphorism must, if it is to be enjoyed, be put into contact and tempered with other material (examples, explanations, stories). Most do not understand this and for this reason one may express what is risky without risk [*Bedenkliches unbedenklich*] in aphorisms, 2, 20[3] (Winter 1876–77).

deeper than the problem of the syntax or syntagma of interpretation is that of the semantics, the meaning of the very concepts and words used in these works. For one so removed from the common, communication is at best a compromise with his thought and its "twilight" ambiguity and half-hiddenness, at worst a betrayal of what is unique and personal to the crude embrace of the vulgar.

"One no longer loves one's knowledge enough as soon as one communicates it."[5] The hermit philosopher perforce uses the common language, but indicates its alienness by placing his words within the frame of quotation marks. Nietzsche's thought on a well-known, indeed common, philosophical *topos* such as freedom is marked by a twofold ambiguity. There are the spaces between the aphorisms, the silences before and after the words, that demand interpretation before there can be any understanding of them. And there are the words themselves: freedom, "freedom," and the almost unutterable, characterized by Nietzsche as "my concept of freedom."[6] But, as we will see, through the empty spaces and beneath the ambiguities the lion's claw of the hermit is decipherable, and it is to this investigation that we now proceed.

I. FREE WILL

I

The traditional philosophical question of "free will and necessity" occupied Nietzsche in some of his earliest writings. Two student essays from 1862, i.e. his nineteenth year, are entitled "Fate and History" and "Freedom of the Will and Fate."[7] Along with the shared themes of fate and the concern with the ambiguity of human independence and autonomy (II, 55, 58) which run through his later writings,[8] there are striking anticipations of well-known formulations and positions. According to the first essay, were a "strong will" to overturn the past, we would join the ranks of "independent gods" and awaken from the dream of history. "Man would rediscover himself, as a child playing with worlds, like a child awakening in a glistening morning. . . ."[9] Not yet the author

5. *Jenseits von Gut und Böse* [*JGB*] 160 (VI, 2, 100).
6. *Götzendämmerung, Streifzüge eines Unzeitgemässen,* [*GD-Str.*] §38 (VI, 3, 133f.).
7. Nietzsche, *Werke und Briefe: Historisch-Kritische Gesamtausgabe* [*HKG*] (Munich: Beck, 1934) II 54–62. Karl Löwith discussed these pieces in his *Nietzsches Philosophie der ewigen Weiderkehr des Gleichen* (Stuttgart: Kohlhammer, 1956; pp. 127–32; originally published 1935). See the translation by J. Harvey Lomax, *Nietzsche's Philosophy of the Eternal Recurrence of the Same* (Berkeley: University of California Press, 1997), pp. 122–27.
8. Cf., e.g., *Der Wanderer und seine Schatten,* (*WS*) 61, "Turkish Fatalism," amor fati in *Die fröhliche Wissenschaft* (FW) 276, and, in *Ecce Homo* (EH), "Why I am a Destiny" (KGW VI, 2, 363–72).
9. The language here not only anticipates the famous parable of *Thus Spoke Zarathustra*

of *Zarathustra*, for whom the final transformation of the spirit is to become a child, playing, the young Nietzsche is not ready to allow humanity to enter the ranks of the child-god. "Free will" as the "unlimited, arbitrary, . . . the infinitely free" is coordinated with and necessarily opposed by fate. "Fate is the infinite force of resistance to free will. Free will without fate is as unthinkable as mind [*Geist*] without the real, good without evil."[10] While a world in which man was free would make him into a god and this world into his plaything, one in which fate was "the only true principle" would turn man into a "plaything of dark causal forces who was not responsible for his errors, free from any moral distinction." Though the youthful Nietzsche suspects that this is in fact the way things are, the man who does not see through the illusion of freedom is the happy one. While human freedom separated from the necessity of fate is dismissed, the converse is seriously considered, and the essay ends with a proposal that would in fact reduce freedom to necessity: "as mind can be merely the infinitely smallest substance, good only the most subtle development of evil from itself," so "free will" may be "nothing but the highest potency of fate."[11]

The focus of the second and shorter essay, "Freedom of the Will and Fate," is on the individual. Freedom of the will for the individual is the same as freedom of thought and is subject to the same limitations. Once it is actualized it is limited by fate's determination of our talents and capacities. Fate "appears stronger than free will," but is nothing but a chain of events of which man as actor is a part. The realm of action is the realm of fate simply, and though the young thinker tries further to equalize the roles of freedom and fate by distinguishing between free, conscious activity and unfree, unconscious activity, his formulations do not get us much beyond Kant's Third Antinomy. The attempt to "dissolve" their opposition in the "idea of individuality" in fact seems only to return us to the problematic of the first essay, in which the individual himself was incorporated into either the impersonal fate of the "ocean of the all," or the massive herd of the "people" of history, or the "humanity" of the world.[12]

(*Z*) I, 1 (VI, 1, 27), but also the final words of Part IV of the work (p. 404), along with the references to Heraclitus, Fragment 52 in *Philosophie in der tragischen Zeitalter der Griechen*, §§ 6–7 (*KGW* III, 2, 322–27) and in *Die Geburt der Tragödie (GT)*, §24. (*KGW* III, 1, 149), along with *Jenseits von Gut und Böse (JGB)*, 57 (VI, 2, 73).

10. *HKG* II, 59.

11. Cf. Spinoza, *Ethica*, I, P 35, Scholium; Hume, "Of Liberty and Necessity," in *An Enquiry Concerning Human Understanding* (ed. Beauchamp, Oxford: Oxford University Press, 1999, pp. 148–64) and Schopenhauer on the Kantian antinomies in the *Kritik der kantischen Philosophie*, appendix to *Die Welt als Wille und Vorstellung, I* in *Sämtliche Werke*, ed. von Löhneysen (Darmstadt: Wissenschaftliche Buchgesellschaft, 1974) I:660–80.

12. *HKG* II, 59.

2

The sense of urgency expressed in the rhetoric of these youthful essays does not lead to any further development of the problem over the next decade and one half, which encompass Nietzsche's discovery of Schopenhauer, his philological studies in Leipzig and teaching in Basel, his encounter with Wagner, and the publication of *The Birth of Tragedy* and the four *Untimely Considerations*. It is possible that Nietzsche found himself a Schopenhauerian *avant la lettre* when it came to this topic and saw little left to add to the master's account. Schopenhauer, too, attempted to affirm both freedom and necessity, though he did this not by trying to combine the two or by dissolving their differences, but rather by separating them while employing a rather heterodox interpretation of Kant's distinction between "intelligible freedom" and "empirical necessity."[13] Although he accepts strict necessity in the phenomenal world, affirming the causal principle's presence in all phenomena, both external and internal to the human actor, and vigorously denies a freely "choosing will" or *Willkür,* Schopenhauer believes that there is an "intelligible freedom" inherent in the will's own willing of its unchanging character, which forms the basis for our sense of guilt, responsibility, and regret.[14] Thus, there is a metaphysical basis for ethical *pathos,* but no actual basis for ethical *action.*

A letter written by Nietzsche only months after his first reading of Schopenhauer in October 1865 may give us a sense of the importance of this aspect of the philosopher's teaching for him: "Three things are my recreations, but rare recreations: my Schopenhauer, Schumann's music, finally solitary walks. Yesterday there was a magnificent thunderstorm in the heavens. I hurried to a neighboring hill . . . and found a hut up there . . . The storm burst forth violently with wind and hail, I experienced an incomparable exaltation and I really knew how we understand nature properly only when we have to flee to her, led by our cares and concerns. What did man and his restless willing mean for me! What did the eternal 'thou shalt,' 'thou shalt not' mean to me! How different the lightning, the storm, the hail, free powers without ethics! How fortunate, how strong they are, pure will, unclouded by intellect!"[15]

---

13. Cf. *Die Welt as Wille und Vorstellung,* I, §54; see also "On the Freedom of the Will," III:565 (§III); "On the Foundation of Morality," III, 706 (§10); the "Transcendent Speculations on the Apparent Purposiveness in the Destiny of the Individual," *Parerga und Paralipomena* I (III, 243–72).

14. Schopenhauer, *Werke* I, 675–80, in the *Kritik der kantischen Philosophie* for Schopenhauer's "supplementation" of the Kantian critical distinction with his own metaphysical one.

15. To Carl von Gersdorff, 7 April 1866, *Kritische Studienausgabe: Briefe (KSB),* (ed. Colli and Montinari, Berlin–New York dtv/de Gruyter 1986), 2:121f.

It was precisely his break with the romantic sensibility so clearly expressed in this letter and exemplified by his association with Schopenhauer's philosophy and Wagner's music that led to the new response to the question of freedom expressed in the "monument of a crisis"[16] that is *Human, All-Too-Human*. The rather disillusioned "humanism" expressed in the title refers at least in part to the demotion of these two erstwhile deities of Nietzsche's intellectual firmament. The work's main task, to use one of its own phrases, is "to overcome metaphysics"[17] and the ambiguous significance of this event is indicated in the title's own duality, with its confirmation of the truth of the human, and its regret at the lost illusions. "We are from the very beginning illogical and hence unjust beings, *and are able to know this*. This is one of the greatest and most insoluble disharmonies of existence."[18]

The conception of the "metaphysical world" as an "all too human" invention entails the rejection of the distinction between "appearance and thing in itself" (the title of *MA* I, 9), the transcendent interpretation of which is a keystone both of Schopenhauer's system and of his interpretation of Kant.[19] Nietzsche's denial of the thing in itself leads to the affirmation that "what we call human life and experience now has continuously *come to be*, indeed is completely in the process of *becoming*, and thus should not be viewed as a fixed quantity."[20] After a discussion of "metaphysical explanations" in aphorism 17, he turns to "The basic questions of metaphysics," the title of MA 18, and denies "belief in unconditional substances" and "belief in identical things" before speaking of "belief in the freedom of the will" as a third "primordial error of all organic beings." Later, in the second chapter of the work, entitled "On the History of Moral Feelings," Nietzsche examines the significance of this belief for our conception of human action and responsibility. Aphorism 39, entitled "The fable of intelligible freedom," is explicitly directed against Schopenhauer's doctrine. An account of the "history of the feelings by means of which we make somebody responsible, i.e., of the so-called moral feelings" leads to the conception that the will must be free if an individual is to be held responsible. Schopenhauer's attempt to combine causal necessity in action with freedom in being, making use of the metaphysical split between appearance and thing in itself, is derided as a "fantastic consequence of intelligible freedom" which is no longer possible with the elimination of the metaphysical realm. Nietzsche fearlessly concludes: "Nobody is responsible for his acts, nobody for his essence. To judge is the same as to be unjust. This is true when the individual

16. *Ecce Homo*, "Human, All-Too-Human," (VI, 3, 321).
17. *MA* I, 20 (*KGW* IV, 2, 37).   18. *MA* I, 32 (*KGW* IV, 2, 48).
19. See, for example, *WWV* I, 564ff.   20. *MA* I, 16 (*KGW* IV, 3, 32).

judges himself. The proposition is as clear as daylight, and yet here everyone prefers to retreat to the shadows and to untruth for fear of the consequences."[21]

The chapter ends with the aphorisms "At the waterfall" and "Non-responsibility *(Unverantwortlichkeit)* and innocence." The first assimilates human action to the unconscious motions of a waterfall, so that "all is necessary, every motion mathematically calculable," though "the actor is stuck in the illusion of a choice of will." The second more regretfully notes that "the complete non-responsibility of man for his actions and his essence is the bitterest pill the knower must swallow," at least insofar as he is accustomed to viewing duty and responsibility as the distinctive calling of mankind. Although the aphorism goes on to try to view such "pains" as "birth pangs," Nietzsche is unable to shake free of the sense of the loss of everything high in the recognition that everything is "all too human." A short aphorism toward the book's end gives a striking formulation to the question at the book's heart: "Truth as Circe. Error has made men out of beasts. Will truth be in a position to turn men back into beasts?"[22]

3

The denial of freedom in this sense is maintained by Nietzsche throughout his works. A whole sequence of aphorisms is devoted to the problem in *The Wanderer and His Shadow*, the book viewed by Nietzsche as the last supplement to *Human, All-Too-Human*.[23] Elsewhere, he gives various, and opposing, genealogies of the rejected idea—for example, in *Beyond Good and Evil* 21 he attaches it to the "vain races" who insist on their "personal right to *their* merit," while in *Genealogy of Morality* I, 13, written barely two years later and as "supplement and clarification to *Beyond Good and Evil*," it is the weak and self-denying who assert that the strong must be free and thus are responsible for not controlling the destructive expressions of their strength.

In one of Nietzsche's last works, the *Twilight of the Idols*, "the error of free will" is the last of the "four great errors," which also include "the error of confusion of cause and effect," "the error of a false causality," and "the error of imaginary causes."[24] The four great errors, then, are all errors in causal attribution, all exemplified by false moral and religious teachings: in the error of confusion of cause and effect (i), vir-

21. *MA* I, 39 (IV, 2, 61f.); cf. Schopenhauer, *Werke* III, 707.
22. *MA* I, 519 (IV, 2, 336).
23. *WS* 9–13; see also *WS* 23 (IV, 3, 183–86; 195f.).
24. *KGW* VI, 3, 82–91. Section numbers in the text in parentheses refer to sections in this chapter.

tue is not (as is believed) followed by happiness, but happiness (in fact) gives rise to virtue (§2); the error of a false causality (ii) is notably present in belief in the "will, spirit, I" (§3); the "familiar, expected, well-remembered" is imposed as an imaginary cause (iii) while the new is excluded, so that "the businessman thinks immediately of 'business,' the Christian of 'sin,' the maiden of 'love'" (§5).[25] The special place of free will in this constellation is shown, not merely by its final position, but by its specificity, as distinct from the generality of the other errors. In fact, it would not be hard to argue that the other three errors are included in the error of free will as well. In his discussion of it, Nietzsche displays none of the qualms notable in his earlier confirmation of complete non-responsibility. "Today, we have no sympathy for the concept 'free will'" (§7). He asserts that it is merely a way to make men feel guilty, attribute responsibility to them (i.e., the error of a confusion of cause and effect) which they cannot possibly possess (i.e., the error of a false causality) and make them worthy of a punishment which is a figment of a medieval imagination (i.e., the error of an imaginary cause).

Free will, then, is the greatest of the four great errors, the error of errors, although a skeptic might object that it might be a further confusion of cause and effect to view it as a *causa sui* and not as a consequence itself of something even more fundamental, perhaps the "anti-nature" of morality, the discussion of which forms the content of the preceding chapter in *Götzendämmerung*, or maybe of a weak will to power. The "immoralist's task" is in fact the "removal of the concept of guilt and punishment from the world and the consequent purification of psychology, history, nature, social institutions, and sanctions." This can only be accomplished with the elimination of the idea of "free will."

In the final section of "The Four Great Errors" Nietzsche moves beyond critique, as he raises and answers the question of "what *our* doctrine can be." That nobody is responsible for who he is or what he does leads to an affirmation of necessity, back to the "fatality" of his earliest essays: the "fatality of his essence or being [*Wesen*] cannot be separated from the fatality of all of that which was and will be." This leads to a further affirmation of the sheer immanence of being. Our being cannot be judged since we are a part of the whole "and there is nothing outside of the whole!"

The elimination of both a providential God and the freedom of the will is necessary if we are to regain a state lost at least since the story of the Garden of Eden overtook humanity. The crucial step from a mere-

---

25. Unsurprisingly, Nietzsche asserts at the beginning of the following section that "the whole realm of morality and religion belongs in this concept of imaginary causes" (§6; op. cit., p. 88).

ly negative non-responsibility to a positive innocence had not yet been taken when Nietzsche confronted the consequences of the inclusion of human acts and thoughts in the causal nexus in *Human, All-Too-Human.* One of the earliest expressions of this positive impulse can be found in *Dawn,* 208, entitled "Question of conscience": "'And in summa, what do you want that is really new?' We no longer want to make causes into sinners and consequences into executioners." The ambiguity of causality and responsibility, present in the Greek term *aitia* itself, must be eliminated. Once we have seen through the doctrine of responsibility and fully affirmed its absence, we are in a new world, a world restored, on the threshold of the playing child of Nietzsche's earliest essays and later inspirations. The concluding words of the chapter in *Götzendämmerung* on the four great errors go beyond the resignation of *Human, All-Too-Human,* focusing not on what has been lost but on what has been recovered. Rather than instituting a world empty of meaning, a world of mechanism, or even one of blind fatality, it announces a great truth: "That nobody is made responsible any longer, the species of being may no longer be reduced to a causa prima . . . with this the *innocence of becoming* is reconstituted. . . . We deny God, we deny responsibility in God: only *with that* do we redeem the world" (§8).[26]

The "innocence of becoming" is the positive consequence of the rejection of free will, and it is the natural counterpart of the image of the *pais paizon* and of the world in which the child plays his creative and destructive games. The return to a pagan world, the elimination of a fallen nature, and the revocation of the punishment of labor and shame, along with the consumption of the fruit of the tree of knowledge that is now also the tree of life—that is the "innocence of becoming" for Nietzsche. It is thus that, after the idols are shattered, the world is redeemed, in the concluding words of *Twilight of the Idols,* by "the last disciple of the philosopher Dionysus . . . the teacher of the eternal return."[27]

---

26. Pp. 90f. See the lengthy note of spring 1888, entitled "The Redemption from All Sin," which seems to be the basis for this section of *Götzendämmerung* (VIII, 3, 15[30]; cf. *The Will to Power* 765). Among the numerous notes that speak of the "innocence of becoming" are VII, 1, 7 [21] (Spring–Summer 1883), 8 [19] (= *WM* 787).26] (Summer 1883), 14 [1] (Summer 1883), 16 [49.84] (Fall 1883), 21 [3] (Fall 1883); VII, 3, 36[10] (June–July 1885). As is well known, Alfred Baeumler brought together many of Nietzsche's unpublished notes that were not included in the posthumous *Will to Power* in a two-volume collection entitled *Die Unschuld des Werdens (The Innocence of Becoming)* (Stuttgart: Kröner, 1931), texts that particularly support Baeumler's heroic, "Heraclitean" interpretation of Nietzsche.

27. *GD,* "What I learned from the ancients," §5 (VI, 3, 154).

II. THE FREE SPIRIT

I

It would seem that, with the redemption of the world, we might have reached an end to our voyage. Yet the thought of a labyrinthine thinker has many false enclosures and dead ends. It is not unusual to have to return to our erstwhile starting points and pick up the thread once again. In such a case we might notice that the work that first rejects freedom, *Human, All-Too-Human,* is subtitled "A Book for Free Spirits"; that *Beyond Good and Evil* both asserts a necessity so unyielding that "almost any word and even the word 'tyranny' would seem useless or at best too weak" (§22) and has a second chapter entitled "The Free Spirit"; and that *Twilight of the Idols* itself, after the unambiguous assertions we have just outlined, has an aphorism in its penultimate chapter entitled "My concept of freedom."[28] We have already spoken of Nietzsche's denial of freedom. We will now have to speak of his affirmation of "freedom" in the "free spirit" before, in our final section, we discuss his new concept of freedom, one so new that it is indistinguishable from the harshest tyranny.

Human, All-Too-Human is a "Book for Free Spirits" one of whose major teachings, as we have seen, is the universal rule of causality and the consequent denial of freedom. This is more than a paradox: it sets up an instability in the free spirit and the Nietzschean project itself. This instability is imaged in the free spirit's solitude, placelessness, homelessness. Free spirits, Nietzsche tells us in *MA 426,* an aphorism entitled "Free spirit and marriage," are like the prophet birds of antiquity: "as the true thinking, truth speaking ones of the present," they must prefer "to fly alone." The final aphorism of the first chapter of the work answers the question that was posed in the chapter's penultimate aphorism: whether the recognition that "the error about life is necessary to life," along with the assertion that "the belief in the value and worthiness of life rests on impure thinking," means that "our philosophy becomes tragedy." "Doesn't truth become hostile to life, to what is better?" According to the final aphorism, only temperament can decide whether one prefers to live in conscious untruth or to live in a truth that seems to attack the very livability of life. One from whom "the usual chains of life have fallen away must be able to renounce many things, almost all things that have value to other men. He must be satisfied with that free, fearless hovering [*Schweben*] over men, customs, laws, and the tradition-

---

28. *GD (Str.)* §38 (ibid., pp. 133 f.).

al evaluations of things." Life "unchained" enforces a kind of existence that is at first unrecognizable as a human life, and the work ends appropriately with a chapter entitled "Man Alone with Himself." Its final aphorism, "The wanderer" (638), acknowledges this problematic "freedom" of the free spirit in a world without freedom in its first line: "Whoever has come to the freedom of reason to even some small degree cannot feel otherwise than a wanderer—though not as a traveler in pursuit of a last goal, because this does not exist." No longer bound by the deceptions of responsibility, faithfulness, meaning, or purpose, he must not allow himself to become attached to anyone or anything. "There must be something wandering in himself which has its joy in change and mutability."

The romantic image of the wanderer, with its Schubertian and Wagnerian resonances, becomes central in Nietzsche's subsequent treatment of the free spirit. As mentioned, Nietzsche's third aphorism book, subtitled the "second and final supplement to the previously published collection of thoughts *Human, All-Too-Human. A Book for Free Spirits*," is entitled *The Wanderer and His Shadow*, after the two personages whose dialogue is supposed to constitute the work. The wanderer images the estrangement and homelessness of the free spirit who has seen through illusions of permanence, while the shadow personifies both his solitude and the insubstantiality of a world released from its metaphysical moorings.

The empty "freedom" of the free spirit/wanderer attains its most striking expression in *The Gay Science*, the last in the series of "aphorism books." Nietzsche himself, in a letter to Lou Salomé, proclaimed that this work marked the end of "the work of six years (1876–1882), of my whole 'free spiritedness [*Freigeisterei*]'!"[29] Chapter II of the work, aphorism 124, warns the traveler against a "nostalgia for land" in his travels on the ocean "in the horizon of the infinite," "as if there were more freedom" on the land, when there is no more land at all, thus imaging the dilemma of a placeless, substanceless freedom. The chapter also serves to introduce the famous aphorism 125, "The mad man," the final metamorphosis of the free-spirited wanderer, now bereft of his shadow or any companion, lighting lanterns at noon in a world unhinged, its horizon expunged, an infinite nothingness through which he wanders after having, in the ultimate assertion and absurdity of his freedom, "murdered God."[30]

29. To Lou Salomé (3 July 1882), *KGB* 6:216f. See also Curt Paul Janz, *Friedrich Nietzsche: Biographie* (Munich: Hanser, 1978) II:162.

30. The images of dislocation in the third book of *The Gay Science* have lost their ambiguity, as the wanderer's destination has become evident to Nietzsche in the work's later affirmation of fate and eternal return, both in the individual conscience's Pindarian watchword to "become what you are" (*FW* 270), the affirmation of the larger world in the *amor fati* with which the fourth book begins (*FW* 276), and with the "highest affirmation that can be attained," the eternal return of the same, with which it all but closes (*FW* 341).

2

What are we to make of such "freedom," and how can we possibly reconcile it with the "causal slavery" that its representative, the free spirit, unveils?[31] Only by remaining separate from the earth and its inhabitants, by "hovering" above the world and its concerns, or by wandering solitary in the desert, an interlocutor of shadows, can the "freedom" of the free spirit be maintained. His freedom is purely negative, a mere separation, as his inquiry is really an attack upon the bonds of the past that have held him fast. But to be *freed* of one set of bonds is not to be *free* simply. Notebook entries written toward the end of the period in which the last of the three books that were included under the name *Human, All-Too-Human* was published show Nietzsche's growing clarity about this. In July 1879, before the publication of *The Wanderer and His Shadow*, he wrote, "one strives for independence (freedom) for the sake of *power*, not vice versa." Freedom is but an instrumentality of power, and Nietzsche's turn from "freedom" to "power," and from free will to strong will, anticipating a commonplace of his later writings (e.g., *JGB* 21) is even more striking in the following, slightly later notebook entry. To say "he has a strong will" "has nothing to do with free will. He is independent from others, thus *free* (as dependent upon himself). The unfree, the weak, is not sufficiently dependent upon himself, and hence is very dependent upon others."[32] In a formulation that echoes yet significantly varies a Kantian one: freedom is not self-legislation but self-dependency.[33]

The first edition of *Human, All-Too-Human* could easily have misled readers about the nature of the freedom of the "free spirit," flanked at its entry as it was by two of the great heroes of the French Enlightenment; its dedication was to Voltaire, "great liberator [*Befreier*] of the spirit," on the centennial of whose death it was published, and its motto, "in place of a foreword," was from Descartes' *Discourse on Method*, the first rule of which is the rule of evident knowledge and the avoidance of prejudice, the rule that guides Nietzsche in his examination of perception, tradition, and metaphysics. The anti-metaphysical and anti-Christian spirit of Voltaire are omnipresent in *Human, All-Too-Human*, as are the Cartesian demands for clarity and evidence in the dissection of

---

31. See, in general, Josef Simon, "Aufklärung im Denken Nietzsches," in Jochen Schmidt, ed., *Aufklärung und Gegenaufklärung in der europäischen Literatur, Philosophie und Politik von der Antike bis zur Gegenwart* (Darmstadt: Wissenschaftliche Buchgesellschaft, 1989), pp. 459–74.

32. *KGW* IV, 3:41 [3], 47 [1] (September, November 1879, respectively).

33. For an explicit recognition of this, see the end of *JGB* 188, where Nietzsche writes "'Thou shalt obey, whomever, and for a long time . . .' this seems to me to be the moral imperative of nature . . ." (VI, 2, 112).

the metaphysical and moral traditions. When it comes to the question of freedom, *Human, All Too Human* seems to reflect the views of the French popularizer of Newton's physics (who was happy to affirm strict necessity while he defended "freedom of thought" in the *Philosophical Dictionary*) rather than the absolutism of Descartes' teaching about the freedom of the will.[34] But even in his earliest days of "free-spiritedness," Nietzsche was unable cheerfully to ignore the contradiction between the free spirit's intellectual *goal*, "liberation" (in Voltaire's terms, *liberté de penser*), and his *teaching* of causal servitude (the Voltairean denial of *liberté*). In 1876, among the earliest remarks on the "free spirit," he wrote the following note: "The image of the free spirit remained unfinished in the previous century: they negated too little and held *themselves* back."[35]

The radicalization of the Enlightenment via its self-reflection was central to Nietzsche's project from the very beginning. And in fact, in the second edition of *Human, All-Too-Human*, published ten years later, Descartes and Voltaire are expunged from the book's beginning, replaced by a preface in the author's own name. No longer holding himself back, he wrote a preface in which he explains what he meant by the "free spirits" of the subtitle. The free spirits whom Nietzsche now admits to having "invented," the shadows to his wanderer, would be those who have undergone a "great separation" [*grosse Loslösung*] (§3) from all that had previously bound them. They are no longer tied to the contingencies of their duties, homes, and loves. The closest the free spirit comes to positive freedom is "willfulness" [*Willkür*]. Rather than manifesting freedom itself, the "free spirit" expresses a "will to *free* will," and his odyssey ends in a "return to life" which involves a reflection upon the "great separation," and in which he gains answers, a whole set of new commandments, "thou shalt's," new ways of being bound to himself and to the world, new ways of being reconciled to his necessary connectedness to the world. "Thou shalt become master of yourself, master of your own virtues"; "thou shalt gain power over your 'for' and 'against'"; "thou shalt learn to comprehend the perspectival in every positing of value." "Thou shalt learn to comprehend the *necessary* injustice in every for and against, injustice as indissoluble from life, life itself as *conditioned* by the perspectival and its injustice." The last of the lessons of power to which the erstwhile free spirit must submit is the lesson of hierarchy, the fixed order of rank: "thou shalt see the problem of the order of rank with your eyes and how power and right and comprehen-

---

34. See, respectively, the paired entries "De la liberté" and "Liberté de penser" in the *Dictionnaire philosophique* (Paris: Gallimard, 1961, pp. 274–77, 277–81) and Descartes, *Meditationes de prima philosophia* IV (*AT* VII, 57).

35. *KGW* IV, 2, 16 [55].

siveness of perspective grow in the heights with one another" (§6). The free spirit, after wandering from his prior homeland and freeing himself from the contingent bonds of his youthful duties and masters, discovers that a life of hovering, wandering, solitary sailing over uncharted seas, a life without perspective and one without binding commitment, is impossible. The "free" insight into the necessary bonds of man leads to a call for self-mastery and self-discipline, the asceticism of the free spirit to which Nietzsche often alludes and which establishes a hierarchy within the self.[36] Nihilism, oblivion, and decadence await those who are not strong enough for this discipline and its separation.[37] For the strong and those capable of "the grand health," the attempt to separate oneself from the bonds of life only shows us our real attachments, and the "will to free will" is a will that runs up against an even stronger will, a will which manifests itself in the necessary hierarchy, the necessary morality present in life itself.

3

The free spirit, and "freedom" as a whole, are relative, transitional concepts in Nietzsche's oeuvre, as in Nietzsche's thought. As the lion in the parable with which *Thus Spoke Zarathustra* begins represents "the creation of freedom for himself and a sacred 'Not' even before duty,"[38] and is situated between the heavily laden camel and the innocent, spontaneous child engaged in the "play of creating," as the "free spirit" is the second chapter between the "prejudices of philosophers" and "the religious essence" in *Beyond Good and Evil*, so "the free spirit" in Nietzsche's own life was only a vanishing moment between submission to the authority of a great philosopher and a great artist and the love of an implacable, tyrannical fate. As he wrote to Lou Salomé: "Spirit? What is spirit to me! What is knowledge to me! I value nothing but *impulses*, and I could have sworn that we had that in common. Just see *past* this phase, in which I have lived for some years—see *behind* it! Don't let *yourself* be deceived about me—*you* don't believe, do you, that 'the free spirit' is my ideal? I am—."[39] But in this letter, and at this point, Nietzsche is unable to fill in the silence surrounding the "free spirit."

In *Beyond Good and Evil* we learn a bit more. Although its second

---

36. See the remarks in *Ecce Homo*, "Menschliches Alllzumenschliches" §5 (VI, 3, 325), where he speaks of *Human, All-Too-Human* as "this monument of a rigorous self-discipline, with which I prepared a quick end for all the 'higher nonsense,' 'idealism,' 'beautiful feelings' and other femininities that I had dragged along with me . . ."
37. See, for example, *JGB* 29 (VI, 2, 43), in the chapter entitled "The Free Spirit."
38. *KGW* VI, 1, 26.
39. *KSB* 6:282 (24 November 1882).

chapter is entitled "The Free Spirit," and it can teach us much about the meaning of this term—for example, we hear of esotericism, masks, semblance, will to power—the free spirit is explicitly replaced by the "free, *very* free spirit," whom we had already met in the preface and who is "something more, something higher, greater, and fundamentally different." It is in aphorism 44 of this work that Nietzsche attempts to settle publicly with the conception that had been of such importance to his own growth. He distinguishes his "free spirit" from those going by the same name in Europe and even in America who are "slaves of the democratic taste, men without solitude, superficial" and believers in "equality of rights" and "sympathy for all that suffers." For such "librespenseurs," "liberi pensatori," "Freidenker," freedom is freedom from suffering: "they want to do away with suffering." Nietzsche's "free, *very* free spirits" do not shrink from affirming the opposite, that "harshness, violence, slavery, secrecy, that what is evil, fearsome, tyrannical" also belong to what elevates man. The "free, very free spirit," the spirit that animates the "new philosopher" of *Beyond Good and Evil*, is the spirit who has finally learned to *detach himself from his freedom*, as the free spirit first detached himself from his bonds. In his recognition of the centrality of the problem of hierarchy he discovers the resolution of the conflict of the world's necessity and the spirit's freedom. In his struggle to master the world, the spirit must master himself, and in the will to self-mastery he discovers a hierarchy within himself, along with the name of the tyrant that is his master: the free spirit is the one who would not shrink from affirming that "the world would be will to power—and nothing else!" (*JGB* 36). No longer bound to his own freedom, he is ready to do what the philosopher has always done, as one animated by the "tyrannical drive itself, the most spiritual will to power" (*JGB* 9): become a man who is a commander and lawgiver and whose "will to truth" is "will to power" (*JGB* 211), one who understands that, for himself as for others, the greatest freedom and the greatest enslavement are indistinguishable.

III. NIETZSCHE'S CONCEPT OF FREEDOM

I

It is tempting to view the process by which the free spirit uncovers both the causal and then fatal necessity at the heart of nature, and then the will to power as the tyrant that determines its own movements, as a prime example of the "dialectic of enlightenment" discovered in the middle of the past century by Max Horkheimer and Theodor Adorno as they reflected on what they saw as the failure of the Enlightenment project in their exile in California as Europe writhed in the bonds of genocide and war. Jürgen Habermas has emphasized the Nietzschean elements in this work,[40] and the authors themselves explicitly express their view that "Nietzsche, as few since Hegel, has understood the dialectic of enlightenment."[41] However, if dialectic is understood in a Hegelian fashion, then the interplay between free spirit and the fatality of nature is not dialectical but agonal. While the Nietzschean free spirit is a vanishing moment Hegelian dialectic depends on two equally valid and opposed elements, each of which is *aufgehoben* (sublated), destroyed yet preserved and elevated into a larger whole.[42] Such an "immanent transcendence" is clearly missing in the interchange between fatality and freedom in the works of Nietzsche's phase of the "free spirit," and the resolution, the personal *amor fati* and the cosmic "eternal return of the same," is not a Hegelian reconciliation but a tragic, if not ironic, capitulation of freedom to fate.

In the winter of 1882–83, preparatory to the publication of the first part of *Thus Spoke Zarathustra*, preceding the "holy book," the "inspired revelation" of the erstwhile free spirit,[43] there is a small set of notes, all of which speak of the "asceticism" of the free spirit, who attempts "only to develop reason," rejecting the comforts of religion, morality, art, and metaphysics, along with "all attributions of value to life." The intermediate result of this process is an existence that is directed toward "always knowing better, hovering above valuations the only consolation." Yet the final result is the discovery that "in the whole process I discovered *living morality, driving force*. I had only dreamed that I was beyond good and evil . . . I held myself back as *value positer*."[44] The portrait of the free spirit in *Human, All-Too-Human* is unmistakable here. Although he believes that he is hovering above the world and its valuations, he is in fact, insofar as he is alive, rooted *in* that world. The consequence of the discovery that he had "held himself back" is made clear in the last of this series of notes:

1. Ascetic attempt to liberate oneself from morality: why? Practical consequence first of all: soldierly poverty, closeness of death. Free spirit

40. Jürgen Habermas, *Der philosophische Diskurs der Moderne* (Frankfurt a.M.: Suhrkamp, 1986), pp. 131, 144–57.

41. Max Horkheimer and Theodor Adorno, *Dialektik der Aufklärung: Philosophische Fragmente* (Frankfurt a.M.: S. Fischer, 1969 [orig. ed. 1944]), p. 50.

42. See Hegel, *Enzyklopädie der philosophischen Wissenschaften in Grundrisse*, ed. O. Pögeler and F. Nicolin (Hamburg: Felix Meiner Verlag, 1969), pp. 102–4 (§§ 81–82).

43. For *Thus Spoke Zarathustra* as "holy book," see letter to von Meysenbug, 20 April 1883 (*KSB* 6:363), repeated to Köselitz, 21 April 1883, ibid., p. 365. For *Zarathustra* as revelation, see *Ecce Homo*, "Thus Spoke Zarathustra" (§§1, 4), VI, 3, 335, 337f.; Janz, II 221–24.

44. KGW VII, 1, 6 [1] (Winter 1882–83).

2. But now we recognize free spiritedness itself as *morality*
To what extent
All feelings are morally colored. What we did was a cure, a means to *life*. Morality appeared as a condition of existence
3. The new *freer* view for morality as condition of existence and its furtherance. Herd—development of the ego. No retribution etc.
4. Attempt at a Beyond Good and Evil.[45]

The free spirit frees himself from the bonds of a particular valuation, in his *agon* with the herd and his age, but frees himself *for* a morality that furthers life. There is no standpoint beyond life; in fact the delusion that there was one is the delusion animating the morality of good and evil. The free spirit in his failure illuminates, for himself and others, the inadequacy, indeed nihilism, of a morality of good and evil. His very unfreedom is central to the new revelation of the inescapability of the circle of life and the ladder of evaluation, the dual doctrines of eternal return of the same and will to power.

2

The free spirit is freed from a view of morality that connects it with freedom, and he prepares to tie himself to a morality of life, to make an attempt at a "beyond good and evil." Three years later Nietzsche wrote a book with that title, arguably his greatest, certainly his subtlest.[46] In Section 260 of this work, in the final chapter, entitled "What is Noble?" Nietzsche gives his first extended exposition of the distinction between "master morality" and "slave morality," whose elaboration was to form such an important part of his next work, *Toward the Genealogy of Morality*.[47] The noble morality of self-glorification and self-affirmation has "the feeling of fullness, of power that wants to overflow, the joy of elevated tension, the awareness of a wealth that would like to grant gifts . . ." It is at odds with the values of "modern ideas" and is itself, when dealing with beings of the "lower ranks," "beyond good and evil." Slave morality arises in reaction to the noble, out of fear of the "power and dangerousness" of the master, while the good is now the harmless "bonhomme." Everywhere that slave morality gains ascendancy "language shows a tendency for the words 'good' and 'dumb' to approach one another."[48]

45. VII, 1, 6 [4].
46. It is the subject of Leo Strauss' only published work wholly devoted to Nietzsche, "Note on the Plan of Nietzsche's *Beyond Good and Evil*" (*Studies in Platonic Political Philosophy* [Chicago: University of Chicago Press, 1983], pp. 174–92). He judges it to be "Nietzsche's most beautiful" work.
47. *KGW* VI, 2, 218.
48. *JGB* 260, VI, 2, 222.

Master morality, "beyond good and evil," arising from the feeling of power, is the morality of life itself, since, as we are repeatedly informed in *Beyond Good and Evil* and most recently in the preceding aphorism [259]), "life is will to power," that is, "*essentially* exploitation, violation, overwhelming of the other and the weaker, suppression, severity, forcing of its own forms, incorporation, and at the very least, exploitation."[49] Aphorism 260 ends with a discussion of a final distinction between master and slave morality. Refinements in reverence and devotion, and love as passion, are regular symptoms of an aristocratic mode of thinking and evaluating, as a part of what Zarathustra would call their "gift-giving virtue."[50] The slave, on the other hand, is animated by a "longing for *freedom*." "The instinct for the happiness and refinements of the feeling of freedom" is an essential part of slave morality. The slave *wants* to be free, insofar as he *is* a slave, while the master realizes his "freedom," which is the expression of his power, i.e., his natural function.

Yet as master he is not free, in a sense that is opposite to the famous unfreedom of the master in Hegel's master-slave dialectic. Master of the slave, he is enslaved by his tyrant, the drive that dominates him as he exemplifies the "terrible basic text of homo natura" that the "free, *very* free spirit" expects to uncover in the "retranslation of man back into nature" that is the "strange and mad task" of this spirit (*JGB* 230). A world that is will to power has no place for freedom, not because it is a "lawful" or regulated world, but because in such a world "laws are completely lacking, and every power draws its final consequence in every moment" (*JGB* 22). For such a world, lacking in laws yet ruled by iron necessity, even the word "tyranny" might seem too weak a metaphor, as he notes in this same aphorism, but it is certainly one of which Nietzsche is fond.[51] In fact, we first meet with it in the aphorism of *Beyond Good and Evil* in which we first read of the "will to power": "philosophy is this tyrannical drive itself, the most spiritual will to power" (*JGB* 9). The slave longs for freedom, the master expresses his passion as he is mastered by it, like the courtly lovers of old, and the philosopher plays the tyrant, commanding and legislating as if he were the "tyrannical drive itself."[52] But

---

49. See the first reference to "will to power" in the work (§9), where it is associated with tyranny and philosophy, and §13 as well with its critique of the teleology of self-preservation and the contrary assertion of life as expression of will to power, alongside the grand, programmatic aphorism in Chapter 2, §36, which concludes that "the world viewed from within . . . would be 'will to power,' and nothing else."

50. VI, 1, 93ff. In §153 we are told that "what is done out of love always happens beyond good and evil."

51. VI, 2, 31 (§22).

52. For the Platonic recognition of this "desire to be tyrant," Nietzsche refers to the *Gorgias* (e.g. 483d ff.) and *Theages* (126a) in notes from the summer 1880 (V, 2, 4 [301]) and spring 1884 (VII, 2, 25 [137]). The former is one of the earliest extended discussions

insofar as "every philosophy in its genesis has been a lengthy tragedy," the philosopher is a victim of hubris and is the mere instrument of a tyrant greater than he: the overpowering will to power itself that masters him as he works to master the world.

3

Have we now reached the terminus of our journey through the labyrinthine thought of the labyrinthine thinker? And if so, is this terminus the way out into the openness of a new world of freedom, or is it a trap in which we will be devoured by a monster? And if it is the latter, was it to our advantage to retreat from the labyrinth's dead ends and to find our way into its heart, or to enter it at all? It is of the nature of a labyrinth that once we are within it is no easier to find our way out than it was to find our way to its center.

Certainly paths have crossed and re-crossed, and in the notebooks of the time following the publication of *Beyond Good and Evil* we see the paths of freedom and will to power intersect increasingly, as also in *Toward the Genealogy of Morality* (II:17, 18), where freedom, or the "instinct of freedom" in those vanquished by "some pack of blond beasts of prey, a conqueror and master race," is said in fact to be the will to power.[53] While the "freedom" of the "free spirit" is a developmental stage in the growth of the soul to ultimate mastery and identification with the tyrannical fate for which man and his concerns are a mere plaything—a necessary separation from the grandeur of the revered past in order to gain a perspective that will permit destruction and replacement or transformation—freedom as a fixed ideal is a mask of the "Machiavellianism of power." Here, a will to power, too weak to realize itself in its own terms, unconsciously disguises itself: "among the suppressed, among slaves of every type as will to 'freedom'—mere *release* seems the goal." As a mere-

---

of the will to power, here called the "feeling of power." It begins: "*All* Greeks (see *Gorgias* of Plato) believed that possession of power as tyrant was the most enviable happiness: its ruthlessness presupposed. *All* were concerned with impeding the advent of the happiest and, if he existed, in thwarting or annihilating him. The supreme happiness in which each believed was located completely in the *feeling of power*." It ends: "Every philosophy had its imperious [*herrische*] side: the Epicureans triumphed having been victorious over the Acheron and the fear of death, the fear of nature: thus, by being masters of nature."

53. This point is made parenthetically in *Toward the Genealogy of Morality* II, 17, 18: "precisely that *instinct of freedom* (speaking my language: the will to power)" (VI, 2, 342). For the other occurrences of this phrase, see II, 16 (338), II:17 (341). See also VIII, 1, 1 [33] (Fall 1885–Spring 1886), i.e., from the same time as *Toward the Genealogy of Morality:* "the most fearsome and thorough longing of man, his drive for power—one calls this drive 'freedom'—must be held in bounds the longest. For this reason has ethics previously, with its unconscious instincts for education and breeding, been concerned with holding the power-lusts in bounds. It defames the tyrannical individual and emphasizes, with its glorification of common fellow feeling and patriotism, the herd's power instinct."

ly negative ideal, freedom is the goal of those most negatively endowed with the animating force of life, as justice and then love are the goals of those who are progressively stronger.[54] In another case, Nietzsche sees the progression as one from freedom to tyranny, from no power to all-power.[55] With the will to power as his reductive tool, Nietzsche engages in a "Critique of Grand Words": freedom is just a 'grand word' for will to power."[56] In another note from the same time he summarizes the movement by which the will to power gains power at all levels of intensity: "One wants freedom as long as one does not yet have power. If one has power, one wants predominance [*Übermacht*]; if one does not attain this (if one is too weak for it), one wants 'justice,' i.e., equal power."[57] As the will to power in actions grand and small seeks resistance and not freedom—indeed, can realize itself only in opposition to another power—so freedom is the most denatured of ideals, the absence of constraint or opposition, indeed a contradiction for a force whose necessary components are growth and predominance.[58]

We are now ready to turn to "My concept of freedom," the title of the thirty-eighth of Nietzsche's "Raids of an Untimely Man" in *Twilight of the Idols*. It is no longer a surprise, if it ever was, that the same book that named "the error of free will" as one of the four great errors, indeed as the exemplary "great error," should contain such a section, and we might even guess at its content in advance. Like the aphorisms that precede ("Whether we have become more moral") and follow ("Critique of modernity"), this aphorism too opposes modern "decadence," the "morality of sympathy," and "democratism," but unlike them, it asserts a contrary teaching. Freedom, the watchword of "modern ideas" and "liberal institutions," is reinterpreted to have a "Nietzschean" sense, one that no longer demands quotation marks.[59]

The aphorism begins with a short critique of "liberal institutions" and their politically guaranteed freedoms as harmful to freedom, since they "undermine the will to power." Nietzsche notes that it is the *fight* for such

---

54. *KGW* VIII, 2. 9 [145] (Fall 1887) (cf. *WM* 776).
55. *KGW* VIII, 2, 10 [77] (Fall 1887) (cf. *WM* 215).
56. *KGW* VIII, 2, 11 [136] (November 1887–March 1888).
57. *KGW* VIII, 2, 10 [82]; Fall 1887 (cf *WM* 784). Other notes that speak of this, or similar, progressions that include freedom are 10 [66] (cf. *WM* 86) and 9 [135] (Fall 1887): here, uniquely, freedom takes second place after the demand for justice from those who have power, but before the demand for "equal rights," "i.e., so long as one does not have the upper hand, one wants to keep one's competitors from growing in power."

58. See VII, 2, 26 [275] (Summer–Fall 1884); VIII, 2, 9 [151] (Fall 1887) (cf. *WM* 656).

59. The understanding of freedom common in "times like today" is rejected as a "symptom of decadence" in a subsequent aphorism (41), that begins "freedom that I do *not* mean . . ."

institutions that actually produces freedom by allowing *illiberal* instincts to reign. "War educates to freedom." Freedom is "self-sufficiency," "distance," toughness, willingness to sacrifice men to one's cause. "Freedom means that the manly, the instincts that rejoice in war and victory, have mastery over the other instincts." The man, and even more the spirit, who has become free, tramples underfoot the welfare of which "Christians, Englishmen, and other democrats" dream. Freedom is measured by the resistance that must be overcome. The highest type of free man can be discovered where the highest resistance has been overcome: "five steps from tyranny, on the threshold of servitude." Nietzsche notes that for individuals the "tyrants" include "implacable and frightful instincts" which summon "the maximum of authority and self-discipline." For peoples, it is only "great danger" that makes something out of them that deserves to be honored. Freedom is mastery, of oneself and of others; freedom involves placing oneself under the harshest conditions, and is visible only as a response to a threat that must be overcome, when one is tyrannized and close to servitude. Those who *are* "free" never become free, and those who become free cannot remain "free" without constantly placing themselves at risk. The first principle of strength is that "it must be necessary to be strong; otherwise one never is."

True freedom, the freedom of the warrior, is inseparable from the necessity that calls it forth and forces it to overcome itself. For this reason it is fundamentally unstable, indeed it *is* this simple instability itself, as the Preface to the Second Edition of *Human, All-Too-Human* put it, not a "free will" but a "will to free will"[60] hovering, now, not between heaven and earth, but between tyranny and servitude, the two poles of a world that is will to power. The aphorism ends with Nietzsche's final clarification about "the sense in which I understand the word freedom: as something that one has and *does not* have, that one *wills*, that one *conquers* . . ."[61]

The conquest of freedom is the final twist in the labyrinth: freedom and necessity are not reconciled, nor are they identified. They are bound together in an *agon* without issue, a war without end. We find, in the labyrinth's center, the same monster that was hidden in it by Daedelus, Minos' faithful servant. Having uncovered it we can only hope that we have also gotten clues to the way out.

60. Preface, §3 (*KGW* IV, 2, 11).
61. *KGW* VI, 3, 134.

Bibliography

Ameriks, Karl. "Pure Reason of Itself Alone Suffices to Determine the Will." In *Kants Kritik der praktischen Vernunft*, edited by Otfried Hoeffe. Berlin: Akademie-Verlag, 2002.

Anderson-Gold, Sharon. *Unnecessary Evil: History and Moral Progress in the Philosophy of Immanuel Kant*. New York: State University of New York Press, 2001.

Anscombe, G. E. M. *The Collected Philosophical Papers of G. E. M. Anscombe*. Oxford: Blackwell, 1981.

———. *From Parmenides to Wittgenstein*. Oxford: Blackwell, 1981.

Aristotle. *Basic Works of Aristotle*. Edited by Richard McKeon. New York: Random House, 1941.

———. *Ethica Nicomachea*. Translated by W. D. Ross. In *Basic Works of Aristotle*, edited by Richard McKeon. New York: Random House, 1941.

———. *Metaphysica*. Translated by W. D. Ross. In *Basic Works of Aristotle*, edited by Richard McKeon. New York: Random House, 1941.

———. *Politica*. Translated by Benjamin Jowett. In *Basic Works of Aristotle*, edited by Richard McKeon. New York: Random House, 1941.

Augustine, St. *Confessions*. Translated by Henry Chadwick. New York: Oxford University Press, 1992.

———. *City of God Against the Pagans*. With an English translation by George E. McCracken. Cambridge: Harvard University Press, 1957.

Ayers, Michael. *Locke*. London: Routledge, 1991.

Benjamin, Walter. *Illuminations*. Edited and with an introduction by Hannah Arendt. Translated by Harry Zohn. New York: Schocken Books, 1969.

Bentham, Jeremy. *Anarchical Fallacies*. In *The Works of Jeremy Bentham*, edited by John Bowring. New York: Russell & Russell, 1962.

Bickerton, Derek. "Pidgin and Creole Languages." *Scientific American* 249 (1983): 116–22.

———. *Language and Human Behavior*. Seattle: University of Washington Press, 1995.

———. *Language and Species*. Chicago: University of Chicago Press, 1990.

———, and William H. Calvin. *Lingua ex Machina: Reconciling Darwin and Chomsky with the Human Brain*. Cambridge: MIT Press, 2000.

Bluhm, William T., N. Wintfeld, and S. Teger. "Locke's Idea of God: Rational Truth or Political Myth?" *Journal of Politics* 42.2 (1980): 414–438.

Blumenberg, Hans. *The Legitimacy of the Modern Age*. Translated by Robert M. Wallace. Cambridge: The MIT Press, 1983.

Bodin, Jean. *Six Books of the Commonwealth*. Abridged and translated by M. J. Tooley. Oxford: Blackwell, 1955.

Boethius. *The Theological Tractates, The Consolation of Philosophy*. Translated by H.

F. Stewart, E. K. Rand, and S. J. Tester. Cambridge: Harvard University Press, 1973.

Braine, David. *The Human Person: Animal and Spirit.* Notre Dame: University of Notre Dame Press, 1992.

Burrell, David. *Freedom and Creation in Three Traditions.* Notre Dame: University of Notre Dame Press, 1993.

———. "Freedom and Creation in the Abrahamic Traditions." *International Philosophical Quarterly* 40 (2000): 161–71.

Cervantes, Miguel de. *Don Quijote de la Mancha.* Barcelona: Galazia Gutenberg, 2004.

Chisholm, Roderick. "Human Freedom and the Self." In *Free Will,* edited by Gary Watson. Oxford: Oxford University Press, 1982.

Chomsky, Noam. *Language and Thought.* Wakefield, RI: Moyer Bell, 1993.

Cicero, Marcus. *On Duties.* Translated by Walter Miller. Cambridge: Harvard University Press, 1997.

Clarke, W. Norris. *Person and Being.* Milwaukee: Marquette University Press, 1993.

Congar, M.-J. "Praedeterminare et praedeterminatio chez S. Thomas." *Revue des sciences philosophique et théologique* 23 (1934): 363–71.

Cowie, Fiona. *What's Within? Nativism Reconsidered.* New York: Oxford University Press, 1999.

Crosby, John F. *Personalist Papers.* Washington, D.C.: Catholic University Press of America, 2004.

———. *The Selfhood of the Human Person.* Washington, D.C.: Catholic University of America Press, 1996.

Darwin, Charles. *On the Origin of Species.* London: John Murray, 1859.

Dennett, D. C. *Freedom Evolves.* New York: Viking, 2003.

Descartes, René. *Discours de la méthode.* Text and commentary by E. Gilson. Paris: J. Vrin, 1966.

———. *Oeuvres.* Edited by Charles Adam and Paul Tannery. Paris: J. Vrin, 1964–1974.

———. *The Philosophical Writings of Descartes.* 3 vols. Translated by John Cottingham, Robert Stoothoff, Dugald Murdoch, and Anthony Kenny. Cambridge: Cambridge University Press, 1988.

di Giovanni, George. "Rehberg, Reinhold und C. C. E. Schmid über Kant und moralische Freiheit." In *Vernunftkritik und Aufklärung,* edited by M. Oberhausen, D. P. Delfosse, and R. Pozzo. Stuttgart–Bad Canstaat: Fromann-Holzboog, 2001.

Donagan, Alan. "Thomas Aquinas on Human Action." In *The Cambridge History of Later Medieval Philosophy,* edited by Norman Kretzmann, Anthony Kenny, and Jan Pinborg. Cambridge: Cambridge University Press, 1982.

Dunn, John. *The Political Thought of John Locke: An Historical Account of the Argument of the Two Treatises of Government.* London: Cambridge University Press, 1969.

Epictetus. *The Discourses, The Manual and Fragments.* 2 vols. Translated by W. A. Oldfather. Cambridge: Harvard University Press: 1925–28.

Filmer, Sir Robert. *Patriarcha and Other Writings.* Edited by Johann P. Sommerville. Cambridge: Cambridge University Press, 1991.

Flew, Anthony. "Compatibilism, Free Will, and God." *Philosophy* 48 (1973): 231–44.

Frankfurt, Harry. "Freedom of the Will and the Concept of a Person." *Journal of Philosophy* 68 (1971): 5–20. Reprinted in Harry Frankfurt, *The Importance of What We Care About*. Cambridge: Cambridge University Press, 1988.

Frege, Gottlob. "On Sense and Reference." Translated by M. Black in *Translations from the Philosophical Writings of Gottlob Frege*, edited and translated by P. Geach and M. Black. Oxford: Blackwell, 1980.

Fukuyama, Francis. *The End of History and the Last Man*. New York: Free Press, 1992.

Gallagher, David. "Desire for Beatitude and Love of Friendship." *Mediaeval Studies* 58 (1996): 1–47.

———. "Free Choice and Free Judgment in Thomas Aquinas." *Archiv für Geschichte der Philosophie* 76 (1994): 247–77.

———. "Thomas Aquinas on the Will as Rational Appetite." *Journal of the History of Philosophy* 29 (1991): 559–84.

Garrigou-Lagrange, R. *God, His Existence and Nature*. 5th ed. Translated by Dom Bede Rose. St. Louis: Herder, 1955.

Gillespie, Michael Allen. *Nihilism before Nietzsche*. Chicago: University of Chicago Press, 1995.

Goethe, Johann. *Maxims and Reflections*. Translated by Elisabeth Stopp. Edited by Peter Hutchinson. New York: Penguin Books, 1998.

Goldwin, Robert. "John Locke." In *History of Political Philosophy*, edited by Leo Strauss and Joseph Cropsey. 3d ed. Chicago: University of Chicago Press, 1987.

Grube, George M. A. *Plato's Thought*. Boston: Beacon Press, 1958.

Habermas, Jürgen. *Der philosophische Diskurs der Moderne*. Frankfurt a. M.: Suhrkamp, 1986.

Harris, Ian. "The Politics of Christianity." In *Locke's Philosophy: Content and Context*, edited by G. A. J. Rogers. Oxford/New York: Oxford University Press, 1994.

Hause, Jeffrey. "Thomas Aquinas and the Voluntarists." *Medieval Philosophy and Theology* 6 (1997).

Heftrich, Eckhard. *Nietzsches Philosophie: Identität von Welt und Nichts*. Frankfurt a. M.: Vittorio Klostermann, 1962.

Hegel, Georg. *Enzyklopädie der philosophischen Wissenschaften in Grundrisse*. Edited by O. Pöggeler and F. Nicolin. Hamburg: Felix Meiner Verlag, 1969.

———. *Philosophy of Right*. Translated by T. M. Knox. Oxford: Oxford University Press, 1967.

Heidegger, Martin. *Being and Time*. Translated by John Macquarrie and Edward Robinson. San Francisco: Harper Collins, 1962.

Henrich, Dieter. *The Unity of Reason: Essays on Kant's Philosophy*. Edited by Richard Velkley. Cambridge: Harvard University Press, 1994.

Herodotus, *Herodoti Historiae*. 2 vols. Edited by Karl Hude. Oxford: Oxford University Press, 1927.

Hobbes, Thomas. *Leviathan*. Edited by Edwin Curley. Indianapolis: Hackett, 1994.

———. *Leviathan*. Edited by C. B. MacPherson. Harmondsworth, UK: Penguin Books, 1968.

———. *On the Citizen*. Edited and translated by Richard Tuck. New York: Cambridge University Press, 1998.

Homer. *Iliad*.

Homer. *Odyssey.*

Horkheimer, Max, and Theodor Adorno. *Dialektik der Aufklärung: Philosophische Fragmente.* Frankfurt a. M.: S. Fischer, 1969.

Hume, David. *Enquiries Concerning Human Understanding and Concerning the Principles of Morals.* Edited by L. A. Selby-Bigge. Oxford: Clarendon Press, 1902.

———. *Hume's Ethical Writings.* Edited by Alasdair MacIntyre. Notre Dame: University of Notre Dame Press, 1965.

———. *A Treatise of Human Nature.* Edited by L. A. Selby-Bigge. Revised by P. H. Nidditch. Oxford: Clarendon Press, 1978.

Huntington, Samuel. *The Clash of Civilizations and the Remaking of the World Order.* New York: Simon and Schuster, 1996.

Husserl, Edmund. *Experience and Judgment: Investigations in a Genealogy of Logic.* Edited by Ludwig Landgrebe. Translated by James S. Churchill and Karl Ameriks. Evanston: Northwestern University Press, 1973.

———. *Formal and Transcendental Logic.* Translated by Dorion Cairns. The Hague: Nijhoff, 1969.

———. *Logical Investigations.* Translated by John N. Findlay. New York: Humanities Press, 1970.

Janz, Curt Paul. *Friedrich Nietzsche: Biographie.* Munich: Hanser, 1978.

Kant, Immanuel. *An Answer to the Question: What Is Enlightenment?* Translated by Mary J. Gregor. In *Practical Philosophy,* edited by Mary J. Gregor. Cambridge: Cambridge University Press, 1996.

———. *Anthropology From a Pragmatic Point of View.* Translated by Mary J. Gregor. The Hague: Martinus Nijhoff, 1974.

———. *The Conflict of the Faculties.* Translated by Mary J. Gregor. New York: Abaris Books, 1979.

———. "Conjectural Beginnings of Human History" (1786). Translated by Emil Fackenheim in *On History,* edited by L. W. Beck (Indianapolis: Library of Liberal Arts, 1963).

———. *Critique of Judgment: Including the First Introduction.* Translated by Werner S. Pluhar. Indianapolis: Hackett, 1987.

———. *Critique of Practical Reason.* Translated by Lewis White Beck. Indianapolis: Macmillan 1956.

———. *Critique of Pure Reason.* Translated by N. K. Smith. New York: St. Martin's Press, 1965.

———. *The End of All Things.* In *Religion and Rational Theology,* edited and translated by Allen W. Wood and George di Giovanni. Cambridge: Cambridge University Press, 1996.

———. *Gesammelte Schriften.* Edited by the Prussian Academy of Sciences. Berlin: de Gruyter, 1902–.

———. *Groundwork of the Metaphysics of Morals.* Edited and translated by Allen Wood. New Haven: Yale University Press, 2002.

———. *Idea for a Universal History from a Cosmopolitan Point of View.* Translated by Lewis White Beck. In *Kant: On History,* edited by Lewis White Beck. New York: Bobbs-Merrill, 1963.

———. *Lectures on Ethics.* Translated by Louis Infield. London: Methuen, 1930.

———. *The Metaphysics of Morals.* Translated by Mary J. Gregor. In *Practical Philosophy,* edited by Mary J. Gregor. Cambridge: Cambridge University Press, 1996.

———. *Observations on the Feeling of the Beautiful and the Sublime.* Translated by

John T. Goldthwait. Berkeley: University of California Press, 1960.

———. *Perpetual Peace*. In *Kant: Political Writings*, edited by H. Reiss. 2d ed. Cambridge: Cambridge University Press, 1970.

———. *Reflexionen zur Religionsphilosophie*. Berlin: Union, 1981.

———. *Religion and Rational Theology*. Edited by Allen Wood and George di Giovanni. Cambridge: Cambridge University Press, 1996.

———. *Religion within the Boundaries of Mere Reason*. Translated by George di Giovanni. In *Religion and Rational Theology*, edited and translated by Allen W. Wood and George di Giovanni. Cambridge: Cambridge University Press, 1996.

Kenny, Anthony. *Aquinas on Mind*. New York: Routledge, 1993.

Knight, Kelvin. *The MacIntyre Reader*. Notre Dame: University of Notre Dame Press, 1998.

Korsgaard, Christine. "Morality as Freedom." In *Creating the Kingdom of Ends*. Cambridge: Cambridge University Press, 1996.

———. "The Normativity of Instrumental Reason." In *Ethics and Practical Reason*, edited by Garrett Cullity and Berys Gaut. Oxford: Clarendon Press, 1997.

———. "Self-Constitution: Action, Identity and Integrity" (The John Locke Lectures at Oxford, England, June 2002).

———. *The Sources of Normativity*. Cambridge: Cambridge University Press, 1996.

Lilla, Mark. *The Reckless Mind: Intellectuals in Politics*. New York: New York Review of Books, 2001.

Livy. *History of Rome*. 2 vols. Translation by Rev. Canon Roberts. New York: E. P. Dutton and Co., 1912.

Locke, John. *An Essay Concerning Human Understanding*. Edited with a foreword by Peter H. Nidditch. Oxford: Clarendon Press, 1979.

———. *Political Essays*. Edited by Mark Goldie. Cambridge: Cambridge University Press, 1997.

———. *The Reasonableness of Christianity: As Delivered in the Scriptures*. Edited by John C. Higgins-Biddle. Oxford/New York: Clarendon Press, 1999.

———. *Two Treatises of Government*. Edited with an introduction and notes by Peter Laslett. Cambridge: Cambridge University Press, 1988.

Lomax, J. Harvey. *Nietzsche's Philosophy of the Eternal Recurrence of the Same*. Berkeley: University of California Press, 1997.

Longinus. *On the Sublime*. Edited and translated by W. Rhys Roberts. 2d ed. Cambridge: Cambridge University Press, 1899.

Loughran, Thomas. "Aquinas, Compatibilist." In *Human and Divine Agency*, edited by F. Michael McLain and W. Mark Richardson. New York: University Press of America, 1999.

Löwith, Karl. *Nietzsches Philosophie der ewigen Weiderkehr des Gleichen*. Stuttgart: Kohlhammer, 1956.

Lucan. *The Civil War*. Translated by Susan H. Braund. Oxford: Oxford University Press, 1992.

MacDonald, Scott. "Aquinas's Libertarian Account of Free Choice." *Revue internationale de philosophie* 21 (1998): 309–28.

Machiavelli, Niccolò. *Discourses on Livy*. Translated by Harvey C. Mansfield and Nathan Tarcov. Chicago: University of Chicago Press, 1996.

———. *Florentine Histories*. Translated by Laura A. Banfield and Harvey C. Mansfield. Princeton: Princeton University Press, 1988.

————. *Il Principe*. Edited by Manfredo Vanni. Milano: Signorelli, 1968.
————. *The Prince*. Translation by Harvey C. Mansfield. Chicago: University of Chicago Press, 1985.
Marcel, Gabriel. *The Mystery of Being*. Lanham: University Press of America, 1950.
Maritain, Jacques. "L'Idée thomiste de la liberté." *Revue Thomiste* 45 (1939): 440-59.
————. *The Person and the Common Good*. Notre Dame: University of Notre Dame Press, 1966.
Marshall, John. *John Locke: Resistance, Religion, and Responsibility*. Cambridge: Cambridge University Press, 1994.
McDowell, John. *Mind and World*. Cambridge: Harvard University Press, 1994.
Melzer, Arthur. "Rousseau and the Modern Cult of Sincerity." In *The Legacy of Rousseau*, edited by Clifford Orwin and Nathan Tarcov. Chicago: University of Chicago Press, 1997.
Mill, J. S. *On Liberty*. Edited by D. Spitz. New York: W. W. Norton, 1975.
————. *Utilitarianism*. Edited by G. Sher. Indianapolis: Hackett, 1979.
Mounier, Emmanuel. *Personalism*. New York: Grove Press, 1952.
Nagel, T. *The Possibility of Altruism*. Princeton: Princeton University Press, 1970.
————. *The View from Nowhere*. New York: Oxford University Press, 1986.
Nietzsche, Friedrich. *Beyond Good and Evil*. Translated by Walter Kaufmann. New York: Random House, 1966.
————. *Briefe: Kritische Studienausgabe*, edited by G. Colli and M. Montinari. Berlin and New York: dtv/de Gruyter, 1986.
————. *Ecce Homo: How One Becomes What One Is*. Translated by Walter Kaufmann. In *On the Genealogy of Morals and Ecce Homo*. New York: Random House, 1967.
————. *The Gay Science, with a Prelude of Rhymes and an Appendix of Songs*. Translated by Walter Kaufmann. New York: Random House, 1974.
————. *Human, All Too Human: A Book for Free Spirits*. Translated by R. J. Hollingdale. Cambridge: Cambridge University Press, 1986.
————. *Werke: Kritische Gesamtausgabe*. Edited by G. Colli and M. Montinari. Berlin and New York: de Gruyter, 1967.
————. *On the Genealogy of Morals*. Translated by Walter Kaufmann and R. J. Hollingdale. In *On the Genealogy of Morals and Ecce Homo*. New York: Random House, 1967.
————. *Thus Spoke Zarathustra*. Translated by Walter Kaufmann. In *The Portable Nietzsche*. New York: Viking Press, 1968.
————. *Twilight of the Idols*. Translated by Walter Kaufmann. In *The Portable Nietzsche*. New York: Viking Press, 1968.
————. *Die Unschuld des Werdens (The Innocence of Becoming)*. Edited by Alfred Baeumler. Stuttgart: Kröner, 1931.
————. *The Will to Power*. Translated by Walter Kaufmann. New York: Random House, 1967.
————. *Werke und Briefe: Historisch-Kritische Gesamtausgabe*. Munich: Beck, 1934.
Pangle, Thomas L. *Political Philosophy and the God of Abraham*. Baltimore: Johns Hopkins University Press, 2003.
Parfit, Derek. *Reasons and Persons*. Oxford: Oxford University Press, 1984.
Parmenides. *Parmenides*. Translation, commentary, and critical essays by Leonardo Tarán. Princeton: Princeton University Press, 1965.
Pegis, Anton C., James F. Anderson, Vernon J. Bourke, and Charles J. O'Neil,

trans. *Summa Contra Gentiles (On the Truth of the Catholic Faith)*. 5 vols. Notre Dame, IN: University of Notre Dame Press, 1975.

Petrarch. *Letters*. Translated by James Harvey Robinson and Henry Winchester Rolf. New York: G. P. Putnam's Sons, 1909.

Pico della Mirandola, Giovanni. *On the Dignity of Man; On Being and the One; Heptaplus*. Translated by C. G. Wallis, P. J. W. Miller, and Douglas Carmichael, with an introduction by Paul J. Miller. Indianapolis: Hackett Publishing Co., 1998.

Pinckaers, Servais, O.P. *Thomas d'Aquin. Somme théologique. Les actes humain, Tome Premier, 1a–2ae, Questions 6–17*. Translated by H.-D. Gardeil, O.P., Nouvelle Édition. Paris: Les Éditions du Cerf, 1997.

———. *Les sources de la morale chrétienne*, 3ᵉ edition. Fribourg, Switzerland: Editions Universitaires, 1993.

Pippin, Robert B. "Hegel, Freedom, The Will: *The Philosophy of Right*, #1–33." In *Hegel: Grundlinien der Philosophie des Rechts*, edited by Ludwig Siep. Berlin: Akademie Verlag, 1997.

———. "Hegel on Institutional Rationality," in *Southern Journal of Philosophy*, Vol. XXXIX, Supplement, "The Contemporary Relevance of Hegel's Philosophy of Right" (2001).

———. "Hegel on the Rationality and Priority of Ethical Life." *Neue Hefte fuer Philosophie* 35 (1995): 95–126.

———. *Hegel's Practical Philosophy: Rational Agency as Ethical Life*. Forthcoming.

———. *Idealism as Modernism: Hegelian Variations*. Cambridge: Cambridge University Press, 1997.

———. "Kant's Theory of Value: On Allen Wood's *Kant's Ethical Thought*." *Inquiry* 43 (summer 2000): 239-65.

———. "The Realization of Freedom: Hegel's Practical Philosophy." In *The Cambridge Companion to German Idealism*, edited by Karl Ameriks. Cambridge: Cambridge University Press, 2000.

Plato. *Complete Works*. Edited, with introduction and notes, by John M. Cooper. Indianapolis: Hackett, 1997.

Pliny the Elder. *Natural History*. Translated by H. Rackham. Cambridge: Harvard University Press, 1938–63.

Pliny the Younger. *C. Plini Caecili Secundi Epistularum Libri Decem*. Edited by R. A. B. Mynors. Oxford: Clarendon Press, 1966.

Plotinus, *Plotinus*. 7 vols. Greek text with English translation by A. H. Armstrong. Cambridge: Harvard University Press, 1966–88.

Plutarch. *Lives*. 2 vols. Edited by Arthur H. Clough. New York: Random House, 2001.

Polybius. *The Histories*. 6 vols. Translated by W. R. Praxton. New York: G. P. Putnam's Sons, 1922–27.

Rawls, John. *Political Liberalism*. New York: Columbia University Press, 1993.

———. *A Theory of Justice*. Cambridge: Harvard University Press, 1971.

Rist, J. M. *The Mind of Aristotle: A Study of Philosophical Growth*. Toronto: University of Toronto Press, 1989.

———. *Real Ethics: Reconsidering the Foundations of Morality*. Cambridge: Cambridge University Press, 2001.

Rossi, Philip. "The Final End of All Things: The Highest Good as the Unity of Nature and Freedom." In *Kant's Philosophy of Religion Reconsidered*, edited by Philip Rossi and Michael Wreen. Bloomington: Indiana University Press, 1991.

Rousseau, Jean-Jacques. *Collected Writings*. Edited by Roger D. Masters and Christopher Kelly. Hanover, NH: University Press of New England, 1990.
———. *The Social Contract*. Translated by Charles Frankel. New York: Hafner Publishing Co., 1947.
Schevill, Ferdinand. *The Medici*. Harper: New York, 1960.
Schmitz, Kenneth. "Personalism and the Existential Act." *Fides Quaerens Intellectum* 1, no. 1 (Summer 2001): 184–99.
Schneewind, J. B. *The Invention of Autonomy: A History of Modern Moral Philosophy*. Cambridge: Cambridge University Press, 1998.
Schopenhauer, Arthur. *Sämtliche Werke*. Edited by von Löhneysen. Darmstadt: Wissenschaftliche Buchgesellschaft, 1974.
Sellars, Wilfrid. *Empiricism and the Philosophy of Mind*. Edited by Robert Brandom. Cambridge: Harvard University Press, 1997.
Seneca. *On Favors*. In *Moral and Political Essays*, edited by John M. Cooper and J. F. Procopé. Cambridge: Cambridge University Press, 1995.
Shanley, Brian J., O.P. "Divine Causation and Human Freedom in Aquinas." *American Catholic Philosophical Quarterly* 72 (1998): 99–122.
Shell, Susan Meld. "Kant as Educator: Reason and Religion in Part One of the *Conflict of the Faculties*." In *Kant's Legacy: Essays in Honor of Lewis White Beck*, edited by Predrag Cicovacki. Rochester: University of Rochester Press, 2001.
Sigmund, Paul E. *Selected Political Writings of John Locke*. New York: Norton, 2005.
Simon, Josef. "Aufklärung im Denken Nietzsches." In *Aufklärung und Gegenaufklärung in der europäischen Literatur. Philosophie und Politik von der Antike bis zur Gegenwart*, edited by Jochen Schmidt. Darmstadt: Wissenschaftliche Buchgesellschaft, 1989.
Simon, Yves R. *A General Theory of Authority*. Notre Dame: University of Notre Dame Press, 1962.
Sokolowski, Robert. *The God of Faith and Reason: Foundations of Christian Theology*. Washington, D.C.: The Catholic University of America Press, 1995.
———. *Introduction to Phenomenology*. New York: Cambridge University Press, 2000.
———. *Presence and Absence: An Investigation of Language and Being*. Bloomington: Indiana University Press, 1978.
Sophocles. *The Ajax of Sophocles*. Translated by R. C. Trevelyan. London: G. Allen & Unwin, 1919.
———. *Plays*. 2 vols. Translated by F. Storr.
Spaemann, Robert. *Personen. Versuche über den Unterschied zwischen 'etwas' und 'jemand'*. Stuttgart: Klett-Cotta, 1996.
Spellman, W. M. *John Locke*. New York: St. Martin's Press, 1997.
Spinoza, Baruch. *Opera*, Volume II. Edited by K. Blumenstock. Darmstadt: Wissenschaftliche Buchgesellschaft, 1989.
———. *The Chief Works of Benedict De Spinoza*. Translated by R. H. M. Elwes. New York: Dover, 1955.
Spruit, Leen. *Species Intelligibilis. From Perception to Knowledge*. Vol. 1 of *Classical Roots and Medieval Discussions*. Leiden: E. J. Brill, 1994.
Stern, Paul. "The Problem of History and Temporality in Kantian Ethics." *Review of Metaphysics* 39 (March 1986): 505–45.
Strauss, Leo. "On the Interpretation of Genesis." *L'Homme* 21, no. 1 (January–March 1981): 5–20.

———. *Studies in Platonic Political Philosophy*. Chicago: University of Chicago Press, 1983.

———. *Thoughts on Machiavelli*. Glencoe, Ill.: Free Press, 1958.

Stump, Eleonore. "Aquinas's Account of Freedom: Intellect and Will." *The Monist* 80 (1997): 576–97.

———. "Augustine on Free Will." In *The Cambridge Companion to Augustine*, edited by Eleonore Stump and Norman Kretzmann. Cambridge: Cambridge University Press, 2001.

———. "Intellect, Will, and the Principle of Alternative Possibilities." In *Perspectives on Moral Responsibility*, edited by John Martin Fischer and Mark Ravizza. Ithaca, N.Y.: Cornell University Press, 1993.

———. "Libertarian Freedom and the Principle of Alternative Possibilities." In *Faith, Freedom, and Rationality: Philosophy of Religion Today*, edited by Jeff Jordan and Daniel Howard Snyder. Savage, Md.: Rowan & Littlefield, 1996.

———. "Sanctification, Hardening of the Heart, and Frankfurt's Concept of Free Will." *Journal of Philosophy* 85 (1988): 395–420. Reprinted in *Moral Responsibility*, edited by John Martin Fischer and Mark Ravizza. Ithaca, N. Y.: Cornell University Press, 1993.

Sumner, L. W. *The Moral Foundation of Rights*. Oxford: Oxford University Press, 1987.

Tacitus. *Agricola, Germania, Dialogues*. Translated by M. Hutton et al. Cambridge: Harvard University Press, 1980.

———. *Histories and Annals*. Translated by C. H. Moore and J. Jackson. Cambridge: Harvard University Press, 1925–37.

Tarcov, Nathan. "Arms and Politics in Machiavelli's *Prince*." In *Entre Kant et Kosovo: Études offertes á Pierre Hassner*, edited by Anne-Marie Le Gloannec and Aleksander Smolar. Paris: Presses de Sciences Po, 2003.

———. "Law and Innovation in Machiavelli's *Prince*." In *Enlightening Revolutions: Essays in Honor of Ralph Lerner*, edited by Stéphane Douard and Svetozar Minkov. Lanham, Md.: Lexington Books, 2005.

———. "Machiavelli and the Foundations of Modernity: A Reading of Chapter 3 of *The Prince*." In *Educating the Prince: Essays in Honor of Harvey Mansfield*, edited by Mark Blitz and William Kristol. Lanham, Md.: Rowman & Littlefield, 2000.

Tertullian. *De anima*. Edited by J. H. Waszink. Amsterdam: J. M. Meulenhoff, 1947.

Thomas Aquinas, St. *La Béatitude*. Edited by S. Pinckaers. Paris: Les Éditions du Cerf, 2001.

———. *Opera Omnia*. Leonine edition. Rome, 1882–.

———. *Summa contra gentiles*. Rome: Editio Leonina Manualis, 1934.

———. *Summa theologiae*. 60 vols. Translated by Thomas Gilby et al. London: Eyre and Spottiswoode, and New York: McGraw-Hill, 1964–73.

———. *Summa Theologiae*. Ottawa: Piana, 1941.

Thucydides. *Historiae*. Edited by Karl Hude. 2 vols. Leipzig: Teubner, 1901.

Trevalyan, R. C., trans. *The Ajax of Sophocles*. London: G. Allen & Unwin, 1919.

Van Inwagen, Peter. "When Is the Will Free?" *Philosophical Perspectives* 3 (1989): 399–422.

Velkley, Richard L. *Freedom and the End of Reason: On the Moral Foundation of Kant's Critical Philosophy*. Chicago: University of Chicago Press, 1989.

Vergil. *Aeneid.*

Voltaire. *Dictionnaire philosophique.* Paris: Gallimard, 1961.

Waldron, Jeremy. *God, Locke, and Equality: Christian Foundations in Locke's Political Thought.* Cambridge: Cambridge University Press, 2002.

Walzer, Michael. *Revolution of the Saints: A Study in the Origins of Radical Politics.* Cambridge: Harvard University Press, 1965.

William of Ockham. *Opera Politica.* 3 vols. Manchester: Manchester University Press, 1940–63.

———. *Opera Theologica.* 10 vols. St. Bonaventure, N.Y.: Franciscan Institute Press, 1967–86.

Williams, Bernard. *Truth and Truthfulness: An Essay in Genealogy.* Princeton: Princeton University Press, 2002.

Wippel, John F. *The Metaphysical Thought of Thomas Aquinas: From Finite Being to Uncreated Being.* Washington, D.C.: The Catholic University of America Press, 2000.

Wolf, Susan. "Asymmetrical Freedom." *Journal of Philosophy* 77 (1980): 151–66.

Wolff, Christian. *Gesammelte Schriften.* New York: Olms, 1976.

Wood, Allen. *Kant's Ethical Thought.* Cambridge: Cambridge University Press, 1999.

Wotyla, Karol. *The Acting Person.* Boston and Dordrecht: Reidel, 1979.

Zeno. *Zeno of Elea. A Text with Translation and Notes.* Edited by H. D. P. Lee. Amsterdam: Adof Hakkert, 1967.

Zuckert, Michael P. *Launching Liberalism: On Lockean Political Philosophy.* Lawrence: University Press of Kansas, 2002.

———. *Natural Rights and the New Republicanism.* Princeton: Princeton University Press, 1994.

Contributors

Seth Benardete (d. 2001) was Professor of Classics at New York University. He also taught at the New School for Social Research, Brandeis University, and St. John's College in Annapolis. He held fellowships in Athens and Florence and was a Junior Fellow at Harvard. Among his books are *Herodotean Inquiries; The Being of the Beautiful: Plato's Theaetetus, Sophist and Statesman; Socrates' Second Sailing: On Plato's Republic; The Bow and the Lyre: A Platonic Reading of the Odyssey; Plato's Laws: The Discovery of Being.*

Jesse Covington is a doctoral candidate in American politics and political theory at the University of Notre Dame. His research interests include public law—particularly civil liberties—and political theory.

Michael Allen Gillespie is the Jerry G. and Patricia Crawford Hubbard Professor of Political Science and Professor of Philosophy at Duke University. He works in political philosophy, with particular emphasis on modern continental theory and the history of political philosophy. He is the author of *Hegel, Heidegger, and the Ground of History,* and *Nihilism before Nietzsche.* He is also co-editor of *Nietzsche's New Seas* and *Ratifying the Constitution.* He is completing a book on the theological origins of modernity. He is the Director of Duke's Gerst Program in Political, Economic, and Humanistic Studies.

Leon R. Kass is the Addie Clark Harding Professor in the College and the Committee on Social Thought at the University of Chicago, and the Hertog fellow in social thought at the American Enterprise Institute. His research interests are in the areas of bioethics, ethics, philosophy, marriage, family, and social mores. His publications include *Toward a More Natural Science: Biology and Human Affairs; The Hungry Soul: Eating and the Perfecting of Our Nature; The Ethics of Human Cloning* (with James Q. Wilson); *Wing to Wing, Oar to Oar: Readings in Courting and Marrying* (with Amy A. Kass); and *The Beginning of Wisdom: Reading Genesis.* In 2001 Dr. Kass was appointed by George W. Bush to chair the President's Council on Bioethics, and he served actively in this capacity until 2005.

Robert B. Pippin is the Evelyn Stefansson Nef Distinguished Service Professor in the Committee on Social Thought, the Department of Philosophy, and the College at the University of Chicago. He is the author of several books on German idealism, including *Kant's Theory of Form; Hegel's Idealism: The Satisfactions of Self-Consciousness; Modernism as a Philosophical Problem;* a collection of his recent essays in German, *Die Verwirklichung der Freiheit;* and *The Persistence of Subjectivity.* He is the winner of the Mellon Distinguished Achievement Award in the Humanities, and was a fellow at the Wissenschaftskolleg zu Berlin.

Robert Rethy is Professor of Philosophy at Xavier University. His area of primary research interest is nineteenth- and twentieth-century German philosophy, with a special interest in Hegel, Nietzsche, and Rosenzweig.

John M. Rist is professor emeritus of Classics and Philosophy at the University of Toronto, and visiting professor at the Institutum Patristicum Augustinianum in Rome. He has published extensively in ancient Greek philosophy, with recent attention to Greek and Latin patristics, theology, and ethics. His publications include *Man, Soul and Body: Essays in Ancient Thought from Plato to Dionysius; Augustine: Ancient Thought Baptized; The Mind of Aristotle; Platonism and Its Christian Heritage; Human Value: A Study of Ancient Philosophical Ethics;* and *Real Ethics.* Professor Rist is a fellow of the Royal Society of Canada and a life member of Clare Hall, Cambridge.

Brian J. Shanley, O.P., is President and Professor of Philosophy at Providence College. He taught for several years in the School of Philosophy at the Catholic University of America. His research concentrates on the thought of Thomas Aquinas. He has been editor of the journal *The Thomist* and is the author of *The Thomist Tradition* as well as several articles on Thomas Aquinas. His translation with commentary of QQ1–13 of the *Summa theologiae* was published as *The Treatise on the Divine Nature* in 2006.

Susan Meld Shell is Professor and Chair of the Department of Political Science at Boston College, she was formerly a fellow at the Bunting Institute of Radcliffe College. Her main research interests include Kant's political, moral, and philosophic writings and contemporary issues in public policy. Her books include *The Rights of Reason: A Study of Kant's Philosophy and Politics* and *The Embodiment of Reason: Kant on Spirit, Generation and Community.*

Robert Sokolowski is the Elizabeth Breckenridge Caldwell Professor of Philosophy at the Catholic University of America, where he has taught since 1963. He specializes in phenomenology, Greek philosophy, and the philosophy of language, and is the author of *Introduction to Phenomenology; Moral Action; The God of Faith and Reason;* and *Eucharistic Presence.* He was awarded the Aquinas Medal by the American Catholic Philosophical Association in 2002.

Eleonore Stump is the Robert J. Henle Professor of Philosophy at Saint Louis University, where she has taught since 1992. Dr. Stump is editor-in-chief of the Yale Library of Medieval Philosophy and was section editor for the philosophy of religion for the new *Routledge Encyclopedia of Philosophy.* The author or editor of fifteen books and anthologies, Dr. Stump's publications include *Reasoned Faith; Philosophy of Religion: The Big Questions;* the *Cambridge Companion to Augustine;* the *Cambridge Companion to Aquinas;* and *Aquinas* in the series Arguments of the Philosophers. Her Gifford lectures, entitled *Wandering in Darkness: Narrative and the Problem of Suffering,* are forthcoming from Oxford University Press.

Nathan Tarcov is Professor in the Committee on Social Thought, the Department of Political Science, and the College at the University of Chicago, where he has served as chair of the Committee on Social Thought and directed the John M. Olin Center for Inquiry into the Theory and Practice of Democracy. He is the author of *Locke's Education for Liberty* and articles on Machiavelli, Locke, Leo Strauss, Quentin Skinner, and American political thought and foreign policy; he is editor and translator with Harvey C. Mansfield of Machiavelli's *Discourses on Livy;* editor with Ruth Grant of Locke's *Some Thoughts Concerning Education;* and editor with Clifford Orwin of *The Legacy of Rousseau.* He is currently writing a book on Machiavelli's *Prince.*

James Thompson is a Ph.D. student in political science, as well as an adjunct faculty member, at the University of Notre Dame. His primary academic interests are in international relations and political theory, and he specializes in particular in the way in which classical and early modern political theory influence international relations theory.

Richard Velkley is the Celia Scott Weatherhead Distinguished Professor of Philosophy at Tulane University. He is author of *Freedom and the End of Reason: On the Moral Foundation of Kant's Critical Philosophy; Being after Rousseau: Philosophy and Culture in Question;* and editor of Dieter Henrich, *The Unity of Reason: Essays on Kant's Philosophy*. He was associate editor of *The Review of Metaphysics* 1997–2006.

Michael P. Zuckert is the Nancy Reeves Dreux Professor of Political Science at the University of Notre Dame. His major research interests are early modern political philosophy, liberal theory, and American constitutional law and history. He has published *Natural Rights and the New Republicanism; The Natural Rights Republic; Launching Liberalism;* and *The Truth about Leo Strauss: Political Philosophy and American Democracy*, co-authored with Catherine Zuckert, as well as many scholarly articles.

Index of Names

Adorno, Theodor, 242–43
Aeschylus, 3
Alberti, Leon Battista, 112
Allison, Henry, 181
Ameriks, Karl, 225n39
Anderson-Gold, Sharon, 181, 201n39
Anscombe, G. E. M., 63, 68, 219
Aristophanes, 23
Aristotle, viiin1, xi, 4, 38, 42, 45, 50, 55, 57–59, 62, 67, 77, 125
Augustine, St., 54–55, 59, 61, 66, 69, 88, 92, 95n16, 96n18, 103n35, 146, 178
Ayers, Michael, 165n68

Bañez, Domingo, 101
Baeumler, Alfred, 236n26
Bellarmine, Robert, 144–45, 164
Benardete, Seth, vii, ix–x, xii
Benjamin, Walter, 205
Bentham, Jeremy, 64
Berdyaev, Nicolai, xiiin2
Bergson, Henri, xiiin2
Bible, xi, xvii–xviii, xxi, 13–14, 18–19, 28, 33, 38, 144–45, 149–50, 154, 161–62, 164, 166, 168–71, 180, 199n34
Bickerton, Derek, 40–42, 45
Blondel, Maurice, xiiin2
Bluhm, William T., 165n69
Blumenberg, Hans, 110
Bodin, Jean, 113–14
Braine, David, 49, 52n23
Bruni, Leonardo, 112
Boethius, Anicius Manlius Severinus, xii
Buber, Martin, xiiin2
Burrell, David, 89n57, 89n58
Buttiglione, Rocco, 56

Caesar, Julius, 129n12, 138n29
Calvin, John, 113, 157

Calvin, William H., 40n1, 45n12
Cervantes, Miguel de, 176n107
Chamberlain, Houston Stewart, 205
Chisolm, Roderick, 87
Chomsky, Noam, 45
Cicero, Marcus Tullius, xii, 61
Clark, W. Norris, xiiin2
Cohen, Herman, 181
Congar, M.-J., 86n49
Covington, J., xvii
Cowie, Fiona, 45n10
Cromwell, Oliver, 176–79
Crosby, John F., xiiin2

Darwin, Charles, 40, 168
Dennett, D. C., 62
Descartes, René, xv, 58, 68, 112, 239–40
di Giovanni, George, 182n2
Dionysius, 86
Donagan, Alan, 78n28
Duns Scotus, John, 88
Dyck, Corey, 202n41

Eliot, George, 94n15, 98
Epictetus, 62
Epicurus, 196–98
Erasmus, 112

Fichte, Johann Gottlieb, xix, 214, 222
Filmer, Sir Robert, xvii, 143–80
Flew, Anthony, 72
Frankfurt, Harry, 95n16
Frederick the Great, 182
Frege, Gottlob, 45
Fukuyama, Francis, 108n2

Gallagher, David, 73n9, 75n17, 77n26, 78n29
Garrigou-Lagrange, R., 99n24

263

www.ingramcontent.com/pod-product-compliance
Lightning Source LLC
Chambersburg PA
CBHW021854020426
42334CB00013B/327